Introduction to
Algorithms &
Data Structures

Michaelle Perez

Australia • Brazil • Canada • Mexico • Singapore • United Kingdom • United States

Introduction to Algorithms and Data Structures
Michaelle Perez

SVP, Product: Cheryl Costantini

VP, Product: Thais Alencar

Senior Portfolio Product Director: Mark Santee

Portfolio Product Director: Rita Lombard

Portfolio Product Manager: Tran Pham

Product Assistant: Anh Nguyen

Learning Designer: Mary Convertino

Content Manager: Caitlin Bonaventure

Digital Project Manager: John Smigielski

Developmental Editor: Deb Kaufmann

VP, Product Marketing: Jason Sakos

Director, Product Marketing: Danae April

Product Marketing Manager: Mackenzie Paine

Content Acquisition Analyst: Callum Panno

Production Service: Straive

Designer: Erin Griffin

Cover Image Source: Yuri Hoyda/Shutterstock.com

For product information and technology assistance, contact us at **Cengage Customer & Sales Support, 1-800-354-9706 or support.cengage.com.**

For permission to use material from this text or product, submit all requests online at **www.copyright.com**.

Library of Congress Control Number: 2023915266

ISBN:978-0-357-67356-0

Cengage
5191 Natorp Boulevard
Mason, OH 45040
USA

Cengage is a leading provider of customized learning solutions. Our employees reside in nearly 40 different countries and serve digital learners in 165 countries around the world. Find your local representative at **www.cengage.com.**

To learn more about Cengage platforms and services, register or access your online learning solution, or purchase materials for your course, visit **www.cengage.com.**

Notice to the Reader

Publisher does not warrant or guarantee any of the products described herein or perform any independent analysis in connection with any of the product information contained herein. Publisher does not assume, and expressly disclaims, any obligation to obtain and include information other than that provided to it by the manufacturer. The reader is expressly warned to consider and adopt all safety precautions that might be indicated by the activities described herein and to avoid all potential hazards. By following the instructions contained herein, the reader willingly assumes all risks in connection with such instructions. The publisher makes no representations or warranties of any kind, including but not limited to, the warranties of fitness for particular purpose or merchantability, nor are any such representations implied with respect to the material set forth herein, and the publisher takes no responsibility with respect to such material. The publisher shall not be liable for any special, consequential, or exemplary damages resulting, in whole or part, from the readers' use of, or reliance upon, this material.

Printed at CLDPC, USA, 10-23

Brief Contents

Contents

Chapter 1

Recursion   1

Chapter 2

Introduction to Data Structures   23

Chapter 3

Designing Efficient Algorithms   49

Chapter 4

Sorting Algorithms   73

Chapter 5

Search Algorithms   105

Chapter 6

Linked Lists, Stacks, and Queues   123

Chapter 7

Hash Tables   165

Chapter 8

Trees   195

Chapter 9

Graphs   253

9.3 Depth-First Traversal   **263**

9.4 Breadth-First Traversal   **268**

9.5 Directed and Undirected Graphs   **271**

9.6 Weighted Graphs   **273**

Chapter 10

Advanced Algorithms   **285**

10.1 Greedy Algorithms   **285**

10.2 Dynamic Programming   **293**

10.3 Dijkstra's Algorithm for the Shortest Path   **306**

10.4 Knuth–Morris–Pratt (KMP) Algorithm   **313**

10.5 Spanning Trees   **325**

10.6 Contours and Regions in Binary Images   **334**

About the Author

Michaelle Perez is a professor of Biomedical Engineering at Galileo University. He has taught mathematics and computer science for the last 20 years. His main interest has been helping students develop the skills necessary to keep learning and tackle complex problems. He has taught a wide range of mathematics and computer science topics to students from high school to graduate school. His current research interest is in applications of computer vision through deep learning, in particular to biomedical images.

Introduction

Once a student has mastered the basic programming patterns in a programming language, the next step is to learn how to use them to solve problems. One of the cornerstones of solving problems is knowing which patterns to apply. This is where algorithms and data structures become fundamental. A computer scientist or programmer familiar with elementary data structures and algorithms can use them to express solutions to problems. Familiarity with data structures and algorithms allows a programmer to tackle unthinkable problems using only a programming language's basic control flow and loops.

The book explores several common ideas: backtracking, depth-first, breadth-first, recursion, divide and conquer, and dynamic programming. The appearance of these ideas in several places shows the student how those could be applied in different contexts. These ideas have proven to be powerful in tackling diverse problems. For example, the breadth-first pattern that uses recursion can be used for searching in a telecommunications network to separate an object of interest in computer vision.

Time complexity and the Big O notation are introduced early in the book using an intuitive presentation. The main objective is that the student could weigh the benefits of using a given algorithm. Having the concepts of time complexity early also serves to better appreciate the benefits of using more elaborate data structures, such as AVL trees and heaps, when implementing a solution.

The concepts presented in this book are fundamental for anyone interested in applying computer programming to solve problems. They provide a strong basis for students wanting to study more specialized structures or advanced algorithms or simply prep for their technical interview.

One of the main characteristics of this book is that it focuses on concepts being language agnostic. That helps the reader to focus on the important ideas, putting aside the technical details of a specific programming language. Nevertheless, the algorithms are presented in a way that makes it easy to grab the pseudocode and implement it in various programming languages. Special care has been put into making the description of the data structures and algorithms useful to different programming languages and paradigms.

Another characteristic is that most algorithms are described in concrete but small cases that illustrate how and why the algorithm works. Then a more formal algorithm is presented through a pseudocode implementation. This also applies to data structures; implementations of all data structures presented in the book are provided, starting with simple user-defined data types, pointers, and arrays.

Organization of the Text

This book is divided into 10 chapters. **Chapter 1** introduces one of the most important algorithmic paradigms: recursion. The introduction uses only arithmetic and basic programming patterns, making it accessible to a beginner programming student. **Chapter 2** introduces the idea of abstract data types and their applications to represent and operate over data. **Chapter 3** introduces time and space complexity from concrete examples and uses those to introduce the Big O notation to create a framework to compare different algorithms. Enough examples are presented so a student can analyze the complexity of complex algorithms. **Chapter 4** explores sorting algorithms and analyzes different aspects of them, such as stability, space complexity, and time complexity. The basic sorting algorithms—bubble sort, selection sort, insertion sort, quick sort, and merge sort—are introduced through detailed examples before presenting a concise version of them through pseudocode. **Chapter 5** introduces the searching principles, giving students the foundation to study more complex searching strategies later in non-linear structures.

Chapter 6 details the fundamental data structures, lists, stacks, and queues. The basic ideas for implementing dynamic data structures are introduced through the linked list and its variations. **Chapter 7** presents the idea of hashing, common strategies, and applications to construct maps and associative arrays. Chapter 8 concerns trees, binary trees, and their variations, including AVL trees, heaps, treaps, and tries. Special attention is given to the advantages of balancing trees and how to balance a tree. **Chapter 9** concerns graphs and the fundamentals of graphs as data structures. This presentation provides all the essential tools to study more advanced graph algorithms. **Chapter 10** details the greedy algorithms family, examples of its applications, and limitations. Dynamic programming is introduced through examples using the top-down approach, its relation to recursion, and tables for memorization. Dynamic programming principles are exemplified through the knapsack problem and the longest common substring problem. Additionally, the Knuth–Morris–Pratt, Dijkstra's, and Prim's algorithms are discussed in detail, and their implementation is shown. Additionally, as examples of the elementary ideas of graphs and abstraction in a different scenario, the elementary algorithms for contour and region finding in binary images are discussed in the book's last chapter.

Features of the Text

This first edition of this textbook has been developed around a clearly established set of learning objectives. Each chapter begins with a list of objectives to prepare students for the chapter content and help them organize their learning experience. Objectives are clearly aligned to the major headings of the chapter and to the end-of-chapter questions, exercises, and projects.

Note | The Note feature provides additional information to supplement the chapter content—for example, helpful tips or background information on a chapter topic.

Best Practices

Best Practices provides tips and tricks for success when learning how to determine and implement data structures and algorithms. These helpful boxes further critical thinking and application skills.

Technical Interviews

The Technical Interview box provides students with examples of the critical thinking problems and questions that they will encounter as they apply for internships and jobs. These tips and tricks help students to successfully apply new concepts in real-world situations.

Quick Checks

Quick Check self-assessments are placed throughout the reading to allow learners to increase understanding of new concepts in-the-moment. In the online reader, these assessments are auto graded and help instructors to confirm student understanding as new material is presented.

Review Questions

Review Questions test student comprehension of the major ideas and techniques presented throughout the chapter. Each question is aligned directly with a learning objective so students can track their learning and review supporting content as needed.

Programming Problems

Programming Problems provide opportunities to apply concepts. These exercises allow students to explore each major programming concept presented in the chapter. Supporting data files are provided in the Cengage resource site when required.

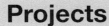

Projects

Projects synthesize multiple learning objectives and concepts within the chapter and allow students to take their skills to the next level by applying new concepts and problem-solving skills in more complex activities. These activities mirror real-world tasks that students are likely to encounter in full stack web development positions.

Chapter Summaries

Chapter Summaries recap the concepts and techniques covered in the chapter and provide students with a bulleted list from which to review content.

Key Terms

Key Terms are identified and defined throughout the chapter and are listed again at the chapter's completion. A glossary at the end of the book lists all key terms in alphabetical order along with their working definitions.

Ancillary Package

Additional instructor resources for this product are available online. Instructor assets include an Instructor Manual, Educator's Guide, PowerPoint® slides, and a test bank powered by Cognero®. Sign up or sign in at www.cengage.com to search for and access this product and its online resources.

- **Instructor Manual:** The Instructor Manual follows the text chapter by chapter to assist in planning and organizing an effective, engaging course. The manual includes learning objectives, chapter overviews, lecture notes, ideas for classroom activities, and additional resources.

- **PowerPoint Presentations:** This text provides PowerPoint slides to accompany each chapter. Slides are included to guide classroom presentations and can be made available to students for chapter review or to print as classroom handouts.

- **Solution and Answer Guide (SAG):** Solutions and rationales to review questions, exercises, and projects are provided to assist with grading and student understanding.

- **Data files:** Data files necessary to complete some of the steps and projects in the course are available.

- **Complete List of Learning Objectives:** A complete list of all objectives addressed in the textbook is available to help instructors plan and manage their course.

- ***Test Bank®:*** Cengage Learning Testing powered by Cognero is a flexible, online system that allows you to:

  - Author, edit, and manage test bank content from multiple Cengage Learning solutions.

  - Create multiple test versions in an instant.

  - Deliver tests from your learning management system, your classroom, or anywhere you want.

Acknowledgments

I want to give special thanks to the Cengage Learning and Freedom Learning Group teams for all their hard work, patience, and dedication to providing students with the best possible product. In particular, thanks to Deb Kaufmann, Mary Convertino, Nicole Spoto, Tran Pham, Pankaj Sharma, Danielle Agostine, Kori Gould, and Caitlin Bonaventure for their valuable comments and suggestions. I am also grateful for the excellent feedback provided by peer reviewers Rajiv Malkan (Lone Star College – Montgomery) and Kyla McMullen (University of Florida). Thanks to my wife, Yenny, and my kids, TD, Laura, and Nina, who filled me with love and enthusiasm while writing the manuscript for this book. And to my mother and sister for their unconditional support.

Dedication

I dedicate this book to the memory of my father, Miguel Perez (1965–2018), my first math and programming teacher and a true example of the power of education to change lives.

Chapter 1

Recursion

Learning Objectives

Upon completion of this chapter, you will be able to:

1.1 Describe the benefits of using recursion.

1.2 Explain how to use recursive methods.

1.3 Explain the difference between direct and indirect recursion.

1.4 Use recursion to solve the Tower of Hanoi problem.

1.5 Use backtracking recursion to enumerate all the subsets of a given set.

1.1 Introduction to Recursion

Recursion is a technique to solve problems where the case at hand is divided into smaller subtasks similar to the original one. Recursion is an important topic to help understand several algorithms, specifically when solving a problem or executing a task that you can split into smaller subtasks.

For example, suppose you want to compute the length of a string of characters. This task is simple when the string has only one character, such as *str1* = "*a*". In this case, the answer is 1. For larger strings such as *str1* = "*abc*", you can think of splitting the original string into *tmp2* = "*a*" and *str2* = "*bc*". Now, to solve the problem, you need to compute the length of the string *str2* and add one (the length of *tmp2*). The problem is reduced to computing the length of a shorter string, *str2*. You can repeat this process by splitting the string *str2* into *tmp3* = "*b*" and *str3* = "*c*". In this case, you can directly compute the length of the string *str3*. You can see this process summarized in **Figure 1-1**.

$$
\begin{aligned}
len(str1) &= len(tmp2) + len(str2) \\
&= 1 + len(str2) = 1 + [len(tmp3) + len(str3)] \\
&= 1 + 1 + len(str3) = 2 + 1 = 3
\end{aligned}
$$

Figure 1-1 Recursive calls made to compute the length of a string

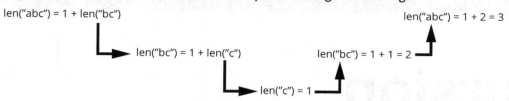

This example illustrates basic recursion structures and why you might want to use them.

The first structure required in recursion is the **base case**, the case in which the function will no longer call itself (recurse). The base case is the most basic case, in which you don't need to divide the task into smaller parts. For the length example, the base case is when the string is a single character.

The other structure is the recursion, the mechanism or description of how you split the current case into smaller cases.

Notice that you could describe the procedure in the example simply by specifying that the length of a string s is 1 if it is a single character. In other cases, it is 1 plus the length of the string s without the initial character. That is an elegant solution to the problem using recursion. Although it would be possible to write your solution using a loop, often using recursion is more straightforward than using a loop. In most cases, using recursion will give clarity to your algorithm.

A **recursive function** is a function that calls itself until it reaches a base case. As with any process, procedure, or function, the procedure must finish in a finite amount of time.

Calculating the Power of a Number Using Recursion

You can use recursion to define a function to compute x^n for any number x and non-negative integer n. Suppose you want to compute $3^0, 3^1, 3^2$, and 3^3. First, remember that $3^0 = 1$ (in general, $x^0 = 1$). Then

$$3^1 = 3^0 \times 3 = 3$$
$$3^2 = 3^1 \times 3 = 3 \times 3 = 9$$
$$3^3 = 3^2 \times 3 = 9 \times 3 = 27$$

From the previous calculations, you might have noticed that to compute 3^3, you used 3^2. This idea can be generalized to any other number, for example, $3^{11} = 3^{10} \times 3$.

The following recursive definition can also express the previous idea:

$$\text{(Base case) } x^0 = 1$$
$$\text{(Recursion) } x^n = x^{n-1} \times x \text{ for } n > 0$$

The pseudocode for such a function might be as follows:

```
power(x,n)
    if n = 0
        return 1
    else
        return power(x,n-1)*x
```

Notice that in the definition of the function `power(x,n)`, you use the same function again; this is what makes this function recursive.

You can use this function to calculate 5^3, as shown in **Figure 1-2**.

Figure 1-2 Recursive calls and returned values made by power(5,3)

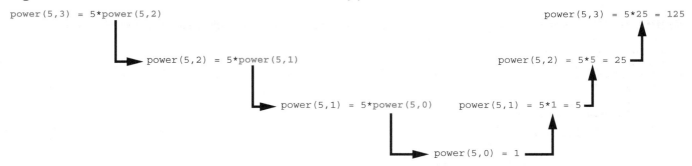

What Is Well-Defined Recursion?

Well-defined recursion is a term used to describe a recursive algorithm that reaches an end state in a finite time and returns the same value every time it is used.

From the previous example, you might have noticed two of the main characteristics that a well-defined recursive function must have:

- The recursive function calls itself using a smaller case of the initial problem. For example, when computing 5^2, the function uses 5^1, a smaller case; not 5^3, a greater case. It is characteristic of a well-defined recursive function that the recursive call is made on a smaller subset or case of the original problem. This characteristic ensures that the function will reach a point where it stops calling itself and returns a value.

- The point where the function stops calling itself is the base case. In the power example in the previous section, the base case is $x^0 = 1$. When the function reaches that case, it stops calling itself, ensuring that the recursive function doesn't go on forever.

It is possible to have more than one base case in a recursive algorithm (as you will see with Fibonacci numbers), but every recursive procedure or function must reach one of those stopping points.

The following example illustrates what can go wrong when defining a recursive procedure.

You want to write a procedure that counts by 2s down. For example, if you start with 20, you want to display 20, 18, 16, 14, . . . and stop before using negative numbers. You use the following implementation:

```
count_down(n):
    display(n)
    if n = 0
        stop
    else
        count_down(n - 2)
```

For a value n of 8, the procedure call `count_down(8)` displays:

$$8 \quad 6 \quad 4 \quad 2 \quad 0$$

For a value n of 9, the procedure call `count_down(9)` never stops. It starts with:

$$9 \quad 7 \quad 5 \quad 3 \quad 1 \quad -1 \quad -3\ldots$$

and it never reaches the base case in the `count_down` function that is $n = 0$.

You can see the recursive calls made in each case in **Figure 1-3**.

Figure 1-3   Top: Recursive calls made by count_down(8) Bottom: recursive calls made by count_down(9)

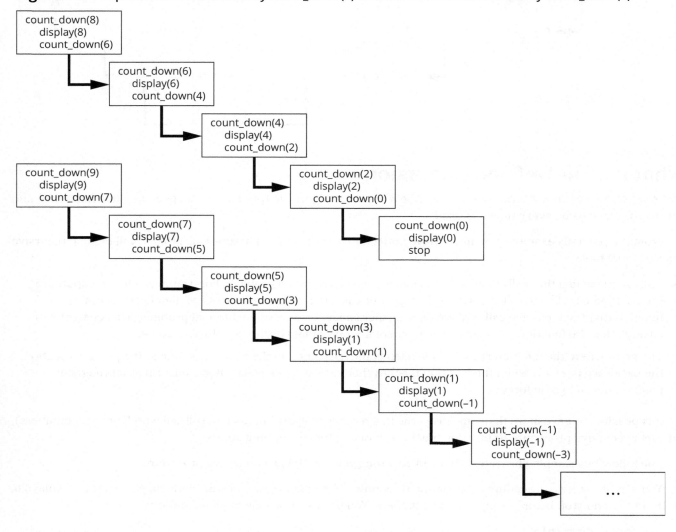

In this case, the recursion is ill-defined because it never stops. You must be careful to avoid such possible cases.

Stack Overflow Errors

When you execute a function call, most programming languages store the parameters of the function in a special memory space called a *stack*, where the parameters are stored until the function returns. Each call of a function uses stack memory. When you use a recursive program, the same function is called multiple times; thus, the required space grows with each call. Since the stack space is limited, it might get full, raising a stack overflow error. A **stack overflow** is an error that occurs when the stack doesn't have space to store necessary data. **Figure 1-4** shows the stack and its relationship to variables in a program.

Figure 1-4   Stack and parameters stored for each function call

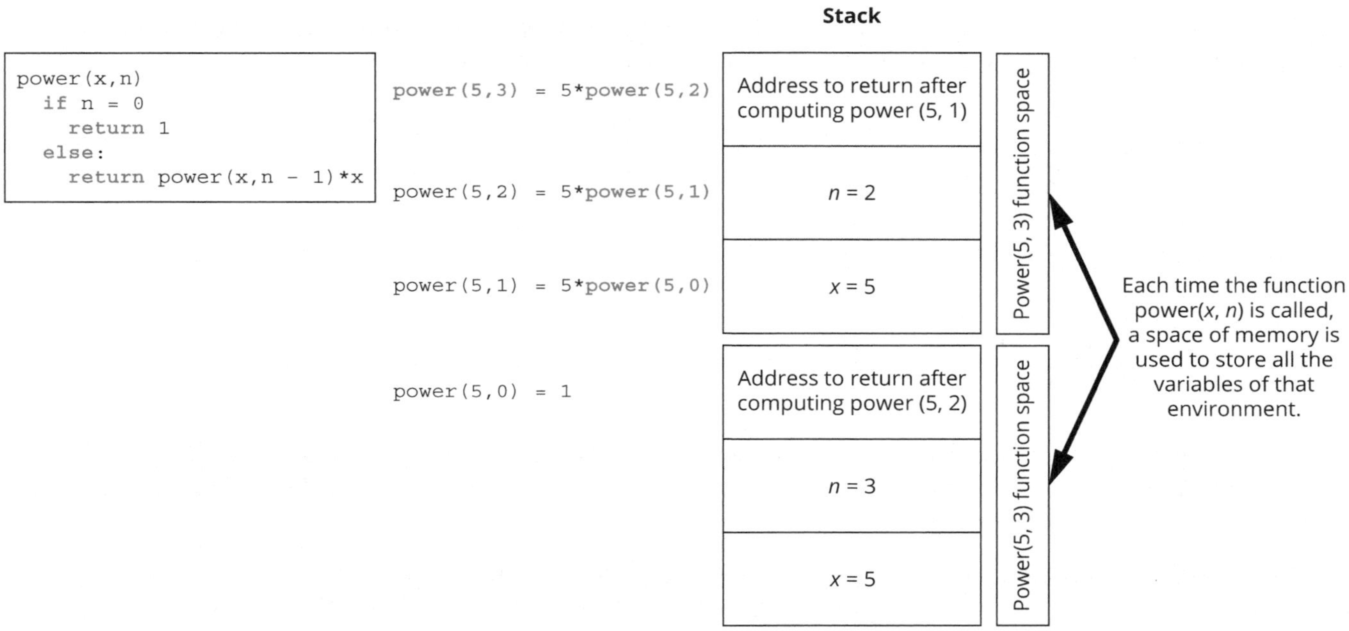

If the recursion is ill-defined, it has no stopping case, and you will eventually have a stack overflow error. However, even if the recursion is well defined, it might require so many calls that the stack gets full before you reach the base case(s).

For example, the recursive version for the computation of the determinant of a square matrix requires a factorial of n recursive calls. A matrix of size 100 will require a factorial of 100 calls. The factorial of 100 is approximately 9×10^{157}, which is a 9 followed by 157 zeros. Making so many recursive calls could fill all the stack space. In such cases, it is necessary to develop a different algorithm, not because the function is ill-defined or flawed but because of memory constraints.

When a recursive function or a loop doesn't reach a point when it stops, at least by design, it is said that the program has entered a **state of infinite recursion**.

The possibility of entering into a state of infinite recursion might be one of the most significant drawbacks of using recursion. But as you will see from exploring several algorithms, using recursion is possible to describe complex algorithms (see the Hanoi Tower problem) with few lines of code. Moreover, studying small cases often naturally leads to a solution using recursion when facing a complex problem.

Note | One way to prevent stack overflow errors is to estimate how many recursive calls are required for the largest case you expect to face. Recall that there is always a limit to how large the numbers or data size you expect a program to handle.

Quick Check 1-1

What is a consequence of having an ill-defined recursive method or function?

Answer: The program enters an infinite recursion, so the function will never reach the base case, resulting in a stack overflow error.

Advantages of Using Recursion

You can translate recursive functions and procedures into iterative functions or procedures. For example, you can implement the power function from a previous section without using recursion as follows:

```
power(x, n)
    if n = 0
        return 1
    else
        val = 1
        for i = 1 to n
            val = val*x
        return val
```

You can see that the number of lines of code is higher and explaining why the code works as intended is not immediately obvious. The use of recursion is not just a way to simplify algorithms. It also enables you to create solutions using the divide-and-conquer strategy.

Using the divide-and-conquer strategy, you try to divide a complex task into smaller subtasks. As you have seen in recursion, the repeated application of this strategy eventually reaches a point where the subtask is so simple that it is possible to solve it directly.

> ## Best Practices

It is almost impossible to find modern software developed entirely by a single programmer. Most software is developed by a team, sometimes by a multidisciplinary team. So you must remember that although recursive algorithms are usually easy to understand, the purpose of each function and procedure should be stated clearly through appropriate documentation.

Tail Recursion

Some modern compilers can transform code written using recursion to iterative methods automatically. But in most cases, using what is called tail recursion can help prevent stack overflow errors. In **tail recursion**, the last command in the function is the recursive call. For example, the following code uses recursion to compute the sum of the numbers from 1 to n.

```
sum(n)
    if n = 1
        return 1
    else
        return sum(n-1) + n
```

Although this uses recursion, the returned value is composed of more than just the returned value of the recursive function. The following code makes use of tail recursion:

```
sum(n, s)
    if n = 1
        return n + s
    else
        return sum(n-1, s + n)
```

Notice that the returned value in the recursive call case is only the recursive function. Some care must be taken when trying to use tail recursion. For example, the following implementation might look like it uses tail recursion:

```
sum(n)
    if n = 1
        return n
    else
        return n + sum(n-1)
```

In the recursive call, the returned value is $n + \text{sum}(n-1)$, so the last command executed is the sum of the two terms n and $\text{sum}(n-1)$. Hence, the last implementation doesn't use tail recursion.

Tail recursion is important because modern compilers create a more efficient code when it is used.

1.2 Examples of Recursive Methods

To better understand how you can implement recursive methods and functions, let's look at how you might use recursion with two functions: the factorial function and the Fibonacci sequence.

The factorial function is used in many statistics, combinatorics, and computer science formulas. It represents the number of permutations or different ways of ordering a list of elements. It turns out that it can be defined through a recursive formula.

The Fibonacci sequence is defined recursively. Each term in the sequence is obtained from the sum of the two preceding ones. This simple definition, done using recursion, is related to a special proportion called the *golden ratio* (approximately 1.618).

The golden ratio appears in nature in several places. For example, the ratio between the size of two contiguous segments of a human finger is usually close to 1.618, the golden ratio.

Computing Factorials with Recursion

The factorial of a non-negative integer n, usually written as "$n!$", is the product of all positive integers less than n. This means:

$$n! = n \times (n-1) \times (n-2) \times \cdots \times 2 \times 1$$

By convention $0! = 1$, which is consistent with the normal convention for an empty product.

Hence, you can compute the factorial as follows:

$$0! = 1$$
$$1! = 1$$
$$2! = 2 \times 1 = 2$$
$$3! = 3 \times 2 \times 1 = 6$$
$$4! = 4 \times 3 \times 2 \times 1 = 24$$
$$5! = 5 \times 4 \times 3 \times 2 \times 1 = 120$$

You can observe a relationship between $n!$ and $(n-1)!$. This relationship leads to a recursive definition of the factorial:

$$n! = n \times (n-1)!$$

Remember that when using recursion, you *reduce* the computation of the function to a smaller case and you must reach a base case. So, you can define the factorial of a function as:

```
factorial(n):
    if n = 0
        return 1
    else
        return n*factorial(n-1)
```

or as:

$$(\text{Base})\ 0! = 1$$
$$(\text{Recursion})\ \text{For } n \geq 1, (n)! = (n) \times (n-1)!$$

Notice that when calling the factorial function, `factorial(10)` does a recursive call to `factorial(9)` and this to `factorial(8)`; thus, at each call, the argument of the function is reduced by one. This guarantees that the function will reach the base case zero.

Computing the Fibonacci Sequence

The Fibonacci sequence is a set of numbers created in a recursive form. It is common to describe the Fibonacci sequence by F_n. The definition of these numbers is: "Each term in the sequence is the sum of the two preceding ones."

The first two terms of the sequence are chosen as 1. Thus, the first terms of the sequence are:

$$F_0 = 1$$
$$F_1 = 1$$
$$F_2 = F_1 + F_0 = 1 + 1 = 2$$
$$F_3 = F_2 + F_1 = 2 + 1 = 3$$
$$F_4 = F_3 + F_2 = 3 + 2 = 5$$
$$F_5 = F_4 + F_3 = 5 + 3 = 8$$

To put it in a more precise way:

$$(\text{Base cases})\ F_0 = 1,\ F_1 = 1$$
$$(\text{Recursion})\ \text{For } n \geq 2,\ F_n = F_{n-1} + F_{n-2}$$

or using pseudocode as:

```
fib(n):
    if n = 0 or n = 1
        return 1
    else
        return fib(n-1) + fib(n-2)
```

This is one example of second-order recursion since the definition of the new number in the sequence depends on the two previous terms. Also, notice how the Fibonacci sequence has two base cases.

If you apply the previous definition to calculate F_4, the result looks like this:

$$F_4 = F_3 + F_2$$
$$= (F_2 + F_1) + (F_1 + F_0)$$
$$= [(F_1 + F_0) + F_1] + (F_1 + F_0)$$
$$= [(1+1) + 1] + (1+1)$$
$$= 5$$

You can see the recursive calls made in **Figure 1-5**.

Figure 1-5 Recursive calls made when computing fib(4)

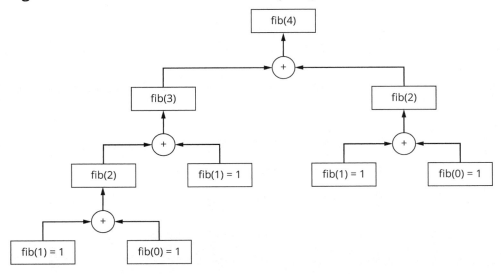

As you might have noticed, making two recursive calls to the function is necessary to compute a single number.

To get an idea of how you can create an iterative implementation for the Fibonacci sequence computation, you can see the computation of F_4 in **Figure 1-6**. This computation starts with F_1 and F_0 and keeps updating values a and b until it reaches the desired number.

Figure 1-6 Iterative computations made to compute fib(4)

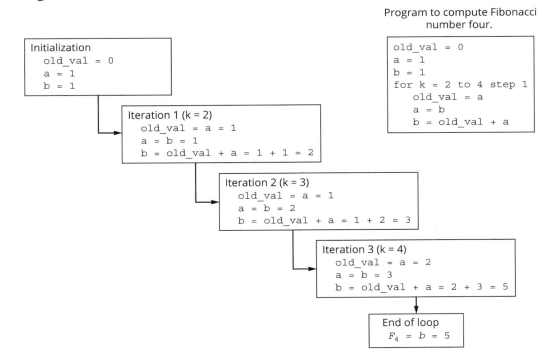

Although the implementation is not very different in the computations made, it is easier to describe the algorithm using recursion than iteration.

Remember the importance of writing easy-to-read code when deciding whether to use a recursive implementation or work hard to transform it into an iterative solution. Easy-to-read code is critical when working with large teams since you won't be able to communicate directly to everybody what you were thinking while writing complex iterative code.

Note | You can have as many base cases as you desire, and the recursion can be of an order as high as you might need.

In the extreme case, it might be that F_n is defined in terms of all the previous cases, although that might be inefficient.

Quick Check 1-2

Why is the definition of Fibonacci numbers an example of second-order recursion?

Answer: The definition of F_n depends on two previous cases and not only on one.

1.3 Direct and Indirect Recursion

You now know that when a function calls itself, it is a recursive function. But it also might happen that the function `foo1` calls another function `foo2`. And now `foo2` makes a call to `foo1`.

This might appear to be a circular definition, something like stating that:

- A recursive definition is one that uses recursive functions.
- A recursive function is one with a recursive definition.

In such a case, you don't have recursion, you have a circular definition. One potential consequence of such circular definitions in code, as discussed before, is entering an infinite recursion state and getting a stack over-flow error.

Thus, using a function `foo1` that calls on `foo2` and `foo2` calls on `foo1` might sound like a circular definition. However, it is possible that each time `foo2` calls on `foo1`, it does it with a smaller argument, and both `foo1` and `foo2` might have a base case. When those conditions are met, you have a well-defined recursive function.

For example, the functions `even(k)` and `odd(k)` are used in the function `count_2k(k)` to display all positive integers from $2k$ to 1.

```
even(k)
    display(2*k)
    odd(k)
```

```
odd(k)
    display(2*k-1)
    if k is not 1:
        even(k-1)


count_2k(k)
    even(k)
```

For a value *k* of 4, you can see the recursive calls made by `count_2k(4)` in **Figure 1-7**.

Figure 1-7   Indirect recursive calls made by the square function implementation

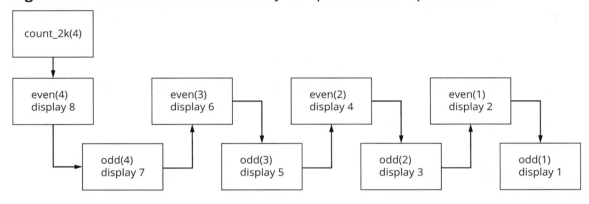

When two or more functions are used in this fashion, it is said that you have indirect recursion. **Indirect recursion** is when a function calls to itself but in an indirect manner. For example, in the `count_2k` implementation, the `even(k)` function calls itself but does it through the `odd(k)` function. **Direct recursion** is when the function calls itself directly. In either case, it is necessary to guarantee that the function won't enter an infinite recursion state.

Computing Squares of Numbers with Direct and Indirect Recursion

You can calculate the square of a positive integer *n* using recursion with the help of the formula:

$$n^2 = n(n-1)+n$$

You can compute the expression *n* (*n* – 1) using the identity:

$$n(n-1) = (n-1)^2 + (n-1)$$

You can verify the identity as follows:

$$(n-1)^2 + (n-1)$$
$$= (n^2 - 2n + 1) + (n-1)$$
$$= n^2 - 2n + 1 + n - 1$$
$$= n^2 - n = n(n-1)$$

Thus, to compute n^2, you can use a function that computes *n* (*n* – 1) and, in the process, the latter function uses $(n-1)^2$. So, you have a solution that uses indirect recursion.

An implementation of that might be as follows:

```
square(n)
   if n = 1
       return 1
   else
       return prod(n) + n

prod(n)
   if n = 1
       return 0
   else
       return square(n-1)+(n-1)
```

For *n* with the value of 3, you can see the sequence of recursive calls in **Figure 1-8**.

Figure 1-8   Sequence of calls made when calling the indirect recursive implementation of square(3)

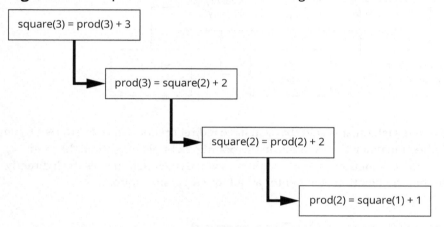

A more direct implementation might use:

$$n^2 = (n-1+1)^2 = (n-1)^2 + 2(n-1) + 1 = (n-1)^2 + 2n - 1$$

In this case, to compute n^2 you use $(n-1)^2$, thus using direct recursion. That looks as follows:

```
square(n)
   if n = 1
       return 1
   else
       return square(n-1) + 2*n - 1
```

For *n* with the value of 3, you can see the sequence of recursive calls in **Figure 1-9**.

Figure 1-9   Sequence of calls made when calling the direct recursive implementation of square(3)

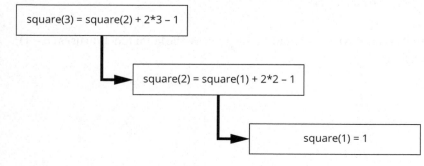

Note | When using indirect recursion, you must be sure that in each cycle of going from one function to another, the parameters are decreasing. If this doesn't happen, you have a circular definition and you are not using indirect recursion.

Quick Check 1-3

How many recursive calls are made to `square(n)` when using the indirect recursive version of `square(n)` with $n = 4$?

Answer: Following the function code, you get the following:

```
square(4) = prod(4) + 4
= square(3) + 3 + 4 = square(3) + 7
= prod(3) + 3 + 7 = prod(3) + 10
= square(2) + 2 + 10 = square(2) + 12
= prod(2) + 2 + 12 = prod(2) + 14
= square(1) + 1 + 14 = 16
```

So, there are four calls to the `square` function.

1.4 The Tower of Hanoi

The Tower of Hanoi is a puzzle where you are given a tower formed by some disks and three pegs. When you start, the disks are stacked in increasing order on one peg. The challenge is to move all the disks from peg A to peg C, moving only one disk at a time, and never put a larger disk onto a smaller one, a concept illustrated in **Figure 1-10**.

Figure 1-10   The Hanoi Tower puzzle

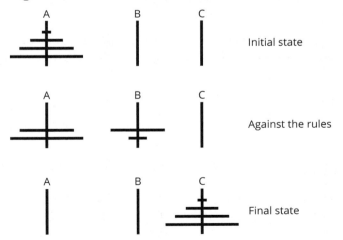

Initial state

Against the rules

Final state

Luckily, you can easily do this task and perhaps even describe the procedure to do it for a small number of disks, like two or three. But describing the solution becomes increasingly difficult as the number of disks grows. Moreover, it might seem like there is no such solution.

From the programming point of view, the solution should be a precise set of instructions on how to move the disks to move the complete tower from one peg to another. You might have already seen that the first step toward a solution is that you move only one disk, which is an excellent base case and doesn't require a complex procedure.

> **Note**
>
> The Tower of Hanoi problem was introduced by French mathematician Edouard Lucas in 1883, and in its original form was about a tower of eight disks. It is associated with a legend called the Tower of Brahma. Sixty-four golden disks form the tower of Brahma and, instead of simple pegs, it has diamond needles. At the beginning of time, God ordained a group of priests to transfer the disk from the first needle to the third. When the job is completed, it is said that the world will end.

Using Recursion to Solve the Tower of Hanoi Problem

When experimenting with two or three disks, you can see that the strategy described in **Figure 1-11** works.

Figure 1-11   Tower of Hanoi solution strategies. Left: Solution for two disks. Right: Solution for three disks

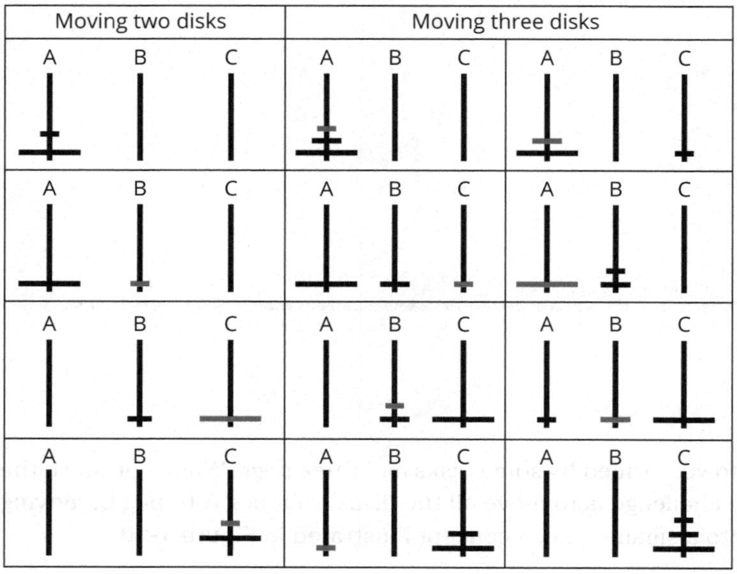

The description might give you an idea of how to apply recursion or divide and conquer.

You can start with the case of two disks. To describe the procedure, let's call the peg where the disks are the source peg, the peg where the disks must be moved the target peg, and the peg left the auxiliary peg. Using the previous notation, the procedure might be as follows:

1. Move the top disk from source peg A to auxiliary peg B.
2. Then move the largest disk from source peg A to target peg C.
3. Move the smallest disk from auxiliary peg B to target peg C.

Using this method, you can describe the process for three disks as follows:

1. Move the top two disks from source peg A to auxiliary peg B. At this point, you might notice that this is against the rules since you can only move one disk at a time. But this is the point to make use of recursion. Moving two disks is a problem that you have already solved.
2. Then move the largest disk from source peg A to target peg C.
3. Finally, move the top two disks from peg B (that is the source now) to target peg C. You now use peg A as an auxiliary peg.

One key aspect here is to notice that you reduce the problem of moving all three disks to moving only two, then moving one, and finally moving two more disks. Reducing the problem to substeps is the key component in recursion.

Next, you can see one possible solution algorithm:

```
tower(n, source, target, auxiliary)
   if n = 1
      move disk-n to target
      return
   else
      tower(n-1, source, auxiliary, target)
      move disk-n to target
      tower(n-1, auxiliary, target, source)
      return
```

As you can see again, a complex procedure can be described in a very elegant way using recursion.

Quick Check 1-4

Given that to move three disks from one tower to another in the Hanoi Tower problem takes seven moves, how many moves are necessary to move four disks?

Answer: 15. By analyzing the solution given in the text, you can see that moving three disks from peg A to peg B is necessary, thus seven movements. Then move the largest disk from peg A to peg C; this is one more movement. At last, move the three disks from peg B to peg C; this requires seven movements. In total, $7 + 1 + 7 = 15$ movements.

1.5 Backtracking: Finding all Subsets

Backtracking is a technique where solutions are constructed from using smaller solutions. It can be done recursively or not.

Why Use Backtracking?

Backtracking is a strategy to find solutions to problems that incrementally build solutions. The search for a solution can be recursive or not. Backtracking usually provides a more systematic way to enumerate all the cases or potential solutions to a problem, which gives some guarantee that there are no missing ones. This is especially important when you face a problem where the number of potential solutions is very large. When randomly searching for a solution, missing one solution, maybe the one you need, is very likely.

In backtracking you might use recursion to incrementally build the solution.

Consider the problem to find a subset S of a set X of positive integers such that the sum of the elements of S is exactly k. For example, for $X = \{1, 2, 3, 4, 5\}$, you want a subset S whose elements add to 6. One possible solution is $\{2, 4\}$.

One approach, the brute-force approach, is to test one by one every subset of X until you find one that satisfies the desired condition. That is a solid strategy to solve the problem. But to find the desired solution it might be necessary to test all possible sets, that is, 2^n where n is the size of the set X. For example, if $n = 10$, you might need to test $2^{10} = 1024$ tests.

Backtracking Solution

Consider the case of finding a subset S from $X = \{2,3,4,8\}$ such that the elements of S add up to 6. Here is a general description of the solution.

1. You start with an empty set, that of course is not a solution since the sum of the elements is 0.

2. Now you have two options: include the 2 in the set or not. The two options should be considered.

(Include 2) If 2 is included, the total sum is 2, which is less than 6, so you keep trying to add more elements to get 6. The next possible element to include is 3, and again you have two possible options, include it or not.

(Include 3) If 3 is included, $S = \{2,3\}$ and the sum is 5 that is less than 6, so you keep searching for numbers to add to S. The next possible element to include or not is 4.

(Include 4) If 4 is included, $S = \{2,3,4\}$ and the total sum is 9 that exceeds 6. You don't need to keep searching this path of options since it will be impossible to reach a number less than 9.

(Not include 4) If 4 is not included, then the next element to consider is 8.

(Include 8) If 8 is included, you get $S = \{2,3,8\}$, since 4 was not included. Then the total sum is 13, which exceeds 6; this is not a potential solution and so 8 shouldn't be included. Since there are no more elements to try, this path has been exhausted.

(Not include 3) Since the option of including 3 didn't provide a solution, now you must test the option of not including 3, so $S = \{2\}$. Then the next element to try to add to S is 4.

(Include 4) If 4 is included, $S = \{2,4\}$. The sum of such elements is 6, which is the desired solution.

A more schematic way of listing the previous procedure is shown in **Figure 1-12**.

Figure 1-12   Subset searching using backtracking

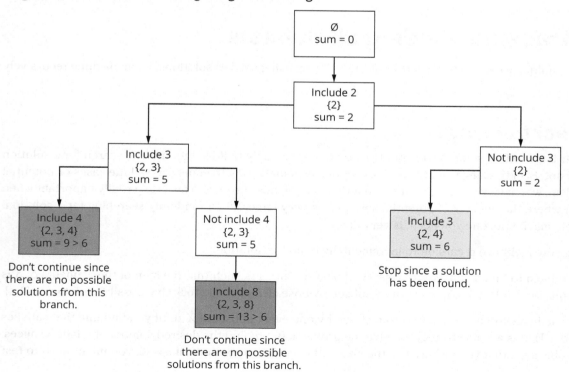

In the following solution, *m* is the index of the element that you have to analyze to include or not and *N* is the size of the set. *S* is the set constructed so far, so when calling the function for the first time you use *S* = {} as the empty set; *k* is the desired value for the sum.

```
subset(X, S, m, N, k)
    S1 = S ∪ {X[m]}
    if sum(S1) = k
        S1 is a solution and finish
    if m+1 <= N
        subset(X, S1, m+1, N,  k)
        subset(X, S, m+1, N, k)
    else
        This path is exhausted
```

You can work an iterative solution and notice that it is necessary to use more lines of code to keep track of all possible combinations.

> **Note** When using backtracking, you must be careful of having a bounding condition. A **bounding function or condition** is used during backtracking to determine if the search must continue or not. A bounding condition tells you if you must keep following a certain path of options or if the path you are following is no longer factual for a solution. In the case of the subset sum problem, the condition is that the sum of the elements of *S* is smaller than *k*.

Technical Interview

When facing a difficult question during an interview, keep in mind two things:

- Most of the time, the interviewer doesn't expect that you know the solution immediately or that you have it memorized. The interviewer wants to see how you approach a problem and how you start to search for a solution.

- As you saw with the Hanoi Tower problem, small cases are sometimes easy to solve and can provide the beginning of a complete solution. Thus, start working with small cases that will help you to make progress toward a general solution. This will also give you a better understanding of the problem you want to solve.

Summary

- A function is called recursive when it calls itself. This call can be in a direct way (direct recursion) or in an indirect way (indirect recursion).

- To avoid having a circular definition or procedure, the recursive function must reach a base case. Usually, the base case is so simple that the answer is immediate and splitting the task into smaller tasks is unnecessary.

- There can be as many base cases as needed and, when using recursion, a function can make as many calls to itself as it needs. The only restriction is that you must ensure that the function reaches a base case in a finite number of steps.

- When a recursive function is ill-defined, it might run forever. This kind of state is called an infinite recursion state. In typical computer architecture, each call to a function uses a space of memory called a stack to store the parameters and variables used to call a function. Since the stack space is finite, the stack gets full when a recursive function enters an infinite recursion state. When the stack runs out of space to store more variables, an error called stack overflow occurs.

- A huge benefit of using recursion is that it provides a way to work from small examples to general solutions. This generalization process helps create an elegant or less complex solution description.

- Recursion can also be used to build solutions incrementally, using a procedure known as backtracking. Although backtracking can be used without recursion, in the same way, a recursive function can be computed iteratively. When using backtracking recursively, you must provide a bounding function or condition used during the search for the solution to decide if more exploration is feasible or if there is no point in keeping up the search through the determined path.

- Recursion provides a powerful technique to approach problems that might seem complicated. A good strategy is to always start with small cases of a problem. Such an approach usually provides you with a base case for a recursive solution, a better understanding of the problem, and, in some cases, a way to generalize your procedure to solve the problem.

Key Terms

backtracking	indirect recursion	state of infinite recursion
base case	recursion	tail recursion
bounding function or condition	recursive function	well-defined recursion
direct recursion	stack overflow	

Review Questions

1. It is possible to define a recursive function without a base case.

   a. True   **b.** False

2. Which of the following are parts of a recursive function definition?

   a. Null cases   **c.** Automatic calling

   b. Base cases   **d.** Composition

3. When your program has a stack overflow error, it is because the program entered an infinite recursion.

   a. True   **b.** False

4. Lucas numbers L_n are defined as follows for a non-negative integer n:

   $L_0 = 2, L_1 = 1$

   For $n > 1$, $L_n = L_{n-1} + L_{n-2}$, what are the values of L_2, L_3, and L_4?

5. Which of the following is true about the Lucas numbers definition given in Question 4?

    a. The function enters into an infinite recursion.

    b. It has two base cases.

    c. It has too many base cases.

    d. The recursion is ill defined since it depends on two values of Lucas numbers and not one.

6. Programmer A is assigned to write a procedure that displays numbers by subtracting 3 starting from n until it reaches a negative number. For $n = 14$, the output should appear as follows:

$$14 \quad 11 \quad 8 \quad 5 \quad 2 \quad -1$$

The proposed pseudocode solution by programmer A is the following:

```
count(n)
if n < 0
    display n
    finish the program
else
    display n
    count(n-3)
```

Which is true about the solution of programmer A?

    a. The recursion is ill-defined because it doesn't have a base case.

    b. It doesn't use recursion.

    c. The recursion is ill-defined since it never reaches a base case.

    d. It uses tail recursion.

7. The number of combinations of n elements into k elements, C_k^n, is the number of subsets with k elements that can be formed from a set with n elements, where n and k are non-negative numbers such that $n \geq k$. C_k^n is also known as the number of ways of choosing k elements from n indistinguishable elements. A recursive definition of it can be made as follows:

$$\text{(Base case 1) } C_n^n = 1 \text{ for any } n \geq 0$$
$$\text{(Base case 2) } C_0^n = 1 \text{ for any } n \geq 0$$
$$\text{(Recursion) } C_k^n = C_{k-1}^{n-1} + C_k^{n-1} \text{ for } 0 < k < n$$

Compute $C_0^0, C_0^1, C_1^1, C_0^2, C_1^2, C_2^2$ using the recursive definition.

8. What prevents backtracking from testing all possible cases when building a solution?

    a. Bounding condition   **c.** Base case

    b. Infinite recursion   **d.** Backtracking stop condition

9. When searching for a solution to a problem that might require recursion, what might be a good strategy to start?

10. When using backtracking to find a subset with sum 10 from $X = \{2, 3, 4, 5, 8\}$, what would be the next step in the algorithm after reaching $S = \{2, 3, 4, 5\}$?

Programming Problems

1. Write a program that uses recursion to display all the odd positive integers, in descending order, from n to 1. **(LO 1.2)**

   For $n = 12$, the program must display: 11, 9, 7, 6, 5, 3, 1

   For $n = 7$, the program must display: 7, 5, 3, 1

2. The Lucas numbers are defined by:

   $L_0 = 2, L_1 = 1$
   For $n > 1, L_n = L_{n-1} + L_{n-2}$

   Write a recursive function that computes the nth Lucas number. **(LO 1.2)**

3. The number of combinations of n elements into k elements, C_k^n, is the number of subsets with k elements that can be formed from a set with n elements, where n and k are non-negative numbers such that $n \geq k$. C_k^n is also known as the number of ways of choosing k elements from n indistinguishable elements. A recursive definition of it can be made as follows:

   $$(\text{Base case 1}) \ C_n^n = 1 \text{ for any } n \geq 0$$
   $$(\text{Base case 2}) \ C_0^n = 1 \text{ for any } n \geq 0$$
   $$(\text{Recursion}) \ C_k^n = C_{k-1}^{n-1} + C_k^{n-1} \text{ for } 0 < k < n$$

   Use the previous definition to write a function that recursively computes all C_k^n for any $0 \leq k \leq n$ and n non-negative integers. **(LO 1.2)**

4. A palindrome is a string that can be read the same way from left to right or from right to left. Given a nonempty string w of size N, check if it is a palindrome or not.

   For example, the string $w =$ "hannah" is a palindrome, but $w =$ "haha" is not a palindrome. Strings with only one character are considered palindromes, thus $w =$ "o" is a palindrome.

   Write a recursive function that checks if a given string is a palindrome. Assume that the chars of the string are indexed starting at 0. **(LO 1.2)**

5. Write a recursive function that receives an array X of size N and displays the elements of the array in reverse order. In this program assume that the array starts at 1. **(LO 1.2)**

   For example, if $X = [1,3,5,7]$ the output should be "7 5 3 1".

   Assume that the indexing starts at zero.

Projects

Project 1-1: The Double Factorial

(LO 1.3) The double factorial of a non-negative integer n denoted $n!!$ is defined by two cases:

1. If n is even, then $n!!$ is the product of all even numbers from 2 to n. For example, $8!! = 2 \times 4 \times 6 \times 8$. The case $2!! = 2$ since it is the only number from 2 to 2. As usual, $0!! = 1$.

2. If n is odd, then $n!!$ is the product of all odd numbers from 1 to n. For example, $9!! = 9 \times 7 \times 5 \times 3 \times 1$.

Use recursive functions to calculate the double factorial of any non-negative integer n.

Project 1-2: Binary Search

(LO 1.3) Suppose you have a sorted array of integers, for example, $X = [2,6,8,12,14,15]$. When asked to find what index corresponds to $n = 14$, you can implement a binary search method using recursion as follows. Given the array X, an index *start* is the least index allowed for the search, an index *last* is the highest index allowed for the search, and the key value is n.

1. Use the mid element between *start* and *last* as the index i.

2. If $X[i]$ is the desired value, then you have found the index.

3. If $X[i]$ is less than the desired value (n), then keep searching only on the second half of the array.

4. If $X[i]$ is greater than the desired value (n), then keep searching only on the first half of the array.

5. Repeat until *start* and *last* can't be recalculated.

For example, with $X = [2,5,8,12,14,15]$, the calls would be:

- $n = 14$, *start* $= 0$, *last* $= 5$. Since $X[2] = 8 < 14$, you search only on the second half of the array.
- $n = 14$, *start* $= 3$, *last* $= 5$. Since $X[4] = 14$, the desired index is 4.

Write a program that realizes a binary search for the key-value n in an array X and returns the index corresponding to the key value. Assume that the key value is present in the array and that the indexes start at 0.

Project 1-3: Movements in the Hanoi Tower Solution

(LO 1.4) You explored one potential solution to the Hanoi Tower problem in the text. But the solution only describes the steps to take in a very abstract way, since it is not so simple to follow all the recursive calls.

For the case with only one disk, the implemented solution requires only one move. For the case with two disks, three movements are required.

Write a program that computes recursively the number of movements necessary to solve the Hanoi Tower problem for n disks.

Project 1-4: All Substrings of a String

(LO 1.5) The substrings of a string are sequences of characters from the original string that preserve the order of appearance. For example, for the string msg = "abcd", the possible substrings are:

"a", "b", "ab", "ac", "bc", "abc", "ad", "bd", "abd", "acd", "bcd", and "abcd"

Notice that not all strings formed with the characters of msg are considered substrings. For example, "bad" is not a substring since "a" is before "b" in msg.

Write a program that lists all possible substrings of a string msg. Assume that all characters in msg are different.

Chapter 2

Introduction to Data Structures

Learning Objectives

Upon completion of this chapter, you will be able to:

2.1 Describe the relationship between data structures and algorithms.

2.2 Explain the use of abstract data types (ADTs).

2.3 Contrast the ADT support in Java, C++, Python, and Go.

2.4 Differentiate linear and non-linear data structures.

2.5 Explain static and dynamic data structures.

2.6 Identify operations of different data structures.

2.1 Basic Data Structures and Algorithms

Most computer programs work by manipulating data, from your email address to the balance of your credit card. For many programs, a simple number is not sufficient to represent objects or entities. For such complex problems, it is necessary to:

- Organize the data necessary to solve the problem and the functions or procedures necessary to manipulate the data (use a data structure).

- Create a solution (an algorithm) for the problem at hand using the data representations, procedures, and functions created in the data structure.

What Is a Data Structure?

A computer represents information using ones and zeros, a binary representation. When using a programming language, you use a layer of abstraction that allows you to use more complex data without representing it exclusively using ones and zeros. Most programming languages allow you to use basic data types. A **data type** is a particular classification of values and operations allowed on those values, as specified by a programming language. For example, most programming languages have an integer data type that enables you to represent integer numbers from a minimum to a maximum value determined by the programming language. The primitive integer data type also has common operations such as addition and multiplication.

A **primitive data type** is a data type or range of values defined by the programming language or compiler. Most programming languages provide built-in primitive data types that allow you to store one number or a character. For example, the Java programming language has eight primitive built-in data types. These are int, byte, short, long, float, double, Boolean, and char. **Table 2-1** shows some of the most common primitive data types.

Table 2-1   Common primitive data types in high-level programming languages (for a 32-bit machine)

Type	Min Value	Max Value	Example
signed integer	−2,147,483,648	2,147,483,648	−1729, 1729
unsigned integer	0	4,294,967,295	3947
Boolean	False	True	True
char	0	255	'a' (91 in ASCII)

As you might imagine, using only these simple data types to solve complex problems would require many code lines, complicated procedures, and functions. One way to mitigate this problem is to create more complex ways to represent, store, and interact with data.

In most programming languages, you build more complicated data types through user-defined data types. A **user-defined data type** uses primitive or other user-defined data types to represent more complex data.

For example, you could define a new data type called Measures that holds the height and weight of a person as follows:

```
type Measures
    fields height, weight


person1 = Measures(170, 200)
person2 = Measures(95, 180)
```

In the previous code the variable person1 is of type Measures with a field height of 170 and weight 200. To use the field values of person1 the notation person1.*field* is used. For example, the following code compares the height of two variables person1 and person2:

```
if person1.height > person2.height
    display("person1 is taller.")
```

For most programming problems, you not only need to store data but also manipulate it. A **data structure** is a particular implementation for storing and managing data. Notice how a user-defined data type can be considered a data structure with no other behaviors besides holding the data in its fields. In some computer science texts, the user-defined data types used by more complex data structures are referred to as records or cells.

Two aspects characterize a data structure: the data it stores and what operations are implemented. For example, the following code provides a data structure known as an ordered pair. An ordered pair is represented as (a,b). The critical characteristic of an ordered pair is the comparison:

$$(a,b) = (c,d) \text{ if and only if } a = c \text{ and } b = d$$

For example, the ordered pair (1, 3) is not equal to the ordered pair (3, 1). The order in which elements are presented in an ordered pair is important. Ordered pairs are a type of data structure called a *fixed size data structure*. It is common to use an ordered pair to hold two values in a single variable.

The following is an implementation for the ordered pair `tuple1` and `tuple2`:

```
type tuple
  fields a, b


compare(tuple1, tuple2)
    if tuple1.a = tuple2.a and tuple1.b = tuple2.b
        return True
    else
        return False
```

Notice the two parts:

- How the data—in this case, the two components of tuple—are stored.
- The operation of comparison of tuples.

Quick Check 2-1

A data structure is characterized by data and operations. True or false?

Answer: True.

A data structure is an implementation for storing and managing data. The data stored and the operations on it characterize a data structure.

What Is an Algorithm?

An informal way to describe an **algorithm** is a set of instructions that uses a set of input values to produce a result. The result produced by an algorithm is called the *output*. The set of output values satisfy a given constraint, making them a solution to a given problem.

A formal definition of algorithm adequate for computer science and programming has specific aspects it must satisfy:

- An algorithm provides step-by-step instructions on using the input values to produce a result. For programming algorithms, the proper steps are determined by the programming language. The key point is that there can't be instructions that are ambiguous or simply invalid.
- The output must provide a solution to the desired problem. Providing a solution means that the output must satisfy a constraint imposed on the output. For example, the following pseudocode provides an algorithm that takes the input of three integers, x, y, and z (the input), and returns the largest of the three.

```
largest(x,y,z)
    val = x
    if y > val
        val = y
    if z > val
        val = z
    return val
```

In this case, the algorithm must solve the problem to find the largest value among the three input values.

- The algorithm must finish after a finite number of instructions are executed, or equivalently it must take only a finite amount of time to finish. For example, the function `largest(x,y,z)` will always finish after executing some of the seven lines of code.

On the other hand, a **computational process** is a set of instructions that uses input values to produce output values, but it is not designed to halt or stop after a finite number of steps. An example of a computational process is a program that waits for a particular key to be pressed to execute a procedure. So, the following code is for a computational process that waits for the Esc key to be pressed, then executes the `beep()` procedure, and then keeps waiting.

```
while(True)
    display("Press a key.")
    key_pressed = input_from_user()
    if key_pressed = 'esc'
        beep()
```

The input and output of an algorithm are not restricted to only primitive data types. They can be any data type or data structure. Even when the input and output of the algorithm are not user-defined data types, the algorithm can use data structures to produce the desired output.

Best Practices

When designing an algorithm to solve a problem many times, some small test cases can help the process. For example, if you need to solve a problem for a million users it could be helpful to try and solve the problem with only four users. Still, it is essential to guarantee that the algorithm will solve the desired problem in more complicated cases. So, it is crucial to design tests for the algorithm to check how it works with inputs other than the ones you had in mind when designing the algorithm. For most modern languages there are tools, such as Microsoft Unit Testing Framework for C++, to write automatic testing functions that can help you to identify errors in the algorithm's logic.

Note | Determining if a routine or instructions will eventually stop can be more complicated than you imagine, even with relatively simple procedures. For example, consider the following recursive function.

A famous mathematical problem, known as the Collatz conjecture (or the Ulam's conjecture or Kakutani's conjecture) is to prove that the function will eventually finish. For example, for a value n of 5, the procedure collatz(5) makes the following calls:

collatz(5) – > collatz(8) – > collatz(4) – > collatz(2) – > collatz(1)

```
collatz(n)
    if n = 1
        return
    else
        if n mod 2 = 0
            collatz(n/2)
            return
        else
            collatz((3*n+1)/2)
            return
```

When the value of n reaches 1, the function stops. The function has been proven to always stop for integer values of n less than 2^{68}.

2.2 Abstract Data Types (ADTs)

High-level programming languages such as Java, Python, C++, Go, and JavaScript provide an abstraction layer through their primitive data types. That means you don't need to worry about how an integer is stored in a computer's physical memory using ones and zeros, nor how to add two integers when stored as ones and zeros. All these programming languages provide a way to add two integers, although the way they provide this functionality, also known as its implementation, might vary between them.

In the same way, **abstract data types (ADTs)** provide a logical description of how data is stored and the operations you can perform with them. How the data is stored, its type, or how the operations are implemented are not specified, only how a user or programmer interacts with it from a conceptual point of view.

An ADT is a mathematical or formal description of how to interact with the data it represents. An ADT's behavior is characterized from the user's point of view. At the same time, a data structure is an implementation of the behaviors of an ADT.

Note	The idea of an ADT was introduced to the world of computer science through the CLU programming language. CLU was a programming language created by Barbara Liskov and her students at the Massachusetts Institute of Technology in 1973. ADTs grew as an effort to improve programming methodologies. At the time, there was a lot of interest in improving the efficiency of the programming process. CLU was also the precursor of other important concepts in computer science, such as object-oriented programming.

The Stack

A **stack** is an ADT where elements of the same type can be stored and retrieved following LIFO order. **LIFO** stands for last in, first out, meaning that the last element inserted is the first to be removed. The name *stack* refers to a physical stack of objects. A stack is a dynamic set. A **dynamic set** is an ADT where data can be added, retrieved, and removed from the set. In **Figure 2-1**, you can see a stack of books and an abstract representation of a stack ADT to model the stack of books.

Figure 2-1   Like a physical stack of books, you can only access the book at the top; when you add a new book to the stack it takes the top position

A stack has two operations to modify the set of stored elements and one to check if the stack is empty or not.

- Push is the operation that inserts a new element into the stack.
- Pop is an operation that returns the last element inserted in the stack and removes it from the stack.
- Empty returns true if the stack is empty and false in another case.

A depiction of a stack and how it changes when using push and pop is shown in **Figure 2-2**.

Figure 2-2   **push inserts a new element at the top of the stack; pop returns the element at the top of the stack**

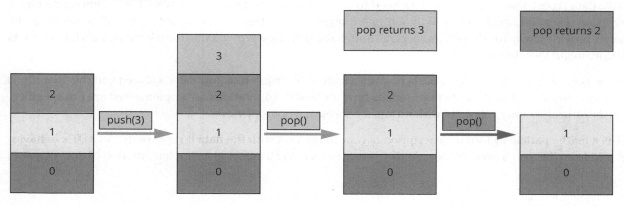

Consider the following code that inserts three elements in stack *s*:

```
s = Stack()
s.push(element1)
s.push(element2)
s.push(element3)
```

If you want to retrieve `element1`, it would be necessary to extract `element3` and `element2` first. It is not possible to access any element of the stack at a given time; any element should be retrieved using the `pop` method.

Quick Check 2-2

What is the output produced by the following code?

```
s = Stack()
s.push(6)
s.push(8)
s.push(9)
s.pop()
display(s.pop())
```

Answer: 8. The Stack ADT follows the LIFO order after the first pop returns the value 9. So, at the top of the stack is the value 8, which is returned by the second pop call.

Why Use ADTs?

ADTs, being a mathematical model in the same way as addition and subtraction, have a consistent behavior through different programming languages. Thus, if you find an ADT with behavior that might be useful to solve a specific problem, you should consider implementing the ADT in a particular programming language.

Several ADTs are commonly used in programs, such as linked lists, queues, priority queues, binary trees, hash tables, disjoint sets, and graphs. These structures have been studied by mathematicians and computer scientists for a long time, and fast algorithms have been designed to implement their operations. Using such ADTs in your algorithms provides you with efficient implementations of the functions.

Since ADTs are a standard tool in programming, most popular ADTs have an implementation in almost every modern high-level programming language. However, most of the time those ADTs are provided by additional libraries. Using the provided implementations allows you to avoid the details of memory management, optimization, and programming that are necessary to implement the operations of many ADTs.

2.3 ADT Support in Popular Programming Languages

Knowing some of the implementations of ADTs that are available in different programming languages is advantageous. The implementation of ADTs in a programming language provides a data structure. Since an ADT is independent of the implementation, various programming languages use different data structures as a basis for their implementations of the standard ADTs.

ADTs in Python

Python provides list, tuple, dict (dictionary), and set as built-in data types. A **built-in type** is a data type that is supported by the language without the use of additional libraries. For example, a list in Python is a built-in data type, so you don't need to implement or use an external library to use the list ADT.

> **Note** | Recall that a primitive data type allows you to store a single value like a number or a character, while built-in data types can be more complex structures. In the Python language the set data structure is provided as a built-in data type. A set can hold several values. Hence, every primitive data type is a built-in data type, but not every built-in data type is primitive. For example, in a specific programming language, a list can be provided by the programming language, which makes lists a built-in data type for that programming language. But a list is not primitive since it stores several elements.

Python provides the module called *collections* when the basic types are not enough and another ADT is necessary. The collections module offers additional features for the built-in types list, tuple, dict, and set.

Many ADTs can be implemented in Python 3.x through classes and the basic built-in types. You can implement the characteristic operations of a given ADT through a class. Classes are used in Python to create user-defined types. For example, the following is an implementation of the stack ADT in Python using classes:

```python
class Stack:

    def __init__(self):
        self.data = [] # Using a list to implement a stack.

    def empty(self): # Check if the structure is empty.
        if len(self.data) == 0:
            return True
        else:
            return False

    def push(self, x): # Adding x at the end of the list.
        self.data.append(x)

    def pop(self, x): # Returns the last inserted element.
        if len(self.data) > 0: # Check if the stack is not empty
            val = self.data.pop()
            return val
        else:
            return None # When the stack is empty returns nothing.
```

Any object of the class stack will have only the methods empty(), push(x), and pop().

ADTs in C++

C++, provides built-in support for arrays. However, it doesn't have built-in types for more complex data structures. The Standard Template Library (STL) supports many ADTs such as double-ended queues, forward lists, lists, maps, queues, sets, stacks, and vectors. To use a data structure from the STL in a program, you must include a file containing the implementation of the desired data structure. In C++, you include files or libraries using the `include` command.

Unlike Python, in C++, lists, maps, and sets are types of containers. A **container** is a data structure that holds objects of the same type. For example, the following code uses a stack from the STL to store some integers and extract them:

```
#include <iostream> // IO library for console programs

#include <stack> // The stack implementation from STL.
using namespace std;

int main() {
  stack<int> x; // new empty stack is created
  x.push(8);
  x.push(6);
  x.push(4);
  x.push(2);

  while(!x.empty()){
    cout << '\t' << x.top();
    x.pop();
  }
}
```

As you can see, the implemented behaviors might vary from one language to another and even from one programmer to another, but the central concept is usually the same. In particular, the implementation of a stack used here includes the `top()` method that returns the value of the last element inserted but doesn't modify the stack. You can think of it as a peeking method that lets you see the next element that pops from the stack. This method wasn't included in the basic operations of the stack ADT.

ADTs in Java

Java doesn't provide built-in types for data structures other than arrays. It provides implementations of linked lists, stacks, queues, binary trees, heaps, hash tables, and graphs through the `java.util` library.

Like C++, the data structures provided by Java through the `java.util` library are containers, meaning all the data stored in them must be of the same class, meaning their implementation inherits from them. The following code makes use of the Stack class to store odd numbers in stack *x* and then displays the numbers in reverse order.

```
import java.io.*;
import java.util.*;

class Example{
  public static void main(String [] args){
    Stack <Integer> x = new Stack<>();

    x.push(9);
    x.push(7);
```

```
        x.push(5);
        x.push(3);
        x.push(1);

        while (!x.empty()){
            System.out.print("\t" + x.pop());
        }
    }
}
```

Notice that this code looks very similar to the C++ example given, especially in the way it manipulates the stack.

ADTs in Go

Go provides built-in basic data structure support for arrays, slices, and maps. The slice data type is the equivalent of a list in Python. The map is an array-like structure that can use data types other than integers as keys. Other ADTs can be implemented using the struct data type. The struct data type in Go is like a class. It encapsulates data but doesn't have methods since Go is not an object-oriented language.

In the following code, you can see an implementation of a stack object in Go.

```
package main

import "fmt"

type Stack []int // Define a new structure of type Stack
                 // containing an array.

func (s *Stack) Empty() bool { // The Empty() function of stack.
    return len(*s) == 0
}

func (s *Stack) Push(val int) {
    *s = append(*s, val) // append inserts val to the end of s
}

func (s *Stack) Pop() (int, bool) {
    if s.Empty() {
        return -1, false   // If the stack is empty
                           // returns no element.
    }else{
        idx := len(*s) -1  // The index of the last element
                           // in the array.
        val := (*s)[idx]   // The value of the last element
                           // of the array.
        *s = (*s)[:idx]    // Remove the last element of the array.
        return val, true   // Returns the top element of the stack.
    }
}
```

Although this implementation is slightly different from the one in Python, you can recognize the same operations: empty, push, and pop. Their use is almost identical, except for the syntactical differences between the languages. You can see the similarities in the following code that uses the previous implementation to create a stack, add even numbers, and display them in the order they are removed from the stack.

```
func main() {
    var x Stack

    x.Push(10)
    x.Push(8)
    x.Push(6)
    x.Push(4)
    x.Push(2)
    x.Push(0)

    for !x.Empty() {
        val, code := x.Pop()
        if code == true {
            fmt.Printf("\t%v", val)
        }
    }
}
```

Best Practices

As you saw in this section, most high-level programming languages have several ADTs implemented through additional libraries. When you start coding an algorithm to solve a given problem, you should start by checking the standard libraries of the chosen language for data structure support.

If you don't find what you need in the standard libraries of a language, you can always use user-defined data types to implement the ADT yourself. Try to use, as much as possible, conventional names for operations and descriptive names for fields. By using the common names for operations, your code will be easier to read and debug.

Quick Check 2-3

Before using a built-in data structure, you must first import the adequate library or module. True or false?

Answer: False. A built-in type or data structure is supported by the programming language without having to use another library or module.

2.4 Linear and Non-Linear Data Structures

A **linear data structure** is a data collection where the elements are organized in such a way that every element has a previous and a following element. In the case of the beginning of the data structure, its previous is null, and for the last element of the structure, its following element is null also.

For example, the array is a linear data structure since every element `array[k]` has a previous element `array[k-1]` and a following `array[k+1]`. In such cases it is common to say that the elements are stored in a sequential manner, that is, for every element there is a previous and a following, except for the first and last elements.

Although the implementation in a particular programming language might use a different data structure, you can only access the elements in the stack following the LIFO order, which makes it a linear data structure.

A more general linear ADT is the list. A **list** is an ADT formed by a sequence of elements (this includes an empty list) where more elements can be added. Sometimes the elements of the list are denoted $a_0, a_1, a_2, \ldots, a_N$ to emphasize that the elements are organized in a sorted way. The subscripts indicate the position of the element in the list. For example, you could refer to a list with the first four odd numbers as $a_0 = 1, a_1 = 3, a_2 = 5, a_3 = 7$ so the element at position 2 (a_2) has a value of 5. Some of the operations for a list L are the following:

- `insert(L, p, x)` inserts the element x at position p of the list L, moving the rest of the elements to the next position. For example, if the list L has the elements $a_0 = 2$, $a_1 = 3$, and $a_2 = 10$ when using `insert(L, 1, -4)`, the list L will then have the elements $a_0 = 2$, $a_1 = -4$, $a_2 = 3$, and $a_3 = 10$.

- `locate(L, x)` returns the position of the element x in the list L.

- `retrieve(L, p)` returns the element of L at position p.

- `delete(L, p)` deletes the element of L at position p, moving all the elements beyond the position p to the previous position in the list. For example, if the list L has the elements $a_0 = 2$, $a_1 = -4$, $a_2 = 3$, and $a_3 = 10$ when using `delete(L, 1)`, the list L will then have the elements $a_0 = 2$, $a_1 = 3$, and $a_2 = 10$.

- `len(L)` returns the number of elements in the list L.

You can see a depiction of a list and how the previous operations affect the list in **Figure 2-3**. Notice that in most programming languages, the indices start at 0.

Figure 2-3 Effect of delete and insert over a list

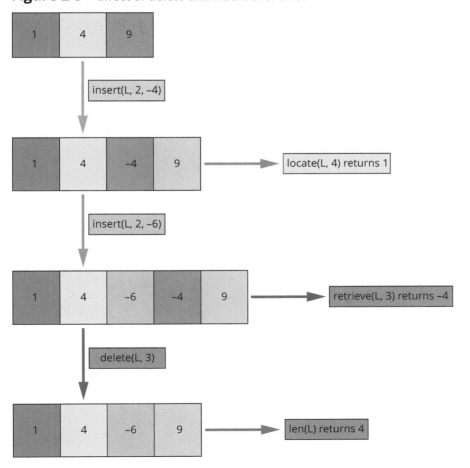

As you can see, the elements in a list are stored and retrieved sequentially, so a list is a linear data structure.

There are other data structures where the data is not stored and accessed sequentially—for example, a graph. A **graph** is an ADT described by a set of vertices V and a set of edges E that connect two vertices. You can see a graphical representation of a graph in **Figure 2-4**.

Figure 2-4   In this graph, arrows indicate connections or edges from one vertex to another

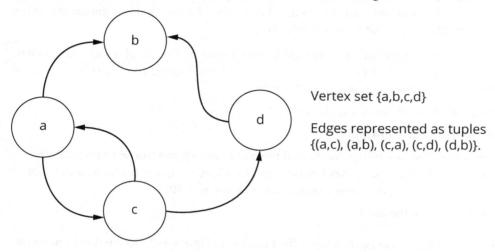

Vertex set {a,b,c,d}

Edges represented as tuples {(a,c), (a,b), (c,a), (c,d), (d,b)}.

A **non-linear data structure** is data that is not structured in sequential order. The data in a graph is not stored linearly, thus it is a non-linear data structure. Thus, saying "the first element of the graph G" doesn't make any sense.

Some of the common graph ADT operations are

- `adjacent(G, v1, v2)` that returns `True` if there is an edge joining the vertex `v1` with the vertex `v2` in the graph G.
- `neighbors(G, v)` returns a list of all vertices v' such that an edge in the graph G joins v with v'.
- `addVertex(G, v)` that adds a vertex v to the set of vertices of the graph G.
- `addEdge(G, v1, v2)` that adds an edge from `v1` to `v2` to the graph G.
- `removeEdge(G, v1, v2)` that removes the edge from `v1` to `v2` of the graph G.

You can see a depiction of how these operations affect a graph in **Figure 2-5**.

Figure 2-5 How different operations affect a graph

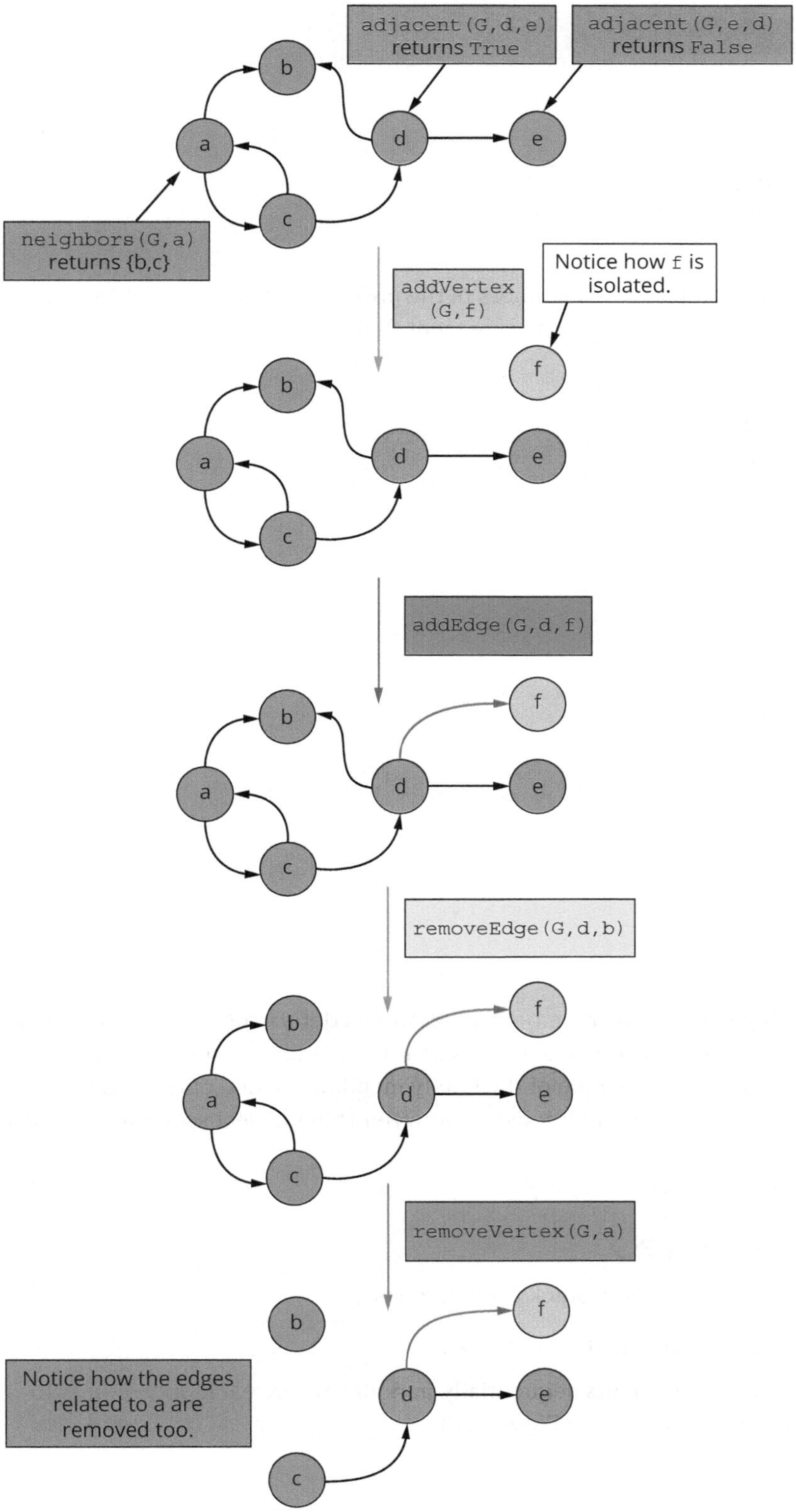

Storing Data in a List versus a Graph

Not every ADT is appropriate for all problems. For example, if you want to store the names of all members of your extended family, a list can capture all the information. Moreover, you could sort the names alphabetically, and a list is good for that task, as shown in **Figure 2-6**.

Figure 2-6   Inserting a new name in position 2 preserves the order in the list

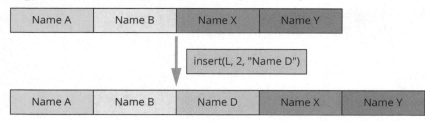

However, if you want to store the familial relationships of the members of the previous list, a linear data structure would not convey the necessary relationship information. A graph can represent that information, as in **Figure 2-7**.

Figure 2-7   Relationships between elements can be represented through edges in a graph

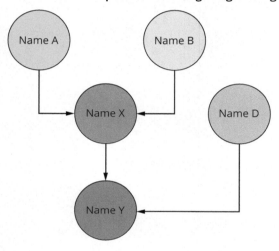

So, the objects to store and the relationship between them are important factors in determining which data structure to use. There is not a single data structure that fits all problems. Even when the objects seem the same it might be that the relationship between them is different as in the example of the family members. When only the names are necessary, a list is a good choice to store them but, when the relationship between them is necessary, a graph is a better choice.

Examples of Linear Data Structures

The most common linear data structures are arrays, linked lists, stacks, and queues:

- An **array** is a fixed-size data structure that stores elements of a fixed type.

- A **linked list** is a non-fixed-size structure that stores elements sequentially in nodes where each node points to the next. You can see depictions of an array and a linked list in **Figure 2-8**.

Figure 2-8   The elements of a linked list are stored in different noncontinuous memory addresses

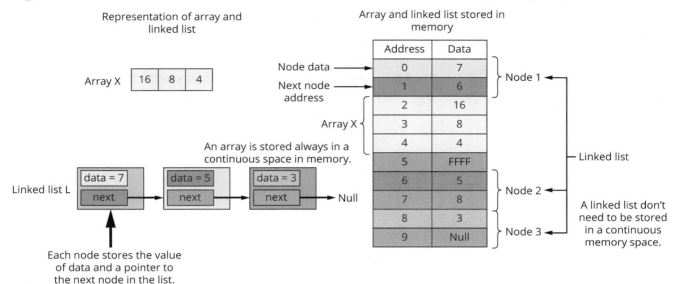

- A stack is a data structure that can be fixed or non-fixed in size, where the elements are stored and retrieved following a LIFO order.

- A **queue** is a data structure that can be fixed or non-fixed in size, where the elements are stored and retrieved following a FIFO order. **FIFO** stands for first in, first out. FIFO means that the first element inserted is the first one deleted or retrieved from the data structure. You can see a depiction of stacks and queues in **Figure 2-9**.

Figure 2-9   Stacks follow the LIFO order for insertion and retrieval, whereas queues follow the FIFO order

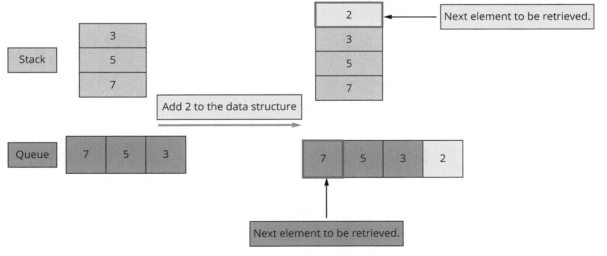

All these structures store data sequentially; that is, you could list all the elements in a specific order.

Quick Check 2-4

In what order are elements of a queue accessed?

Answer: FIFO. First in, first out means that the first element inserted is the first retrieved and removed from the queue.

Examples of Non-Linear Data Structures

The most common non-linear data structures are trees and graphs:

- A **tree** is a data structure where data is organized hierarchically through links. In a tree, the data is encapsulated in nodes composed of the datum and the links to other nodes. The main difference with linked lists is that the links don't follow a linear sequence and that one node can point to more than just another node. In **Figure 2-10**, you can see a depiction of a particular type of tree called a binary search tree. The tree data structure's details are covered in a later chapter.

Figure 2-10   Binary search tree

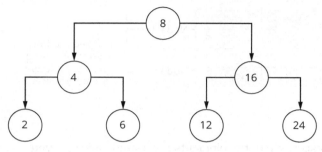

- A graph is a data structure composed of vertices and edges linking two vertices.

You can use linear data structures to implement non-linear data structures and the other way around. For example, you can implement a linked list as a tree where each node has only one link. **Figure 2-11** depicts a linked list implemented using a binary tree.

Figure 2-11   Using a graph to represent a list of three elements

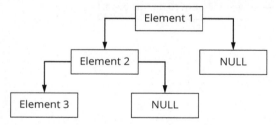

> **Note** When using more complex data structures, it is common to use non-linear data structures to implement linear ADTs. Using graphs or trees to represent lists might not seem intuitive, but they accelerate the operations if additional constraints are imposed on the lists. For example, it is common to use a binary tree to accelerate the search process.

2.5 Static and Dynamic Data Structures

When you declare or use a variable in a program, it requires memory to be reserved to store the variable. When you declare or create a data structure, you usually don't know in advance how much data will be stored, so it is difficult to declare the data structure without knowing how much space must be reserved to store it.

One solution is to require the user (the programmer) to give the structure size when it is created. A **static data structure** has a fixed size.

All data structures are fixed size due to memory limitations and implementation details. But at least from the algorithmic design point of view, having the possibility of using a data structure that doesn't require you to determine its size from the start and lets you extend it as you need it is convenient. A **dynamic data structure** has a non-fixed size. So you can grow or reduce the size of a dynamic data structure as needed throughout the program's operation.

Arrays versus Lists

In most programming languages, an array is implemented by reserving a fixed size of continuous memory and pointing to the start of the chunk of reserved memory. Data in an array is accessed through an index that indicates its position from the beginning of the reserved memory space. You can see that illustrated in **Figure 2-12**.

Figure 2-12   Arrays are stored in a continuous space of memory

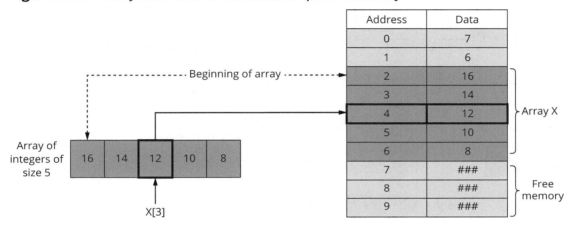

A list doesn't have a fixed size, so it grows each time a new item is inserted. Some implementations of a list use fixed-size memory spaces, such as arrays. When the fixed size is insufficient, it is linked to another fixed-size memory space. The linked list is an example of a data type where the reserved space can hold only one data element at a time. The idea of this implementation is illustrated in **Figure 2-13**.

Figure 2-13   A list implementation using fixed-size arrays; with this implementation the array data is not in a
continuous memory space

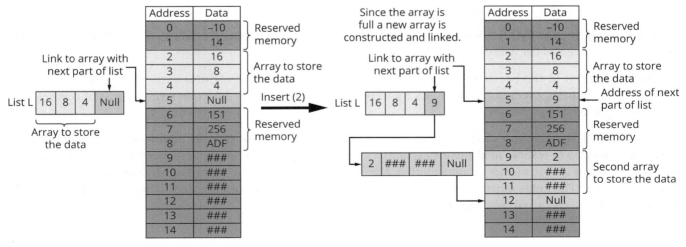

Best Practices

There is a tradeoff between balancing the memory overhead from using a list and its simplicity. It is possible that by using a list, you reserve space that might never be used, as shown in **Figure 2-14**. With other implementations, it is also possible to have slower access to the elements stored in the list.

Figure 2-14   When using a list, some memory could be reserved but never used, depending on the size of the arrays

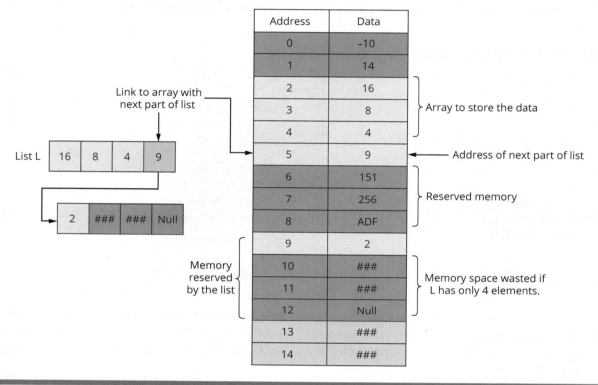

When to Use a Static Data Structure

Some languages, such as Python, don't have arrays; they only have lists, a dynamic data structure. In other languages such as C++, Java, and Go, arrays exist as a built-in data type.

As pointed out in the previous section, access is faster and more straightforward when you use an array. Nevertheless, if during execution it is necessary to resize an array, that can be expensive in terms of running time and memory use.

For example, suppose you want to resize the array X = [1, 2, 4] to store an additional three integers. First, it will be necessary to reserve new memory space to store six integers. Reserving more memory each time the array needs to grow may lead to memory fragmentation. **Memory fragmentation** is when holes of free memory exist between reserved spaces. The holes of free space might not be large enough to store necessary objects, thus rendering the space useless. You can see this in **Figure 2-15**.

Figure 2-15 When resizing an array, the freed space (in orange in the figure) might not be suitable to store new objects, resulting in wasted memory space

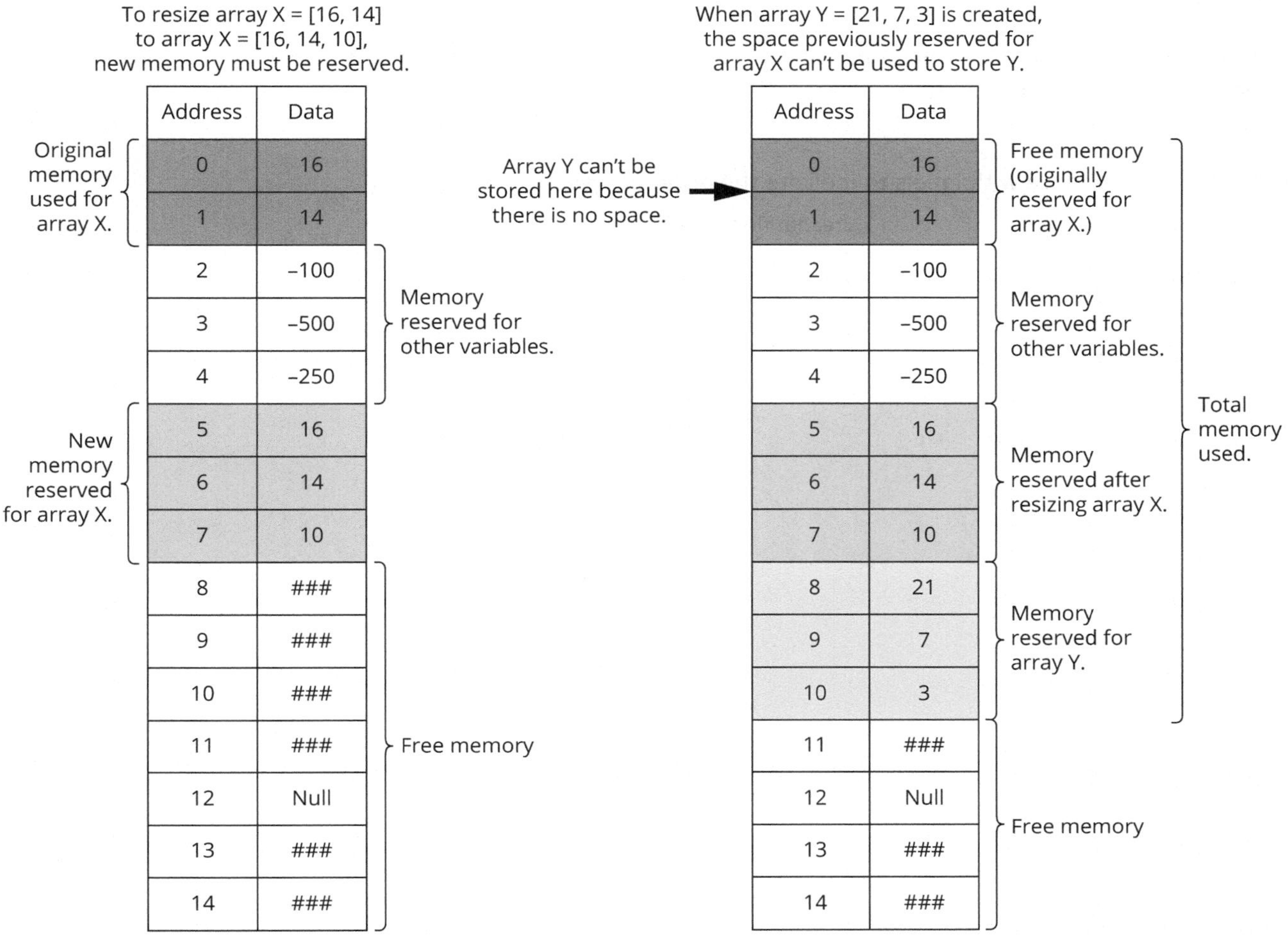

The second step after you reserve the necessary memory space for the resize is to copy the existing data of the array. Not only must the information in the old place be copied to the new location, but any reference to this array, usually done by a pointer, must be updated.

A static or fixed-size data structure is an ideal tool when you know the size of the data to be stored. It also might be a good idea to use a static structure for simple tasks or where performance is a critical aspect of the program.

> **Note** When implementing a complex algorithm using only arrays, you might get a higher execution time. Getting a higher execution time when using an array might be due to a slower implementation for an operation such as a locate. Consider that the support for dynamic data structures in most modern programming languages uses the fastest algorithms and the implementations have been thoroughly revised.

2.6 Common Operations of Data Structures

Traversing a Data Structure

Suppose you have the data structure `TimeWorked` storing the number of months that the members of a project have been working. After the end of the month, the data in `TimeWorked` must be updated, increasing the time worked on the project. So, it will be necessary to visit each element stored in `TimeWorked`.

Traversing a data structure is a term used for the operation of enumerating all the elements of the data structure. There is not a single way of traversing a data structure, but every way of traversing must list all the elements in the data structure.

Figure 2-16 illustrates three common ways of traversing a binary tree. Notice that a binary tree doesn't have a single logical way to list its elements.

Figure 2-16   Binary tree with labels to indicate the order of traversal

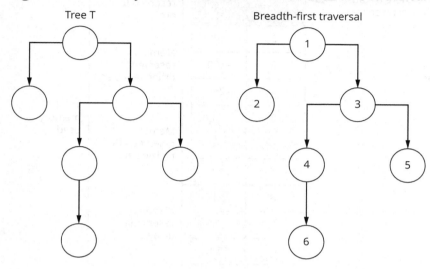

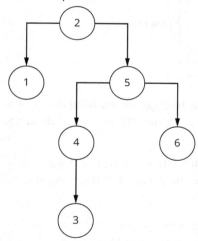

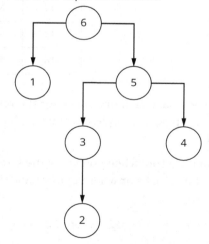

> **Note**   When you use a data structure and want to traverse it, you must ensure that you are not destroying or changing the data in the structure during the traverse. For example, it might be that you need to list all the elements in a stack for testing or debugging purposes. If you use the pop() operation, the returned element is deleted from the data structure. In this case, you are not traversing the structure but emptying the stack.
>
> The previous situation is one of the reasons why some implementations of ADTs provide more than the basic ADT operations. For example, the stack structure in Java extends the Vector data structure, and thus it inherits the methods of the Vector structure. The methods of the Vector class can be used to traverse the data in the stack without removing the contents.

Searching for an Element

When traversing a data structure, you must visit all data structure elements. But when you are searching for a specific element, that might not be necessary. Moreover, it is desirable to reach the object you are searching for with the least number of steps possible.

Suppose you are searching for the value $x = 8$ in the array `NumArray = [2, 8, 1, 4, 2, 11]`. It is possible to go through the values stored in `NumArray` and compare them with $x = 8$ until you get a match as shown in the following code.

```
found = False
i = 0
while (i < 6 and not found)
    if NumArray[i] = 8
        found = True
    i = i + 1
if found
    return i
else
    return -1
```

Notice that, during the execution of the previous code, i takes the values 0 and 1. The loop doesn't access all elements of the array, only those necessary before finding the desired value $x = 8$.

One aspect to consider when searching for an element in a data structure is that the data structure might store elements of a user-defined data type. For example, suppose that in the data structure `TimeWorked` you want to keep the name and number of months a person has been working on a project. To use abstraction, you can define a user-defined data type member with two fields, name and time. In that way, `TimeWorked` will store elements of type `members`. When searching for a member, you might be interested only in the name or the time worked. The field used to search is called a **key**. A key is a field from a data type that is used to retrieve an element from a data structure. In most cases, in order to have consistency, the key value should be unique to each element.

A data structure is often optimized to search for a particular key as fast as possible. So it is usually necessary for you to think about which fields are more convenient as keys when storing data in a data structure.

Modifying a Data Structure

The most common operations to modify a data structure is to add new elements or remove elements.

These operations make sense only in dynamic data structures since static data structures can't grow or shrink in size. The insertion and deletion operations in linear data structures are usually more straightforward than in nonlinear data structures.

For example, in **Figure 2-17**, you can see two ways of inserting a new node into a binary tree.

Figure 2-17 A new node can be connected to an existing tree in different ways; in the two possibilities shown here, the search property is preserved

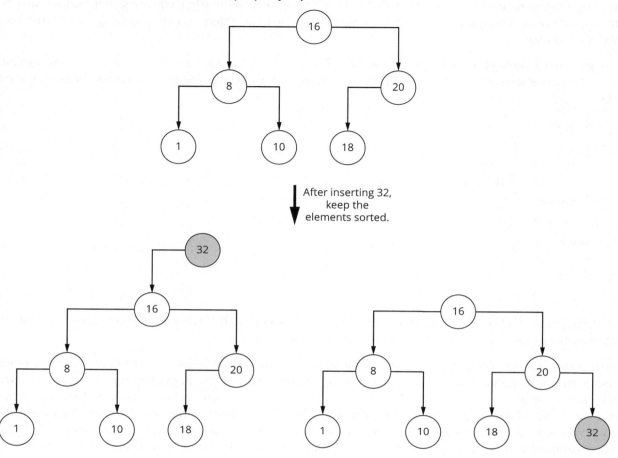

On the left in Figure 2-17, a new node with data 32 is inserted at the top and the whole tree becomes its left branch. On the right in the figure, a new node with data 32 is also inserted, but this time as the right branch of the node with data 20.

In many cases, it is desirable to order the elements stored in a data structure. For example, it might be required to keep the elements in sorted order. In the following code, you can see an implementation of a function that inserts a new integer, x, to a list, L, and keeps the elements in ascending order.

```
sorted_insert(L, x)
    N = len(L)                              The length of the list
    for i=0 to N-1 step 1               iterates over each element of L
        var = retrieve(L, i)
        if var > x                        If the current element is larger, inserts
                                                        the new element
            insert(L, i, x)
            return
    insert(L, N, x)                   If wasn't inserted, the element is larger than all
                                          others and should be inserted at the end of the
                                                                                list
    return
```

Notice that in the previous example there is no need to write a new function to delete an element and keep the order of the elements in the list. Since all elements are sorted by the value x, it is possible to consider the pair (i, x) as a key.

Technical Interview

When given a problem or challenge, it is useful to answer the following questions:

- What type of data is the input? Are they integers? Are negative numbers allowed?
- Is there a limit on the size of the data?
- Is the data received in a specific data structure?

These questions will help you choose the proper data structure for your solution algorithm. Once you have those answers, you can use a high-level approach to the problem, using generic names for the ADTs such as queues, stacks, lists, and dictionaries. Using generic structures is a good strategy even if the interview is in a specific language since this will provide you with a road map to implement your solution.

Quick Check 2-5

When you add a new element to any queue, the queue stays sorted since the element is stored at the end of the queue. True or false?

Answer: False. This is only true if the key value is the position of the element in the queue. Imagine a queue of people waiting to buy something. If the key value is the height of a person, then the queue doesn't stay sorted when a new element is added.

Summary

- Every variable in a program must have a data type. The data type describes what values can be stored in the variable along with the permissible operations.
- Most programming languages provide built-in data types such as integers, Boolean, and characters.
- You can define more complex data types called user-defined data types. They are a useful abstraction to manage several values corresponding to a single entity like the height and weight of a person.
- A data structure is a particular implementation for storing and retrieving data. You can use data structures to solve problems through the design of algorithms.
- A more precise definition of an algorithm requires the algorithm to solve a problem correctly (satisfy the given constraints of the problem), using a finite number of steps or instructions and in a finite amount of time.
- An ADT (abstract data type) is a mathematical model that provides a logical description of how data is stored and the operations on it. When an ADT is implemented, it becomes a data structure.
- Most high-level modern programming languages provide support for ADTs. That means they provide tools to implement common data structures such as stacks, lists, queues, maps, and tables.
- Some programming languages, such as Python and Go, provide basic data structures as built-in types. Other languages, such as Java and C++, provide data structures through classes of their standard libraries.
- Data structures can be classified by the way the data is stored. When stored sequentially, the data structure is called linear, and when it is not stored sequentially, it is called non-linear.

- Data structures can be classified according to whether you can add new data to it or not. Arrays are fixed size; you can't add more data, but you can modify the data stored in an array.

- Most data structures provide ways to traverse, search, insert, and delete elements. In practice, implementing such operations might require additional constraints. For example, a specific order for traversal is searched by a specific key and inserted or deleted, keeping a particular property in the data structure.

Key Terms

abstract data type (ADT)	dynamic set	non-linear data structure
algorithm	FIFO	primitive data type
array	graph	queue
built-in type	key	stack
computational process	LIFO	static data structure
container	linear data structure	traversing a data structure
data structure	linked list	tree
data type	list	user-defined data type
dynamic data structure	memory fragmentation	

Review Questions

1. Data structures are constructed exclusively by using primitive data types.

    a. True   **b.** False

2. You can use a data structure when designing an algorithm, but you can't use an algorithm as part of a data structure.

    a. True   **b.** False

3. Which of the following is true about an ADT?

    a. ADT stands for abstract data type.
    b. An ADT is an implementation of a data structure.
    c. ADT stands for advanced data type.
    d. An ADT provides a mathematical model, not an implementation.

4. What is the output of the following program?

```
s = new Stack()
s.push(10)
s.push(7)
s.push(5)
s.pop()
s.pus(9)
s.pop()
display(s.pop())
```

5. All programming languages provide only fixed-size data structures as built-in data types.

    a. True   **b.** False

6. Remember that Go is not an object-oriented language. How could you implement ADTs that are not part of the built-in data types?

7. Which languages provide built-in data types for dynamic data structures?

    a. Java   **c.** C++

    b. Python   **d.** Go

8. Which of the following are linear data structures?

    a. Graph   **c.** Queue

    b. Linked list   **d.** Tree

9. You are responsible for writing a program to store information about clients, sales representatives, and showrooms. Every sales showroom has sales representatives, and each sales representative has its clients. What data structure is more appropriate to store the data?

10. Consider graph *G* given in **Figure 2-18**. What is the value returned by `neighbors(G, v3)`?

Figure 2-18   Graph for Review Question 10

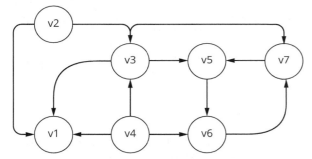

Programming Problems

1. Suppose `studentList` is a list ADT that contains the name and average of a group of students. Every element of the `studentList` is a user-defined data type with a string field name and an integer field average. Write a program that displays the name of the two students with the highest average. **(LO 2.4, 2.5)**

2. Suppose `groceryList` is a list ADT that contains the user-defined data type `ingredient`. The `ingredient` data type has the field's name and price. Write a program that computes the sum of all the prices of each ingredient in the list. **(LO 2.1, 2.4, 2.5)**

3. Sometimes, a stack has an operation called `top(S)` that returns the element at the top of the stack, which is the element returned by `pop(S)` but doesn't remove this element. Write the `top(S)` operation using the stack ADT defined in the text. **(LO 2.2, 2.6)**

4. Write a function that calculates the total accumulated on a stack of numbers. That is, it traverses the stack and adds all the elements of the stack. **(LO 2.4, 2.5)**

5. Using a stack, write a function that reverses a string. For example, when using `reverse(arr, N)`, where `arr` is the array of characters "hello" and N is the array's length, then the result should be `"olleh"`. **(LO 2.1, 2.2, 2.4)**

Projects

Project 2-1: Balanced Parentheses

(LO 2.1, 2.2, 2.5) When writing a mathematical expression, one aspect to verify is that the parentheses are balanced. That means that for each opening parenthesis, `"("`, there is one closing parenthesis, `")"`. For example, the following are strings with balanced parentheses:

`"(a(b+c)(d+(fg)h)d)"`, `"(((ab)))"`, `"(a)(b)()()((()()))"`

The following are examples of strings with unbalanced parentheses:

`"(ab(c)(d)(())"`, `"()())"`, `"(()()"`

Use a stack to write a program that verifies if a string has balanced parentheses `"("`, `")"`.

Project 2-2: Lexicographic Order

(LO 2.2, 2.5, 2.6) The lexicographic order is defined for tuples by

If $a > c$, then (a,b) is greater than (c,d).

If $a = c$ and $b > d$, then (a,b) is greater than (c,d).

For example, the lexicographical order *(3, 1)* is greater than *(1, 10)*, *(8, 11)* is greater than *(8, 9)*, and *(2, 5)* is smaller than *(5, 2)*.

Implement a `lex_insert(L, a, b)` function that inserts a tuple (a,b) into the list L and keeps the element in L sorted in ascending lexicographical order.

Project 2-3: Binary Digits

(LO 2.2, 2.5, 2.6) A way to compute the digits of the binary representation of a number in decimal representation is by repeatedly dividing the number by two and computing its residues. For example, for 55 the procedure is as follows:

```
55 / 2 = 27 remainder 1 (6th digit)
26 / 2 = 13 remainder 1 (5th digit)
13/2 = 6 remainder 1 (4th digit)
6/2 = 3 remainder 0 (3rd digit)
3/2 = 1 remainder 1 (2nd digit)
1/2 = 0 remainder 1 (1st digit)
```

The binary representation of *55* is *110111*. Notice how the digits are the residues, but they are in reverse order. To sort them in the proper order, you can use a stack.

Use a stack to write a code to display the binary representation of a number x.

Project 2-4: Palindrome Generator

(LO 2.2, 2.5, 2.6) A palindrome is a string that reads the same from left to right or right to left. For example, the following strings are palindromes:

`"fababaf"`, `"fabaabaf"`, `"aaa"`, `"aa"`

Notice how a palindrome can have an even or an odd number of characters.

Write a function that receives a string txt and builds a palindrome of even size by reversing the characters of txt. For example, when `txt = "abc"`, the result should be `"abccba"`.

Chapter 3

Designing Efficient Algorithms

Learning Objectives

Upon completion of this chapter, you will be able to:

3.1 Describe the efficiency and complexity of designing algorithms.

3.2 Apply Big O notation to describe an algorithm's efficiency.

3.3 Measure an algorithm's best, worst, and average-case time requirements as a function of size.

3.4 Determine the space complexity of algorithms.

3.5 Discuss the tradeoffs of using a heuristic algorithm.

3.1 Efficient Algorithms

When constructing the solution to a problem, you might try different strategies and find that more than one is successful. So how do you choose between different solutions? There can also be factors specific to a given problem like how much memory is available. If you are working with an embedded device like a refrigerator, the amount of available memory might not be as large as in a desktop computer. On the other hand, when programming for a device used in the manufacturing industry, high speed might be critical. Another aspect that might affect the selection of the algorithm is the programming language chosen to implement a solution.

Memory and time are two related resources in programming that play a critical role in designing algorithms. As you will see later, there are different types of memory, and each type has limitations in amount and speed. A solution's time requirement can be defined in different ways as well and can vary depending on various factors.

Analyzing Algorithms

The **analysis of algorithms** is the process of finding the more efficient algorithm, usually measuring how long it will take to produce a solution. Although the central aspect is the time it takes to complete, other factors might be relevant when analyzing an algorithm, such as how much memory is necessary to implement a given solution.

> **Note** | The analysis described in this chapter applies to a computer with a single processor. Some computers can run several pieces of code at the same time. A **parallel algorithm** is designed to run several pieces of code simultaneously. The analysis is slightly different when running several pieces of code simultaneously and assembling all the output into a single result. Such analysis is part of the more specialized topic of parallel algorithms and is not covered here.

Comparing Algorithms

Although measuring algorithm completion time is a good heuristic, there are reasons that make it an inefficient measurement in practice.

- First, measuring the completion time requires the implementation of the algorithm and its profiling. **Profiling** is a type of analysis in software engineering where speed of execution, memory usage, and other factors are measured.

- The time it takes to run might vary significantly depending on factors that don't depend on the algorithm itself. Like the hardware on which the implementation is run, the programming language and the compiler can greatly affect an algorithm's execution time.

- What input should be used to measure the algorithm's completion time? Depending on the input, some algorithms might be faster in certain cases but perform poorly in others.

The previous reasons are why the algorithm's complexity is used instead of the exact amount of time it takes to complete a task. The **complexity of an algorithm** is a function that measures the number of resources needed by an algorithm as a function of the input size.

The **time complexity** of an algorithm measures the computational time needed by the algorithm. When measuring computational time, the number of steps or basic instructions is used as an approximation for time complexity. Doing so avoids dependence on the hardware, compiler, or programming language.

The Fibonacci numbers are a sequence where each sequence term is the sum of the two previous terms. This is except for the first two, which are defined as 0 and 1. Consider the following function that receives a positive integer n as input and computes the nth Fibonacci number:

```
foo(n)
    a = 0
    b = 1
    tmp = 0
    if n = 0 or n = 1 return n

    for i = 2 to n step 1
        tmp = a
        a = b
        b = tmp + a
    return b
```

When the function is called with a parameter n, the `for` loop is repeated $n-1$ times. Each time the loop is executed, three operations are executed. Thus, the total number of steps is given by the first four steps of the function, followed by $3(n-1)$ steps of the `for` loop and one for the `return` statement. So you can express the number of steps of `foo (n)` as:

$$f(n) = 4 + 3(n-1) + 1 = 3n$$

Even if you can't specify the exact time the algorithm will take to complete, you can estimate how it grows with each value of n. In the best case, the time the algorithm takes to complete is perfectly proportional to $f(n)$. There is no perfect relationship in practice, but they are certainly correlated. You can see in **Figure 3-1** the function $f(n)$ and the time it takes to compute `foo (n)`.

Figure 3-1   Left: average running time of procedure. Right: plot of $f(n)$

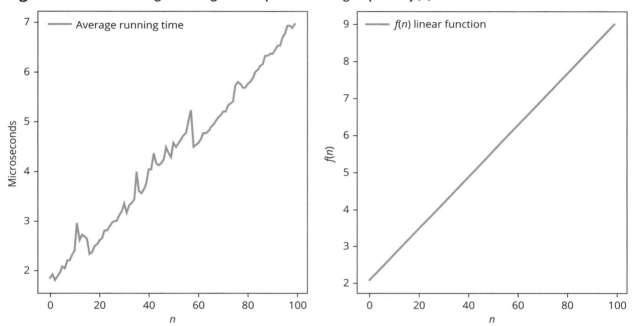

So if you use $f(n)$ as a measure of the complexity of the algorithm, you can compare it to other algorithms. Given the relation between $f(n)$ and the time the algorithm takes to complete, you can deduce that smaller values of $f(n)$ imply more efficient algorithms.

Quick Check 3-1

Consider the following function:

```
foo1(n)
    val = 1
    for i = 1 to n step 1
        val = val*(1 + i^2)
    return val
```

What function relates to the number of instructions of `foo1 (n)`?

Answer: $f(n) = n + 2$

Before the `for` loop, there is only one instruction. The loop executes n times and the value is returned at the end. Thus, $f(n) = 1 + n + 1 = n + 2$ instructions are executed.

3.2 Big O Notation

When analyzing the complexity of an algorithm, simply using the number of steps taken to execute as a function of the input size has some drawbacks.

First, small differences in algorithm design affect the resulting function $f(n)$. Slight differences in the number of steps used to code the algorithm might lead you to think that there is a significant difference between the two algorithms. In the past, when memory and processing power were very limited, these small details were important. Today, modern compilers create optimizations that make small differences in style irrelevant. For example, the following two functions return the same result.

```
foo1(n)
    sum = 0
    for j = 0 to n-1 step 1
        for k = 0 to n-1 step 1
            sum = sum + j + 2*k
    sum = sum + n
    return sum



foo2(n)
    sum = 0
    for i = 0 to n-1 step 1
        tmp_sum = 0
        for j = 0 to n-1 step 1
            tmp_sum = tmp_sum + i + 2*j
        sum = sum + tmp_sum
    sum = sum + n
    return sum
```

Notice that in `foo1(n)`, the first loop over the variable j is executed n times. Also, in each cycle of the first loop, a second loop with n iterations is called. Thus, the total number of operations computed is $f_1(n) = (n \times n) + 3$. The 3 comes from the two assignments made at the beginning and end of `foo1(n)` plus the return statement at the end. Thus, you know that the time required to execute a call to `foo1(n)` is proportional to $f_1(n) = n^2 + 3$.

In `foo2(n)`, there is a loop like the one in `foo1(n)`. The most inner loop executes n iterations. But the outer iteration executes two assignments, one for `tmp_sum` and one for `sum`, and the n iterations of the inner loop. Notice that there are also two assignments made outside of the loops, one at the beginning and one at the end of the code. Thus, the running time is proportional to $1 + n(1 + n + 1) + 1 = n^2 + 2n + 3$.

It is natural to think that there is a significant difference between $f_1(n)$ and $f_2(n)$. It turns out that for large values of n they are almost the same. You can see how similar they are in **Figure 3-2** where $f_1(n)$ and $f_2(n)$ are plotted.

Figure 3-2   Plot of $f_1(n)$ and $f_2(n)$. For large values, it is almost impossible to distinguish between the two functions

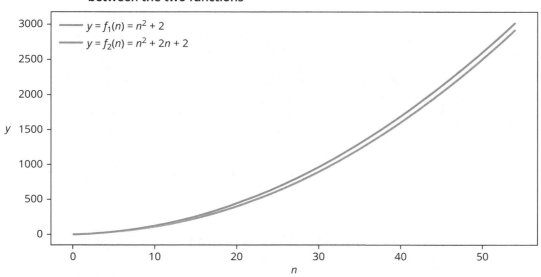

To express the similarity between the complexity of the functions `foo1` and `foo2`, it is common in computer science to use a mathematical concept called rate of growth. The **growth rate** of a function $f(n)$ is the type or order of the highest-order term. It is common to say that the growth rate is determined by the term that dominates the value of $f(n)$ for large values of n.

For example, $f(n) = 3^n + n^2$ has order 3^n or exponential order. To understand why 3^n or the exponential part dominates, **Table 3-1** shows some values of the function and each term in the expression to assess its size as the input n increases. In the example shown in the table, the terms of $f(n) = 3^n + n^2$ are calculated for various values of n. Notice the term that contributes the most to the overall size of $f(n)$.

Table 3-1   Sample values for the function $f(n)$

n	$f(n)$	3^n	n^2
1	4	3	1
2	13	9	4
3	36	27	9
4	97	81	16
5	268	243	25
10	59149	59049	100
20	3486784801	3486784401	400

Notice that for large values of n the value of $f(n)$ is mostly composed by 3^n. Thus, you can say that the order of $f(n)$ is the dominant term of $f(n)$.

Comparing Functions for Big Numbers

Using the growth rate to analyze algorithms is convenient because:

- The growth rate is not affected by small changes, such as rewriting arithmetic expressions.
- The growth rate directly relates to the amount of time it takes an algorithm to run.

Determining the growth rate of a function is part of a mathematical toolset called asymptotic analysis. **Asymptotic analysis** is a set of techniques used to describe the limit behavior of a function. The limit behavior of $f(n)$ refers to the properties of the function for very large values of n, or when n approaches infinity.

The growth rate is one property used to describe the asymptotic behavior of a function. In other words, you can use the growth rate to summarize the behavior of a function $f(n)$ for large values of n.

Most of the time, you will be interested in knowing how your algorithm behaves when the input size is large. For small input values, the differences in the running time of two algorithms might be imperceptible to a user. On the other hand, when the input size is large, the differences might be so great that a user might even think the program is idle. Asymptotic analysis is an ideal tool to study an algorithm's running time since it focuses on large input values.

To illustrate the difference between smaller and larger input values, **Figure 3-3** displays the plots for n^4, 4^n, and $n!$.

Figure 3-3   Left: For small values of n, it seems like the factorial function is faster. Right: For large values of n, the factorial grows much faster

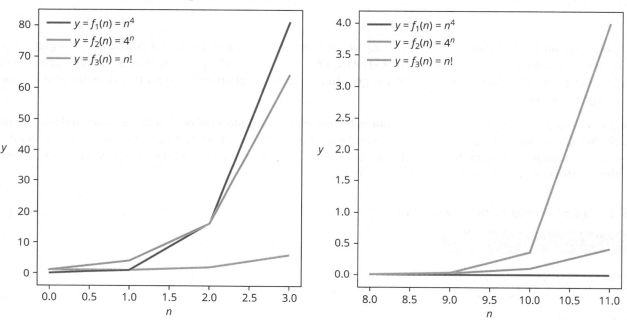

In this figure, imagine that n is the number of files to process and the lines are comparing the complexity of three different algorithms whose growth rates are n^4, 4^n, and $n!$. In the left plot, you can see that for small values of n it might seem that the smaller values are from $n!$. On the other hand, for large values of n, $n!$ is much larger than both n^4 and 4^n. So, for two or three files, the algorithm with complexity $n!$ would be faster. It would be almost eight times faster than the other two. But for 15 files, it would take around 1,200 times more time than the other two algorithms.

Using asymptotic analysis, you can focus on the performance of an algorithm for large inputs, when the running time is more critical.

Quick Check 3-2

What is the dominant term of $f(n) = 3^n + n^9$?

Answer: 3^n. The exponential function 3^n grows much faster than a polynomial function n^9. Thus, the exponential is the dominant term.

Upper Bounds for Functions

So far, you have seen that to express the complexity of an algorithm, a function that expresses the number of steps $f(n)$ in terms of input size n is used. To summarize its behavior for large input sizes, you use the growth rate expressed through the dominant term of $f(n)$.

For example, instead of saying that function `foo(n)` has complexity $f(n) = n^4 + 6n$, you say that it has a complexity of the order of n^4. Since the main point of expressing the complexity of algorithms is to compare their efficiency, it is common to use Big O notation. **Big O notation** gives an asymptotic upper bound for a function. This upper bound defines a function that will be greater than the result of its bounding function for large values of n. This notation is usually represented by $f(n) = O(g(n))$.

Mathematically, what $f(n) = O(g(n))$ means is that starting from some number $n_0 > 0$, and for some positive number c, the following holds:

$$0 < f(n) \leq cg(n)$$

For example, consider $f(n) = 2n^2 + 1$, then $f(n) = O(n^2)$. To see that:

$$2n^2 + 1 \leq 3n^2 \quad \text{for all} \quad n \geq 1$$

The Big O notation is not very precise because it only provides an asymptotic upper bound. That means that the relation holds for functions that grow faster. More precisely, note that $n^2 = O(n!)$, and $n^2 = O(2^n)$. In effect, since:

$$n^2 \leq n! \text{ for } n \geq 4 \text{ and } n^2 \leq 2^n \text{ for } n \geq 4$$

This is shown in **Table 3-2**.

Table 3-2   Values for n, n^2, 2^n, and $n!$

n	n^2	2^n	$n!$
1	1	2	1
2	4	4	2
3	9	8	6
4	16	16	24
5	25	32	120
6	36	64	720

You can see a plot of common functions used to describe the complexity in **Figure 3-4**.

Figure 3-4 The factorial grows faster than the exponential, and the exponential grows faster than the polynomial

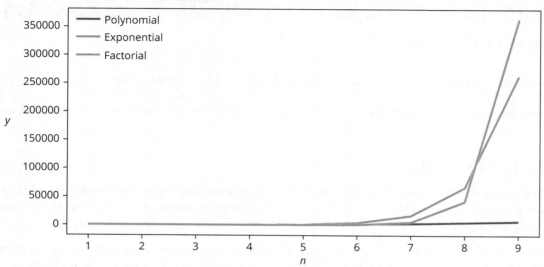

The plot illustrates the case that if you have to choose between an algorithm with $O(n^2)$ complexity and one with $O(n!)$ complexity, you should pick the one with $O(n^2)$ complexity since it will be faster.

Other notations exist for describing the complexity bounds of an algorithm. The lower bounds of an algorithm's complexity are described using Omega notation. **Omega notation** gives an asymptotic lower bound for a function, usually represented by $f(n) = \Omega(g(n))$.

Mathematically, $f(n) = \Omega(g(n))$ means that starting at some value n_0 and for some number C:

$$f(n) \geq Cg(n) \geq 0$$

You can consider this as the symmetric part of $O(f(n))$; for example, $2^n = \Omega(n^2)$. In effect, $n \geq 4$ holds $n^2 " 2^n$. It was previously mentioned that $n^2 = O(2^n)$.

The last notation is Theta notation. **Theta notation** gives an asymptotic equivalence, $f(n) = \Theta(g(n))$ when $f(n) = O(g(n))$ and $f(n) = \Omega(g(n))$. For example, $3n^2 + 2n + 1 = \Theta(n^2)$. Since:

$$0 \leq 3n^2 + 2n + 1 \leq 6n^2 \quad \text{for all} \quad n \geq 1$$

Then $3n^2 + 2n + 1 = O(n^2)$. And since:

$$0 \leq n^2 \leq 3n^2 + 2n + 1 \quad \text{for all} \quad n \geq 1$$

Then $3n^2 + 2n + 1 = \Omega(n^2)$. Thus, the result is $3n^2 + 2n + 1 = \Theta(n^2)$.

The Theta notation is more restrictive than Big O and Omega notation. For example, you already saw that $n^2 = O(n!)$ but $n^2 \neq \Theta(n!)$, as it is impossible to multiply $n!$ by a number in such a way that $c\,n! " n^2$ for large values of n.

Figure 3-5 displays plots of the behavior when $f(n) = \Omega(h(n)), f(n) = O(g(n))$, and $f(n) = \Theta(f_2(n))$.

Figure 3-5   Growth rate determines the relation

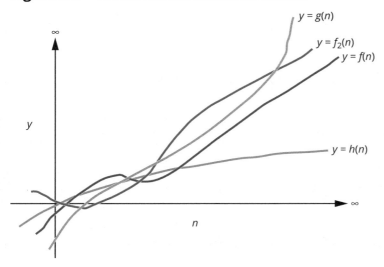

Note	The Big O notation has been used in a mathematical area called number theory since the late 1800s. Mathematician Paul Bachmann introduced it. By 1970 the Big O notation was popularized in computer science by mathematician and computer scientist Donald Knuth. Knuth wrote the first complete treatise on algorithm analysis, a series of books called *The Art of Computer Programming*. In this series, Knuth introduces the Omega notation and the Theta notation.

Principles for Asymptotic Analysis

Suppose a function $f(n)$ describes the number of operations necessary to execute an algorithm with an input of size n. The next step to analyze the algorithm's efficiency would be to get asymptotic bounds $O(f(n))$, $(f(n))$, or $\Theta(f(n))$. These bounds can be used to compare different solutions for a problem.

As previously mentioned, if you have an algorithm with complexity $O(n^2)$ and another with $O(n!)$, the first one is more efficient for large values of n. Recall that when analyzing algorithms for comparison, the focus is on large input sizes because it is in these cases where performance is more critical.

In **Figure 3-6** you can see a comparison between the most common complexities.

Figure 3-6 Commonly used complexities in algorithms

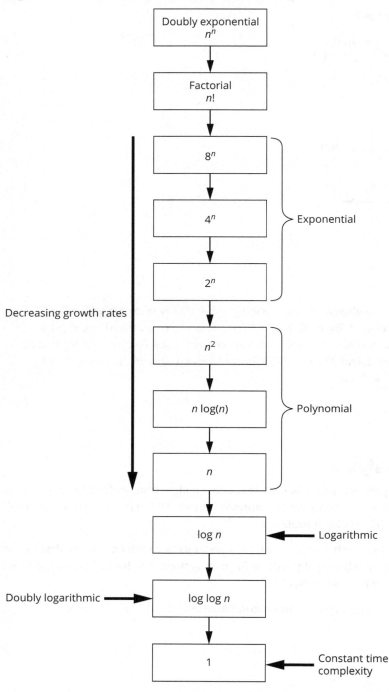

From Figure 3-6 you can infer that an algorithm with complexity $O(n^3)$ is more efficient than one with complexity $O(4^n)$.

Some other properties allow you to keep a simple expression for the complexity when using Big O notation.

- If c is a constant number, then $O(cf(n)) = O(f(n))$. For example, $3n^2 = O(n^2)$ and $6n^2 = O(n^2)$, since multiplying by a constant doesn't change the dominant term.

- If $f(n) = O(g(n))$, then $O(f(n) + g(n)) = O(g(n))$, since the dominant term will be in $g(n)$.

- If $f(n) = O(g(n))$ and $g(n) = O(h(n))$, then $f(n) = O(h(n))$. This property is referred to as transitivity or the transitive property.

> ## Technical Interview

When solving an algorithm, the first objective is to have a working solution. Before trying to have a solution with the best complexity possible, focus on creating a solution without paying much attention to the running time. Once you have an answer, you can focus on reducing the time complexity. One strategy to reduce the time complexity is to focus on the loops that generate the dominating term in the complexity. Sometimes it is possible to reduce some loops by a mathematical identity such as:

$$1 + 2 + 3 + \ldots + n = \frac{n(n+1)}{2}$$

3.3 Algorithm Time Complexity

To compute the time complexity of an algorithm, one key point is to compute the function $f(n)$ that relates the input size with the number of steps needed to execute the algorithm.

There are many properties that simplify the analysis of an algorithm because the end result of the analysis is to get an asymptotic bound of $f(n)$ and not $f(n)$ itself.

> ## Best Practices

Having an estimate of the complexity of your code is important even when performance is not the main goal of your code. In practice, over time software has to deal with input sizes that weren't contemplated when the code was written. Having an estimate of the complexity of each part of a project can give you clues about which parts are key points to optimize so your software is able to escalate with the demands of the users.

Basic Asymptotical Analysis

To compute a bound for the function $f(n)$, there are some basic results:

- The running time of a `for` loop is the running time of the statement inside the loop multiplied by the length of the `for`. For example, suppose that the running time of the function `foo(m)` is given by $g(n) = 3n^2$. Then the following code makes n calls to the function `foo(m)`.

```
var = 0
for m = 1 ... n
    var = var + foo(m) + 3
```

Thus, the running time of the code is:

$$f(n) = 1 + n * g(n) = 1 + n * 3n^2 = 1 + 3n^3$$

The dominant term in the expression is n^3. Thus, the complexity of the code is $O(n^3)$.

- Suppose that `foo1(n)` and `foo2(n)` have running time $f_1(n)$ and $f_2(n)$, respectively. Then when running `foo1(n)` and `foo2(n)`, the running time would be $f_1(n) + f_2(n)$. When using asymptotic notation, the dominant term of f_1 or f_2, depending on which one is "larger" or "smaller," will be the bound for the running time.

- In a conditional loop, for example, `while k < n`, if the variable k grows or decreases exponentially, then the resulting running time will be $O(\log n)$. For example, consider the following code:

```
log_foo(n)
    k = 1
    while k < n
        k = k*2
```

Notice that for $n = 8$, the value of k goes:

$$k = 1 \quad k = 2^1 \quad k = 2 * 2 = 2^2 = 4 \quad k = 2^2 * 2 = 2^3 = 8$$

Thus, the number of iterations will be $\log_2 n$. Hence, the complexity has bound $O(\log n)$.

In **Figure 3-7** you can see the number of iterations executed by `log_foo(n)` for values of n from 1 up to 200.

Figure 3-7   Blue shows the number of iterations in the while loop. Orange shows the plot of a logarithmic function

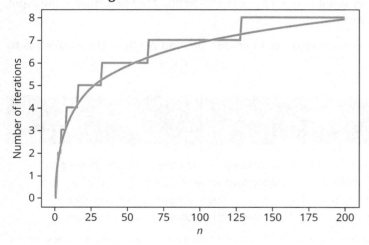

To exemplify the basic principles for asymptotic analysis, consider the following code where the input size is n:

```
key = n
accumulate = 0
while key > 1
    key = key/2
    accumulate = accumulate + key
accumulate = max(100, accumulate)

for i = 1 to n step 1
    sum = 0
    for j = 1 to n step 1
        sum = sum + 2*j
    accumulate = accumulate*sum
```

The first two lines are executed in constant time since they don't depend on the size of the input n. The `while` loop has a logarithmic running time at each iteration and the `key` value is reduced by half. So far, the running time complexity could be expressed by $O(2 + \log n)$. But the dominant term in $O(2 + \log n)$ is $\log n$, so the complexity might be expressed as $O(\log n)$.

The last part of the code is a nested loop. Start analyzing the algorithm by determining the bound for the inner loop:

```
for j = 1 to n step 1
    sum = sum + 2*j
accumulate = accumulate*sum
```

This loop has n iterations, thus the running time is $O(n)$. The outer loop runs for n iterations so the result of the complete loop:

```
for i = 1 to n step 1
    sum = 0
    for j = 1 to n step 1
        sum = sum + 2*j
    accumulate = accumulate*sum
```

would be $O(n * n) = O(n^2)$. Joining the two parts of the code, the complexity could be expressed as $O(\log n + n^2)$. Since n^2 is the dominant term in the expression $\log n + n^2$, the code has $O(n^2)$ complexity.

Best Practices

The ideal case for the time complexity of an algorithm is $O(1)$. That an algorithm is $O(1)$ means that it will take a fixed amount of time regardless of the input size. The next best option is to have a growth rate dominated by $\log n$. For example, an algorithm that has complexity $O(\log(\log n))$ is faster than one with $O(\log n)$. In practice, exponential complexity algorithms are impractical for large input values, and you should avoid them whenever possible.

Best, Worst, and Average Case

The number of instructions that an algorithm executes can't always be given as a single mathematical expression such as n^2, 2^n, or $n!$. Sometimes the number of instructions that will execute depends on input values. For example, consider the following code:

```
complex_foo(n)
    val = 0
    if n mod 2 = 1
        for k = 1 to n step 1
            val = val + k
    else
        key = 1
        while key < n
            key = 2*key
            val = val + key
```

Notice that when n mod 2 = 1, a for loop with n iterations is executed. In other words, when n is odd, the complexity is $O(n)$. But when n mod 2 = 0, a while loop is executed. The while loop has complexity $O(\log n)$. So, if you are using an even number, there is a better running time $O(\log n)$ than if you use an odd number where the running time is $O(n)$.

When analyzing an algorithm to implement, the difference in running time depending on different values of the input might be relevant. To provide such information, it is common to consider the following:

- **Best-case running time** describes the best possible running time, which happens when the algorithm executes the least number of instructions. The best-case running time is usually given by an asymptotic lower bound $(f(n))$. For example, you could say that the function `complex_foo(n)` used earlier has complexity $(\log n)$. The **best-case scenario**, or simply the **best case**, is the input configuration for which the running time is the best. For example, the best case for the `complex_foo(n)` is when n is odd.

- **Worst-case running time** describes the worst possible running time, which happens when the algorithm executes the maximum number of instructions. The worst-case running time is usually given by an asymptotic upper bound $O(f(n))$. For example, you could say that `complex_foo(n)` is $O(n)$. The **worst-case scenario**, or **worst case**, is the input configuration for which the running time is the worst. For example, the worst case for `complex_foo(n)` is when n is even.

- **Average-case running time** describes the average over all possible complexities for an algorithm. The average case is usually given as an asymptotic equivalence $\Theta(f(n))$. In most cases getting the average case running time is very hard. To compute the average running case, it is necessary to know how likely it is to get each type of input. In the case of `complex_foo`, the two types of input, relevant to the complexity analysis, are even and odd numbers. Since no additional restrictions are given over the value of n, then it is equally likely to get one even or odd number. Hence, the average running time will be $\frac{1}{2}O(n) + \frac{1}{2}O(\log n) = O(n)$.

It is always true that the best case is less than or equal to the average case, and the average case is less than or equal to the worst case. Focusing on the worst case is common because it gives an upper bound for the running time. The average case might require additional tools from probability theory to compute and some hypotheses about the distribution of inputs.

Quick Check 3-3

Consider the following function:

```
foo(number_array, x)
    n = len(number_array)
    i = 0
    while i < n
        if x < number_array[i]
            return i
        else
            i = i + 1
    return -1
```

What is the worst case for `foo(number_array, x)`?

Answer: When x is larger than all the elements in `number_array`.

When x is larger than all the elements in `number_array`, the function has to iterate over all the elements of `number_array`. That is the worst case. In such a case, the `while` loop executes n iterations. So, the worst-case running time has complexity $O(n)$.

Complexity of Search in an Array

Suppose that you need to write a program that finds the index associated with a key value *x* in an array `arr` of integer numbers sorted in ascending order. Consider the following two options, a linear search and a binary search:

```
linear_search(arr, x)
    index = 0
    keep_searching = True
    if index < len(arr) and keep_searching
        if arr[index] = x
            keep_searching = False
        else
            index = index + 1
    if not keep_searching
        return index
    else
        return -1


binary_search(arr, x)
    start = 0
    end = len(arr)
    found  = False
    while start <= end and not found
        index = (start + end)/2
        if arr[index] = x
            found = True
        else
            if x > arr[index]
                start = index + 1
            else
                end = index - 1
    if not found
        return -1
    else
        return index
```

Figure 3-8 is an illustration of the execution of `linear_search(arr, x)`, `binary_search(arr, x)` for `arr = [0, 3, 5, 7, 11, 13, 17, 19]`, and *x* = 5.

Figure 3-8 Steps taken in a linear search (left) versus steps in a binary search (right)

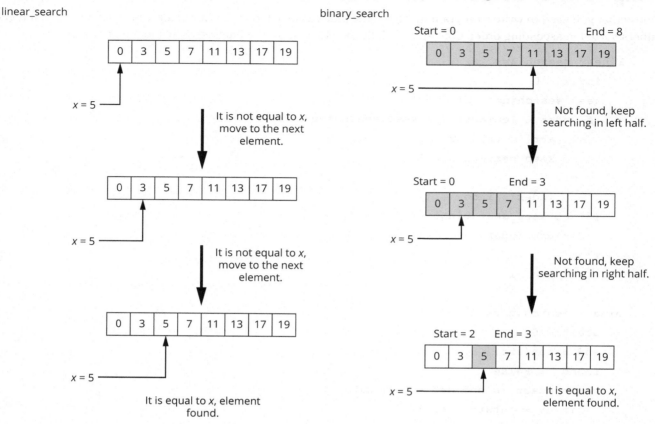

To analyze the `linear_search(arr, x)` algorithm, consider the following:

- The best case is when the key value is the first element in the array. In this case that is when `x = 0`. In such a case, only one iteration is executed. Thus, `linear_search(arr, x)` is (1) in the best case. Saying that `linear_search(arr, x)` is (1) means that the number of instructions executed by the function is constant in the best case.

- The worst case is when the key is not present in the array or is the last element in the array. Consider $x = 6$ in `arr = [0, 3, 5, 7, 11, 13, 17, 19]`. The algorithm starts with `index = 0` and increases by one at each iteration. To reach the value of 19, the index must reach the value of 7. Reaching 7 means that the operation is executed the same number of iterations as the length of the array. Hence, you can say that the algorithm is $O(n)$.

To analyze `binary_search(arr, x)`, you search for the best and worst case for the algorithm as follows:

- The best case is when the key value is in the middle index, that is, when the key value is at the index's first value `(start + end)/2`. For example, for `arr = [0, 3, 5, 7, 11, 13, 17, 19]`, if $x = 11$, when the algorithm starts, `index = (0 + 8)/2 = 4`. Thus, `arr[index] = arr[4] = 11`. So `binary_search(arr, x)` is (1) in the best case.

- The worst case is when the algorithm executes the maximum possible number of iterations. Notice that the algorithm keeps searching for the key value each time in a smaller range of values, from `arr[start]` to `arr[end]`. See Figure 3-8.

As you can see at each step, the number of possible values for index is reduced by a factor of 2. Hence, `binary_search(arr, x)` is $O(\log n)$. The worst case for the `binary_search(arr, x)` is also when the value x is not present in `arr`.

3.4 Space Complexity of Algorithms

Another key aspect to consider when deciding what algorithm to implement is how much memory the algorithm will use. It turns out that the amount of memory used by an algorithm can directly affect the running time.

The relation between memory usage and running time is due to the fact that there are multiple types of memory within a computer. Modern computers have different ways to store data, which reside in different parts of the computer.

In most cases, the instructions are executed in the CPU. The CPU has a set of registers and memory. The CPU memory has the fastest access time; however, it is quite small compared to the amount of memory in a hard drive. The disadvantage of hard drive memory storage is that it takes much more time to access. As an estimate, suppose that it takes 1 second to read data from the CPU (this is called L1 Cache memory); then it would take 10 days to read data from a hard drive. Fortunately, reading data from a CPU takes around 1 nanosecond (10^{-9} second).

Understanding the memory needs of an algorithm is also a key aspect when working with embedded devices. A program running on your desktop has much more available memory than a program running on a smartwatch.

> **Note**
>
> When analyzing the space complexity of algorithms, it is common to count each cell or node of an abstract data type (ADT) as a single unit. When counting each node or cell of an ADT as a single unit, it is reasonable to assume that each cell or node uses approximately the same amount of memory. This hypothesis is valid if the nodes are comprised of static data structures. However, it is possible to have a list that stores vectors; in this case, you shouldn't count each node using a single memory unit because vectors can grow.

Space Complexity

The **space complexity** of an algorithm describes the amount of memory an algorithm uses as a function of the input size. As with time complexity, space complexity is given as an asymptotic bound.

For space complexity, there are also best-, worst-, and average-case scenarios. The best case is when the amount of memory used is the minimum, and the worst case is when the amount of memory used is the largest. The average case estimates how much memory is required for the average case.

Best Practices

To improve the space complexity of a solution, try using a different data structure. For example, if it is necessary to rearrange a set of values, a linked list might be the best choice. To rearrange, the linked list elements only require changing the pointers, which might reduce the necessary memory.

Space Complexity of Reversing a String

Consider the problem of reversing a string of characters. For example, if `str = "hello"`, the output should be `"olleh"`. To solve the problem, consider the following function that receives the string `str` to reverse.

```
reverse(str)
    stack = new Stack()
    n = len(str)
    for i = 1 to n step 1
        stack.push(str[i])
```

```
reverse_str = ""
for i = 1 to n step 1
    char = stack.pop()
    reverse_str = reverse_str + char


return char
```

In this case, the space complexity of the algorithm is better given as a function of n = len(str). Notice that the algorithm makes use of a stack. As in the case of instructions for the running time, it is not necessary to have an exact measure of the memory used. So, when using an integer variable x and a char c for the space, complexity is not required to distinguish that x is four times larger than c. It is usually only considered that two variables are necessary. Generally, if x bytes store one element in the stack, then bytes are used to store m elements.

Based on the previous observation, the function uses a stack with n elements and the string reverse with a maximum length of n. Thus, the space complexity can be described by the function $f(n) = 1 + n + n = 2n + 1$. The one in $f(n)$ represents the memory used to store n = len(str), the first n represents the space used to store the stack once it is full, and the last n represents the memory used to store the new string reverse(str).

Once you have $f(n) = 2n + 1$, you may observe that reverse(str) has a space complexity $O(n)$.

3.5 Heuristic Algorithms

A heuristic is a strategy or pattern that has proven effective when solving a problem. Heuristics do not always lead to the best solution but, in many cases, that is the best you can do.

When working with a modern computer, an algorithm with running time $O(n^2)$ might take hours to complete. An algorithm with running time $O(2^n)$ might require more time than the age of the universe to complete. Hence, even if an algorithm to solve a problem is known, it might be a better strategy to use a heuristic to construct a potential solution and test it.

Computationally Expensive Problems

Suppose that you want to go from city A to city B. If there are many routes joining the cities, there are a couple of things that should be determined to choose the best route.

- What metric is being used to determine the "best" route? Are you interested in reaching B in the least amount of time? Or do you want to visit as many cafes on the road as possible?

- What information is available? For example, you might not have a perfect description of the traffic conditions at the expected travel time.

Given the previous observations, you might consider a satisfactory journey to reach city B before nightfall and to get a cup of coffee on the road.

When approaching a complex problem such as going from city A to city B, it might be impossible to get a "perfect" solution, whatever "perfect" might mean. To get a solution that satisfies some constraints, what is the best strategy?

For traveling from city A to city B, you could ask someone who has previously traveled between the destinations to give you useful pointers to design your travel. In this case, the pointers are heuristics of how to build a solution (travel route).

Even in algorithmic problems in computer science, there are problems so complex that computing an optimal solution might take much more time than is reasonable to wait. In such cases, using a heuristic might be the best approach.

When using heuristics, consider the following:

- You might not get the optimal solution. Heuristics might guide you to a solution but not necessarily the best solution. Using the example of traveling from city A to city B, you might use your friend's suggestions and arrive at city B at 6:00 p.m. But another person taking a different route might arrive at 4:00 p.m. So, your friend's heuristic leads you to a solution but not necessarily the best (fastest) one.

- The solution obtained might be only approximate. If your objective was to reach city B before 6:00 p.m., the heuristics given by your friend might help you arrive by 6:15 p.m. But without the heuristics, you might spend the night driving.

When using heuristics to solve a problem, remember that they might not be the perfect solution but are often a necessary tool.

Knapsack Problem

Suppose that you are given a bag that can carry a certain maximum weight. There are also certain objects you might want to put in the knapsack, each with a profit value. The **knapsack problem** consists of finding a combination of elements that don't exceed the given weight and provide the most profit.

For example, suppose you have a bag that supports 13 kg. There are five items with a profit of 1 and a weight of 2 and six objects with a profit of 3 and a weight of 3. You can see a summary of this information in **Table 3-3**.

Table 3-3   Summary of weight, profit, and how many items of each type are available

Type	Weight	Profit	Available
Type 1	2	2	4
Type 2	3	3	3

One viable solution might be to take three items of weight 4 and get a profit of 9. Obviously, that is not an optimal solution.

If you use a brute-force approach to solve the problem, $4 * 3 = 12$ possible solutions exist. Notice that if you add five options of a new type of element, the possibilities are now $5 * 4 * 3 = 60$. So, with each new type of item, the options grow exponentially.

The fact that the number of tests grows exponentially hints at why using heuristics is useful.

One of the possible heuristics to use is the greedy choice. The **greedy heuristic** observes that choosing the locally optimal solution might lead to a globally optimal one. Using the greedy heuristic, you take the option that at this moment gives you the most profit.

In the example, this heuristic could be stated as choosing as many items as possible with the highest profit for the weight still available.

In **Figure 3-9**, you can see the choices made with the greedy heuristic for the knapsack problem.

Figure 3-9   Local choices made by the heuristic

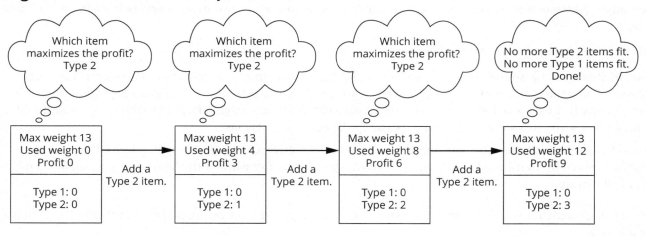

Notice that the optimal solution for this problem is a profit of 12, choosing four of the 2 kg items and one of the 3 kg items. Also notice that this is not the same as the solution using the greedy heuristic with one item at a time.

In the worst case, it might be necessary to check all possible combinations to find a global optimal. So, if there are n items in total, it would be necessary to try 2^n possibilities. While using the heuristic there are at most n decisions to make, although at the cost of missing the optimal solution.

> **Note**   You can use a heuristic extracted from your users' data when facing a complex problem in a given context. For example, when planning a route to take, you might use your knowledge of the local traffic conditions to design a planning algorithm.

Summary

- The complexity of algorithms expressed through a function of the input size provides a tool to compare their performance. The complexity allows you to focus on the performance of an algorithm for large input values where the performance is more critical.

- Asymptotic analysis is used to compare complexities because it focuses on the limit behavior of functions. Asymptotic analysis is used to compare the behavior of the functions for large values of their arguments.

- The notation for upper, lower, and equivalent bounds $O(f(n))$, $(f(n))$, and $\Theta(f(n))$ provide a mechanism to reduce a function to its growth rate.

- Time complexity is directly related to the running time of an algorithm. When studying the time complexity of an algorithm, you usually focus on the worst case. The worst case is the instance where the algorithm executes the largest number of instructions.

- Space complexity is related to an algorithm's memory usage. As with time complexity, space complexity focuses on the worst case most of the time.

- Practical algorithms have a polynomial complexity at the most. When a solution algorithm has an exponential time complexity, it might require an unreasonable amount of time to produce a solution. When the input size is small, an exponential time complexity might be okay, but for large numbers, it makes the solution algorithm useless.

- When solving complex problems where there is no solution algorithm, or when the solution has a large time complexity, you can apply heuristics to get an approximate solution.

- Heuristics might not provide an optimal solution but will provide an approximate solution in a more reasonable amount of time.

Key Terms

analysis of algorithms	greedy heuristic	space complexity
asymptotic analysis	growth rate	Theta notation
average-case running time	heuristic	time complexity
best-case running time	knapsack problem	worst-case running time
best-case scenario or best case	Omega notation	worst-case scenario or
Big O notation	parallel algorithm	worst case
complexity of an algorithm	profiling	

Review Questions

1. The only aspect to study in algorithm analysis is the running time of an algorithm.

   a. True   **b.** False

2. The complexity of an algorithm measures what magnitude as a function of the size of the input?

   a. Running time used by the algorithm
   b. Memory used to store secondary data
   c. Hours invested in writing the algorithm
   d. Resources needed by the algorithm

3. Consider $f(n) = 2^n + n$. Which of the following is true?

   a. $f(n) = O(n)$ **c.** $f(n) = O(2^n)$
   b. $f(n) = O(\log n)$ **d.** $f(n) = O(1)$

4. Asymptotic analysis is related to the behavior of $f(n)$ for what magnitude of values of n?

   a. Large   **c.** Average
   b. Small   **d.** Worst

5. Which of the following is correct?

   a. $\log n = O(1)$ **c.** $\log n = O(n^2)$
   b. $2^n = O(n^2)$ **d.** $n! = O(2^n)$

6. Which of the following is correct?

   a. $\log n = \quad(1)$ **c.** $\log n = O(1)$
   b. $1 = \Theta(\log n)$ **d.** $1 = \quad(\log n)$

7. Suppose that $f(n) = O(\log n)$ and $g(n) = O(f(n))$. What relationship exists between $g(n)$ and $\log n$?

8. Consider the code:

```
val = 0
for k = 1 to n step 1
    for j = 1 to n+1 step 1
        val = val + (k+1)
    val = k*val
```

What is the time complexity of the code?

9. Consider the following function to compute the largest power of 2 that divides an integer x.

```
foo(x)
    if x mod 2 = 0
        return foo(x/2) + 1
    else
        return 1
```

What is the worst case of the `foo(x)` function?

10. Consider the following function to compute the largest power of 2 that divides an integer x.

```
foo(x)
    if x mod 2 = 0
        return foo(x/2) + 1
    else
        return 1
```

What is the best- and worst-case running time of `foo(x)` in terms of x?

Programming Problems

1. Write a program that receives two positive integers m and n, where m and n are greater than one, and computes the largest power of n that divides m. Describe its best and worst case. Notice that in this case, the best and worst case are described in terms of m and n, not only in terms of one of the inputs. **(LO 3.3)**

2. When solving an algorithm to reverse the order in a string array, a stack can be used to store the order of the elements. Another strategy is to do it inline. When doing the operation inline, the algorithm modifies the same array used as input. This has the advantage of reducing the space complexity. Write a program that reverses the order of the elements in an array `arr` and has space complexity $O(1)$. **(LO 3.3, 3.4)**

3. Consider the knapsack problem with the following type of items, their costs, and profits:

Type	Weight	Profit
1	3	7
2	2	8
3	5	6

Write a program that receives as input w, $n1$, $n2$, and $n3$. w is the maximum weight allowed, $n1$ is the maximum number of items of type 1 allowed, $n2$ is the maximum number of items of type 2 allowed, and $n3$ is the maximum number of items of type 3 allowed. The algorithm must return the optimal solution to the knapsack problem. **(LO 3.5)**

4. Consider the knapsack problem with the following type of items, its costs, and profits:

Type	Weight	Profit
1	3	7
2	2	8
3	5	6

Write a program that receives as input w, $n1$, $n2$, and $n3$. w is the maximum weight allowed, $n1$ the maximum number of items of type 1 allowed, $n2$ the maximum number of items of type 2 allowed, and $n3$ the maximum number of items of type 3 allowed. The algorithm must return a viable solution computed using the greedy heuristic. **(LO 3.5)**

5. Consider a list of integer `number_list` with their elements sorted in ascending order. Using the same approach as in `linear_search`, write a program that inserts a new key element x keeping `number_list` sorted. **(LO 3.3)**

Projects

Project 3-1: Linearly Sorting Arrays

(LO 3.2, 3.3, 3.4) Write a program that receives a list `number_list` of integers in random order. The program must return a new array with the same elements sorted in ascending order.

For this problem, use the linear approach. Using the linear approach means that you search for the minimum element from the list by traversing the complete list; once the minimum is found it is copied as the first element of the sorted array and deleted from the list. Then repeat the previous process with the remaining elements until there is no element to be copied. Compute the time complexity in the worst case, then compute the space complexity in the worst case.

Project 3-2: Linear Sorted Insertion

(LO 3.2, 3.3, 3.4) Write a function that receives a sorted list `number_list` of integers and uses the same strategy as in the binary search to insert a new element x in such a way that `number_list` stays sorted. Compute the time complexity in the worst case, then compute the space complexity in the worst case.

Project 3-3: Backtracking 0-1 Knapsack

(LO 3.2, 3.3, 3.4, 3.5) Consider the knapsack problem and suppose that the list of weights and profits is given in the arrays `weights` and `profits`. One case of the knapsack problem is the 0-1 knapsack problem where the available number of items of each type is one. The problem consists of deciding which elements must be included in the bag. Write a function that receives the maximum weight W, the array `weights`, and the array `profits` and returns the maximum profit possible in the 0-1 knapsack problem enumerating all the possibilities.

Project 3-4: 0-1 Knapsack with Heuristics

(LO 3.5) Consider the knapsack problem and suppose that the list of weights and profits is given in the arrays `weights` and `profits`. One case of the knapsack problem is the 0-1 knapsack problem where the available number of items of each type is one. The problem consists of deciding which elements must be included in the bag. Write a function that receives the maximum weight W, the array `weights`, and the array `profits` and creates an approximate solution to the 0-1 knapsack problem using the greedy heuristic.

Project 3-5: Change Coins Problem with Heuristics

(LO 3.5) Consider the following instance of the "change coins" problem. Suppose that you have coins of the following denominations: 1 cent, 3 cents, and 5 cents. The problem consists of using as few coins as possible for a given amount x.

Write a program that solves the change coins problem described in the previous paragraph using the greedy heuristic.

Chapter 4

Sorting Algorithms

Learning Objectives

Upon completion of this chapter, you will be able to:

4.1 Analyze various sorting algorithms.

4.2 Implement a solution using bubble sort.

4.3 Implement a solution using selection sort.

4.4 Implement a solution using insertion sort.

4.5 Implement a solution using quicksort.

4.6 Implement a solution using merge sort.

4.1 Introduction to Sorting Algorithms

Sorting is a famous computer science problem and probably one of the most studied. Sorting algorithms are important because they usually work as a building block for more complex algorithms.

Having things in a predetermined order is a great way to be efficient. The benefits of an ordered environment also apply to data structures. However, sorting is also time-consuming for data structures, as it is in real life, hence the importance of designing efficient procedures to sort things.

When given a sequence (or array) of N integer numbers, such as $a_0, a_1, \ldots, a_{N-1}$, the **sorting problem** consists of producing a new sequence $b_0, b_1, \ldots, b_{N-1}$ with the same values in such a way that $b_0 \leq b_1 \leq \ldots \leq b_{N-1}$. For example, from the sequence $a_0 = 7, a_1 = 3, a_2 = 5, a_3 = 11$, the sorting problem produces the new sequence $b_0 = 3, b_1 = 5, b_2 = 7, b_3 = 11$ (the sequence sorted in ascending order).

When describing the solutions for the sorting problem, the input is specified as an array of N integer numbers. However, most of the algorithms presented in this chapter can apply to most linear data structures. Also, notice that the description of the algorithms focuses on using integer values in ascending order, but the algorithms can apply to any data type if you can compare the objects in the array.

When you have two objects x and y of a certain data type to sort, you need a function to compare them, such as `comp(x,y)`. `comp(x,y)` returns exactly one of the following:

- `'equal'`
- `'greater'`
- `'lesser'`

Any function used to sort objects must follow some rules to provide consistent results, such as:

- `comp(x,x)` = `'equal'` (symmetry of equality property)
- If `comp(x,y)` = `'equal'`, then `comp(y,x)` = `'equal'` (symmetry of equality property)
- If `comp(x,y)` = `'greater'`, then `comp(y,x)` = `'lesser'` (antisymmetry property)
- If `comp(x,y)` = `'equal'`, then `comp(x,z)` = `comp(y,z)` (transitive property for equality)
- If `comp(x,y)` = `'greater'` and `comp(y,z)` = `'greater'`, then `comp(x,z)` = `'greater'` (transitive property for inequality)

A function used to sort a certain type of objects and that follows the previous rules is called a **comparison function** (in discrete mathematics a comparison function is also called a partial order).

> **Note**
>
> The previous discussion of the sorting problem uses numbers sorted in ascending order. As you might imagine, it might be necessary to sort the numbers of an array (or objects of a different data type) in descending order. Fortunately, given any comparison function, such as the comparison between two integers, it is always possible to create the **inverse comparison**. The inverse of comparison function `comp(x,y)` is one that returns `'lesser'` when `comp(x,y)` is greater, and `'greater'` when `comp(x,y)` is `'lesser'`.
>
> Using the inverse comparison when solving the sorting problem produces a sequence in descending order for the original comparison function. In the following code snippet you can see an implementation of the inverse comparison for the comparison function `comp(x,y)`.
>
> ```
> inverse_comp(x,y)
>     if comp(x,y) = 'greater'
>         return 'lesser'
>     if comp(x,y) = 'lesser'
>         return 'greater'
>     return 'equal'
> ```

You can use different functions to sort objects for a specific data type. For example, suppose you define the data type *Student* with a string field for the name, one integer field for age, and one real number field for height in centimeters. In the following code, you can see two different comparison functions for two students and how the ideas applied to integer values can be straightforwardly translated to real values:

```
type Student
    fields name, age, height

age_comp(x, y)
    if x.age = y.age
        return 'equal'
    else
        if x.age > y.age
            return 'greater'
        else
            return 'lesser'
```

```
height_comp(x, y)
    if x.height = y.height
        return 'equal'
    else
        if x.height > y.height
            return 'greater'
        else
            return 'lesser'
```

Having the comparison functions `height_comp` and `age_comp` allows you to sort an array of data of type Student by height or age, applying the same algorithm, using only the appropriate comparison function.

> **Note**
>
> It is common in many programming languages to use a numeric value instead of `'equal'`, `'greater'`, and `'lesser'`. The ideas used in this chapter can be translated to such cases. For example, it is common to use 0 instead of `'equal'`, a negative number for `'lesser'`, and a positive number for `'greater'`. In such a case, the previous example for the `height_comp(x,y)` function would be as follows:
>
> ```
> height_comp(x, y)
>     if x.height = y.height
>         return 0
>     else
>         if x.height > y.height
>             return 1
>         else
>             return -1
> ```
>
> Or, using the fact that the `height` field is a numeric data type, it is possible to use the following implementation:
>
> ```
> height_comp(x, y)
>     return x.height-y.height
> ```
>
> When using a numeric value instead of the equal, greater, and lesser, the properties of a comparison function are translated as follows:
>
> - comp(x,x) = 0 (symmetry of equality property)
> - If comp(x,y) = 0, then comp(y,x) = 0 (symmetry of equality property)
> - If comp(x,y) > 0, then comp(y,x) < 0 (antisymmetric property)
> - If comp(x,y) = 0, then comp(x,z) = comp(y,z) (transitive property for equality)
> - If comp(x,y) > 0 and comp(y,z) > 0, then comp(x,z) > 0 (transitive property for inequality)

Finding the Video with Most Likes

Consider the following situation. Suppose you have a video streaming service where you provide thousands of students with access to programming tutorial videos. The number of videos increases as time passes, and you need to add more servers to keep providing the service. You decide to invest in a high-speed server, but the space is insufficient for all the videos. So, you choose to put some videos on the faster server and the rest on the older servers. How do you decide what videos to put on which servers?

There are many strategies you could use, but one that might be reasonable is to put the most liked videos on the faster server since people are more likely to look for those. To execute that strategy, you need to sort the videos by the number of likes each video received.

Moreover, as the content of your service grows, it might be necessary to create ways for users to search through the content, such as searching using the date of publication. To make the search process less time-consuming, you should sort the content. By sorting the content, users spend less time looking at items that are not relevant to them.

> ## Best Practices
>
> When solving a problem, if you notice that retrieving the necessary objects is becoming cumbersome, ask yourself if sorting the objects by certain values will make the retrieval easier or faster.
>
> With many problems, having the data or objects sorted in a certain way simplifies the solution. Although taking the time to sort the objects might seem like an expensive process, in the long run, this ordering can improve code readability and execution time.

What Is a Sorting Algorithm?

Recall that the sorting problem consists of taking a sequence of objects $a_0, a_1, \ldots, a_{N-1}$ and producing a new sequence with the same values $b_0, b_1, \ldots, b_{N-1}$ such that $b_0 \leq b_1 \leq \ldots \leq b_{N-1}$.

A **sorting algorithm** is any algorithm that solves the sorting problem. When studying a sorting algorithm, it is usual to consider integer values for the sequence. However, that doesn't mean you can only apply sorting algorithms to integer values. As mentioned before, using any comparison function that follows the reflexive for equality, symmetric for equality, antisymmetric, and transitive property is possible.

When using data types composed of more than one field, it is common to sort them based on a set of fields. The fields used to compare two objects are known as **keys**. When describing a sorting algorithm, you usually use only the key values fields and not all fields of the data type. But, in practice, you operate with data of a given data type including all its fields.

Notice that the key value might not be unique when discussing sorting and searching algorithms. For example, if you use the `Student` data type with the field `age` to sort a list of students from the youngest to the oldest, there might be two or more students of the same age. In this case, deciding how to sort the objects might require using other fields.

When the key values are not unique, some situations require that objects are kept in the same relative order. A **stable sorting algorithm** is an algorithm that maintains the relative order of the input values in the output sequence for elements with the same key value. In **Figure 4-1**, you can see some input sequences, the expected result for stable sorting algorithms and a sort by an unstable algorithm.

Figure 4-1   **Stable and unstable sorting of records**

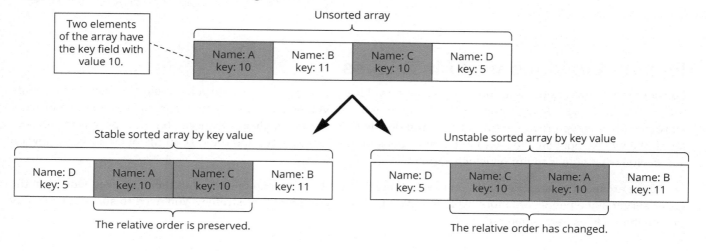

In Figure 4-1 the unsorted array has the key value 10 repeated in the first and third position of the array. The sorted result at the left had produced an output as expected for a stable sorted algorithm since the data with name A is before the data with name C, as they were before sorting. On the other hand, the sorted result at the right did not preserve the relative order of the data with name A and the data with name C, since the data with key C is before the data with key A in the sorted array.

What about non-numerical types? It is also possible to sort non-numerical values, for example, by alphabetical order. In such a case, a comparison function might be such that `comp("hello", "bye")` = `'greater'`.

Types of Sorting Algorithms

Not all sorting algorithms are the same, although the output is always a sorted sequence. The following are some characteristics used to classify them:

- *You can compare them by complexity.* The more time-consuming part of a sorting algorithm is usually the number of comparisons. As you might expect, sorting a sequence requires many comparisons. The best sorting algorithms have a complexity $O(n \log n)$.

- *You can categorize a sorting algorithm by the number of swaps.* When sorting a sequence, it will be necessary to move the values in the sequence. A **swap** or **inversion** is a change in the order of elements of the sequence, where the kth element is in the jth position and the jth element is in the kth position. For example, given the input array $X = [5,3,7,2,9]$, you swap the elements at positions 2 and 3 (assuming the index starts at 0), giving a result of $X = [5,3,2,7,9]$. It is always possible to put a sequence in order using only swap operations. **Figure 4-2** illustrates using sequence swaps to sort an array.

Figure 4-2   Sorting using swaps

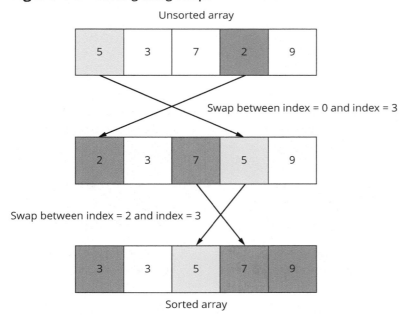

Unsorted array

Swap between index = 0 and index = 3

Swap between index = 2 and index = 3

Sorted array

As in the case of the running time, you summarize the relationship between the number of swaps and the input size using asymptotic notation. Recall that asymptotic notation is a mathematical tool used to describe the relationship between the resources used by an algorithm in terms of the input size.

- *You can use auxiliary memory.* When sorting a sequence of values, it is possible to use an auxiliary structure to keep track of useful data. For example, you can traverse part of a structure, identify the maximum element so far, and store its value in another array. In such a case, the array where the partial maximum is stored is called an *auxiliary structure*. The amount of additional auxiliary memory needed, that is, the space complexity, is another characteristic by which sorting algorithms get classified. When an algorithm has a space complexity of $O(1)$ or $O(\log n)$, the algorithm is an **in-place sorting algorithm**.

- *You can classify sorting algorithms by whether an algorithm is stable.* That means the algorithm keeps the same relative order of the input for repeated key values.

> **Note**
>
> Sorting is an essential part of file and database administration systems that comprise large amounts of data that are impossible to keep in the main memory. For such cases, another characteristic becomes critical for a sorting algorithm: external memory use. A sorting algorithm that uses external memory, such as hard drives or cloud storage, is called an **external sorting algorithm**.
>
> You should access the hard drive or cloud storage as little as possible to load the necessary data to the main memory. That means that, for example, it is more efficient to make a read to the external data storage work with the data in main memory and make a single write than constantly reading and writing to memory each time one piece of data is modified. The reason is that the difference in speed between access to the main memory (RAM) and accessing the hard drive is enormous. On average, reading data from RAM takes around 50 nanoseconds (5×10^{-8} sec), while reading data from a hard drive, on average, takes 5 milliseconds (5×10^{-3} sec). That is an increment of 100,000 times!

4.2 Bubble Sort

Bubble sort is a simple sorting algorithm that traverses parts of the input array swapping elements to put the largest of the current sub-array at the last position. Bubble sort is the most basic sorting algorithm. The name *bubble sort* comes from the idea that a large element will move to the top of an array, like a bubble that moves to the surface of the water.

> ### Technical Interview
>
> If you are asked to sort a sequence in a job interview or code challenge, bubble sort is probably not a good choice. Although it is simple to remember and implement, it has the worst running time. Therefore, you should consider other sorting algorithms, especially if performance is critical.
>
> However, you can use bubble sort with a small number of elements or when testing to see if an idea will work out. A good strategy might be to use bubble sort to check if your plan solves the problem at hand. If it does, then change the sorting method to use a more appropriate algorithm.

Bubble Sort Example

Consider the array $X = [1,7,3,2,4]$. The idea behind bubble sort is that the 7 must rise to the top, or last position, of the array in order to produce an array sorted in ascending order. The difficulty is that, unlike you, the algorithm doesn't have a global view of the entire array, so it must simultaneously execute comparisons of two elements. Therefore, you can start by comparing $X[i]$ and $X[i + 1]$ from the starting position to the end. If $X[i] > X[i + 1]$, then $X[i]$ is out of place, so the elements are swapped. In **Figure 4-3**, you can see the sequence of comparisons and swaps executed.

Figure 4-3   Comparisons and swaps made in bubble sort

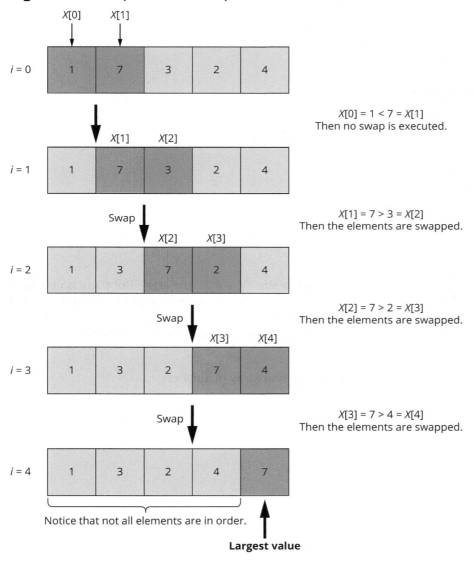

$X[0] = 1 < 7 = X[1]$
Then no swap is executed.

$X[1] = 7 > 3 = X[2]$
Then the elements are swapped.

$X[2] = 7 > 2 = X[3]$
Then the elements are swapped.

$X[3] = 7 > 4 = X[4]$
Then the elements are swapped.

As you can see, the resulting array has the largest value in the last position. But the first elements are not in the correct order. Hence, the next step is to apply the same procedure to the first four elements of the array. **Figure 4-4** shows the sequence of comparisons and swaps made.

Figure 4-4 Bubble up operation done in bubble sort in the second iteration

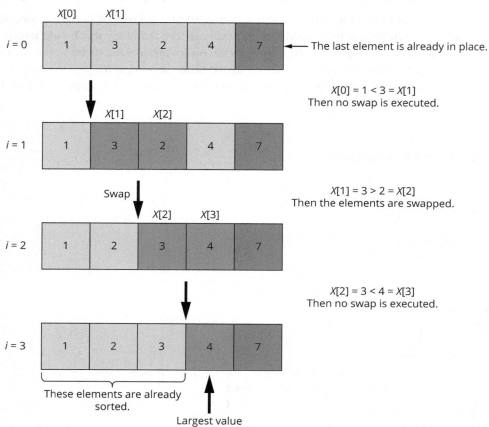

Notice that before completing all comparisons, the algorithm has already sorted the array. But there is no way of knowing this without continuing with the process. This is because the algorithm must keep bubbling up the largest value among the first three elements to the top of the array, although there won't be any change. So, the comparisons execute to ensure that the algorithm really sorted the array. This is one of the main reasons why bubble sort is the least efficient algorithm among those discussed in this text.

In **Figure 4-5**, you can see how bubble sort operates over a different array of numbers.

Figure 4-5 Sequence of swaps done in bubble sort

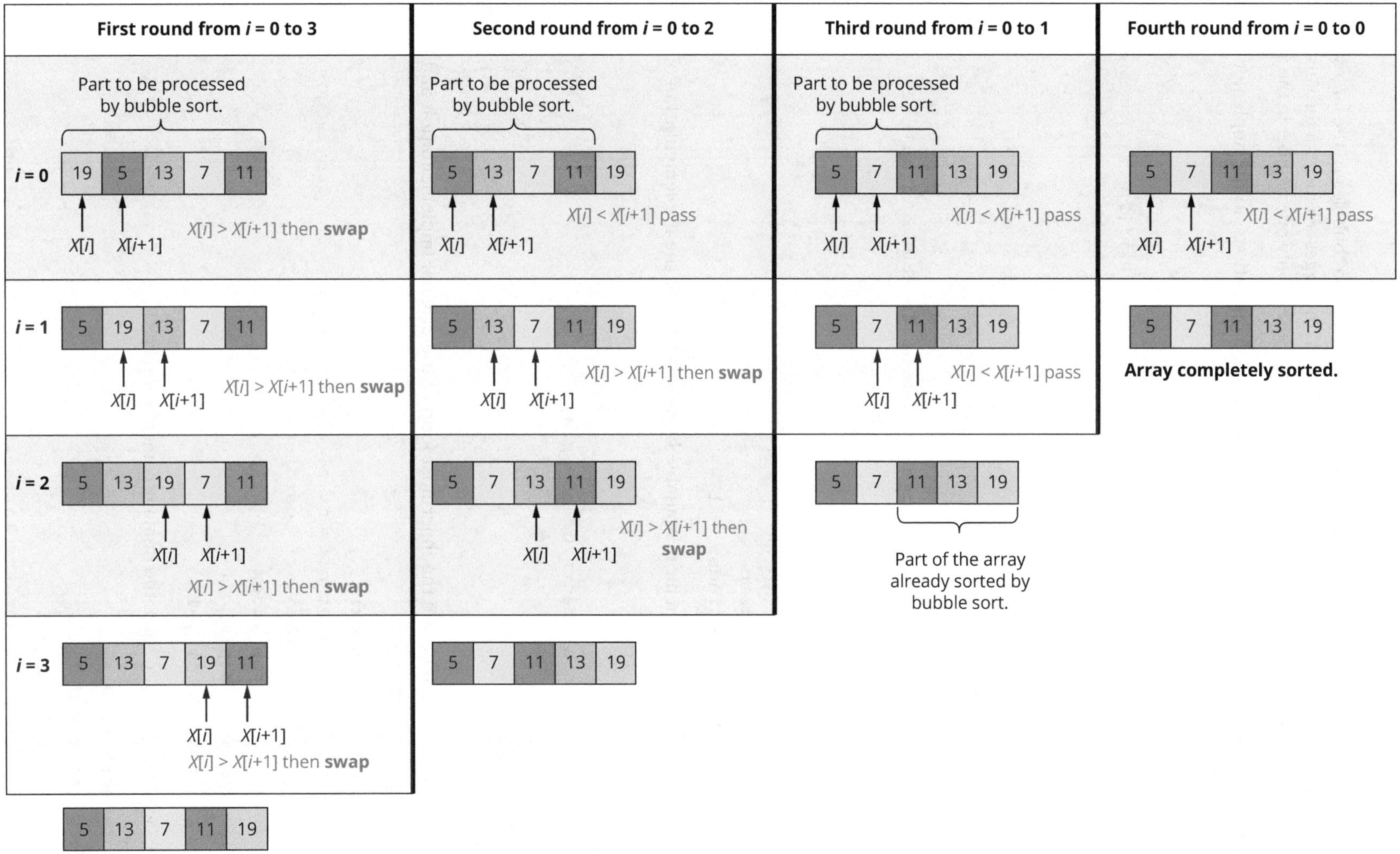

Bubble Sort Details

Recall that sorting an array X of size N using bubble sort first uses swaps to "bubble up" the largest element of the array X to the top of the array (position $N-1$). The next step is to "bubble up" the largest element of the sub-array $X[0],\dots,X[N-2]$, and then keep "bubbling up" for each sub-array $X[0],\dots,X[k]$ until there is only one number in the sub-array.

The following implementation of bubble sort uses only basic operations. In the implementation, X is an array of integer values of given size N:

> **Note** | In this text, a double semicolon (; ;) and a light blue color is used to mark comments in pseudocode.

```
bubble_sort(X, N)
;; bubble sort implementation
   top_index = N-1
   while top_index > 1
   ;; At each iteration the largest element is "bubbled up"
      for j = 0 to top_index-1 step 1
         if X[j] > X[j+1]
            temp = X[j]
            X[j] = X[j+1]
            X[j+1] = temp
      top_index = top_index - 1
```

You can make the implementation more readable by separating out the implementation of the swap operation as follows:

```
swap(X, i, j)
   ;; Swap of two elements of an array
   temp = X[i]
   X[i] = X[j]
   X[j] = temp
```

Also, recall that you can separate the innermost loop of the original implementation and put it in a `bubble_up` function:

```
bubble_up(X, top_index)
   ;; Moves the largest element of the sub-array of X from 0 to
   ;; top_index to the last position in the array.
   for j = 0 to top_index - 1 step 1
      if X[j] > X[j+1]
         swap(X, j, j+1)
```

Using the two previous functions, the final implementation is:

```
bubble_sort(X, N)
   top_index = N-1
   while top_index > 1
   ;; At each iteration the largest element is "bubbled up"
      bubble_up(X, top_index)
      top_index = top_index - 1
```

> ## Quick Check 4-1

What is the result of `bubble_up(X,3)` for $X = [3,1,5,2,7]$?

Answer: $X = [1,3,2,5,7]$.

Notice that `bubble_up` uses $j = 0,1,2$. When $j = 0$, there is a swap since $3 > 1$, $X = [1,3,5,2,7]$. For $j = 1$, the comparison is $X[1] = 3 > X[2] = 5$, so there is no swap. Lastly, for $j = 2$, the comparison is made between $X[2] = 5$ and $X[3] = 2$. So, a swap results in $X = [1,3,2,5,7]$.

Performance of Bubble Sort

Review the last implementation of the bubble sort algorithm:

```
bubble_sort(X, N)
    top_index = N-1
    while top_index > 1
        bubble_up(X, top_index)
        top_index = top_index - 1
```

Notice that the `while` loop executes N times. Therefore, to compute the complexity of the bubble sort, it is necessary to compute the complexity of `bubble_up(X,top_index)`. The function `bubble_up()` iterates through `top_index-1` elements, so its complexity is $O(top\_index)$. Since the largest possible value of `top_index` is $N-1$, the `bubble_up()` function has a worst-case complexity of $O(N)$, since you only use the dominant term. Hence, the complete `bubble_up` function has complexity $O(N\,O(N)) = O(N^2)$.

Notice that bubble sort only uses the auxiliary variables `top_index` and `j`. Thus, its space complexity is $O(1)$ and it is an in-place sorting algorithm.

> **Note**
>
> In computer science, a quadratic complexity such as $O(N^2)$ is considered acceptable, but it might not be acceptable in practical terms. For example, if you have 10 million records (10^7) and assume that your computer can read them and execute instructions at 1 billion operations per second (10^{-9}), then to sort all the records it will take approximately:
>
> $$(10^6)^2 \times 10^{-9} \times \frac{1}{60 \times 60} \approx 27 \text{ hrs}$$

4.3 Selection Sort

Selection sort is a sorting algorithm that iteratively searches for the smallest element and swaps it into the appropriate place. Selection sort is like bubble sort in that, in both cases, they solve part of the problem in a subsequence, but selection sort reduces the number of swaps necessary to sort the array. The difference between selection sort and bubble sort might seem insignificant, but if you are sorting an array of records with integer keys and large amounts of data in other fields, swapping the records in memory might be computationally expensive.

Regarding the number of swaps, selection sort is better than bubble sort, although the time complexity remains the same.

The characteristics of selection sort make it a good choice when working with large files and a small number of keys. In addition, the algorithm's simplicity might compensate for its poor performance in minor cases when using more complicated algorithms might not be worth the work needed to implement them.

Selection Sort Example

Selection sort iteratively finds the index of the minimum element and swaps that with the current position. For example, given $X = [3,7,1,2,4]$, you start by finding the minimum in the array. In this case, $X[2] = 1$. Then, you swap the elements at positions 2 and 0 and get:

$$X = [1,7,3,2,4]$$

In **Figure 4-6**, you can see the series of comparisons made to find the minimum in the array.

Figure 4-6 Selection process done in selection sort

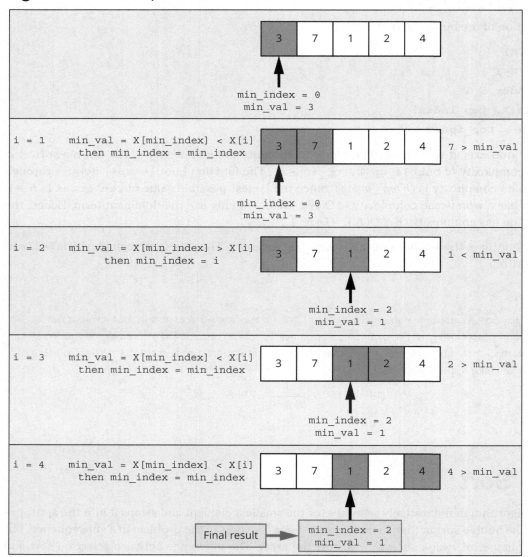

After the initial iteration, you search for the minimum element in the sub-array from $i = 1$ to the end, meaning the minimum of the sub-array [7, 3, 2, 4]. In this case, the swap is between $X[3] = 2$ and $X[1] = 7$. This process repeats until there is only a subsequence of length 1. You can see the complete sequences of swaps in **Figure 4-7**.

Figure 4-7   Swaps made in selection sort

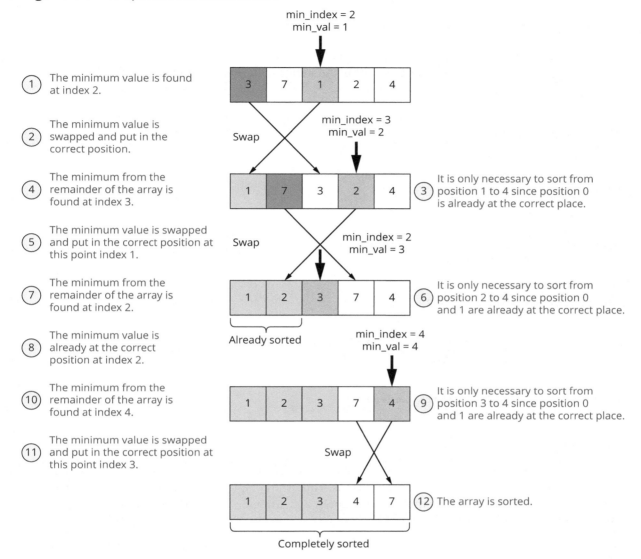

① The minimum value is found at index 2.

② The minimum value is swapped and put in the correct position.

④ The minimum from the remainder of the array is found at index 3.

⑤ The minimum value is swapped and put in the correct position at this point index 1.

⑦ The minimum from the remainder of the array is found at index 2.

⑧ The minimum value is already at the correct position at index 2.

⑩ The minimum from the remainder of the array is found at index 4.

⑪ The minimum value is swapped and put in the correct position at this point index 3.

③ It is only necessary to sort from position 1 to 4 since position 0 is already at the correct place.

⑥ It is only necessary to sort from position 2 to 4 since position 0 and 1 are already at the correct place.

⑨ It is only necessary to sort from position 3 to 4 since position 0 and 1 are already at the correct place.

⑫ The array is sorted.

Selection Sort Details

There are a few steps to consider when implementing selection sort:

- From a starting position (initially $X[0]$), find the minimum in the sequence.
- Swap the minimum and the value located in the starting position.
- Repeat the process by moving the starting position by 1 to the right until the array is in the correct sort order.

Here is the pseudocode for the selection sort implementation:

```
selection_sort(X, N)
    for i = 0 to N-2 step 1
    ;; At each iteration find the index of the minimum element
        min_idx = i
        for j = i+1 to N-1 step 1
            if X[min_idx] > X[j]
                min_idx = j
```

```
temp = X[min_idx]
X[min_idx] = X[i]
X[i] = temp
```

It is possible to rewrite the previous implementation using two auxiliary functions swap and find_min. You can find an implementation for swap in the bubble sort algorithm. An implementation of find_min is as follows:

```
find_min(X, start_index, N)
    ;; Find the index of the minimum element of X from
    ;; start_index to N-1
    min_idx = start_index
    for i = start_index + 1 to N-1 step 1
        if X[min_idx] > X[i]
            min_idx = i
    return min_idx
```

Then, the selection sort algorithm implementation is:

```
selection_sort(X, N)
    for start_index = 0 to N-2 step 1
        ;; Find the index of the minimum element
        min_index = find_min(X, start_index, N)
        ;; Put the minimum element at the beginning
        ;; of the subarray
        swap(X, min_index, start_index)
```

Performance of Selection Sort

From the implementation of the find_min function of the selection sort algorithm shown in the previous section, you can see that the loop executes N-1-start_index comparisons. Thus, the complexity of the select procedure might be written as $O(N-1-start\_index)$. The longest of those loops is for start_index = 0 when it becomes $O(N-1) = O(N)$, since the dominant term (N) is the relevant term.

Now the selecton_sort method implemented in the previous section calls the find_min function $N-1$ times; thus, selection sort has complexity:

$$O((N-1)\,O(N)) = O(N^2 - N) = O(N^2)$$

So, the time complexity of selection sort is $O(N^2)$. Notice that the number of swaps made by selection sort is $O(N)$. Since there are only the auxiliary variables min_index, start_index and i, the space complexity of the selection sort is $O(1)$. Thus, selection sort is an in-place algorithm.

4.4 Insertion Sort

You might have noticed that the number of comparisons made with bubble sort and selection sort is always the same, independent of how the values in the input array were sorted.

With selection sort and bubble sort, the same number of comparisons is made for $X = [3, 2, 5, 1]$ and for $Y = [1, 2, 3, 4]$, although the number of swaps is certainly less for Y than for X.

Insertion sort is a sorting algorithm that creates a sorted array by sequentially inserting each new data in the appropriate position. Insertion sort takes advantage of the starting subsequence when sorted. Therefore, a sorting algorithm is an **adaptive sorting algorithm** if the complexity changes based on whether the array is presorted.

Insertion Sort Example

An insertion sort will sort a sub-array, inserting the next element in the correct position of the array. To illustrate this, consider the array $X = [7, 1, 2, 3, 4]$. With insertion sort, you already sorted the sub-array $[7]$. The element to consider for insertion is $X[1] = 1$. Since $7 > 1$, it is inserted before 7. Now the array is $X = [1, 7, 2, 3, 4]$. Next, the algorithm sorts the subsequence $[1, 7]$ and the element to consider for insertion is $X[2] = 2$. You can see the sequence of comparisons made to insert $X[2] = 2$ and $X[3] = 3$ in **Figure 4-8**.

Figure 4-8   Comparisons made in insertion sort

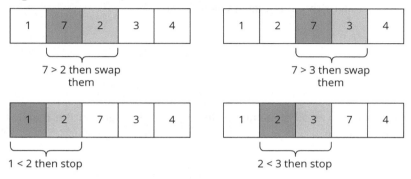

Notice that the insertion process is shorter if the value considered for insertion is closer to its correct position. In **Figure 4-9**, you can see the comparisons and swaps made by insertion sort for the array $X = [1, 2, 3, 5, 7]$.

Figure 4-9   Insertion sort is more efficient when the array is presorted

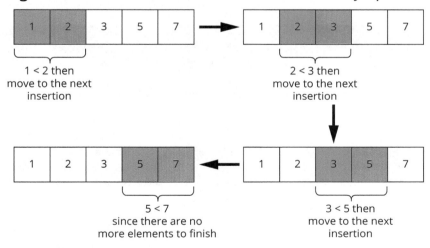

Insertion Sort Details

To implement an insertion sort:

- For the presorted subsequence $[a_0, \ldots, a_k]$, find the correct position for the element a_{k+1}.
- Insert the element a_{k+1} in its correct position in the sorted subsequence.
- Now, repeat for the new sorted subsequence until you have sorted all elements.

The insertion operation can vary depending on the data structure used, but for arrays, it is more convenient to use swaps to implement it. Look at the following insertion sort function:

```
insert(X, insert_index)
    insert_key = X[insert_index]
    j = insert_index
    while j >= 0 and X[j-1] > insert_key
        swap(X, j, j-1)
        j = j-1
```

When using the `insert` function, the insertion sort algorithm implements as follows:

```
insertion_sort(X, N):
    For i = 0 to N-2 step 1
        insert_index = i + 1
        insert(X, insert_index)
```

Another implementation using the `insert` function moves all elements in the array to the right until it reaches the index, where the algorithm should insert the new element.

```
insert(X, insert_index)
    insert_key = X[insert_index]
    j = insert_index
    while j >= 0 and X[j-1] > insert_key
        X[j] = X[j-1]
        j = j - 1
    X[j] = insert_key
```

Quick Check 4-2

Consider the array $X = [2, 5, 3]$. How many swaps will you execute when using insertion sort? Use the version of the implementation with the swap.

Answer: One swap. Since the subsequence [2, 5] is already in sort order, it is only necessary to insert the value 3. Inserting the value 3 only requires swapping it with the 5.

Performance of Insertion Sort

First, notice that, as with bubble sort and selection sort, you can implement insertion sort in-place. Since insertion sort only uses auxiliary variables j, insert_index, and insert_key, its space complexity is $O(1)$.

The worst case for the insert(X, insert_index) function is when the array X[insert_index] is smaller than all the elements $X[i]$ with i < insert_index. So, the complexity of the insert function is $O(insert\_index)$ since, in the worst case, the insert function makes insert_index comparisons. Also, the insertion sort algorithm makes $N - 1$ insertions; hence, the complexity of the insertion sort is:

$$O((N-1)\,O(insert\_index)) = O((N-1)\,O(N)) = O(N^2)$$

> **Note** Insertion sort is in a special classification for sorting algorithms called online. You can execute an **online sorting algorithm** with partial knowledge of the data it needs to sort. For example, you can execute insertion sort for an array $X = [3, 5, 2]$, and later find out that there are other numbers and that the actual array was $X = [3, 5, 2, 7, 1]$. That won't be a problem, as you can continue with insertion with $i = 2$. You don't have to start over.
>
> Notice that not all sorting algorithms are online. For example, the bubble sort and selection sort algorithms need to know all the values in the first pass.

4.5 Quicksort

Quicksort is a sorting algorithm that divides an array in two parts then applies the same strategy to each part to sort the whole array, which means that it uses the strategy of divide and conquer. Quicksort reduces the problem of sorting an array of N elements into sorting two arrays with lengths less than N. The key point is that the partition is done in-place, putting all elements greater than a pivot value q on the right and all less than q on the left. In computer science, a **pivot value** is an element of an array (it could be a multidimensional array like a matrix) selected as a reference to perform certain operations. In the case of quicksort, the pivot value is used to split the array in two sub-arrays.

> **Note** The quicksort algorithm was invented by mathematician and computer scientist Tony Hoare. He was trying to solve the problem of language translation. At the time, dictionaries were stored on magnetic tape to translate the words from one language to another. Hoare thought it would be easier to sort the words in the text in alphabetical order. Trying to find an effective way of sorting words with the limited memory available for computers in those days, he devised the quicksort algorithm. The invention of the quicksort shows how important sorting problems are in computer science and programming.

Quicksort Example

The quicksort algorithm uses a pivot value. Since there is no real strategy for choosing the pivot value, the algorithm selects the rightmost value in the array. When using the pivot value, the original array splits into two sub-arrays: one with elements less than the pivot value and the other with values greater than the pivot value.

For example, to apply quicksort to $X = [6, 7, 2, 3, 9, 1, 4]$, the first pivot value is `pivot_value = 4`. Thus, X could be split as `x_left = [2, 3, 1]`, `pivot_value = 4`, and `x_right = [9, 6, 7]`. Then, you can apply quicksort to each sub-array `x_left` and `x_right`. This application would require reassembling the sub-arrays and the pivot value into a single array again, thus the array gets rearranged as $X = [2, 3, 1, 4, 9, 6, 7]$. Then, `x_left` is the sub-array from `low = 0` to `left_high = 2`. And `x_right` is the sub-array from `right_low = left_high + 2 = 4` to `high = 6`. In **Figure 4-10**, you can see how repeating that process will work until the array gets sorted.

Figure 4-10 Quicksort process of splitting and sorting

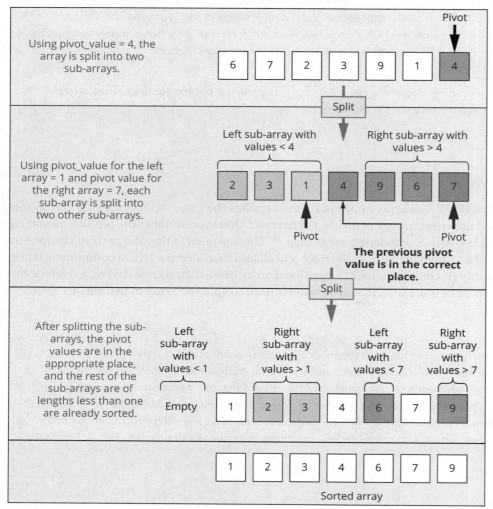

So, the key to the quicksort algorithm is rearranging the values, forming `x_left` and `x_right`. To illustrate how to accomplish this using swaps, suppose that `left_high = -1`, which means that the `x_left` sub-array is empty. And `right_low = 0`, with `pivot_value = 4` and `pivot_index = 6`. To create the correct values for `left_high` and `right_low`, you traverse the array and, when the algorithm finds an element less than `pivot_value`, it moves `left_high` one unit to the right. You can see this process illustrated in **Figure 4-11**.

Figure 4-11   Splitting in quicksort using only swaps

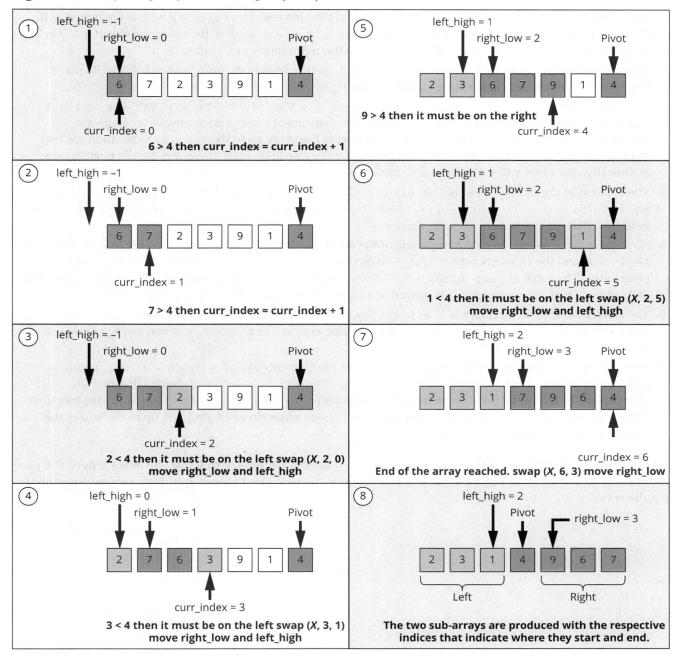

A detailed description of the steps in Figure 4-11 is as follows:

1. Starting with `left_high` = -1 and `right_low` = 0, the element at `curr_index` = 0 is compared with the pivot value. Since the value at `curr_index` is 6 > `pivot_value` = 4, the current element is left at its place and the current index is moved one element to the right, thus `curr_index` = 1.

2. The value at `curr_index` is 7 > `pivot_value` = 4, so the element at `curr_index` is left at its place. Then the current index is moved one element to the right, thus `curr_index` = 2.

3. The element at the `curr_index` is 2 < `pivot_value` = 4, then `right_low` = `right_low + 1` = 1 and `left_high` = `left_high + 1` = 0. Thus, the elements at `curr_index` and `left_high` are swapped. Notice that the elements from the beginning of the array up to the `left_high` position are less than the pivot value, and the elements from the `right_low` position up to the `curr_index` position are greater than the pivot value. Finally, `curr_index` = `curr_index + 1` = 3.

4. The element at the `curr_index` is 3 < `pivot_value` = 4, then `right_low` = `right_low + 1` = 2 and `left_high` = `left_high + 1` = 1. And the elements at `curr_index` = 3 and `left_high`= 1 are swapped. Last, `curr_index` = `curr_index + 1` = 4.

5. Notice that the elements from the beginning of the array up to the `left_high` position are less than the pivot value, and the elements from `right_low` position up to `curr_index` position are greater than the pivot value. The value at `curr_index` is 9 > `pivot_value` = 4, then the element at `curr_index` is left at its place. Then the current index is moved one element to the right, thus `curr_index` = 5.

6. The element at the `curr_index` is 1 < `pivot_value` = 4, then `right_low` = `right_low + 1` = 3 and `left_high` = `left_high + 1` = 2. And the elements at `curr_index` = 5 and `left_high` = 2 are swapped. At last, `curr_index` = `curr_index + 1` = 6.

7. `curr_index` = 6 has reached the last position, thus the elements at `curr_index` = `pivot_index` = 6 and `right_low` = 3 are swapped. Then `right_low` = `right_low + 1` = 4. Notice that now all elements at the left of the pivot value (from the beginning of the array up to `left_high` = 2) are less than the pivot value, and all the elements at the right of the pivot value (from `right_low` up to the end of the array) are greater than the pivot value.

Notice that to identify the left and right parts of X, it is only necessary to know the index where the pivot value ends up in the array. In **Figure 4-12**, you can see how the new pivot values split for a second time into the two sub-arrays.

Figure 4-12   The second iteration of splits in quicksort

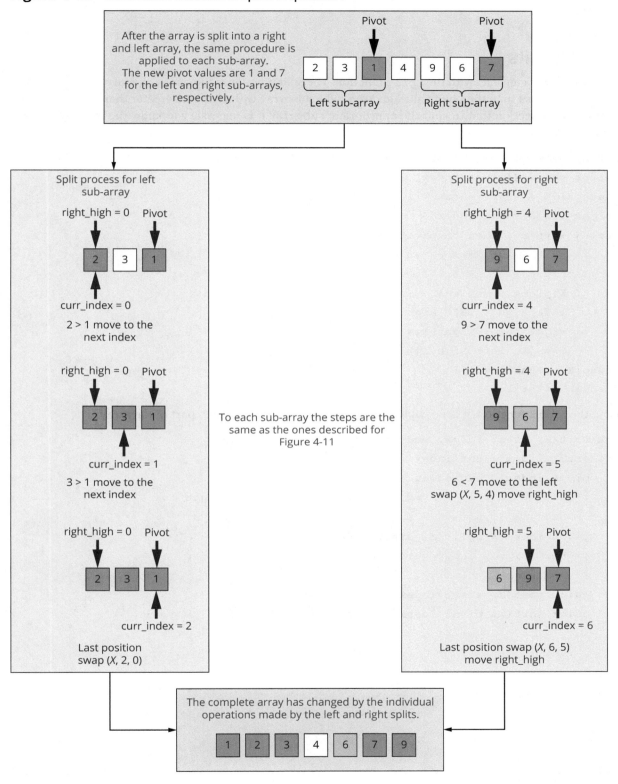

Each time the array splits, the size of the resulting arrays is at least one less than the original; thus, the algorithm will eventually stop.

Quicksort Details

To write the quicksort, you can start with the `split` function. The split function is the one in charge of creating the left sub-array with elements less than the pivot value, and the right sub-array with elements greater than the pivot value. Recall from the previous section that to split the appropriate sub-array it is necessary to know the starting position (`start_index`) and a pivot index that is the same as the last position.

```
split(X, start_index, pivot_index)
    pivot_val = X[pivot_index]
    left_high = start_index - 1
    right_low = start_index
    for j = start_index to pivot_index-1 step 1
    ;; If an element is less or equal to pivot_val
    ;; then put it at the left side of the array by using swap.
        if X[j] <= pivot_val
            left_high = left_high + 1
            right_low = right_low + 1
            swap(X, left_high, j)
    swap(X, right_low, j)
    return right_low
```

Then, using the `split` function, it is possible to use recursive calls to sort each part of the array:

```
quick_sort(X, start_index, end_index)
    if start_index < end_index
        pivot_index = end_index
        ;; The split function returns the pivot_index = right_low - 1
        ;; and also modifies X to produce the two sub-arrays.
        pivot_index = split(X, start_index, pivot_index)
        ;; Recursively apply quick sort to the left sub-array
        ;; and right sub-array.
        quick_sort(X, start_index, pivot_index-1)
        quick_sort(X, pivot_index+1, end_index)
```

Quick Check 4-3

Suppose $X = [3, 11, 9, 6, 2, 1, 5]$. What is the result after using `split(X, 0, 6)`?

Answer: [3, 2, 1, 5, 11, 9, 6]

The following illustrates the sequence of values for `left_high`, `right_low`, and `X`, notice that the bolded values are the values in the left partition of the split:

- `pivot_val = 5, left_high = -1, right_low = 0`
- `j=0, pivot_val=5 > X[j]=3 then left_high = 0, right_low =1, X = [3, 11, 9, 6, 2, 1, 5]`
- `j=1, pivot_val=5 < X[j]=11, left_high = 0, right_low = 1, X = [3, 11, 9, 6, 2, 1, 5]`
- `j=2, pivot_val=5 < X[j]=9, left_high = 0, right_low = 1, X = [3, 11, 9, 6, 2, 1, 5]`
- `j=3, pivot_val=5 < X[j]=6, left_high = 0, right_low = 1, X = [3, 11, 9, 6, 2, 1, 5]`
- `j=4, pivot_val=5 > X[j]=2, left_high = 1, right_low = 2, X = [3, 2, 9, 6, 11, 1, 5]`
- `j=5, pivot_val=5 > X[j] = 1, left_high = 2, right_low = 3, X = [3, 2, 1, 6, 11, 9, 5]`
- `swap(X, 3, 6), left_high = 2, right_low = 4.`
- `X=[3, 2, 1, 5, 11, 9, 6], left_high = 2, right_low = 4`

Performance of Quicksort

Since all the operations made by the quicksort algorithm are swaps, and those are made in-place, the space complexity of quicksort is $O(1)$. That makes quicksort an in-place algorithm.

The worst case for quicksort is when the `split` function produces an empty array and an array of size $N - 1$. If this occurs at each recursive call of the quicksort, then each call will use $N - 1$ comparisons. Thus, its complexity is $O(N^2)$. You can see an illustration of this in **Figure 4-13**.

Figure 4-13   In quicksort the worst case is when the array is presorted

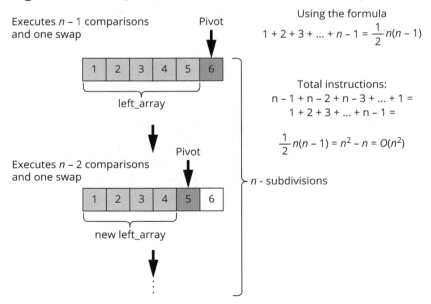

Executes $n - 1$ comparisons and one swap

Pivot

left_array

Executes $n - 2$ comparisons and one swap

Pivot

new left_array

Using the formula
$$1 + 2 + 3 + \dots + n - 1 = \frac{1}{2}n(n - 1)$$

Total instructions:
$$n - 1 + n - 2 + n - 3 + \dots + 1 =$$
$$1 + 2 + 3 + \dots + n - 1 =$$

$$\frac{1}{2}n(n - 1) = n^2 - n = O(n^2)$$

n - subdivisions

Although this gives a worst case for quicksort, like bubble sort, selection sort, and insertion sort, it differentiates on average. Most of the time, the `split` function will produce a well-balanced partition. A balanced partition means that each part is approximately the same size. If that is the case, then the number of recursive calls is approximate $\log N$. Thus, the average complexity is $O(N \log N)$. You can see such a case illustrated in **Figure 4-14**.

Figure 4-14   On average the array won't be presorted and quicksort is more efficient

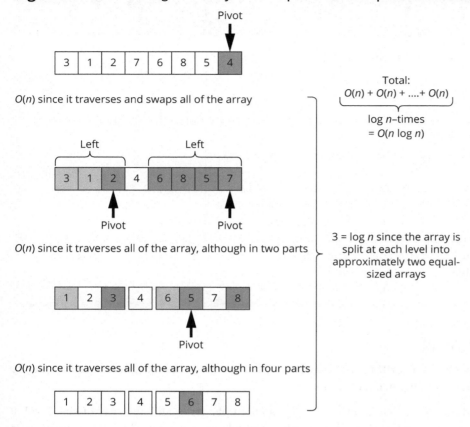

O(n) since it traverses and swaps all of the array

Total:
O(n) + O(n) + ...+ O(n)
log n–times
= O(n log n)

O(n) since it traverses all of the array, although in two parts

3 = log n since the array is split at each level into approximately two equal-sized arrays

O(n) since it traverses all of the array, although in four parts

Moreover, when the size of N grows, the probability of getting balanced parts in quicksort increases. That makes the quicksort algorithm the most practical in-place sorting algorithm for large-size arrays.

4.6 Merge Sort

Merge sort is a not in-place sorting algorithm that splits an array recursively into smaller parts; each part is sorted and then join the parts to produce the desired sorted array. Merge sort also uses the divide-and-conquer strategy. Recall that in quicksort, most of the work occurs when splitting the original array to guarantee that each part has certain characteristics. However, in merge sort, the merging part of the algorithm is where most of the work occurs. As you will see in this section, the split made in merge sort is quite simple. In contrast, the merge part of the algorithm requires a more complex sequence of steps.

| Note | Mathematician John von Neumann usually gets the credit for inventing the merge sort algorithm. He also made significant contributions to physics (especially quantum theory), economics, engineering, and computer science. |

Merge Sort Example

The merge sort algorithm starts by splitting an array into two almost equal-sized parts. When the array has an odd length N, you can use the integer part of $N/2$. So, if your array has length 15, the integer part of 15/2 is 7. So, you split the original array into two sub-arrays, one with 7 elements and the other with 8, to have a total of 15 elements.

After splitting an array, you recursively call the merge sort algorithm until you reach the base case. The base case for merge sort occurs when the array has length one. In such a case, the array is already in sorted order. For example, given the array $X = [6, 5, 3, 9, 4]$, you can see X being recursively split into two sub-arrays in **Figure 4-15**.

Figure 4-15   Splitting process done in merge sort

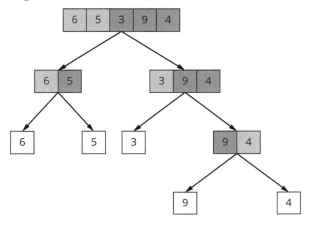

After reaching the point where the sub-arrays are in sorted order, the merging process should have occurred. In **Figure 4-16**, you can see the merging process.

Figure 4-16   Merge sequence done in merge sort

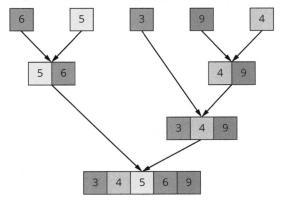

You can use an auxiliary array (`aux_array`) of the same size as the original array for the merge process. When merging two sub-arrays, traverses are simultaneous, and the smaller element copies to `aux_array` until there are no more elements to add. Then, the elements stored in `aux_array` get copied to the original array X. You can see the process illustrated in **Figure 4-17**.

Figure 4-17   Merge sort using the auxiliary array to merge two sub-arrays

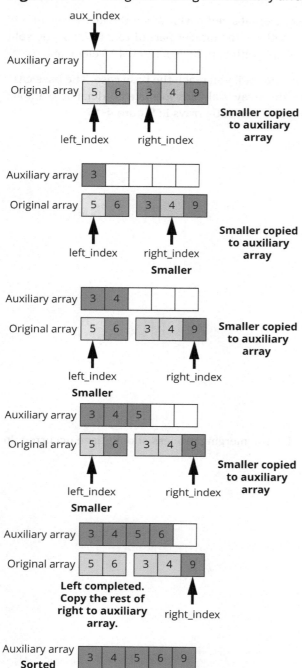

Merge Sort Details

As pointed out in the previous section, most of the work is done in the merge part of the algorithm while requiring that the two arrays, already sorted previously, merge. So, for example, when merging two sub-arrays of array X, you need the start position (`start_index`), the middle position (`mid_index`), and the end position (`end_index`) to complete the algorithm. Additionally, it is also necessary to provide the `aux_array` used to sort the elements:

```
merge(X, aux_array, start_index, mid_index, end_index)
    start_left = start_index
    end_left = mid_index - 1
    start_right = mid_index
    end_right = end_index
    left_index = start_left
    right_index = start_right
    aux_index = start_index
    while left_index <= end_left and right_index <= end_right
    ;; This loop traverses both sub-arrays simultaneously
    ;; and copies the values in the appropriate place at X.
        if X[left_index] <= X[right_index]
            aux_array[aux_index] = X[left_index]
            left_index = left_index + 1
        else
            aux_array[aux_index] = X[right_index]
            right_index = right_index + 1
        aux_index = aux_index + 1

    while left_index <= end_left
        ;; If there are still elements at the left side not copied
        ;; in the previous loop they are copied into X.
        aux_array[aux_index] = X[left_index]
        left_index = left_index + 1
        aux_index = aux_index + 1

    while right_index <= end_right
        ;; If there are still elements at the right side not copied
        ;; in the previous loop they are copied into X.
        aux_array[aux_index] = X[right_index]
        right_index = right_index + 1
        aux_index = aux_index + 1

    for i = start_index to end_index step 1
        ;; All the rest of elements in aux_array are copied into X.
        X[i] = aux_array[i]
```

You should separate the merge process into three stages:

```
while left_index <= end_left and right_index <= end_right
    if X[left_index] <= X[right_index]
        aux_array[aux_index] = X[left_index]
        left_index = left_index + 1
    else
        aux_array[aux_index] = X[right_index]
        right_index = right_index + 1
    aux_index = aux_index + 1
```

Here, you set it up to copy the elements of the left and right parts to the auxiliary array, depending on which is the smallest. You can see an illustration of this part of the process in Figure 4-17.

In Figure 4-17, one of the two parts did not get completely copied to the auxiliary array, so the next part copies the missing elements:

```
while left_index <= end_left
    aux_array[aux_index] = X[left_index]
    left_index = left_index + 1
    aux_index = aux_index + 1


while right_index <= end_right
    aux_array[aux_index] = X[right_index]
    right_index = right_index + 1
    aux_index = aux_index + 1
```

And finally, you copy the part of the auxiliary array not used in the merge process to the original array X:

```
for i = start_index to end_index step 1
    X[i] = aux_array[i]
```

Once you implement the merge operation, you can complete the merge sort as follows:

```
merge_sort(X, aux_array, start_index, end_index)
    if start_index < end_index
        ;; Compute an index to split the original array
        mid = integer((start_index + end_index)/2) + 1
        ;; Apply merge sort to each sub-array
        merge_sort(X, aux_array, start_index, mid-1)
        merge_sort(X, aux_array, mid, end_index)
        ;; Merge the two sorted sub-arrays into a single one
        merge(X, aux_array, start_index, mid, end_index)
```

Performance of Merge Sort

To determine the time complexity of the merge sort algorithm, review the example shown in **Figure 4-18**.

Figure 4-18   Merge sort divides each array by two so it will have log(n) levels

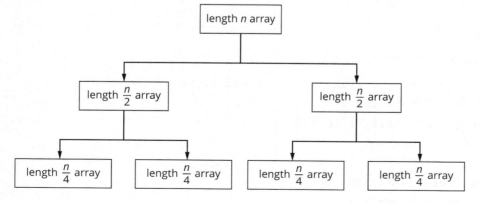

The length n array is traversed at each level of the description in Figure 4-18, so the complexity is $O(N)$ at each level. But at each step, the size of the arrays divides by two, and the number of levels becomes $O(\log N)$. Thus, the complexity of the merge sort algorithm is $O(N \log N)$. The merge sort algorithm has the best time complexity in the worst case. Still, since it is necessary to use the auxiliary array to complete the merge operations, its space complexity is $O(N)$.

Best Practices

Table 4-1 summarizes the key characteristics of time and space complexity for sorting algorithms.

Table 4-1   Characteristics of sorting algorithms

Algorithm	Worst-Case Time	Average-Case Time	Space Complexity	Notes
Bubble sort	$O(N^2)$	$O(N^2)$	$O(1)$	
Selection sort	$O(N^2)$	$O(N^2)$	$O(1)$	Fewer swaps
Insertion sort	$O(N^2)$	$O(N^2)$	$O(1)$	Online
Quicksort	$O(N^2)$	$O(N \log N)$	$O(1)$	Best on average and in-place
Merge sort	$O(N \log N)$	$O(N \log N)$	$O(N)$	Best running time but not in-place

Summary

- Given a sequence (or array) of N numbers $a_0, a_1, \ldots, a_{N-1}$, the sorting problem produces a new sequence, $b_0, b_1, \ldots, b_{N-1}$, with the same values in such a way that $b_0 \le b_1 \le \ldots \le b_{N-1}b_{N-1}$.

- All the algorithms discussed in this chapter contain numerical elements in an array. However, all algorithms can be changed by simply changing the expression $x <= y$ for a comparison function. It is also possible to modify the algorithms to get an array sorted in descending order by using the inverse comparison function.

- It is common to face problems that require sorting data directly. Sorting data can help tackle a difficult problem while reducing complexity, even when sorting the data is not mentioned explicitly in the problem description.

- A sorting algorithm is an algorithm that solves the sorting problem. Sorting algorithms are classified by complexity, the number of swaps necessary, how they handle repeated key values (stable or unstable), and their space complexity (in-place or not).

- Bubble sort is the simplest sorting algorithm but not recommended for any serious task since it lacks advantages over other sorting algorithms. Bubble sort has $O(N^2)$ complexity. Bubble sort traverses the array several times and swaps elements until the array is in complete sort order.

- Selection sort has complexity $O(N^2)$, but the number of swaps it makes is $O(N)$. That makes selection sort a good choice when swapping elements of the array is computationally expensive.

- Insertion sort has worst-case complexity $O(N^2)$, but this can change if the sequence has some parts already sorted. Since the algorithm's complexity is affected by whether the array is in sort order, the algorithm is adaptive. Selection sort is also an online sorting algorithm, which means that it can start sorting when it only has partial knowledge of the data it needs to sort.

- Quicksort uses a divide-and-conquer strategy where an array divides into two sub-arrays: the first sub-array of all elements less than a pivot value and the second array of all elements greater than the pivot value. Then, quicksort recursively sorts each sub-array. The process of subdividing an array is known as split and is the more complex part since it makes no use of any auxiliary array. Quicksort algorithms are in-place with worst-case complexity $O(N^2,),),)$, but this happens only when the array is already in sort order. In practice, the quicksort algorithm commonly has a complexity of $O(N \log N)$.

- Merge sort can also use a divide-and-conquer strategy. Merge sort divides the original array into two sub-arrays recursively. Once the sub-arrays have length one, the algorithm merges pairs of sub-arrays. The merge process creates a new sorted sub-array. Merge sort uses an auxiliary array to merge the sub-arrays. Thus, merge sort is not an in-place algorithm. The complexity of merge sort is $O(N \log N)$.

Key Terms

adaptive sorting algorithm	inverse comparison	quicksort
bubble sort	inversion	selection sort
comparison function	keys	sorting algorithm
external sorting algorithm	merge sort	sorting problem
in-place sorting algorithm	online sorting algorithm	stable sorting algorithm
insertion sort	pivot value	swap

Review Questions

1. When using the `bubble_up(X, 0)` sort with the array $X = [2,1,8,3,5]$, how many swaps are executed?

   a. 0

   b. 1

   c. 3

   d. 6

2. When using bubble sort with the array $X = [2,1,8,3,5]$, how many swaps are executed? Don't count the swaps, like `swap(X, 1, 1)`.

   a. 0

   b. 1

   c. 3

   d. 5

3. How many swaps execute when using the `insert` function of the insertion sort algorithm for $X = [1,8,3,5]$ with `insert_index = 2`?

   a. 0

   b. 1

   c. 2

   d. 3

4. How many swaps execute using the insertion sort algorithm for $X = [1,8,3,5]$?

   a. 0

   b. 1

   c. 2

   d. 3

5. Which of the following algorithms is an online sorting algorithm?

   a. Bubble sort

   b. Insertion sort

   c. Merge sort

   d. Quicksort

6. Which of the following algorithms performs better if the array's beginning is partially sorted?

   a. Bubble sort

   b. Insertion sort

   c. Merge sort

   d. Quicksort

7. Suppose you have an array of type *encyclopedic_files* composed of a critical integer value number and a string field. The string field is very large most of the time. Which swap-based algorithm is more appropriate to sort the array or *encyclopedic_files*?

8. When using the `split` method in quicksort, what results if applied to the array $X = [2, 1, 8, 3, 5]$ and the `pivot_index = 4`?

9. Can you say that insertion sort is a stable sorting algorithm?

10. Can the quicksort algorithm be considered a stable sorting algorithm?

Programming Problems

1. Suppose the data type `Student` has two fields: a string name and a number average. Given an array of students, `studentArray`, modify the selection sort algorithm to sort the students by the number average in descending order. **(LO 4.1, 4.3)**

   For example, given: `[Student('A', 2.4), Student('B', 3.0), Student('C', 3.9), Student('D', 2.5)]`, the result should be: `[Student('C', 3.9), Student('B', 3.0), Student('D', 2.5), Student('A', 2.4)]`

2. Use selection sort to sort a list of names `X = ['name 2', 'other name', 'name1']` by the length of the name. For example, after sorting the array X, the result should be `X = ['name1', 'name 2', 'other name']`. **(LO 4.1, 4.3)**

3. Write a program that computes the number that appears the maximum number of times in an array `intArray`. Ensure that the algorithm has complexity $O(n \log n)$. Suppose that only one of the values in the array is the correct answer. **(LO 4.1, 4.6)**

4. Write a program that returns the length of the longest consecutive sequence of numbers present in an array X. Suppose there are no repeated numbers. For example, if $X = [8, 3, 2, 1, 10, 9, 7, 6, 21]$, then the longest sequence of consecutive integers is 6, 7, 8, 9, and 10. The next one is 1, 2, and 3. **(LO 4.1, 4.2, 4.6)**

5. A rational number or a fraction $\left(\frac{a}{b}\right)$ can be represented by two fields, the numerator (a) and denominator (b), with a non-zero denominator. When working with rational numbers, equality and comparison greatly depend on both parts. For example, below you can see the conditions for equality:

$$\frac{a}{b} = \frac{c}{d} \qquad ad = bc$$

and for greater than:

$$\frac{a}{b} > \frac{c}{d} \qquad ad > bc$$

Write an ADT (abstract data type) to represent a rational number and write the comparison function, so it is appropriate to sort rational numbers. **(LO 4.1)**

Projects

Project 4-1: Union of Sets

(LO 4.1, 4.2, 4.3, 4.4. 4.5, 4.6) Sets are special since their elements characterize them. For example, if there is a repeating element, such as {1, 2, 3, 1}, you should simplify it to {1, 2, 3}.

Write a program that takes as input two arrays X, Y, their lengths N, M, and an array `union_array` of length $N + M$. The program returns the union of X and Y, where the `union_array` stores $X \cup Y$.

So, for example, if $X = [1, 3, 4]$, $Y = [1, 3, 6]$, then the program should return [1, 3, 4, 6, Null, Null].

Project 4-2: Intersection of Sets

(LO 4.1, 4.2, 4.3, 4.4, 4.5, 4.6) Sets are special since their elements characterize them. For example, if there is a repeating element, such as {1, 2, 3, 1}, you should simplify it to {1, 2, 3}.

Write a program that takes as input two arrays X, Y, their lengths N, M, and an array `intersection_array` of length $max\{N, M\}$. The program returns the intersection of X and Y, storing $X \cap Y$ in the `intersection_array`. Make sure that the program has a time complexity of $O(N \log N)$, where $n = max\{N, M\}$.

So, for example, if $X = [1, 3, 4]$, $Y = [1, 3, 6]$, then the program should return [1, 3, Null].

Project 4-3: Randomized Quicksort

(LO 4.1, 4.5) The performance of quicksort depends on the pivot value. It is possible to increase the probability that even if all elements in the array are already sorted, the algorithm won't reach $O(N^2)$. Instead, the algorithm will choose the pivot randomly, providing more chances for a balanced split. Therefore, at each step, the `pivot_index` will be a random number between `start_index` and `end_index`.

Write a modified version of quicksort that uses random pivots. This sorting algorithm is called randomized quicksort.

Project 4-4: Closest Pair Problem

(LO 4.1, 4.6) Write a program that, given an array of numbers X, finds the pair of numbers with the smallest distance between them. Ensure that your algorithm runs in $O(N \log N)$, where N is the array's length. Your code should check that the array has a length of at least two items.

For example, if $X = [7, 12, 31, 9, 25, 2]$, the program should return 7, 9.

In case of a tie between two elements, for example, with $X = [7, 9, 11]$, the pair with the smallest sum should be chosen. So, in this case 7, 9, although 9, 11 have the same distance.

Chapter 5

Search Algorithms

Learning Objectives

Upon completion of this chapter, you will be able to:

- **5.1** Discuss various search algorithms.
- **5.2** Apply sequential search algorithms to a problem.
- **5.3** Apply a binary search algorithm to a problem.
- **5.4** Apply a recursive binary search algorithm to a problem.

5.1 Introduction to Search Algorithms

Data structures are created to organize information. One of the main purposes is to use that data to accomplish some tasks. For example, a new user-defined data type employee might be created to store how much a company must pay its employees. To simplify access to the information, the employee data type will have an integer number employee_id that works as a unique identifier. Other fields, such as name, date of birth, address, and phone number, are stored in the same data type. To organize all the employees' data, you might want to store it in a larger data structure, such as an array or a list. Using a user-defined data type makes the data better organized. But other tasks, other than just storage, are required. One of the most common is searching for the address of a specific employee using the employee_id number. In such cases, you are not interested in some employees but in one specific employee. The operation of retrieving a specific employee is called a **search process**.

Generally, when referring to a data structure, each piece of data, like the employee data type mentioned in the previous paragraph, becomes the type of data being searched. It is common to refer to the data stored using the user-defined data type as **records** or **nodes** of the larger data structure. Thus, searching refers to retrieving a record with specific characteristics from a data structure.

A **search algorithm** is designed to provide a way to access a particular record or node in a data structure. When executing a search algorithm, the nodes or records are characterized by a key. A **key** is a set of fields used to compare two objects in search and sort algorithms. It is common to require that the key be uniquely assigned to each record. The idea is that the same answer is provided each time the search algorithm is used with a particular key. For example, when searching by first name in a list of employees, two employees might have the same name. So, two different search algorithms might give different results. To avoid such difficulties, most of the time it is assumed that the set of fields that form the key can be used to uniquely identify a record. The key of interest is called the target value. The target value is a particular combination of fields that compose the key.

In computer science, search algorithms are commonly described using integer values. But with few exceptions, you can extend the algorithms described for integers to any data type. The only requirement is to have a comparison function for key values.

Notice that to study efficient search algorithms, you need a function that helps you compare two objects and determine if they are equal. You will see that sorting is a tool that can speed up the search process. Searching data structures that are already sorted gives the best results in many scenarios. You can see an array of records sorted alphabetically by the field name in **Figure 5-1**.

Figure 5-1 A set of records sorted alphabetically using the name field

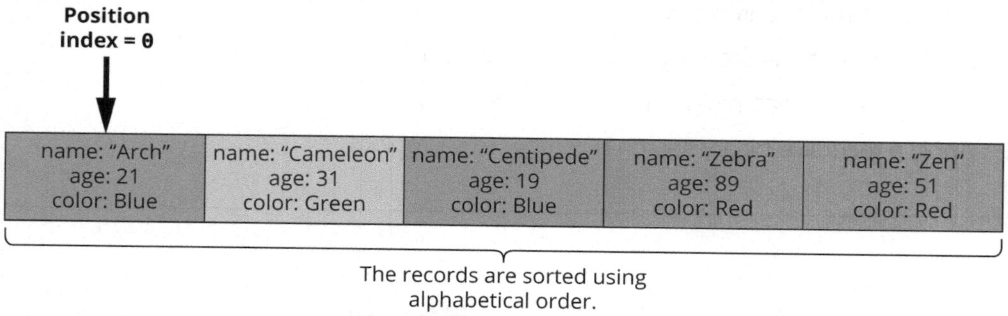

Finding a Friend's Phone Number

When searching for a friend's contact information on your phone, you most likely use a search algorithm. In fact, in most modern devices, more than one type of algorithm and a significant number of data structures are used.

Suppose that you need to access the contact information of a friend named Alex. In this case, a record might contain the name, email, photo, phone number, and more. The key for the records in this data structure is the name, in this case, Alex. "Alex" is the target value that you are searching for. You are looking for the contact with the name "Alex," supposing there is only one such contact.

Notice that the objective is not simply to get back "Alex" as an answer; the objective is to get all the information on the record that matches the name Alex. A search algorithm returns a pointer to the desired record so you can use it to access the information in the record. For example, suppose your contact information is stored in an array. In this case, a search algorithm returns the index of the contact associated with the name "Alex."

In **Figure 5-2**, you can see an array that stores different names. When searching for the target value "Alex," the result is the index number 2. The index number works as a pointer in the array where the desired record can be found.

Figure 5-2 A search algorithm must provide a way to retrieve the record with the key value that matches the target value

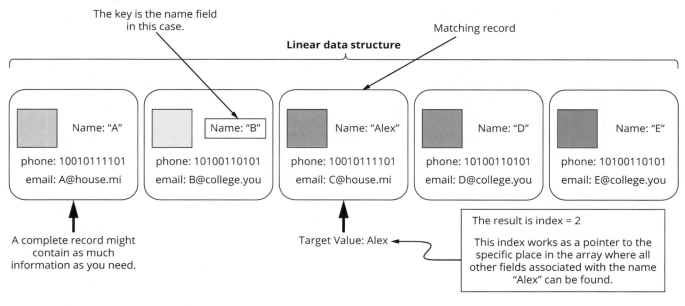

Sorted and Unsorted Searches

Suppose your phone doesn't have a search function. If your contacts are sorted in alphabetical order, finding the contact of your friend "Jordan" is easier compared to searching for "Jordan" in an unsorted list.

When implementing a search algorithm, it is essential to know whether the records are sorted. Let's look at the case of searching for "Jordan" on your phone.

If the records are sorted, you can scan a couple of names and deduce if you have to look forward or backward. If you see the name "Andrew," you know you need to keep going. But if you find the name "Zelda," then you know that you must move backward. If you reach a point where the names are:

... "Insta," "Karl," ...

Then you know that the name "Jordan" is not in your contacts since it should be after "Insta" and before "Karl," following the rules of alphabetical order. You can see this situation illustrated in **Figure 5-3**.

Figure 5-3 Looking for the contact information with name "Jordan"

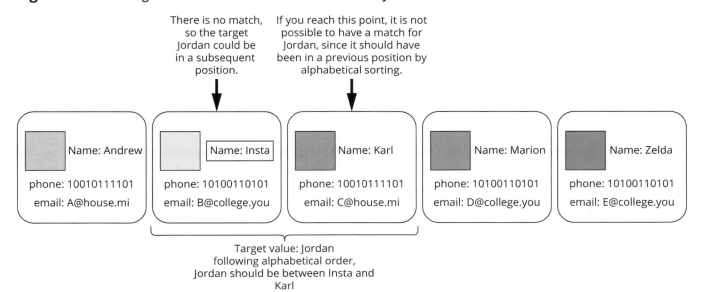

In contrast, if the records are not sorted, you can't reach conclusions without checking all records. If you see the name "Andrew," you can't know if "Jordan" is before or after it. When searching in an array of unsorted records, you must check each record until you find the desired one.

Note	As you might have experienced, the search function of a phone doesn't give you back the contact information of just an exact match. The comparison function uses a string-matching algorithm to determine if a record is part of the answer.

> A **string-matching algorithm** finds if a given string is part of a larger text. For example, if using a string-matching algorithm to compare "Alex" with the name field of your contacts, you could get the following as matching:
>
> - "Alex Holiday"
> - "Alexandria"
> - "Alexey"
> - "Dr. Alex Central Hospital"
>
> Although slightly related to search algorithms, string-matching algorithms use additional tools to produce more efficient results.

Quick Check 5-1

When traversing a sorted array of integers, you reach a point where the values are $X[i] = 7$, $X[i+1] = 14$, and $X[i+2] = 21$. Which of the following is a valid conclusion?

    a. The target value 31 is not present anywhere in the array.
    b. The target value 5 is not present anywhere in the array.
    c. The target value 8 is not present anywhere in the array.

Answer: c. Notice that the value 31 might be present in the array but only for $X[j]$ with $j > i+2$. Also, 5 could be present but only for $X[j]$ with $j < i$. But if $X[j] = 8$, then $i < j < i+1$ since $X[i] = 7 < 8 < X[i+1] = 14$. But there is no possible value of an integer j between i and $i+1$.

5.2 Sequential Search

Sequential search is a search algorithm implemented in a linear data structure where the data structure is traversed until the record with the matching key is found.

Recall that in a linear data structure, the data is organized sequentially. The sequential organization of the data provides a natural way to traverse the structure. For example, an array `X = ["a", "b", "Alex", "c", "d"]` is naturally traversed as `X[0] = "a"`, `X[1] = "b"`, `X[2] = "Alex"`, and `X[3] = "d"`.

The sequential search executes a loop that retrieves every record's key value and compares it with the search key.

You can see a sequential search executed on a non-sorted linear data structure in **Figure 5-4**. Notice that in the case the target is not present, it will be necessary for the algorithm to traverse the entire data structure before concluding that the target is not present.

Figure 5-4   Sequential search over an unsorted array

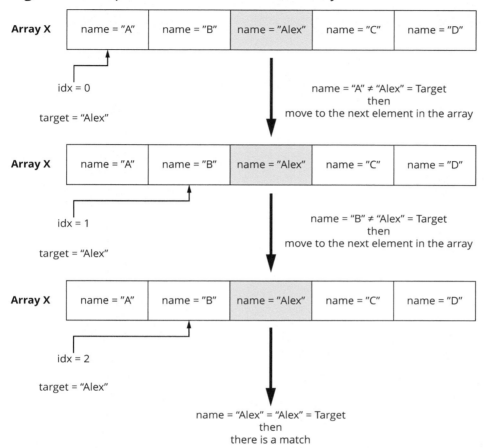

Sequential Search Algorithm Details

Suppose X is an array of integers and `target` is the target value. An implementation of a sequential search algorithm that returns the index of the first occurrence of the `target` value is described below.

```
sequential_search(X, target)
    N = len(X)
    for j = 0 to N-1 step 1
        if X[j] = target
            return j
    return Null
```

As mentioned before, this algorithm must check all records until the target value is found. If the algorithm reaches the end of the array without a match, then Null is returned, indicating that the target was not found in the array.

When the input array X is sorted, it is possible to modify the sequential search algorithm to take advantage of the sorted nature of the elements. The key observation to make is if the current value X[k] is larger than the target value. It is impossible to find the target value within the indices $j > k$. Since the array is sorted if `target < X[k]`, then `target = X[j]` for some j < k; otherwise, the target value is not in the array.

An implementation that uses the previous observation is below.

```
sorted_sequential_search(X, target)
   N = len(X)
   ;; By checking if the target is not in the range from
   ;; X[0] to X[N-1], the following loop can be avoided.
   if target < X[0] or target > X[N-1]
      return Null
   j = 0
   while j < N
      if X[j] > target
         ;; In this case the target is not present for i < j
         ;; Thus, it must be that it is not in the array.
         return Null
      if X[j] = target
         return j
      else
         j = j + 1
   return Null
```

Time Complexity of Sequential Search

Consider the case where the array X is not sorted, or you can't assume it is. In the unsorted case, the worst possible case is that the target value is not present in the array or it is present in the very last position.

In **Figure 5-5**, you can see that while the algorithm traverses the array if the target is not found in the current position, there is no way to ensure that it won't be present in a later position. In the case of Figure 5-5, the target is found only at the very last position. When the target is not present, you can only reach that conclusion when the last position is reached.

Figure 5-5   Worst case for sequential search in the unsorted case

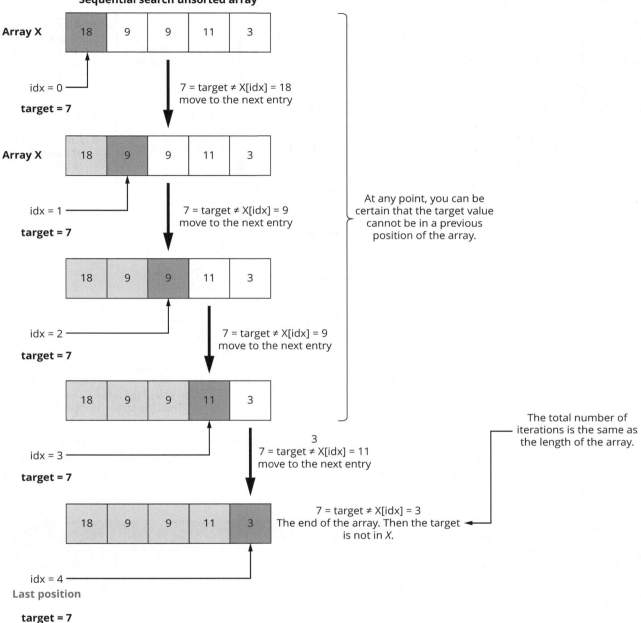

So, when the target element is in the last position or if it is not present, the algorithm traverses the whole array. Traversing the whole array means the loop makes N = len(X) iterations. Thus, the complexity of the sequential search for the unsorted case is $O(N)$.

In practice, the sorted case has a better performance on average. This is because in the sorted case, if the target value is not present, it could be a point where you can reach that conclusion without traversing the whole array. In **Figure 5-6**, you can see such a case for a target value of 7.

Figure 5-6   **Worst case for sequential sort in the sorted case**

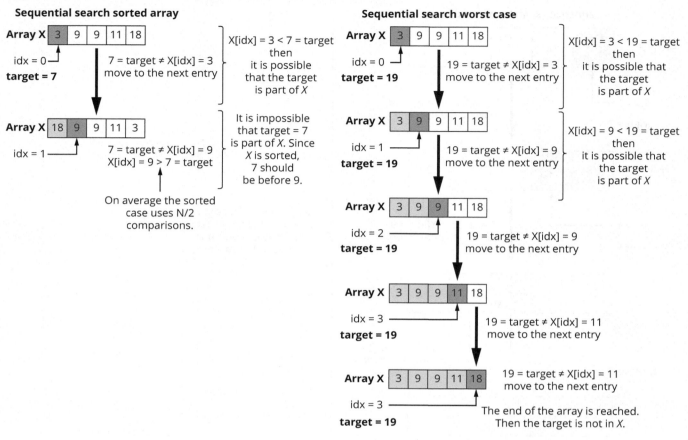

In Figure 5-6, you can also notice a case when the target value is 19. Since the target value is the last possible value, the sequential search traverses the whole array before finding the target. So the worst case is when the target value is the last element in the array. In the worst case, the loop will execute $N = len(X)$ iterations. Thus, the complexity of the sequential search in the sorted case is $O(N)$.

Best Practice

Sequential sort is considered a naive solution to the searching problem. But its simplicity makes it a good candidate when the linear data structure is small.

When the data structure is substantial, it might not even fit in memory without an additional data structure. Then it is convenient to sort the structure. However, the cost of sorting the structure might be quite high. But in the long run, it will significantly improve performance.

Note

In this chapter, search algorithms are described using an array. But as mentioned before, you can apply the algorithms to most linear data structures. The only exceptions are structures with some inserting and retrieving policies, for example, queues and stacks.

In the case of a stack, the data structure is designed to keep the elements sorted in a way that has nothing to do with a key value. Applying direct search algorithms such as sequential search is impossible in such cases. Moreover, if you are in a scenario where you need to search the elements of a stack, you might have chosen the wrong data structure for your problem.

Quick Check 5-2

Suppose that the target value is present in the array X. Is the number of instructions executed by the sequential search algorithm the same for the sorted and unsorted cases?

Answer: No. Suppose that the target value is the minimum value of the array. In the sorted case, the value is found in the first iteration. For the unsorted case, the value could be in the last position of the array.

5.3 Binary (Interval) Search

Binary search is a search algorithm in sorted arrays that finds the target value by splitting the array in two at each iteration. The algorithm starts by finding the element in the middle of the array. Then the middle element is compared with the target value. If the target is equal to this element, the algorithm stops. In other cases, the left or right half is chosen depending on whether the target value is larger or smaller than the current value. This process is repeated within half of the array interval until the target value is found or there are no more possible subintervals.

In **Figure 5-7**, you can see a binary search executed over an array of 11 elements. In the case of the figure, the target value is at position 7, but only 3 iterations are necessary to locate the target.

Figure 5-7   Basic binary search procedure

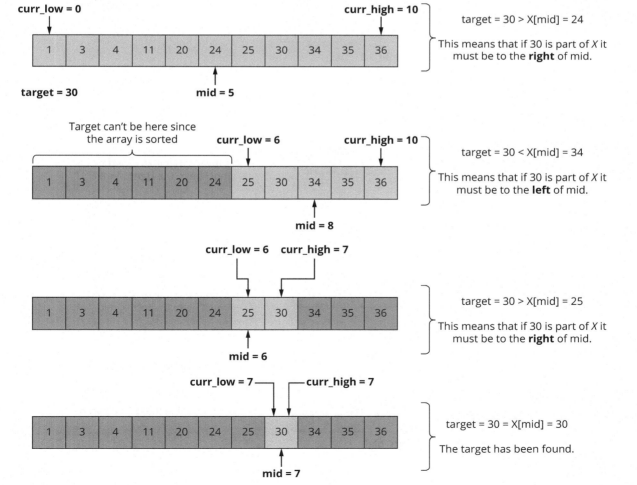

The binary search uses the principle of divide and conquer. At each iteration, the problem space is divided in half. This algorithm is usually implemented using recursion; however, an iterative version also exists, as is shown in the following section.

Searching Without Checking All Elements

Binary search is an algorithm that doesn't need to check every element in the data structure to find the target, even if the element is not present.

In **Figure 5-8**, you can see the steps that the binary search uses to find a target that is not in the array X.

Figure 5-8   Binary search indices used to know where the sub-array starts and ends and provide a way to see that an element is not in the array

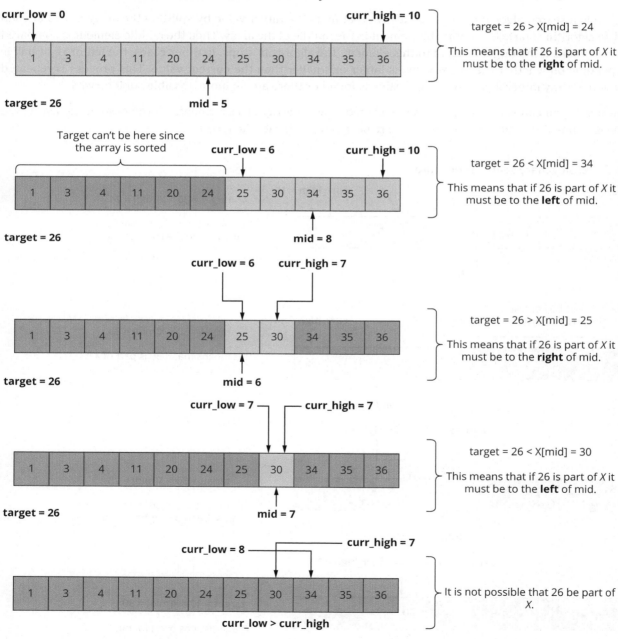

One thing to notice about the binary search algorithm is that the last value of mid gives the index where to insert a new element to keep the array sorted. Such an index might be helpful in dynamic data structures such as lists. **Figure 5-9** is an example of using a binary search to insert a new element within a list.

Figure 5-9   Inserting an element using binary search

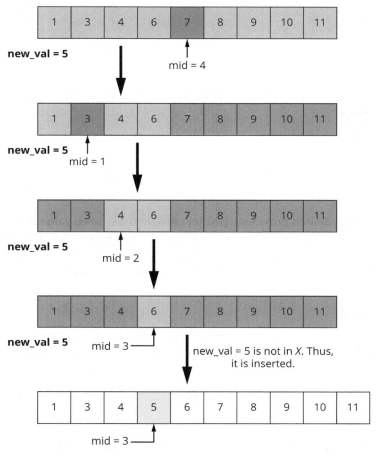

Binary Search Algorithm

Here is an implementation of the binary search algorithm for a sorted array X and a target value target:

```
binary_search(X, target)
    current_low = 0
    current_high = len(X) - 1

    while current_low <= current_high
        mid = integer((current_low + current_high)/2)

        if X[mid] = target
            return mid
        else
            if X[mid] > target
                current_high = mid - 1
            else
                current_low = mid + 1
    return Null
```

One detail about binary search is that it might not give the index of the first occurrence of the target value. Consider that in some applications, you might want the first occurrence of the target value. You can see such cases in **Figure 5-10**.

Figure 5-10 Binary search might not give the index of the first occurrence of a value

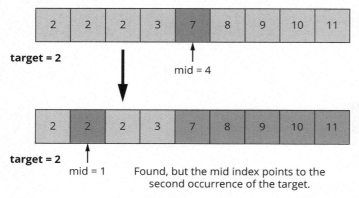

If the first occurrence of the target value is needed, binary search provides a pointer close to the desired value. Since you know that the array is sorted, the pointer gives reference to the first occurrence if the previous index is different from the target value. If the previous position is equal to the target value, it is an earlier occurrence. By traversing the structure back until no more occurrences of the target value are found, at that point the first occurrence has been found.

Time Complexity of Binary Search

Notice that at each iteration, the value of `current_low` or `current_high` is changed by the mid value. Since `mid = (current_low + current_high)/2`, it follows that mid decreases by half, as well as the difference between `current_low` and `current_high`.

You can see an illustration of how the value difference between `current_low` and `current_high` varies in two cases of binary search in **Figure 5-11**.

Figure 5-11 At each iteration, the length of the interval where the target value might be is reduced by half

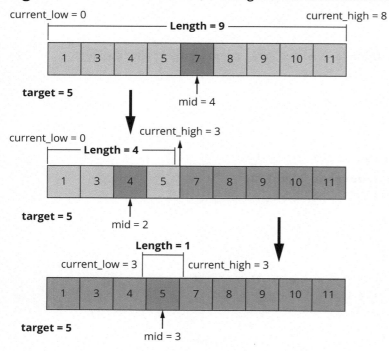

The previous examples show that, given a data structure of size N, the number of iterations to complete a binary search will be close to $\log(N)$. This is because at each step the length of the array with possible options is divided by two at each step. Thus, the binary search algorithm has time complexity $O(\log N)$.

Note	The idea of the binary search algorithm is quite old. John Mauchly was the first to publish a version of the algorithm. He described the algorithm in a publication about digital computers in 1946. Mauchly described a version of the algorithm that works only for arrays with a length of the form $2^n - 1$ for some positive integer n. In 1960, in the journal *Proceedings of Symposia in Applied Mathematics*, D.H. Lehmer mentioned a general version of binary search that worked for arrays of any length.

Quick Check 5-3

Given the array X = [1, 2, 2, 2, 3, 3, 3, 6, 9, 10, 12, 14, 16, 21, 21], what is the index given by the binary search algorithm for a target value of 3?

Answer: 5. When executing the binary search algorithm, the sequence of values for current_low, mid, and current_high is the following.

- 0, 7, 14; X[7] = 6 choose left subarray
- 0, 3, 7; X[3] = 2 choose right subarray
- 3, 5, 6; X[5] = 3 target found.

Notice that index 5 corresponds to the array's second instance of the value 3.

Technical Interview

Binary search is a great algorithm, and you can use a sorting algorithm to apply binary search to an unsorted array. Such convention of operations would take $O(n \log n)$ to sort and $O(\log n)$ for each target that you need to search. Supposing that the number of searches needed is $f(n)$ then the complexity of a solution that uses binary search and a sorting algorithm is $O((n + f(n)) \log n)$. Notice that the term $O((n + f(n)) \log n)$ is composed of $O(n \log n)$ that represents the complexity of sorting the array first, and $O(f(n) \log n)$ that represents the number total complexity of making $f(n)$ searches after the array is sorted.

You can calculate the complexity of using sequential search in a solution similarly. In this case, there is only the number of searches needed $f(n)$ and each one will take $O(n)$. Hence, the complexity of a solution that uses sequential search has complexity $O(n \, f(n))$.

So, the key point when comparing the two approaches is $f(n)$. If $f(n) = \Omega(\log n)$, this means that $f(n)$ grows at a rate almost logarithmic. Then, a sequential search will have lower complexity than sorting first.

This is an example of how you could explain when one approach is better than the other.

5.4 Recursive Binary Search Method

Recall that to solve a problem using recursion, you divide it into a smaller subproblem that is similar to the original one. When using recursion, it is necessary to have a base case, the case in which the function will no longer call itself (recurse). The other part is the recursion, which is the mechanism or description of how you split the current case into smaller cases.

The binary search algorithm can be described using recursion. As you might have noticed, finding the mid element and comparing it to the target value is repeated each time to a smaller sub-array. That makes the binary search algorithm an excellent candidate to be described using recursion.

Binary Search Using Recursion

The simplest case in the binary search method is when the array has only one element. In such a case, the only thing to do is to compare the element to the target value and return the corresponding index.

The binary search recursion algorithm consists of doing a binary search in the two sub-arrays: the one from `low` to `mid-1` or `mid+1` to `high`, depending on which of those could contain the target value.

Notice that the distance between `low` and `high` is reduced by half at each iteration. Thus, the sub-array is eventually going to have a length of 1. When the sub-array reaches length 1, the algorithm reaches the base case.

You can see a recursive implementation of the binary search algorithm for an array X and a target value `target` below.

```
recursive_binary_search(X, target, low, high)
    if low > high
        return Null
    else
        mid = integer((low + high)/2)
        if X[mid] = target
            return mid
        else
            if target < X[mid]
                return recursive_binary_search(X, target, low, mid-1)
            else
                return recursive_binary_search(X, target, mid+1, high)
```

Space Complexity of Binary Search

Recall that in most computer architectures, the parameters are stored in memory when you call a function. So calling a function requires a memory space equal to the data used inside the function.

For a recursive function, each call requires reserving new space in memory for the parameters.

The non-recursive implementation of the binary search algorithm makes use of the variables `current_low`, `current_high`, `mid`, `target`, and a pointer to X. This means that the space complexity is constant since the memory used doesn't depend on the size of the array X. Notice that the array X is not copied but only a pointer to X is used. Hence, the space complexity of the non-recursive binary search is $O(1)$.

Now for the recursive binary search algorithm, a recursive call is made instead of iterating like in the non-recursive version. Hence, at each call, the amount of memory is reserved, specifically to store `low`, `high`, `target`, and the pointer to X. Therefore, the space complexity of the algorithm is $O(\log N)$, which is the same as the number of iterations of the non-recursive implementation.

In **Figure 5-12**, you can see how memory use increases at each recursive call.

Figure 5-12   More memory is required at each recursive call during the search

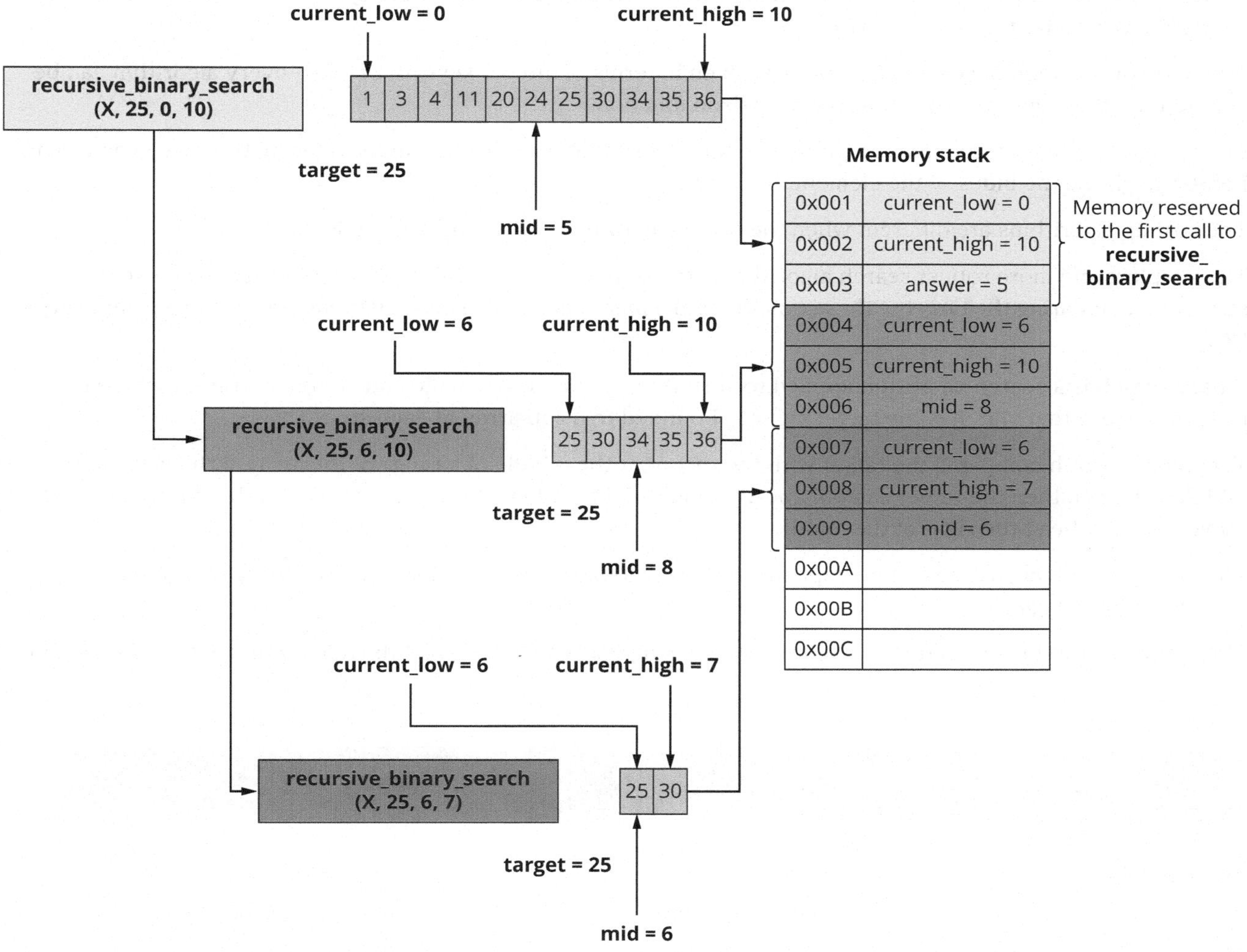

Best Practice

When designing a software solution, you must consider the possibility that the data structure you are using might grow to a considerable size. In such cases, consider using a more specialized data structure. Another approach might be to insert new elements into the data structure, keeping other elements sorted. In this way, it will be possible to use binary search. So, the added cost of inserting is rewarded in a faster search.

Summary

- Search algorithms are an important class of algorithms in applications. Search algorithms are designed to retrieve a record having a target value as a key.

- The basic description of search algorithms is given in terms of integer keys. But almost every algorithm can be adapted to other types of keys using a comparison function.

- The result of a search algorithm is a pointer to the record that matches the target value. In the case of arrays, the pointer might be the index of the element in the array.

- The sorting algorithms are different when the data structure is sorted and when it is not.

- The simplest and more robust search algorithm is the sequential search. Sequential searching traverses a data structure, comparing the target with each node until a match is found. The sequential search has a complexity of $O(n)$.

- Binary search is a search algorithm applied to sorted arrays. It uses a divide-and-conquer strategy where the possible record that matches the target value is bounded to a sub-array at each step.

- The binary search compares the target with the record at the middle of a range of the array. If the value in the middle is higher, then the target can only be at the left of the middle. If the value at the middle is lower, then the target can only be at the right of the middle.

- The binary search algorithm can be implemented using loops or using recursion. The binary search has a complexity of $O(\log n)$.

- The recursive version of binary search has a space complexity $O(\log n)$ while the non-recursive version has $O(1)$.

Key Terms

binary search	record	sequential search
key	search algorithm	string-matching algorithm
node	search process	target value

Review Questions

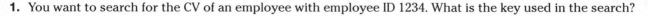

1. You want to search for the CV of an employee with employee ID 1234. What is the key used in the search?

   a. The employee's CV

   b. The employee Name

   c. The employee ID

   d. A pointer to the CV record

2. Suppose `comp(x,y)` is a comparison function. If `comp(Tony,Roy) = 'equal'` and `comp(Roy, May) = 'less'`, what is the value of `comp(May, Tony)`?

3. Suppose X = [1, 1, 4, 4, 7, 9, 5, 2, 2, 5] is an array of length 10. How many comparisons are made by sequential search for the array X and target value 5?

    a. 4   **c.** 7

    b. 5   **d.** 10

4. Which is the best case complexity of sequential sort?

    a. $\Omega(1)$ **c.** $\Omega(n)$

    b. $\Omega(\log n)$ **d.** $\Omega(n \log n)$

5. The worst case for sequential search in the sorted and unsorted case is the same.

    a. True   **b.** False

6. Binary search has two implementations for sorted and unsorted arrays.

    a. True   **b.** False

7. Recursive binary search has the same time complexity as non-recursive binary search.

    a. True   **b.** False

8. Suppose that to solve a certain problem, you use $O(\log n)$ searches in an unsorted array. Besides the searches, the solution only needs a constant number of operations. What is the complexity of your solution if you use sequential search?

9. Suppose X = [1, 3, 5, 7, 11, 13, 17, 19, 23, 29, 31]. How many comparisons are made by the binary search algorithm when searching the target value 7 in the array X?

10. Suppose that to solve a certain problem you use $O(n \log n)$ searches in an unsorted array. Besides the searches, the solution only needs a constant number of operations. What is the complexity of your solution if you sort the array first and then use binary search?

Programming Problems

1. Given an array of positive integers X and a number M, write a program that finds two numbers a, b in X such that $a + b = M$. **(LO 5.1, 5.2)**

2. Suppose X is a sorted array and Y is an unsorted array. Write a program that returns `True` if all Y elements are in X and `False` in other cases. **(LO 5.1, 5.3)**

3. Suppose that X is an array of records of type student. The student data type has the fields name, age, and height. Both age and height are numerical values. The age key sorts the array X. Write a function that finds a student in X with a given age and height. Notice that you can't suppose that the students are sorted by height. **(LO 5.1, 5.3, 5.4)**

4. Construct a frequency histogram of an array of values without using an auxiliary array. The frequency histogram counts how many times each value appears in an array. For example, for X = [1, 2, 3, 1, 2, 3, 4, 1, 1, 2, 1], the program should display [5, 3, 2, 1]. The value 5 means that the lowest number in the array X, 1 in this case, is present in five different positions in X. The value 3 means that the next lowest value, in this case 2, is present in three different positions in X. **(LO 5.1, 5.2, 5.3, 5.4)**

5. Write a program that inserts a new element X in a sorted list in a way that the list is sorted after the insertion. **(LO 5.1, 5.2, 5.3)**

Projects

Project 5-1: First Occurrence Search

(LO 5.1, 5.3, 5.4) Recall from the chapter that the binary search doesn't always return the first occurrence of the target value. Modify the binary search algorithm discussed in the text to return the target value's first occurrence.

Project 5-2: Interpolation Search

(LO 5.1, 5.3) Binary search uses the middle of the array as a point to split and reduce the range where the target value might be. An improvement to that strategy might be to use a linear function to try to predict a better index to reduce the range. When using interpolation search instead of the middle, a linear function predicts the new index.

For a sorted array and index values `low` and `high`, the new value will be:

```
new_index = low + (target - X[low])*(high - low)/(X[high] - X[low])
```

as long as `X[high]` and `X[low]` are different. So `new_index` is the analog of `mid` for the interpolation search.

Implement the interpolation search for an array `X` and a target value `target`.

Project 5-3: Stable Sorted Insertion

(LO 5.1, 5.2, 5.3) Given a sorted list X, write a program that inserts a new element according to the following conditions:

- If the element is present in X, then your solution must insert the new value after all the other occurrences with the same key as the new value.
- If the element is not present in X, it should be inserted so that the list X continues to be sorted.

Project 5-4: Exponential Search

(LO 5.1, 5.2, 5.3) Given a sorted array X with length N, the exponential search algorithm uses a two-stage process:

- First, find a sub-interval where the target value might be.
- Then use a binary search over the range found in the previous step.

The array grows exponentially to estimate the sub-interval where the target value might be. Start with `start_index = 0`. If this corresponds to the target value, then the problem is solved.

For other cases, let's start with `p = 1`. If `X[p] <= target`, the algorithm expands the range by duplicating `p = p*2`. Repeat until `X[p] > target` or you reach the end of the array.

Now you know that the target value is between the indices `p/2` and `p`.

Implement the exponential search algorithm.

Chapter 6

Linked Lists, Stacks, and Queues

Learning Objectives

Upon completion of this chapter, you will be able to:

6.1 Differentiate between linked list, stack, and queue abstract data types.

6.2 Apply appropriate operations for a linked list element.

6.3 Apply appropriate stack methods.

6.4 Apply appropriate queue methods.

6.5 Implement array-based stacks and queues for a given problem.

6.1 Abstract Data Types: Linked Lists, Stacks, and Queues

Stacks, queues, and linked lists are linear, dynamic abstract data types (ADTs). The fact that they are linear means that there is a single expected way to traverse the elements in the data structure. In the case of stacks and queues, the way the elements are inserted and retrieved characterizes the ADTs. **Figure 6-1** illustrates the real-life analogs of stack and queue ADTs.

Figure 6-1   A queue of people and a stack of books

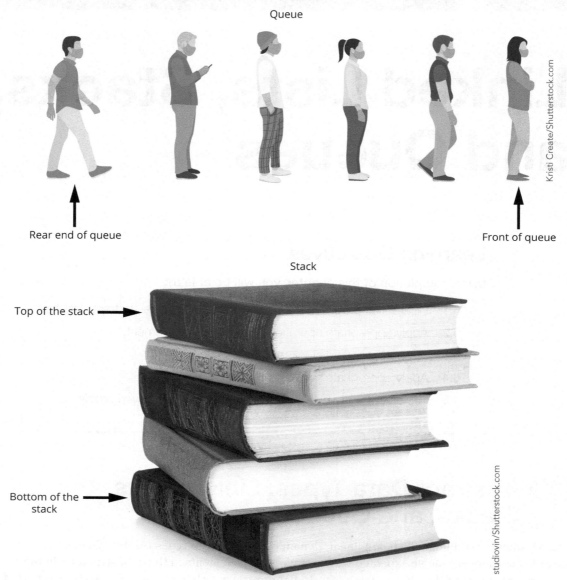

Linked lists are other basic dynamic data structures. They allow growth without reconstructing or copying the existing data into a new location in memory.

Computer science has two ways to share information between procedures and functions. The first is **by value**, meaning the function or procedure receives a copy of the object. That means any change in the object won't affect the original object outside of the function or procedure. For example, suppose that foo(x,y) receives both integer values x and y by value:

```
;; This function modifies the values x, y.
foo(x,y)
    y = "Sheep"
    x = "Bird"


x = "Dog"
y = "Cat"
display(x, y)
```

```
;; x and y are sent by value, so new copies of them are used inside
;; foo().
foo(x,y)
;; During the execution of foo only the local copies of x and y
;; were modified, so the values of x and y remain "Dog" and "Cat."
display(x, y)
```

The previous code snippet displays two lines:

```
Dog, Cat
Dog, Cat
```

Both lines are the same since the values of the variables x and y outside `foo` are unaffected; that is, `foo` receives copies of x and y that are independent of the x and y outside the code of `foo`.

The other way to pass parameters is by reference. When passing parameters **by reference**, a pointer or link to the stored object is sent to the function or procedure. When passing a parameter by reference, all changes made inside the function or procedure are preserved when the function or procedure terminates.

Suppose the function `foo(x,y)` now receives the parameters x and y by reference:

```
;; This function modifies the values x, y.
foo(x,y)
    y = "Sheep"
    x = "Bird"

x = "Dog"
y = "Cat"
display(x, y)

;; x and y are sent by reference, so every modification of x and y
;; is kept after the procedure finishes.
foo(x,y)
;; After the execution of foo the variables x and y have different
;; values since they were changed by foo that receive x and y by
;; reference.
display(x, y)
```

The previous code snippet displays two lines:

```
Dog, Cat
Bird, Sheep
```

In this case, x is changed to the value `"Bird"` and y is changed to the value `"Sheep"` inside `foo(x,y)`. What `foo` receives are references to the x and y outside of `foo`. Then any change to x and y is preserved once the function terminates.

> **Note**
>
> All functions receive their ADT parameters by reference in this chapter. In some programming languages, it is necessary to simulate pass-by-reference because the language always passes its parameters by value. For example, to use passing by reference in the C language, you use pointers to the objects as parameters instead of modifying their properties. That means that the address where the data is stored in memory is passed to the function. In this way, the function accesses the given address and modifies the data directly in memory.

Linked Lists

A linked list is a dynamic linear ADT where each element (called a **node**) has a pointer to the next element in the linked list. Linked lists are one of the simplest ways of providing dynamic data structures in the typical computer architecture, as shown in **Figure 6-2**.

Figure 6-2   A linked list includes nodes, keys, data, and next pointers. This way of linking nodes allows the linked list to grow as needed and use non-continuous memory spaces

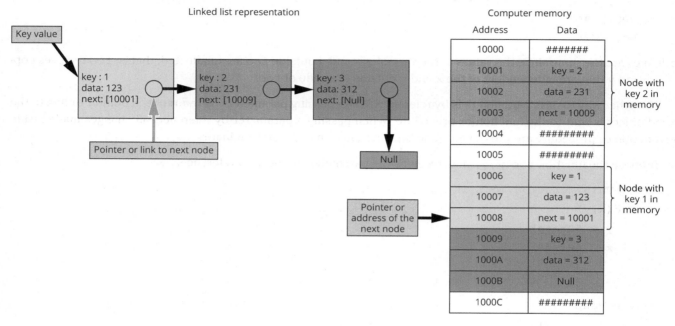

Recall that an array's size must be specified upon creation, and this size does not change. The compiler reserves a continuous block of memory to store the elements of the array. One of the main advantages of arrays is equal-time random access. **Equal-time random access** means that any array element takes the same time to be accessed. In terms of Big O notation, every time an algorithm reads from an array, it takes $O(1)$, or constant time.

Unlike an array, a linked list is dynamic. That means you can grow or shrink the linked list as much as you want or until your computer's memory runs out. A linked list uses nodes to grow dynamically. A node from a linked list is a user-defined data type that holds a key value, a pointer to the next element in the linked list, and possibly more data. The key value is used to sort or identify each component of the linked list.

The pointer to the next element is the key to the dynamic growth of the linked list. To construct a linked list, you only need the key value and possibly the data you want to store. You create a new node with the key value and data, and the compiler reserves only the necessary memory to store a single node. The value of the next pointer of the node is set to `Null`. **Null** is a term used to denote a reference to an invalid or non-existent object. Think of Null as the empty set, in the sense that it is a set but it has no elements. So Null is a reference to nothing.

To gain access to the linked list, you use the head pointer. The **head pointer** is a pointer or reference to the first element in a linked list. There is also the **tail pointer**, which references the last element of a linked list. Usually, the tail pointer references a node with the next pointer `Null`.

The nodes, pointers to the nodes, head pointer, and tail pointers characterize a linked list. That means any linked list implementation must be done through nodes with at least one link to an adjacent element.

To insert a new node in the linked list, you create the node, so the compiler reserves the necessary memory to store the new node. Then the next pointer of the last element of the linked list is set to the new node. To keep the structure of the linked list, the next pointer of the last node is Null. Keeping all the linked list nodes in contiguous memory addresses is unnecessary. You can see such a scheme in **Figure 6-3**.

Figure 6-3   Insertion of a new node in the linked list. First, a new node is created to hold the data. The node requires a space of memory. Then the next link of the tail is updated

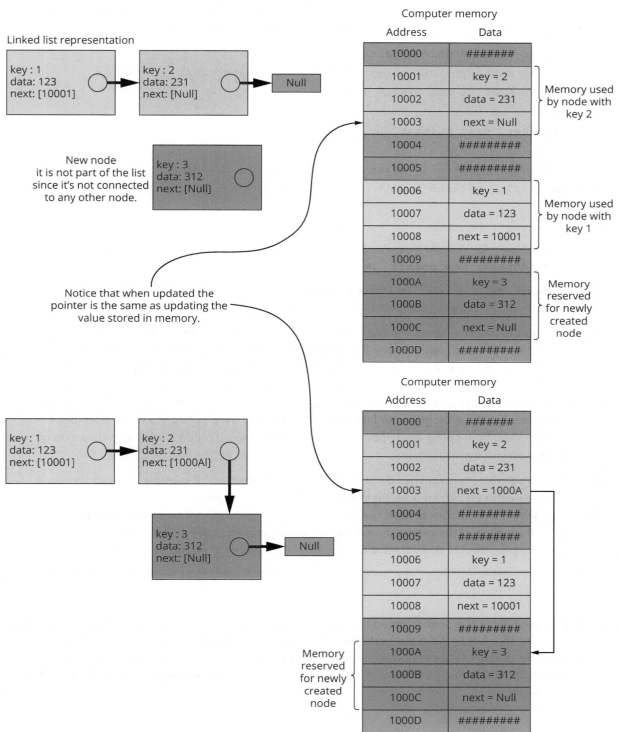

Best Practice

One common problem when writing dynamic data structures such as linked lists is memory leakage. **Memory leakage** can happen when your program keeps memory reserved even when it is no longer using it and can no longer access the stored content.

In low-level programming languages, the programmer must manually reserve the memory necessary to create a new node. The following code snippet describes one possible way to do that:

```
;; New user-defined data type node
;; The node data type has a key value and a pointer next_pointer to
;; the next node in the linked list.
type node
    fields key, next_pointer


;; Enough memory space is reserved for storing a new node.
address = allocate(size(node))


;; A new node is constructed by new node(1, Null)
;; and is stored in address by the command store().
store(in address, new node(1, Null))
```

The problem comes when the node is no longer needed. When you no longer need the reserved memory, it must be freed. The program can then use the freed memory to store another object.

Suppose you forget to free the memory and change the next pointer to another node. Then you can no longer use the node or its associated memory. Forgetting to free the memory can exhaust the memory reserved for your program, raising an error during its execution. These bugs are challenging to detect since they happen only under particular circumstances. For example, suppose that a user wants to add a new node with a name field. If the user fails to spell the name correctly several times, it might create several new nodes, one for each attempt. If the programmer fails to free the memory used during the failed attempts, this memory will be blocked from being used. If this happens several times, it might lead to an exhaustion of memory, even if the actual list is small in size.

Most high-level programming languages don't allow manual management of memory. The programming language liberates the memory when an object is destroyed. High-level programming languages such as Java, C#, GoLang, Python, and JavaScript have garbage collectors. A **garbage collector** is a subroutine in charge of analyzing which parts of the reserved memory are no longer being used and freeing them. With garbage collection, the programmer doesn't have to manually free memory that is no longer in use.

A variation of the linked list is the doubly linked list. In a **doubly linked list**, each node has an additional pointer called the **previous pointer** that holds the node's address preceding the current node. The previous pointer in the nodes of a doubly linked list points to the previous element. A doubly linked list uses a head pointer that points to the first element of the linked list and a tail pointer that points to the last element in the linked list. See **Figure 6-4** for an illustration of a doubly linked list.

Figure 6-4 A doubly linked list comprises nodes with a next and previous pointer. The prev and next pointers allow moving from head to tail or tail to head

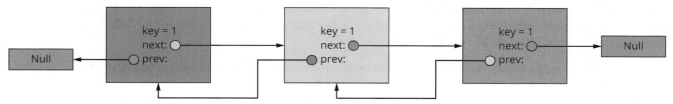

One of the main advantages of a linked list over an array is that rearranging the order of an element is more straightforward in the linked list. But linked lists don't have equal-time random access.

Stacks

You can think of a stack as a linked list where the elements are added and removed only at one end, much like adding or removing books only from the top of a stack of books. Stacks are characterized by two operations, `push()` and `pop()`. The `push()` operation adds a new element to the stack, and the `pop()` operation removes an element from the stack.

The insertion and retrieval of elements in a stack follow the LIFO (last in, first out) scheduling policy. A **schedule policy** is a rule that dictates in which order the elements in a data structure are retrieved. The array and list have a random access policy. **Random access policy** means there is no specific order to insert or retrieve an element. In a linked list, you can insert a new node in any place in the linked list.

The LIFO schedule policy establishes that the last element inserted is the first to be retrieved. So, in the same way as a physical stack, the last element to be placed in the stack is the first you take out. See **Figure 6-5** for a depiction of a stack with the `push()` and `pop()` operations.

Figure 6-5 A stack's `push()` and `pop()` operations

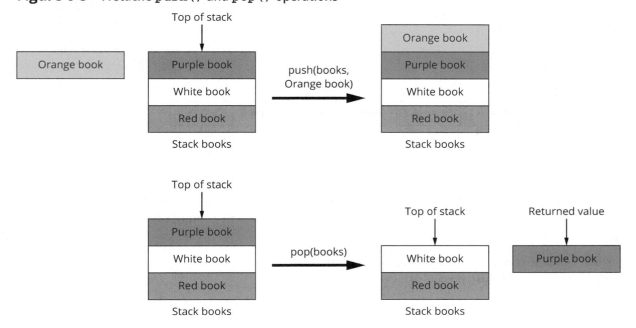

In addition to the push() and pop() operations, it is common for a stack to have a top() operation (sometimes called peek()) and an empty() operation. The top() operation returns a reference to the element at the top of the stack, but doesn't remove it from the stack. In another case, the empty() operation returns True if the stack is empty and False in other cases (sometimes called is_empty()). Keep in mind that in practice, the only thing you can be sure about implementing the stack is the LIFO policy.

It is common to use the terms underflow and overflow when discussing stacks and other data structures. **Underflow** is when you try to delete or retrieve an element from an empty data structure. **Overflow** is when you try to insert a new element into a data structure with a size limit after it has reached its maximum capacity. Since a stack can be fixed or non-fixed, a stack may overflow. Because the memory of any computer is finite, it is always possible to overflow the memory.

The way an underflow or overflow is managed depends on the specific programming language and sometimes on the programming style.

Queues

As its name suggests, a queue is a linear data structure that behaves like a queue of people. The main characteristic of a queue is the FIFO (first in, first out) policy. FIFO means that the first element inserted must be the first to be retrieved.

The two primary operations of a queue are enqueue() and dequeue(). The enqueue() operation inserts a new element into the queue, and the dequeue() operation removes the first element of the queue. **Figure 6-6** depicts a queue with the enqueue() and dequeue() operations.

Figure 6-6 A queue's enqueue() and dequeue() operations

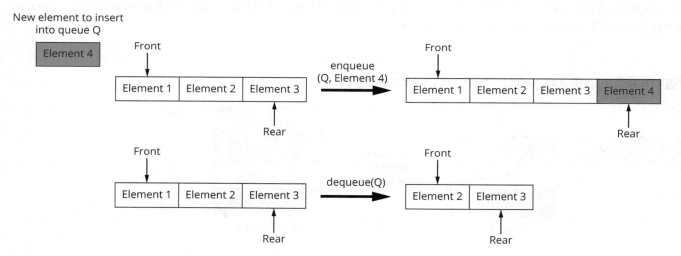

In addition to the primary operations, a queue has front() and rear() functions that return the first and last elements of the queue, respectively. The queue also has the empty() operation that returns True if the queue is empty and False otherwise.

The underflow concept also applies to queues. The underflow happens when you use dequeue() in an empty queue. For a fixed-size queue, it is also possible to overflow.

Quick Check 6-1

Suppose Q is an empty queue. What is the result of the following code?

```
enqueue(Q, 10)
enqueue(Q, 5)
enqueue(Q, 0)

display(Q.rear())

dequeue(Q)
dequeue(Q)
dequeue(Q)
dequeue(Q)
```

Answer: The program displays 0, and then the queue underflows. Since a queue follows the FIFO policy, the rear is the last element inserted, in this case, 0. The queue empties out after the first three dequeue() calls. Then when using dequeue() again, the linked list underflows.

6.2 Common Linked Lists Operations

Linked lists are a great model of a dynamic data structure. Many of the principles used to operate over them are critical to operating on more complicated data structures.

One aspect that makes linked lists so valuable is their flexibility. With an appropriate procedure, merging, joining, or even intersecting two linked lists efficiently is possible.

Why Use Linked Lists?

Arrays provide constant random-access time, but inserting a new element in a specific position is difficult. Linked lists are a more flexible tool.

Linked lists provide constant-time unsorted insertion knowing beforehand how large the linked list will be. Knowing how long it will take to do an insertion and guaranteeing that it will always take the same time (at least approximately) might be critical in real-time applications, such as storing the data from an accelerometer. Restoring the velocity and position from the acceleration is best if the readings are evenly spaced in time.

Moreover, an array might reach its maximum capacity, and you might need to store more data. In such a case, it might be necessary to create a new array of a larger size. Once the array is created, the computer blocks out the necessary memory. At last, it is necessary to copy all elements from the old array to the new one.

The link between nodes in a linked list is a pointer to the next node. So, to join two linked lists, it is only necessary to make the next pointer of one linked list's tail equal to the other's head. This can be done without creating a new copy of the data or reserving enough memory to fit the joined data of the two linked lists.

Singly Linked Lists

The insertion of a new linked list element could be unsorted, sorted, random, or at an index. When inserting a new element in a linked list in an unsorted manner, there are three options:

- **Insert at the tail.** In this case, the new node is inserted after the current tail. You can see an implementation in the following code where new_node is the node to insert and L is the linked list.

```
;; Function that inserts new_node to the tail of the linked list L.
tail_insert(L, new_node)
    if L.tail = Null
        ;; If tail is null, then the list is empty and the new
        ;; node is the head and tail.
        L.tail = new_node
        L.head = new_node
    else
        ;; If the tail is not null, then the new node is put after
        ;; tail. That means that new_node is next to tail.
        L.tail.next = new_node
        ;; Since the new node is now the last one, tail must
        ;; point to new_node.
        L.tail = new_node
    new_node.next = Null
```

> **Note**
>
> Be careful of overwriting a pointer unintentionally when using dynamic data structures. Overwriting a pointer might lead to missing information and corrupting the data structure. Sometimes the differences between a correctly implemented modification and a terrible error are subtle. To see such possibilities, consider the following code snippet:
>
> ```
> ;; This code wrongly executes an insertion of new_node
> ;; to the tail of the linked list L.
> wrong_insert(L, new_node)
>     ;; For illustration purposes, suppose that new_node = A
>     ;; and L.tail points to B.
>     L.tail = new_node
>     ;; Now L.tail points to A.
>     L.tail.next = new_node
>
>     ;; Since L.tail points to A, L.tail.next is A, hence
>     ;; A.next is A creating a loop in the linked list.
>     new_node.next = Null
> ```
>
> When using the wrong_insert method, the linked list L is corrupted. The steps taken by wrong_insert are illustrated in **Figure 6-7**.

Figure 6-7 How updating the next pointer before the tail pointer leaves a linked
list in an inconsistent state

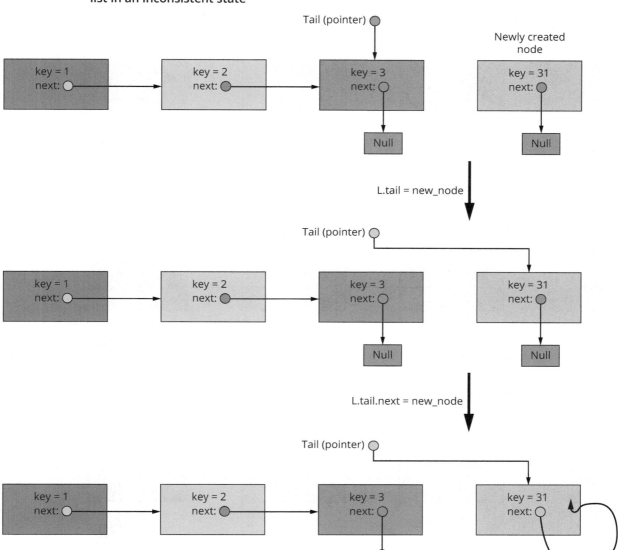

- **Insert at the head or front.** In this case, the new node is inserted at the front of the linked list and becomes the new head. You can see the procedure illustrated in **Figure 6-8**.

- **Insert at a given index.** Since the nodes in a linked list are organized sequentially, it is possible to associate a numeric position to each element. To add the node new_node at the position k into a linked list L requires updating the node's pointer at $k-1$ position and new_node.

Figure 6-8 Inserting a new node to the front of a linked list requires changing the new node's next pointer and the linked list's head pointer

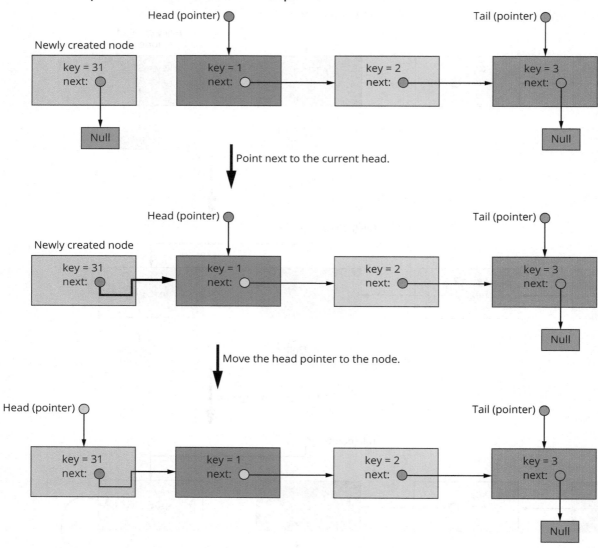

Here is an implementation to insert new_node at the position *k* in a linked list L:

```
insert_at(L, new_node, k)
    ;; The current variable will be used to move from one node to the
    ;; next one until the right position is found.
    current = L.head
    idx = 0
    ;: If the head is Null, the only possible place to insert
    ;; a new node
    ;; is at the head, that means that k must be 0.
    if L.head = Null
        if k > 0
            return -1
```

```
        else
            ;; If the new node must be inserted at position 0, then it
            ;; becomes the new head and tail of the list L.
            L.head = new_node
            L.tail = new_node
            new_node.next = Null
            return 1


    ;; If the linked list is not empty, then we search for the correct
    ;; position.
    ;; That is when idx is the same as k-1 or while idx < (k-1).
    while not current.next = Null and idx < (k-1)
        idx = idx + 1
        current = current.next ;; current point to the next node.
    ;; In case you want to insert a new node at a position that
    ;; exceeds the length of the list, an error message should be sent.
    if current.next = Null and idx < k-1
        return -1
    ;; In case the end of the list is reached, then new_node must
    ;; be inserted at the tail and replace L.tail.
    if current.next = Null and idx = k
        current.next = new_node
        L.tail = new_node
        new_node.next = Null
        return 1


    ;; If none of the previous special cases occurs, then current is
    ;; pointing to the node right before the position k.
    next_node = current.next
    ;; next_node is used as a temporary variable
    current.next = new_node    ;; now new_node is right after current
    new_node.next = next_node ;; now new_node is linked to the rest
                               ;; of the list.
```

Notice that it is necessary to make some validations during the process to avoid trying to operate with a Null object.

On the other hand, it is possible to make sorted insertions in a linked list. Since one node only has a link to the next, it is only possible to use sequential methods for searching.

The following code snippet shows how new_node could be inserted into a sorted linked list L.

```
sorted_insert(L, new_node)
    current = L.head ;; Starting a search process from head.
    while not current.next = Null and current.next.key < new_node.key
        ;; While the current pointer hasn't reached the tail and the
        ;; key value is less than the target value the current
        ;; pointer is moved to the next node.
        current = current.next
```

```
new_node.next = current.next  ;; link the new node to the next
                              ;; in the list
current.next = new_node       ;; the new node is inserted right
                              ;; after current
```

The procedure is illustrated in **Figure 6-9**.

Figure 6-9   How a linked list is traversed to insert a new node in a sorted list

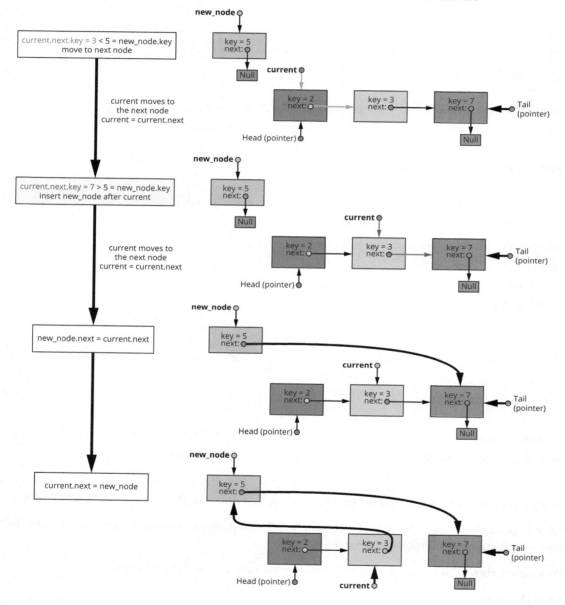

When removing a node or part of the linked list, it is imperative to be careful. If you are using a low-level programming language, remember to free the reserved memory for the deleted node. Failing to free the memory might lead to memory leakage problems. Be careful not to leave the data structure in an inconsistent state, as shown earlier in Figure 6-7.

To remove the node at the position k from a linked list L, you can follow the next steps:

- Get a reference or pointer `curr` to the node at the `k-1` position.
- The node to eliminate `old_node` is `curr.next`.
- Link the node `curr` to the next node of `old_node`.

You can see the process illustrated in **Figure 6-10**.

Figure 6-10   Deleting a node that is not at the tail nor the head

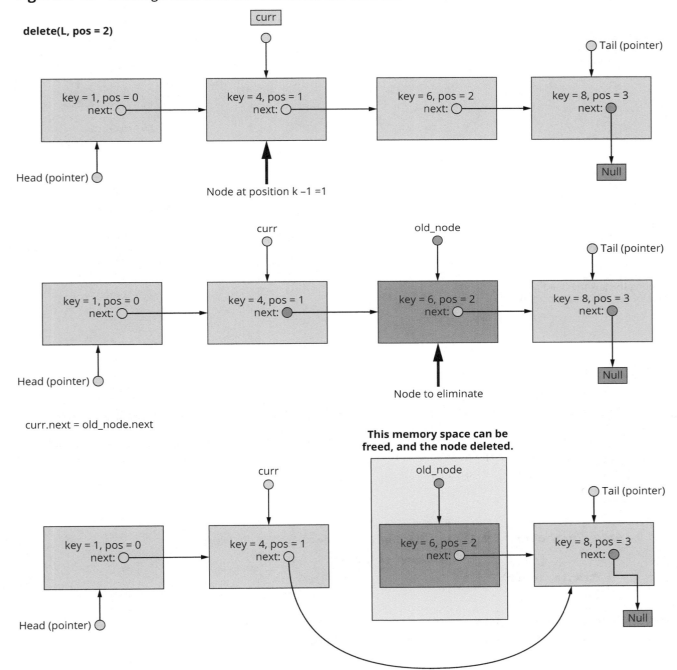

Notice that you must handle some exceptional cases. One is when there is only one element in the linked list. Another is how to handle the case where the given index exceeds the length of the linked list. You can see illustrated in **Figure 6-11** how failing to handle special cases might lead to a data structure in an inconsistent state.

Figure 6-11 Deleting the head element of a linked list can lead to problems. Additional verifications are necessary to avoid a linked list with inconsistent data

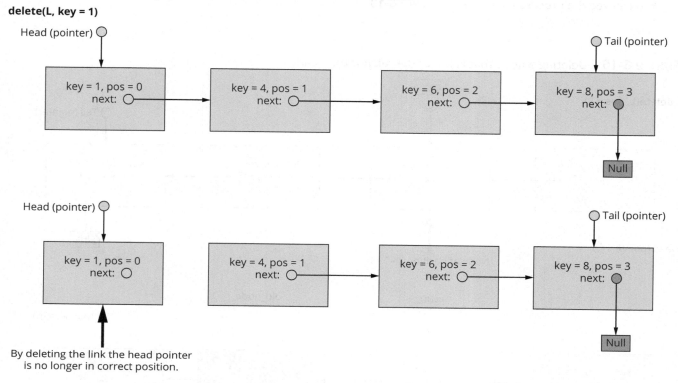

delete(L, key = 1)

By deleting the link the head pointer is no longer in correct position.

Doubly Linked Lists

When working with a doubly linked list, some of the procedures described for a singly linked list are simplified since you have access to the previous element. But also you must be careful to update the previous pointer of each node.

With the additional link, it is possible to traverse the linked list in any direction from a given node. For example, the double link allows you to traverse the linked list in two directions: forward and backward. The following code snippet shows the backward traversing of a linked list L.

```
backward_display(L)
    curr = L.tail ;; The backward traverse starts from the tail
    while not curr = Null ;; The head has been reached when
                          ;; prev is Null
        display(curr)
    curr = curr.prev
```

When modifying an unsorted doubly linked list, there are the same possibilities as for a singly linked list. An element can be inserted or deleted from the head, the tail, or between two nodes.

You can apply the ideas presented for a singly linked list to a doubly linked list. You can implement insertion, deletion, and search the same way for singly and doubly linked lists. But you can use the previous pointer to make a more straightforward procedure. To illustrate this, suppose that L is a doubly linked list, and you want to delete the node with the key value x. The following code implements the procedure.

```
remove_key(L, x)
    ;; Start by searching for the node with the desired key value.

    curr = L.head
    while not curr.key = x and not curr.next = Null
        ;; While the curr.key is not the key value, move to the next node
        ;; or stop if a Null value has been reached.
        curr = curr.next

    if not curr.key = x
    ;; If the desired key hasn't been found, then return an error code.
        return -1

    ;; In other cases curr must be pointing to a node with a key value
    ;; equal to x.
    curr.prev.next = curr.next
    curr.next.prev = curr.prev
```

One of the main advantages of linked lists is that it is easy to split and merge them. For example, the following code splits a linked list L into all elements before a node with key value x and all nodes after.

```
    curr = L.head

    while not curr.key = x and not curr.next = Null
        curr = curr.next

    if curr.key = x
        L_before = L
        curr.prev.next = Null
        tail = L.tail
        L_before.tail = curr.prev

        curr.prev = Null
        L_after = new List(head = curr, tail = tail)
```

The procedure is illustrated in **Figure 6-12**.

It is possible to use linked lists as the base for implementing other linear dynamic data structures such as stacks, queues, and sets.

Figure 6-12 Splitting a linked list. It is only necessary to change the pointers of the nodes where the split is done

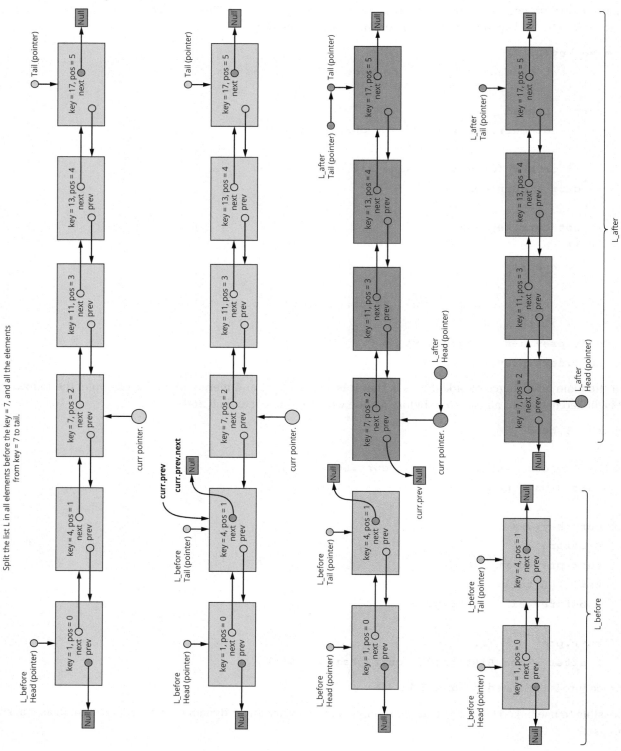

Circular Linked Lists

Another type of linked list is the circular linked list. A **circular linked list** is a doubly or singly linked list where the tail's next pointer points to the head, and the previous pointer of the head points to the tail if it applies. You can visualize a circular linked list as a ring like the one shown in **Figure 6-13**.

Figure 6-13   An illustration of a circular linked list. Each node has a next and previous pointer. The head has the previous pointer to the tail, and the tail has the next pointer to the head

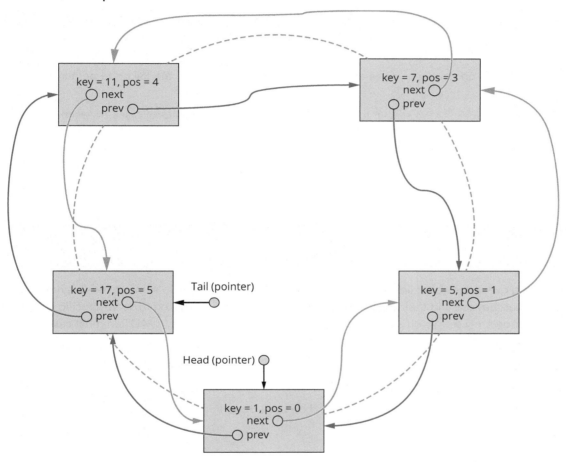

Notice that the insertion and deletion in a circular linked list are almost identical to the one for doubly linked lists. One key difference is in the traversing. If you try to traverse a circular linked list the same way as a doubly linked list, your program will enter an infinite loop. That is because the next pointer might never reach a null value. It is necessary to use a different stop condition, such as when the next pointer reaches the head again. Here is an implementation for a forward traverse of a circular linked list:

```
traverse(L)
    curr = L.head ;; The curr pointer used to traverse
                  ;; the list starts at the head.
    display(curr)
```

```
while not curr.next = L.head
    ;; Since the list is circular, the only way you might
    ;; know that you have traversed the whole list is if
    ;; you return to the head.
    curr = curr.next
display(curr)
```

Quick Check 6-2

In a circular linked list with only one element, to what node is the previous pointer of the tail node pointing?

Answer: To itself. The tail node doesn't always point to a particular node. The only exceptional cases are when it points to itself when only one node is in the linked list and when it points to the head when only two nodes are in the linked list.

Technical Interview

It is common to be asked questions about linked lists in general technical interviews. In some cases, it is not just required to know what they are and their essential operation. You may also be asked to solve specific problems for them. You don't rely simply on search, insert, and delete operations of a list ADT. In most cases, you are expected to take advantage of the pointer used by the nodes.

One example of such a problem is the following. Given a linked list, L, delete the nth element from the end. Suppose that the length of the linked list is greater than n.

One solution using the retrieve_position, len, and delete operations is the following:

```
N = len(L)

out_node = retrieve_position(L, N - n - 1)
delete(L, out_node.key)
```

The previous code snippet is a perfectly valid answer, but for a singly linked list, it requires in the worst case two traverses of the complete linked list. A more efficient approach that takes advantage of the pointer and the linked list to avoid having to traverse the list several times is the following. Use two-pointers back and curr. Initially, back points to the head and curr points to the nth position of the list. It is necessary to start traversing part of the list with curr to put it in its initial position. Then move to curr and back one node at a time until curr reaches the tail. Then back points to the node to be deleted.

```
prev = Null
back = L.head
curr = L.head
```

```
k = 0
while k < n
    ;; First curr will point to the n-th position from the start.
    curr = curr.next
    k = k + 1

;; curr is at the position n while back is at the head, position 0.
while not curr.next = Null
    ;; Each time you move curr one position, you also move back one
    ;; position. That means that when curr reaches the last position
    ;; N = len(L), then back is at the N - n - 1 of the list.
    ;; So back points to the node that is to be removed.
    prev = back
    back = back.next
    cur = curr.next

if back = L.head
    L.head = back.next
else
    prev.next = back.next
```

In the previous code snippet, you can see an implementation of a solution described in the previous paragraph.

So, when presented with a problem related to linked lists, it is convenient to think of a solution at the level of a pointer and not just at the level of the list ADT.

6.3 Common Stack ADT Methods

Any stack data structure must have two primary operations: push() and pop(). The way these operations are implemented is of no importance as long as the implementation enforces the LIFO policy.

Stacks can have a maximum size or grow as large as necessary. There is no theoretical limit for the stack ADT, but it must be possible to add and remove elements. Or it could have a maximum size given by the implementation.

Why Use Stacks?

Because stack is characterized by the LIFO policy, the objects are returned in the reverse order in which you insert them.

The analogy of a physical stack of objects shows how to solve problems using a stack.

One way to implement a stack is by using the linked list. You can get the desired behavior by removing and inserting only one end of the linked list. It is possible to implement the pop and push operations using either end.

Main Stack Operations

The two primary operations of a stack are pop(), which removes an element from the stack, and push(), which inserts an element into the stack. The LIFO policy requires that the last element pushed into the stack must be the one to be deleted when the pop() operation is used.

The following code uses a linked list L to implement a stack. In this implementation, all operations are made at the end of the stack.

```
pop(L)
    ;; Since the tail pointer must be updated when an element is
    ;; removed, it is necessary to reach the node right before
    ;; the tail to replace the tail pointer.
    curr = L.head
    while not curr.next = L.tail
        curr = curr.next

    ;; The tail pointer is replaced, and the last element is returned.
    ;; The last element of the list is the top of the stack.
    top = L.tail
    L.tail = curr
    L.tail.next = Null
    return top


push(x)
    ;; Push only requires inserting the node x at the tail.
    curr = L.tail
    if curr = Null
        ;; If the stack (L) is empty, tail and head should be updated.
        L.tail = x
        L.head = x
    else
        ;; If tail is not null only, tail should be replaced to put x at
        ;; the top position that is the tail of the list.
        curr.next = x
        L.tail = x
        x.next = Null
    return 1
```

Figure 6-14 illustrates how the linked list is modified by the push and pop operations and a depiction of the stack.

Figure 6-14   A stack with push and pop operations that modify the linked list used as the data holder

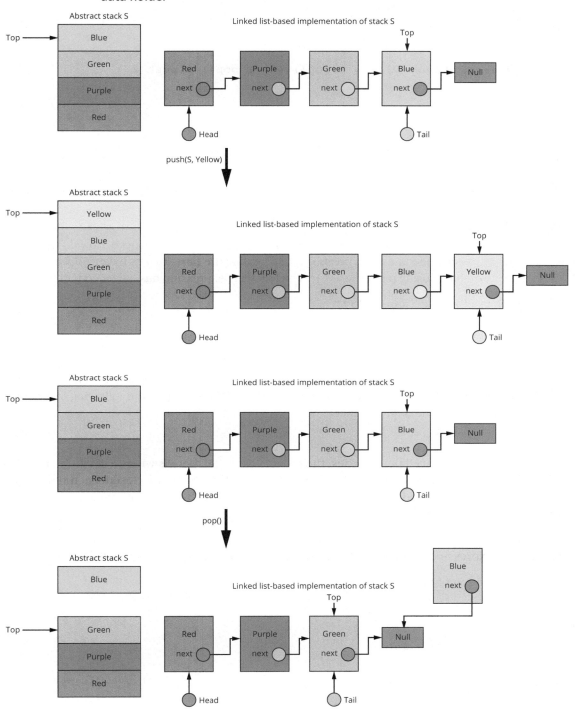

Quick Check 6-3

Suppose that in a stack S the following operations are executed:

```
S.push(+) S.push(3) S.push(2) x = S.pop() y = S.pop() S.push(x - y)
```

What are the elements of the stack?

Answer: [+ – 1]

After the initial insertions, the stack is [+ 3 2]. The two pop operations make $x = 2$ and $y = 3$. The push insert $2 - 3 = -1$ at the top of the stack.

Keeping Parentheses Balanced with Stacks

To see some potential applications of the stack, consider the problem of keeping parentheses balanced. How do we ensure that every open parenthesis has a closing one in a valid position? A string has the parentheses balanced when every open parenthesis "(" has a corresponding closing parenthesis ")". The following expression has balanced parentheses:

```
"((aaa)(aba))((abb(a)(b))(aa(aaa)(a)))"
```

while the next one doesn't:

```
"((aaa)(a)) )"
```

You might have noticed that you can't keep track of how many parentheses must be closed using a simple counter. Notice the order in which the open and closed parentheses appear is critical. For example, the following expression has as many open as closing parentheses but is not balanced.

```
"( ) ) ( ( )"
```

To determine if an expression has balanced parentheses, the order is essential. Here is where a stack can be helpful to keep track of how many parentheses are still open and in which order they should be closed. Each time a new parenthesis is opened, a new element is added to the stack `parenthesis_stack`. And each time a parenthesis is closed, an element is removed from the stack.

At the end of the expression, the stack must be empty to conclude that the expression has balanced parentheses. Moreover, if while analyzing the expression, the stack gets underflow, then the expression is not balanced.

Here is a complete implementation of the previous description:

```
is_balanced(expr)
   N = len(expr)
   parenthesis_stack = new Stack()
   for i = 0 to N-1 step 1
      if expr[i] = '('
         ;; If the character is an open parenthesis, then a one
         ;; is added to the stack.
         parenthesis_stack.push(1)
      if expr[i] = ')'
         ;; If the character is a closing parenthesis, then an
         ;; element should be removed from the stack.
         if parenthesis_stack.empty()
            ;; An underflow has occurred. This indicates that
            ;; there were more deletions than insertions, thus
```

```
        ;;   parenthesis is unbalanced.
        return False
    else
        parenthesis_stack.pop()
;; If the stack is empty, then the number of open parentheses is
;; the same as the number of closed parentheses.
if parenthesis_stack.empty()
    return True
else
    return False
```

> **Note** | The stack concept was developed by mathematician A.M. Turing in 1947. Turing developed the idea, but instead of the push() and pop() operations, he used the bury and un_bury operations. Turing developed this idea to keep track of functions calling and returning values.

6.4 Queue ADT Methods

Any queue data structure must have two basic operations, enqueue() and dequeue(). As with the stack, the most critical aspect is writing an implementation that enforces the FIFO policy.

In some applications, you might want to restrict the queue size or even have a limit given by the implementation. The important part is that the implementation provides an interface to the user through the enqueue() and dequeue() operations. A programmer might know what to expect if the FIFO policy is correctly implemented.

Why Use Queues?

The FIFO characteristic of a queue makes it perfect for any shared resource where all requests have the same priority, such as for a printer that is shared among all members of an office. All printing requests enter a queue. When the job at the front of the queue is completed, the following one starts. **Figure 6-15** depicts an OS's queue use in scheduling jobs.

Figure 6-15 A series of queues to schedule the execution of processes in a computer. A user sends a program or command that enters the job queue. From the job queue, a process enters the CPU. From the CPU, the process may require input or a network. In such a case, it enters a different queue

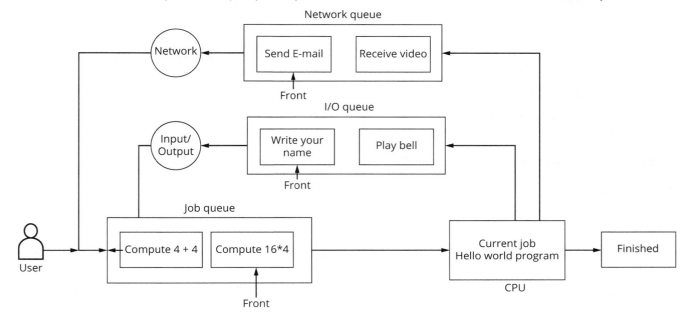

Main Queue Operations

As mentioned, the two primary operations of a stack are enqueue() and dequeue(). The enqueue(Q, x) operation inserts a new element *x* to the queue Q, and the dequeue(Q) operation deletes the first element inserted or enqueued into Q.

A pointer to the head and another to the tail are necessary to implement a dynamic queue using a linked list. A simple strategy might be to enqueue new elements after the tail and dequeue the element pointer by head. The following code uses a linked list L to implement a queue.

```
enqueue(L, x)
    ;; If the list is empty, head and tail must be modified.
    if L.tail = Null
        L.head = x
        L.tail = x
        x.next = Null
        return 1
    ;; In other cases put the new element after the
    ;; rear that is the tail of the linked list.
    L.tail.next = x
    L.tail = x
    return 1



dequeue(L)
    if L.head = Null
        display("Underflow")     ;; This means that the list was empty.
        return Null
    if L.head.next = Null
        ;; If the list is left empty, then tail and head
        ;; should be updated.
        x = L.head
        L.head = Null
        L.tail = Null
    else
    ;; In other cases, since a queue returns the front element, the head
    ;; of the list must be returned.
        x = L.head
        L.head = x.next
    return x
```

Figure 6-16 illustrates how the previous implementation works.

Figure 6-16 A queue and how a linked list implements the queue behavior. How the `enqueue` and `dequeue` operations affect the linked list used to implement the queue ADT

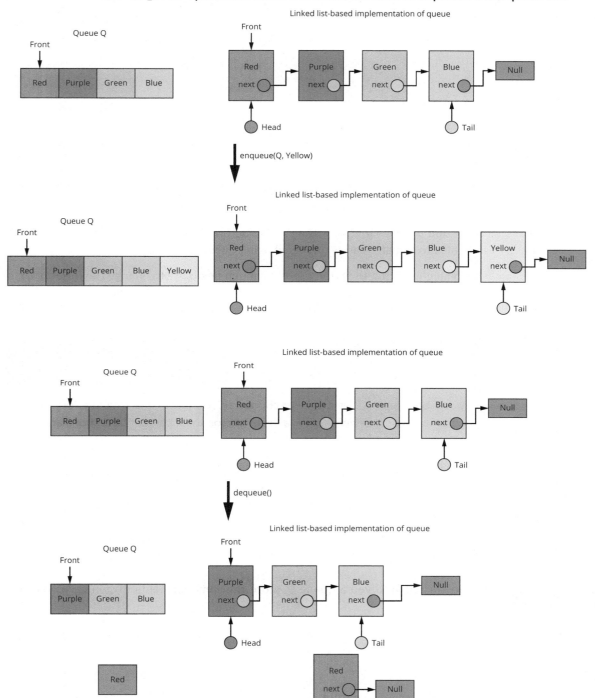

> ## Quick Check 6-4

Suppose you want to implement a queue using a linked list, as in this section. What code will be returned by the `rear()` function?

Answer: `L.tail`

In the implementation of the insertion and deletion of this section, every new element is put in the tail. Hence, `rear()` will return the object that `L.tail` points to.

Printing Elements of a Queue in Reverse Order

Queues are great for modeling anything that behaves following the FIFO structure. Objects such as queues of printing jobs, processes in a computer, or data files to transfer can be modeled using queues.

One drawback of queues and stacks might be that they don't provide much flexibility to change the order of their elements. One strategy to manipulate the elements in a queue or stack is to use auxiliary data structures.

> ## Best Practice

Choose your data structures wisely and beforehand. It is crucial to choose an adequate data structure for each problem. Instead of using a generic data container such as a list or vector, think of what operations are necessary.

Although it is possible, as shown before, to use a linked list to implement the behaviors of a stack or queue, that defeats the purpose of using an ADT. Using an ADT should help make the code more modular and readable. The abstraction layer provided by the ADTs rules helps others to read your code and to know what behavior to expect.

For example, consider the following problem. Given a queue Q, store the same elements of Q in reverse order. Suppose Q is empty, and you execute:

```
enqueue(Q, 2)
enqueue(Q, 3)
enqueue(Q, 5)
```

The order in which the elements are deleted by the `dequeue()` operation is 2, 3, and 5. The task is to change Q to return the elements in the reverse order, that is, 5, 3, 2.

One strategy to do this is to combine a stack and a queue. Stacks are ideal for reversing elements' order since that is what the LIFO policy ensures. The idea is illustrated in **Figure 6-17**.

Figure 6-17   A queue and a stack ADT can reverse the orders of elements in a queue. Notice that using ADTs makes the procedure simpler to explain

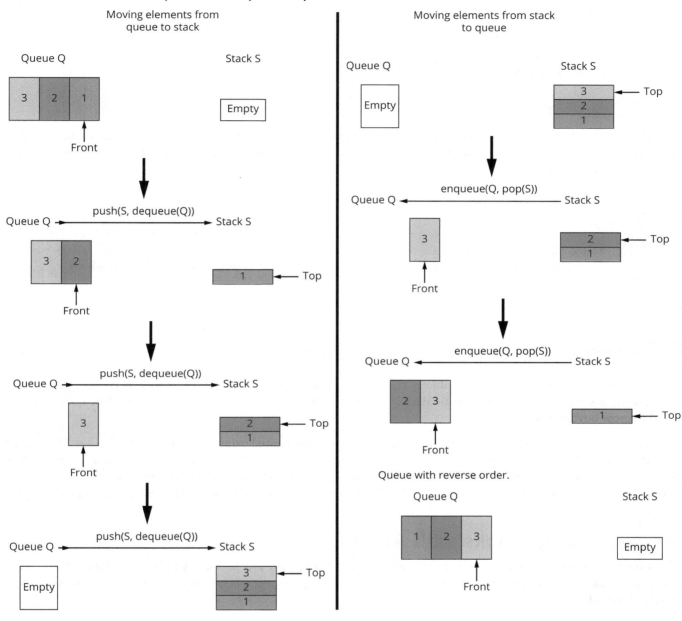

The following code snippet implements a solution to the problem.

```
reverse(Q)
   S = new Stack()
   ;; Every element of the queue Q is stored in the stack S.
   while not empty(Q)
      x = dequeue(Q)
      push(S, x)
```

```
;; Every element in the stack S is stored in Q.
;; Given the LIFO property of S, the elements are
;; in reverse order in Q.
while not empty(S)
    x = pop(S)
    enqueue(Q, x)


return 1
```

This solution has a $O(n)$ time complexity and a $O(n)$ space complexity; that is, each loop in the function reverse (Q) makes $n = $ len(Q) iterations, hence the $O(n)$ time complexity. And since it requires a stack that stores n elements, the space complexity is $O(n)$.

> **Note**
>
> Notice that ADT doesn't have a traverse() function for a queue and stack that returns all elements in the ADT. This limitation is functional from a design point of view. Suppose it is necessary to traverse the data structure with some frequency. Then you must consider if the stack or queue is the more appropriate ADT.

6.5 Array-Based Stacks and Queues

When a simple data type in a small number is stored in a stack or queue, it becomes unnecessary to use a complex dynamic data structure as a base. A static data structure might be good enough because the stack or queue doesn't need to grow beyond a specific limit.

As you will see in this section, the stack and queue can be implemented using an array as a data holder. That means that the data is stored in an array. Recall that the objective of using an ADT such as a stack is to provide a standard interface that can help a programmer to understand how a program behaves. Even when the underlying data holder has a fixed size from the programmer using the ADT implementation, the stack doesn't have a fixed size but a limit size.

Implementing Stacks with Arrays

For a stack implementation using an array to have the stack properties, it is necessary to keep the index at the top or use a particular value. In the case of an array of non-primitive data types, it is possible to use the NULL to signify the end of the stack.

Instead of using a particular value to indicate the end of the stack, you can use a user-defined data structure field. A user-defined data type can hold all the necessary information to implement the stack. You can see such a data type here.

```
type stack_array
    fields N, data_array[N], idx = -1
```

The field N is the only input to create the stack_array object. N indicates the maximum size of the stack. data_array is an array of size N to hold the elements of the stack. And idx will be a variable used to indicate where the top of the stack is located. You can see how those are used, illustrated in **Figure 6-18**.

Figure 6-18 Using an array to implement the stack ADT. How the push and pop operations modify the array and the auxiliary index idx

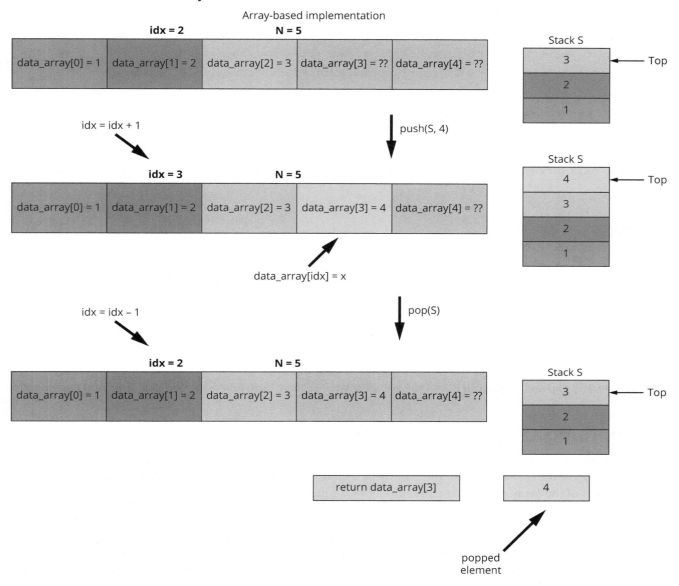

The following code implements the ideas presented in Figure 6-18.

```
empty(S)
    ;; An index of -1 indicates that the stack is empty.
    if S.idx = -1
        return True
    else
        return False


top(S)
    ;; The value of idx indicates the position of the top of the queue.
    if S.idx = -1    ;; This indicates that the stack is empty.
        return Null
```

```
    else
        return S.data_array[S.idx]

push(S, x)
    ;; To push a new element, it's stored after the top at idx+1.
    if S.idx = N - 1 ;; If there is no more space, there is overflow.
        display("Overflow")
        return -1

    S.idx = S.idx + 1
    S.data_array[S.idx] = x
    return 1

pop(S)
    if S.idx < 0
        display("Underflow")
        return -1
    ;; Retrieve the element at idx and change the value of idx.
    x = S.data_array[S.idx]
    S.idx = S.idx - 1
    return x
```

In this case, the pop and push both have time complexity $O(1)$ since both functions don't use any loop to complete.

Implementing Queues with Arrays

Two things are necessary to enforce the FIFO policy and use all available space in an array. First, you need an index for the tail or head of the queue. Second, there must be a shift in the position of the elements in the array. You must shift the elements of the array during the enqueue(x) or dequeue() operations.

In the same way that the index pointing to the top of the stack was necessary, now you must keep track of where the tail is. That assumes every element inserted into the queue is put at the tail position. But it also is necessary that after a dequeue(), all elements in the array shift one position to the left. The shift frees one space to store a new element and puts the element at the front of the queue, always at position 0. **Figure 6-19** illustrates how to execute the enqueue(Q, x) and dequeue() operations and how to use the tail index.

So an array_queue data structure implemented using an array will have a tail field and an array to store the elements of the queue.

```
type array_queue
    fields N, data_array[N], tail = -1
```

Figure 6-19 An implementation of the queue ADT using an array. How the array and the auxiliary index tail are modified by the `enqueue` and `dequeue` operations

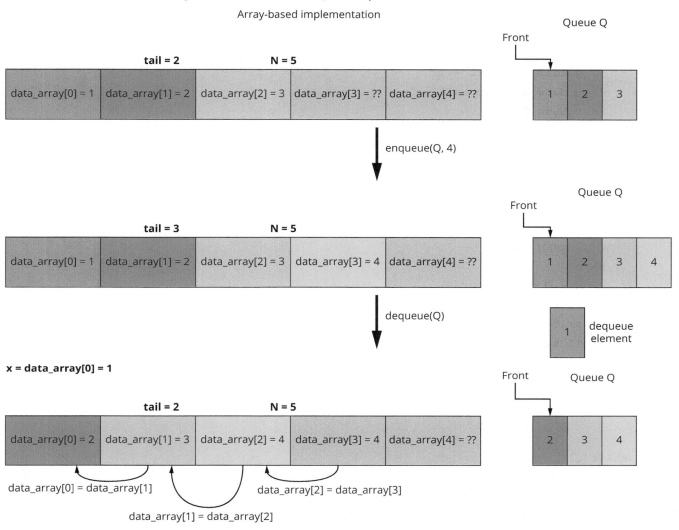

When implementing a new operation, you must ensure that all the data is consistent. So, if a new element is added when using an array-based implementation, the tail pointer must be updated for a queue to access the last element in the queue (rear). The following code snippet implements the operations described in Figure 6-19.

```
front(Q)
    ;; The front of the queue is at the position of the tail index.
    if Q.tail = -1
        return Null
    else
        return Q.data_array[0]


empty(Q)
    if Q.tail = -1
        return True
    else
        return False
```

```
enqueue(Q, x)
    if Q.tail >= N-1
        display(overflow)
        return -1
    else
        Q.tail = Q.tail + 1
        Q.data_array[Q.tail] = x
        return 1


dequeue(Q)
    ;; Given the FIFO policy of a queue, the element
    ;; at position 0 is returned.
    if Q.tail = -1   ;; Special case of empty queue
        display("underflow")
        return -1
    else
        x = Q.data_array[0]
        ;; All other elements must be moved one position to keep the
        ;; data in the correct configuration.
        if shift(Q) = 1   ;; This means that the shift was
                          ;; completed correctly.
            return x
        else
            return Null


shift(Q)
    ;; Moves all elements to one previous position.
    for k = 0 to Q.tail - 1 step 1
        Q.data_array[k] = Q.data_array[k+1]
    Q.tail = Q.tail - 1
    return 1
```

Notice that in this case, the shift operation has a loop that makes `Q.tail - 1` iterations. In the worst case, that is the same as N. Hence, the time complexity of the `dequeue(Q)` operation is $O(N)$.

Note

A similar implementation for the queue is possible. In this case, you store the front index and shift the data in the array each time a new element is inserted into the queue. In this case, the element is always inserted at position 0.

This additional implementation allows you to have the heaviest processing during insertion or deletion. So the decision of implementation use depends on when the time is a more critical factor during insertion or deletion.

Summary

- Stacks, queues, and linked lists are linear data structures. They are dynamic since the number of elements can change.

- The elements in a stack, queue, or linked list are stored sequentially. Hence, they are linear ADTs.

- There are two ways a function can receive its parameters: by value or by reference.

- When receiving a parameter by value, the function receives a new copy of the parameter. Every change made inside the function's code won't affect the copy outside the function's code.

- When receiving a parameter by reference, a function receives a pointer or a link to the same object. Every change made to the parameter inside the function will be kept when the function terminates.

- A linked list uses nodes to store its data. Each node stores the data and links or pointers to adjacent elements in the list.

- A singly linked list or simply a linked list uses nodes with only a next pointer. The next pointer is a reference to the next node in the list.

- A doubly linked list uses nodes with the next and previous pointers. The next pointer is a reference to the next node and the previous pointer is a reference to the previous node in the list.

- A linked list usually has a head pointer that references the beginning of the list and a tail pointer that points to the end.

- Beware of memory leakage in low-level programming languages. One instance where memory leakage happens is when you forget to free the memory used to store objects that are no longer in use.

- The stack is a linear ADT characterized by the LIFO schedule policy.

- LIFO stands for last in, first out. Last in, first out means that the first element being deleted from the stack is the last inserted element.

- The two primary operations of a stack are `pop()` and `push()`, which delete and insert elements to the stack, respectively.

- The queue is a linear ADT characterized by the FIFO schedule policy.

- FIFO stands for first in, first out. Hence, in a queue, the first element inserted is the first to be deleted.

- The two primary stack operations are `enqueue()` and `dequeue()`, which insert and delete elements from the queue, respectively.

- Insertions and deletions in a linked list always have three possible cases in which you modify the tail, the front, or in between.

- Be careful handling each case correctly, or you could put your linked list in an inconsistent state. Such inconsistencies arise, especially when reassigning the next or previous pointers. Recall that a pointer is the only way to recover all elements in the linked list.

- Doubly linked lists provide more flexibility to navigate the data structure. The only way to reach a node is through one of the adjacent nodes.

- A circular linked list is a doubly or singly linked list where the tail's next pointer points to the head and the previous pointer of the head points to the tail if it applies.

- The stack data structure operates on only one end of the data structure. That means if you implement the stack using another data structure, such as a list, all elements are inserted and removed from one end of it. The previous actions enforce the LIFO policy.

- When implementing a queue using a linked list, it will be necessary to add elements to both ends of the list. But the FIFO policy can be unforced, inserting elements at the front or the tail.

- Stacks and queues can be implemented using an array as a data holder. That limits the size of the elements they can hold, but from the programmer's point of view, they are still dynamic data structures.

- When implementing a queue using an array, it is possible to implement an insertion with complexity $O(n)$ and deletion $O(1)$. But it is also possible to implement an insertion with complexity $O(1)$ and deletion $O(n)$.

Key Terms

by reference	head pointer	previous pointer
by value	memory leakage	**push()** operation
circular linked list	node	random access policy
doubly linked list	Null	schedule policy
equal-time random access	overflow	tail pointer
garbage collector	**pop()** operation	underflow

Review Questions

1. If x is passed by value and y is passed by reference to foo(x,y), what is displayed by the following code?

```
foo(x,y)
   y = x + 1
   x = 5
x = 3
y = 7
foo(x,y)


display(x,y)
```

2. Given the following code, what is the value of L.head.key?

```
L = new LinkedList()


for i = 1 to 9 step 1
   curr = new Node(key = i)
   if L.tail = Null
      L.tail = curr
      L.head = curr
   else
      if i mod 2 = 0
         L.tail.next = curr
         L.tail = curr
```

```
        else
            curr.next = L.head
            L.head = curr
```

3. What is the output of the following code?

```
    S = new Stack()

    for k = 0 to 10 step 1
       push(S, k)
       for j = 0 to 5 step 1
          push(S, j*k)

    display(pop(S))
```

4. Consider the following code snippet:

```
    Q = new Queue()

    k = 10
    while k > 0
        enqueue(Q, k)
        k = k - 1

    while k < 5
        dequeue(Q)
        k = k + 1

    display(front(Q), rear(Q))
```

What is displayed by the code snippet?

5. When does an overflow occur in a stack data structure?

6. Stack, queue, and linked list ADTs have a single expected way to be traversed. What classification is given to them because of that?

7. If you implement a stack data structure using an array of size 100 as a data container, then your data structure becomes a static data structure.

   a. True
   b. False

8. Which policy enforces that the last element inserted be the last to be deleted?

   a. LIFO
   b. FIFO
   c. LIT
   d. Linked list

9. Which policy enforces the last inserted element be deleted first?

   a. LIFO
   b. FIFO
   c. LIT
   d. Linked list

10. In a non-empty circular doubly linked list *L*, what is the value of `L.tail.next`?

    a. `Null`
    c. `L.tail`

    b. `L.tail.prev`
    d. `L.head`

11. Consider the following code:

```
S = new Stack()


push(S, 1)
push(S, 2)
push(S, 3)
push(S, 4)
```

How many times must you use `pop(S)` to get the `S.top = 2`?

    a. 1
    c. 3

    b. 2
    d. 0

12. Consider the following code:

```
Q = new Queue()


enqueue(Q, 1)
enqueue(Q, 2)
enqueue(Q, 3)
enqueue(Q, 4)
```

How many times should you use `dequeue(S)` to get the `S.front = 2`?

    a. 1
    c. 3

    b. 2
    d. 0

13. Suppose three nodes with key values 1, 2, and 3 are stored sequentially in a circular linked list. What is the value of the node `curr` after the following code?

```
curr = L.head
for j = 1 to 6 step 1
    curr = curr.next
```

    a. 1
    c. 3

    b. 2
    d. Null

14. Suppose you use an array to implement the Stack ADT, and your friend uses a linked list. Both add eight nodes with only a numeric data type to the linked list. You suppose that every numeric value, including the pointers, uses the same memory space and that the array-based implementation's limit is eight elements. Which implementation uses more memory?

    a. The array-based
    c. The linked list

    b. Both use the same
    d. It is not possible to estimate

Programming Problems

1. Suppose each node in a linked list has the fields year, total, and id. The id works as a numerical key. A programmer noticed that the total value was wrong. Each year greater than 2020 must have a total of 50% higher. Write a program that fixes the linked list. **(LO 6.1, 6.2)**

2. A bank has three desks to solve complaints. Each desk can only attend to one person at a time and have a maximum of five people in a queue waiting. Each person is identified with a unique integer ID number. Write a program that inserts a new person at the queue with the least number of persons waiting and returns -1 if all the queues are full and has the function of removing the person being attended at a given desk j and adding a new person at desk j from the queue for desk j. You can see an example of the desired behavior in **Figure 6-20**. **(LO 6.1, 6.4, 6.5)**

Figure 6-20   A model of how this program should model the three desks and queues when a new customer is inserted, and how to model when one desk is free

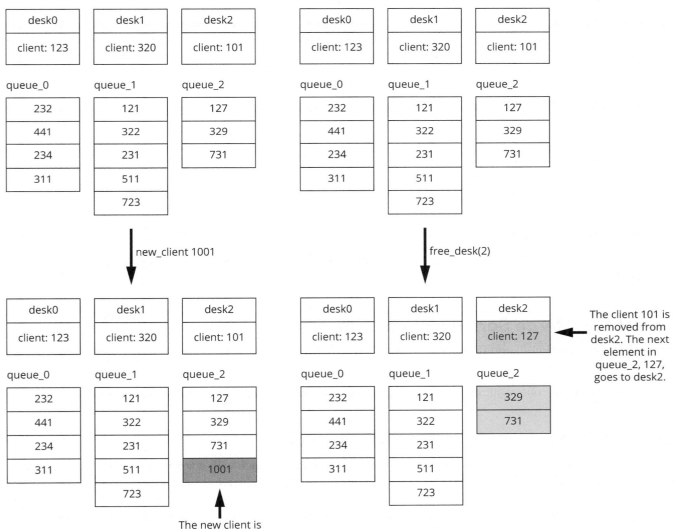

3. Write an implementation of the stack data structure using a queue as a data container. You can use an auxiliary queue to implement the `push`, `pop`, `top`, and `empty` operations. **(LO 6.3, 6.4)**

4. Write a queue implementation using a stack as a data container. You can use an auxiliary stack to implement the `enqueue`, `dequeue`, `front`, `rear`, and `empty` operations. **(LO 6.3, 6.4)**

5. The company has two stores. In the whole company, each employee has a unique integer id. The data of the employees in the first store are in a doubly linked list `store1` sorted by id in ascending order. The employees of the second store are stored in the list `store2` sorted by id in descending order. Write a program that creates a linked list with the employees of `store1` and `store2` using a user-defined data type that stores an integer value for `employee_id`. **(LO 6.1, 6.2)**

Projects

Project 6-1: Bubble Sort in Linked Lists

(LO 6.1, 6.2) The bubble sort algorithm extracts the maximum element of array A from position 0 to j and puts it in the j position. By varying the value of j from 0 to $N-1$, the bubble sort puts all elements of array X in order. You can see an implementation of bubble sort below.

```
bubble_sort(X, N)
    top_index = N-1
    while top_index > 1
        for j = 0 to top_index-1 step 1
            if X[j] > X[j+1]
                temp = X[j]
                X[j] = X[j+1]
                X[j+1] = temp
        top_index = top_index - 1
```

Suppose that L is a doubly linked list storing integer values as keys. Implement the bubble sort algorithm for a singly linked list L.

Project 6-2: Merge Sort in Linked Lists

(LO 6.1. 6.2) Suppose that $L1$ and $L2$ are sorted linked lists. Write a procedure to merge $L1$ and $L2$ into a single sorted linked list L that contains the elements of both lists.

A method similar to the one required is used to implement the merge sort algorithm for linked lists.

Project 6-3: Retrieving in a Doubly Linked List

(LO 6.1, 6.2, 6.4) Suppose that a doubly linked list L has several nodes, each with a key value from a set. The doubly linked list is sorted by id. Each node has a field name. A subset of key values has been stored in a stack S. Write a program that searches the name associated with each key value stored in S. Your program must start searching an element x starting at the position of the previous value searched. For the first element, you should start at 0.

For example, suppose you have a linked list L

(0, "A") <=> (1, "B") <=> (2, "C") <=> (3, "D") <=> (4, "E") <=> (5, "F") <=> (6, "G")

If the first value to search is 3, then the pointer `curr` starting at the head will have to move three times to the right, so it points at 3. If the next element to search is 5, it is expected that you start with `curr` pointing at 3 and move it two times to the right. If the next element is 4, it is expected that you start with `curr` pointing at 5 and move it one position to the left.

Project 6-4: Evaluating Arithmetic Expressions

(LO 6.1, 6.3) An arithmetic expression like $3 + 2 * 9$ is said to be in infix notation. Infix notation means that the operators $*, +, -, \div$ are between the two operands.

1. If a character is a number, for simplicity, you can assume that only single digits are used. Then push any to the operand stack any number.

2. If a character is an operand, then

    a. If the operator stack is empty or the top is an operator with less precedence, then push the character to the operator stack.

    b. If the operator stack top has more or equal precedence than the character, then pop from the operands and operate and calculate the result accordingly to the operator at the top. Push the result to the operand stack. Repeat until the top of the operator stack has less precedence or is empty.

3. If a character is a parenthesis, then

    a. If it is an open parenthesis, push it to the operator stack.

    b. If it is a closing parenthesis, pop the operators and two operands. Compute the result of the operation over the operands and push it to the operands stack. Repeat until an open parenthesis is found and pop it.

The procedure is illustrated in **Table 6-1** for the expression $3 * ((3 + 1) * 5 + 7) - 11$.

Table 6-1   Procedure for Project 6-4

Index	Character	Execute	S1(operand)	S2(operator)
0	3	push(3) to S1	3	
1	*	push(*) to S2	3	*
2	(	push("(") to S2	3	*(
3	(	push("(") to S2	3	*((
4	3	push(3) to S1	3 3	*((
5	+	push(+) to S2	3 3	*((+
6	1	push(1) to S1	3 3 1	*((+
7	)	pop 3,1 from S1 and + from S2	3	*((
7	)	compute 3 + 1 pop "(" from S2	3	*(
7	)	push(4) to S1	3 4	*(
8	*	push(*) to S2	3 4	*(*
9	5	push(5) to S1	3 4 5	*(*
10	+	+ has less precedence than *	3 4 5	*(*

(continues)

Table 6-1   Procedure for Project 6-4 (*continued*)

Index	Character	Execute	S1(operand)	S2(operator)
10	+	pop * from S2 and 5, 4 from S1	3	*(
10	+	compute 4*5 and push to S1 push + to S2	3 20	*(+
11	7	push(7) to S1	3 20 7	*(+
12	)	pop until a) is found	3 20 7	*(+
12	)	pop 7, 20 and +	3 20 7	*(
12	)	compute and push 7 + 20 to S1 and pop S2	3 27	*
13	-	- has less precedence than *	3 27	*
13	-	pop 27, 3, and * stack empty		
13	-	compute 3*27 and push 81 to S1 and push - to S2	81	-
14	11	push(11) to S1	81 11	-
14	END	pop 11, 81 and -	70	

Write a program that receives a string name `exprs` with an arithmetical expression that only uses single-digit numbers, +, *, (, and). Assume that the string has no white spaces. The program must evaluate the expression using the two-stack algorithm described in the problem.

Chapter 7

Hash Tables

Learning Objectives

Upon completion of this chapter, you will be able to:

7.1 Discuss hashing and hash tables.

7.2 Explain insert, delete, and search operations in a hash table.

7.3 Describe how hash codes are commonly generated for different data types.

7.4 Explain why hash code compression is required.

7.5 Employ chaining, linear probing, and double hashing collision handling techniques.

7.6 Measure the efficiency of hashing.

7.1 Introduction to Hash Tables

Hash tables and hashing are techniques that can be used to associate simple indexes with more complicated key values, such as associating a string name composed of several characters with a simple index. The index indicates in which place the information associated with that specific name might be found. Creating such an association requires solving some technical issues such as how to make the index unique, that is, how to reduce a string, probably composed of several characters, to a single number. In the following sections, common strategies to solve these issues are discussed.

A great feature of arrays is a property called equal-time random access. Equal-time random access means that the time required to write or retrieve the data on a given array position is always constant. In other words, it has time complexity $O(1)$. On the downside, you can only access the data through the index, and the index is a simple integer.

In many applications, such as phone books, you might want to access the data as fast as in an array but use the name of a contact instead of a number. Or you may want to use a user-defined data type as a key. This user-defined data type can be composed of several fields such as a phone number that includes the area code.

A way to provide fast access, as fast as in an array, using complex data types as indices could be to imagine the keys and data like a table of contents (TOC) where the key is analogous to the topic and the data values are the actual content, as shown in **Figure 7-1**. You can find the correct page number for the desired content using the TOC. So, by using something similar to a TOC, you can find the desired position in an array given the key you are searching.

Figure 7-1   A TOC uses the page number as a pointer to the actual location of the content

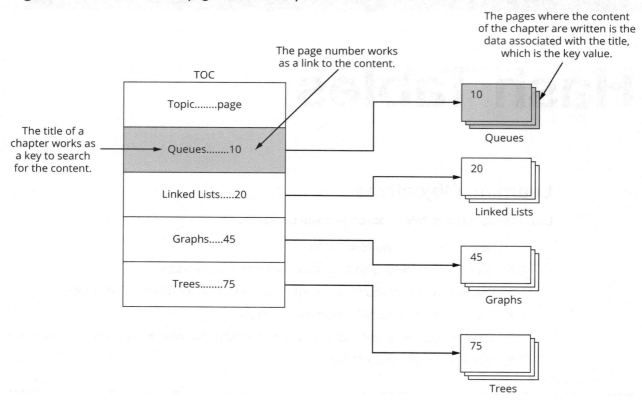

An **associative array** is an ADT (abstract data structure) that stores key and data value pairs so that each key appears at most once in the ADT. This allows you to insert, delete, search, and modify the associated data using the key value. This is similar to the way you access the content of an array using an index that indicates the position in the array.

The following elements and behaviors characterize an associative array A:

- A set K of possible key values.
- insert(A, key, data) inserts data associated with the key value key.
- delete(A, key) removes data associated with the key value key if it exists in the associative array A.
- search(A, key) returns the associated data to the key value key if it exists in the associative array A and Null in other cases.

A naive way to implement an associative array is to use an array that stores user-defined data types with one field for the key and one for the data. The rest of the operations can be implemented using search algorithms.

For example, suppose that all possible keys are the names of departments in a college:

[Math, Economics, English, Physics, Computer Science]

For each department, the associated data is the name of the department director, the number of majors in the field, and the year of creation. One implementation for such an associative array using only user-defined data types and arrays is shown here.

```
;; New data type department
type department
    fields
        Director, majors, year
```

```
type assoc_array
   fields
       m, data_array = new array[m]


A = new assoc_array(m = 5)          ;; Array of size 5


;; function to implement at TOC
translate(name)
   if name = "Math"
      return 0
   if name = "Economics"
      return 1
   if name = "English"
      return 2
   if name = "Physics"
      return 3
   if name = "Computer Science"
      return 4
   return Null


insert(A, key, data)
   ;; First the index where the data should be stored is computed
   index = translate(key)
   if not index = Null
      ;; If the key is valid the data is stored at index
      A.data_array[index] = data
      return 0
   else
      return -1


delete(A, key)
   index = translate(key)
   if not index = Null
      A.data_array[index] = Null
      return 0
   else
      return -1


search(A, key)
   index = translate(key)
   if not index = Null
      data = A.data_array[index]
      return data
   else
      return -1
```

The previous implementation can be used to store the data of the different departments in a very efficient way since each operation takes a constant number of operations. In other words, it has time complexity $O(1)$. Also, its use provides very readable code. You can see how the data can be inserted and retrieved in the following code snippet.

```
;; Creating the data for the English and CS departments

english_data = new department("Prof. Shakespeare", 121, 1613)
cs_data = new department("Prof. Turing", 420, 1936)

;; Inserting the data for the English and CS departments

insert(A, "English", english_data)
insert(A, "Computer Science", cs_data)

;; Searching and displaying the data of the
;; English and Math department

data = search(A, "English")
display("Data for English department")
display(data)

data = search(A, "Math")
display("Data for Math department")
display(data)
```

The output provided by the previous code is similar to the following:

```
Data for English department
Director: Prof. Shakespeare
Majors: 121
Foundation: 1613

Data for Math department
Null
```

Although the previous implementation is very efficient, its application is limited due to two main points:

- If the set of possible keys is too large, manually writing a function such as `translate(key)` becomes completely impractical.

- The number of elements to be inserted might not be known, not even approximately. Sometimes, the number of possible key-data pairs is too large to use a single array to store all the values.

For the second point, one solution might be using a dynamic data structure such as a linked list. A better solution might be using non-linear dynamic data structures such as trees.

Supposing that the second point is not a problem, a way to address the implementation of the `translate(key)` function without having to write it manually is by using a hash function. A **hash function** is a function that maps a set of keys, K, to a set of integers, $V = \{0, 1, \ldots, N - 1\}$. The value returned by a hash function when applied to a particular key value x in K is called the **hash code** of x.

An example of a hash function is the `len(txt)` function that returns the length of a string `txt`. Suppose that you need to store the data of all departments in a college. The existing departments are:

```
[Math, Economics, English, Physics, Computer Science]
```

Using the `len(key)` function instead of using the `translate(key)` function for each department name, an index in the array is assigned. Now, if a new department called "Law" needs to be added, it can be inserted at position 3 of the array since `len("Law")` = 3, as shown in **Table 7-1**.

Table 7-1   Hash code associated with each key value in the list of departments

Key value	Index len(key)
"Math"	4
"English"	7
"Economics"	9
"Computer Science"	16
"Physics"	7
"Law"	3

Note | You might have noticed that both the English and Physics departments have a key length of 7. This would create a collision, an issue discussed later in this chapter.

Why Hash Tables?

A **hash table** is an implementation for an associative array that uses a hash function to create an integer key value to store the data associated with a key value. Usually, a hash table uses a data structure such as an array to store the data; that is, to get the equal-time random access property. But a hash table might use any other data structure to store the data. In some cases, a combination of fixed size and dynamic data structures is used to overcome the limits in the size of an array.

One key point in implementing a hash table is the choice of a hash function. The problem is to build a function that gives a single number for a (probably complex) key in such a way that it is efficient to compute. Fortunately, practical experience has provided some guiding techniques and functions that provide great results in most cases. One of the most useful cases is when the key values are strings. A function that assigns a numeric value for each letter is usually used in such cases. An example of such an assignment is given in **Figure 7-2**.

Figure 7-2   To each letter in the English alphabet, a non-negative integer is assigned by the `ord` function

Letter x	Value ord(x)
a/A	0
b/B	1
c/C	2
d/D	3
e/E	4
f/F	5
g/G	6
h/H	7
i/I	8
j/J	9
k/K	10
l/L	11
m/M	12
n/N	13
o/O	14
p/P	15
q/Q	16
r/R	17
s/S	18
t/T	19
u/U	20
v/V	21
w/W	22
x/X	23
y/Y	24
z/Z	25

Once each letter has a numeric value assigned, it is possible to compute a single number for each string key value. One such function is implemented in the code snippet below. Notice that the function that assigns a numerical value to each character is denoted by `ord(c)`.

```
hash0(key)
    N = len(key)
    hash_code = 0
    for i = 0 to N step 1
        hash_code = hash_code + ord(key[i])
    return hash_code mod 20
```

The mathematical description of the function `hash0(key)` for a string $a_0a_1a_2 \cdots a_{N-1}$ is as follows:

$$\text{hash0}(a_0a_1a_2 \cdots a_{N-1}) = \left(\sum_{i=0}^{N-1} \text{ord}(a_i) \right) (\text{mod}\, 20)$$

When applied to the key values "Math", "Computer Science", and "Law" the results are as follows:

```
key1 = "Math"
key2 = "Computer Science"
key3 = "Law"
```

```
display(hash0(key1)) ;; Result 18
display(hash0(key2)) ;; Result 14
display(hash0(key3)) ;; Result 13
```

The steps to compute such a hash function are summarized as follows:

1. Compute the value `ord(char)` for each character `char` that composes the key value.
2. Add all the values of `ord(char)` and store them in S.
3. Compute the residue of S modulus 20.

All the intermediate values necessary to compute the hash code for the keyword "Math" are shown in **Table 7-2**.

Table 7-2 Intermediate computations for `hash0("Math")`

	i	Key[i]	Ord(key[i])
	0	'M'	12
	1	'a'	0
	2	't'	19
	3	'h'	7
sum			38
Sum modulo 20			18
hash0('Math')			18

Notice that the value 20 for the modulus in this case is completely arbitrary. In practice you usually choose a number that corresponds to the size of the data array used.

This procedure allows us to efficiently search, insert, and modify the data associated with a key value inside an array. Since in practice the keys will have certain characteristics, including a size limit, a hash function such as the one described earlier is bounded by a constant time complexity $O(1)$. If the associated data is stored in an array at the position `hash(key)`, then the retrieval, storage, and modification are also bounded $O(1)$. Hence, you have a data structure with almost equal-time random access based on a string key value.

Quick Check 7-1

Compute `hash0("Mark")` using the process described before and the values given in Figure 7-2.

Answer: 19 Using the `ord()` function as described in Table 7-2, it follows:

	i	Key[i]	Ord(key[i])
	0	'M'	12
	1	'a'	0
	2	'r'	17
	3	'k'	10
sum			39
Sum modulo 20			19
hash0('Mark')			19

When to Use a Hash Table

The case in the previous section highlights one of the best properties of hash tables: the ability to use almost any arbitrary data type as a key and insert, retrieve, and modify the associated data with equal-time random access.

Since a hash table uses an array that is a fixed-size data structure, then hash tables are fixed size in essence. The size of the array must be established beforehand. Since arrays are stored in contiguous memory locations, it is not easy to extend the array size if necessary. This is one of the biggest drawbacks of hash tables. Another drawback of establishing the array size or the number of key-data pairs to store beforehand is that the hash function determines the index. That might lead to unused space in the array if the hash function does not produce all possible positions as hash codes.

The ideal scenario to use a hash table is when the number of keys to be used is much smaller than the entire set of possible keys. For example, suppose that you store key data pairs where the key is the name of a department in a college. The department name might be restricted to a string of at most 20 characters; assuming that only lowercase letters and no symbols are used, the number of possible keys is:

$$26^{20} = 19,928,148,895,209,409,152,340,197,376$$

Although a college might have many different departments, it is very unlikely that the number of departments will reach more than a thousand. Hence, the number of actual keys is smaller than the set of all possible keys.

Note	Hash tables implement associative arrays, meaning each key value must appear only once in the data structure. But there are other cases where hash functions and similar ideas can be used. One of those is the creation of indices. An **index** is a data structure that associates values of a field with the set of key data pairs where the value is present. You can see an example of an index in **Figure 7-3**.

Figure 7-3 An index over the field department, created over a hash table that stores the key-data pair of majors and major information

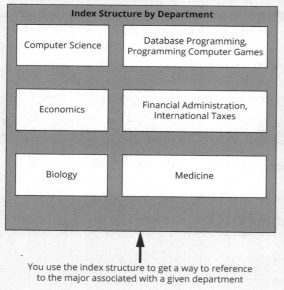

Index Structure by Department	
Computer Science	Database Programming, Programming Computer Games
Economics	Financial Administration, International Taxes
Biology	Medicine

You use the index structure to get a way to reference to the major associated with a given department

Structure of Majors Data Types	
Database Programming	Department: Computer Science Students: 300 Campus: Central
Programming Computer Games	Department: Computer Science Students: 160 Campus: North
Financial Administration	Department: Economics Students: 120 Campus: Central
International Taxes	Department: Economics Students: 80 Campus: South
Medicine	Department: Biology Students: 125 Campus: Central

The data structure Majors Data Types is an associative array so it uses the major name to get the associated information. Using the index you can search the majors in a given department

One way to implement an index is through a hash table that associates the field used for the index to an array with pointers to the key-data pairs stored in the hash table. You can see an illustration of this in **Figure 7-4**.

(continues)

Figure 7-4 An illustration of how an index can be implemented using a hash function, an array of pointers, and linked lists

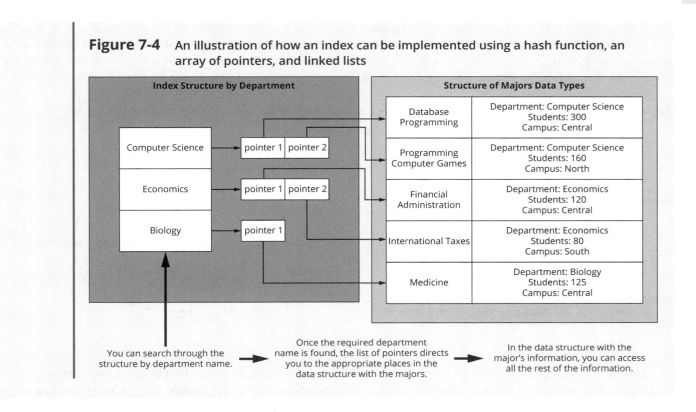

Perfect Hashing and Collisions

As described in the previous section, the ideal scenario for a hash table is when the number of keys to be used is known or smaller than the whole set of possible keys. In an ideal case, the hash table size should be the same as the number of keys used. In **Figure 7-5**, you can see such a case.

Figure 7-5 A set of five keys stored perfectly in an array of length 5 using a hash function $f(n) = 3n \bmod 5$

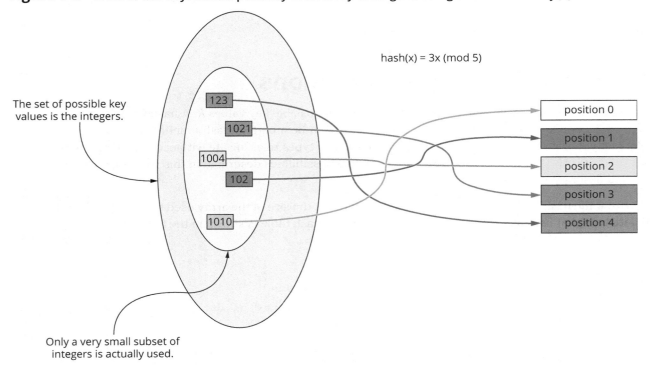

Unfortunately, it is rare that all keys directly map to different positions using a hash function. In a hash function $h(x)$, a **collision** occurs when two different key values have the same hash code. There are common strategies to handle collisions when using hash functions to construct associative arrays. The two most robust solutions are in the later sections of this chapter. In **Figure 7-6**, you can see an illustration of collisions for a simple hash function.

Figure 7-6   Two different values have the same resulting hash code. Such occurrences are collisions

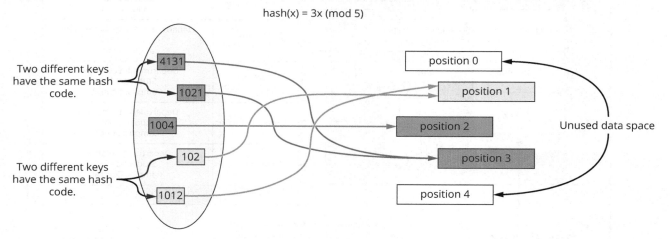

A **perfect hash function** is a hash function $h(x)$ over a set of key values S such that there are no collisions. For a small set of key values, it is always possible to construct a simple perfect hash function, as shown at the beginning of this section. It is necessary to build such a function for more complex sets dynamically.

Note   On how to use random numbers to build such functions, see Fredman, M. L., Komlós, J., & Szemerédi, E. [1984]. Storing a sparse table with $O(1)$ worst case access time. *Journal of the ACM, 31*[3], 538–544; and Verma, N. [2021]. *Universal classes of hash functions.* https://mathsanew.com/articles/universal_classes_hash_functions.pdf. For a set of up to 10 million, there are algorithms like the ones developed by Dietzfelbinger to build perfect hash functions in Dietzfelbinger, M., Karlin, A., Mehlhorn, K., Meyer auf der Heide, F., Rohnert, H., & Tarjan, R. E. [1994]. Dynamic perfect hashing: Upper and lower bounds. *SIAM Journal on Computing, 23*[4], 738–761.

7.2 Primary Hash Table Operations

When implementing a hash table, you need to know the set of possible key values K. A hash function $h(x)$ generates an integer hash code for each key value. $h(x)$ does not need to be a perfect hash function, although that might be desirable. And you need an array of size m pointers to the data types to associate with each key value or an array of the associated data type. You can see a depiction of the two possibilities described in this paragraph applied to a set of names and descriptions in **Figure 7-7**.

Notice that the hash function, in this case, is independent of the size of the array used to store the data. The user-defined data type that uses an array of objects to implement a hash table is shown in the following snippet.

```
type hash_table
    fields
        hash_function ;; Hash function associated
        m             ;; Integer size of the array of data
        data_array    ;; Array of size m of data
```

Note that the field `hash_function` is a function that receives a key value as a parameter.

Figure 7-7 In a hash table, each key value is associated through a hash function to a position in the array

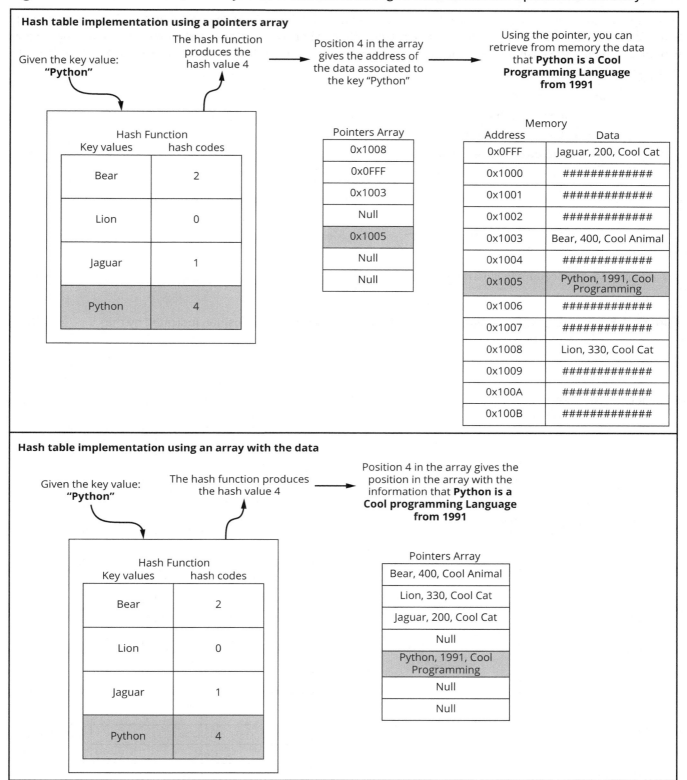

Insertion in Hash Tables

To study how to insert elements in hash tables, suppose a hash table is implemented as in the previous section. To start, assume that you are working only with perfect hashing. When you want to insert a new element `key` associated with `data`, you use the hash function and store the data in the position indicated by the hash code. Such implementation is shown below.

```
insert(H, key, data)
    hash_code = H.hash_function(key)
    idx = hash_code mod H.m
    if not H.data_array[idx] = Null
        ;; In case the index is already used return an error code
        return -1
    else
        H.data_array[idx] = data
        return 0
```

The previous procedure is illustrated in **Figure 7-8**.

Figure 7-8   Inserting a new element requires changing the value at the position indicated by the hash function by the associated data

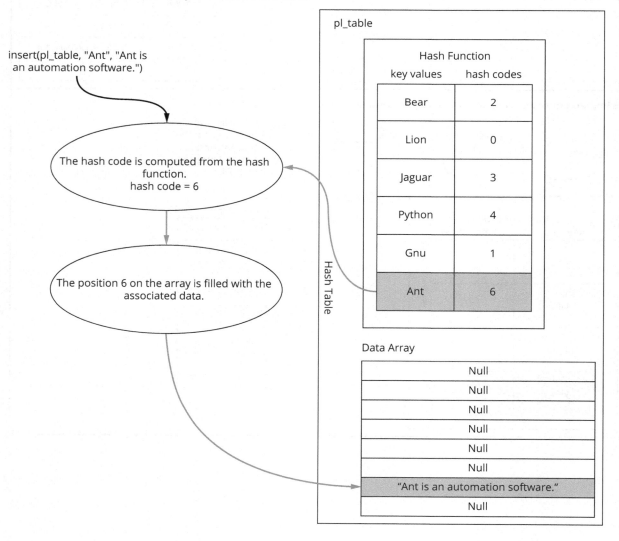

Using an array of pointers instead of an array of data allows you to use the memory better. Since only the space necessary to store the pointers is stored in the array, only the space necessary for the pointers must be in contiguous memory space. There is no memory reserved for each data element until it is used.

For example, suppose the data associated with each key value contains 20 integer fields. An array to store 100 of such data elements requires enough contiguous space to store 2,000 integer values. Even if you only need to insert a single element in the hash table, you will still need to reserve space for 100 elements. On the other hand, by using pointers to data, it is only necessary to reserve contiguous space for 100 pointers. After each insertion, the space necessary to store the 20 new fields is allocated as needed. But when no element has been inserted, only the space for 100 pointers is reserved. You can see how the insertion procedure works using pointers in **Figure 7-9**.

Figure 7-9   When using an array of pointers, the memory where the actual data is stored does not have to be in a single contiguous space. Moreover, until a new element is inserted, the space used by the hash table is only the space necessary to store the array pointers

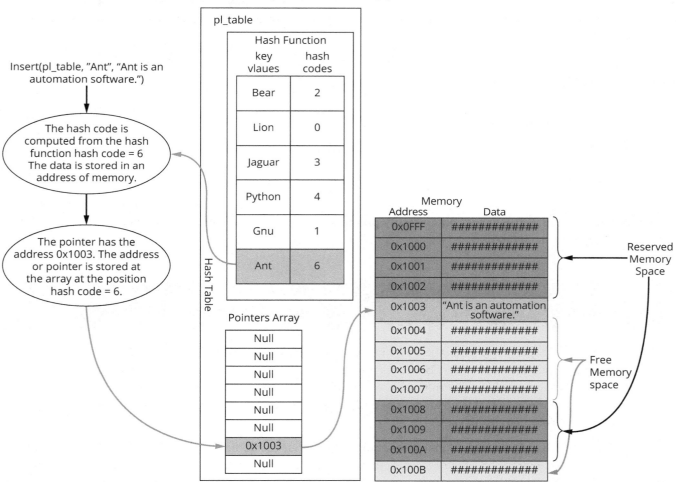

> ## Note
>
> The concept of pointers and their direct use is visible only in low-level programming languages such as C, Rust, Go, and C++. In those programming languages, you can directly access the pointers.
>
> Pointers are not explicitly used in higher-level programming languages such as Python, Java, C#, and JavaScript, but all of them use pointers in the background.
>
> In the pseudocode in this book, the convention is that when you use a variable that stores a user-defined data type, it accesses the associated object. In the case of a low-level programming language, you don't access the pointer but the object the pointer is addressing. In a high-level language, you access the object itself, although in the background, the language uses a pointer.

Deletion in Hash Tables

Since a hash table is an implementation of an associative array to refer to any item in the table—read it, modify it, or delete it—it must be referred to by a key value. Hence, the delete operation for the hash table uses a key value associated with the data you want to delete.

An implementation that works for a hash table that uses pointers or an array with a specific user-defined data type is shown here.

```
;; delete procedure on a hash table
delete(H, key)
    hash_code = H.hash_function(key)
    idx = hash_code mod H.m
    H.data_array[idx] = Null
```

When using an array of a specific data user-defined data type, setting the position to Null will overwrite the data stored in that position. If the array contains only pointers, then the data might still exist in memory but can't be accessed through the hash table.

Technical Interview

Be aware of the programming language used during an interview. As pointed out before, low-level programming languages make it possible to access pointers directly. Hence, in such cases, knowing that removing a pointer to an object *doesn't delete the object or free the associated memory* is a key distinction. Failing to free the memory that is no longer needed leads to one of the many problems in memory management, called memory leakage.

On the other hand, although high-level programming languages do not explicitly mention pointers, you should know if parameters are passed to a function by value or reference. The use of parameters by reference is almost the same as using pointers, but you do not have to worry about memory leakage. Nevertheless, if you understand that a function might be using pointers "under the hood," you might solve unexpected behaviors that otherwise are very complicated to understand.

Search Keys in Hash Tables

When searching for a key in a hash table, a pointer to the requested element is provided; since the hash function is to provide quick access to the position associated with a key value, this operation can be performed in $O(1)$. Below you can see an implementation of the search operation.

```
search(H, key)
    hash_code = H.hash_function(key)
    idx = hash_code mod H.m
    return H.data_array[idx]
```

Once you have access to the associated data, it is possible to modify the fields. Notice that with the code provided in this section, it is possible to make small modifications to the hash table data structure to achieve more specific objectives, such as editing only one field of the associated data.

Suppose you have an image represented as a multidimensional array of integers from 0 to 31. That means that to each pair of indices i and j, there is another associated array of numbers (r, g, b). This three-element vector (r, g, b) represents a pixel of an image, where the color displayed is a combination of red, green, and blue according to the values in the three-element vector. You can see how such an image would look rendered by your monitor if encoded in an RGB scheme in **Figure 7-10**.

Figure 7-10   An example of a 128×128 image encoded in RGB using 5 bits

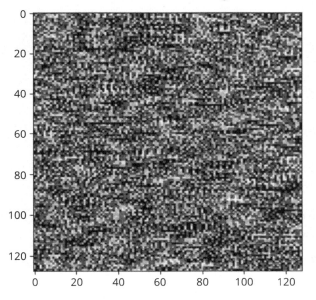

Suppose that you are precisely interested in the colors black (0,0,0), white (31, 31, 31), red (31, 0, 0), and blue (0, 0, 31). In the image, analysis is common to compute a frequency histogram. A **frequency histogram** is a function or table that counts how many times certain values repeat in an object. For example, you might be interested in computing a frequency histogram for the colors black, white, red, blue, and others for a given image img. You can see such a frequency histogram shown in **Figure 7-11**.

Figure 7-11 The result of counting how many times the colors black, white, red, blue, and other appear in the pixels that compose the image shown in Figure 7-10. Such counting is called a frequency histogram

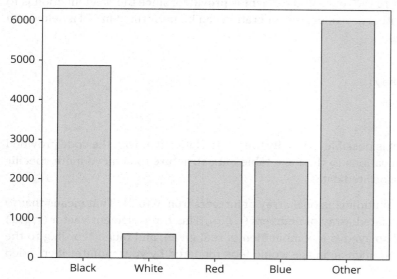

A hash table with perfect hashing is an excellent tool for computing the desired histogram. A handcrafted hash function such as the following can be used for simplicity.

```
color_hash(color)
    if color = [0, 0, 0]
        return 0 ;; black color
    if color = [31, 31, 31]
        return 1 ;; white color
    if color = [31, 0, 0]
        return 2 ;; red color
    if color = [0, 0, 31]
        return 3 ;; blue color
    return 4 ;; Any other color
```

Once a perfect hashing has been constructed, it is possible to compute the histogram traversing the array of colors and adding all the values. To hold the desired data, you can use a user-defined data type and a hash table.

The computation is the most natural part of the code, shown below, and a bar plot of the result is in Figure 7.11.

```
type color_bin:
    fields
        name  ;; The color name
        count ;; How many pixels of that color have been found
        RGB   ;; the RGB representation
```

```
freq_hist = new hash_table(hash_function,
                                   color_hash,
                                   m = 5)


new_color = new color_bin(name = "black",
                          count = 0,
                          RGB = [0, 0, 0])

insert(freq_hist, new_color)

new_color = new color_bin(name = "white",
                          count = 0,
                          RGB = [31, 31, 31])

insert(freq_hist, new_color)

new_color = new color_bin(name = "red",
                          count = 0,
                          RGB = [31, 0, 0])

insert(freq_hist, new_color)

new_color = new color_bin(name = "blue",
                          count = 0,
                          RGB = [0, 0, 31])

insert(freq_hist, new_color)

new_color = new color_bin(name = "other",
                          count = 0,
                          RGB = Null)

insert(freq_hist, new_color)


for i = 0 to 63 step 1
   for j = 0 to 63 step 1
      color = search(freq_hist, img[i, j])
      color.count = color.count + 1
```

Notice that the main advantage of the use of a hash function in this implementation is that the innermost part of the for loop is executed in constant time. Without using a hash function, it will only require four comparisons to associate the color with the appropriate color count. But in other cases, for example, when counting all possible colors, the total number of comparisons would be $256 \times 256 \times 256 = 16777216$, which is more comparisons than the total number of pixels. In such cases, the reduction of complexity by the use of hash functions is significant.

Quick Check 7-2

What is the complexity of deleting an element from a hash table? Assume perfect hashing.

Answer: $O(1)$

Since the deletion of an element requires finding the corresponding key-value pair in the data array and setting the corresponding position to Null, it follows that the complexity is the same as the one for searching, that is, $O(1)$.

7.3 Hash Functions and Hash Codes

This section discusses common strategies to generate hash codes that are of general use and have been proven to work well in practice.

The strategies described in this section focus on two basic data types: integers and strings. One more strategy is to combine different hash codes. This is because every user-defined data type that might be used as a key is composed of those two data types.

It might seem that real or floating-point numbers are missing, but, given the fact that floating-point numbers are affected by rounding errors, it is not possible to use hash functions effectively on them.

Hash Functions for Integer Keys

When working with integer keys, one way to produce hash codes is by using modular hashing. **Modular hashing** uses the residue of a key modulus m, where parameter m is related to the size of the array used to implement the hash table. To reduce the possibility of collisions, a parameter k is used. The precise definition of the hash function is as follows:

$$h(x) = (kx) \bmod m$$

Using a value of $m = 29$ and $k = 7$, you can see the result of the previous function for a set of keys in **Table 7-3**.

Table 7-3   Key values and the corresponding hash code for each one. Notice that there are two collisions in the hash codes for the keys 101 and 9381

x	10	101	1212	102817	9181	9381	817161
kx	70	707	8484	719719	64267	65667	5720127
h(x)	12	11	16	26	3	11	22

To choose the parameter m, one heuristic is choosing the size of the array of the hash table. For the parameter k, the best option is to use a random number.

Since most of the time you will not know what key values will be used in advance, it is hard to design a hash function or choose parameters that produce a perfect hashing or something as close as possible. Using random numbers in some form, the parameters have shown to be a good choice in practice.

Another way to introduce some degree of randomness is the mid-square method. The **mid-square method** is an algorithm to produce a hash code by squaring the key value and using the middle digits as hash code.

For the mid-square algorithm, you must choose a number of digits r to choose from the square. After that, the key value is squared, and the r digits in the middle are used as hash code, as shown in **Table 7-4**.

Table 7-4 A set of integer keys and the hash codes for a parameter $r = 3$

x	10	101	1212	102817	9181	9381	817161
square	100	10201	1468944	10571335489	84290761	88003161	667752099921
$h(x)$	100	20	689	133	290	3	520

Notice that in cases where the length of the square n is such that $n - r$ is odd, then the right part is given one more digit of length. For example, for 84290761, there are $\dfrac{8-3}{2} = 2$ digits at the left and 3 digits at the right. The mid-square procedure can be used several times, which leads to a lower probability of collision due to the randomness introduced by the square operation.

> ## Quick Check 7-3
>
> What is the value of the mid-square hash with $r = 3$ for the key $x = 1256$?
>
> **Answer: 775**
>
> The square of $x = 1256$ is 1577536. Since the length of the square is 7, then the mid-square value is the one beginning after the second position, that is, 775.

Polynomial Hash Codes

Polynomial hash codes are an algorithm to compute hash codes for strings that converts each character into a numerical value and then computes a polynomial function using the numerical value of each character as coefficients.

For simplicity, suppose that only the letters a, e, i, o, and u are used. By assigning the numeric values as shown in **Table 7-5**, the hash code requires a parameter p that is usually chosen as a large prime number.

Table 7-5 Numeric value assigned to each letter to compute the polynomial hash code of strings

character	a	e	i	o	u
value	0	1	2	3	4

Once the string of characters $\omega = a_0 a_1 a_2 \cdots a_{N-1}$ has been transformed to an array of integer values `X = [n1, n2, …, nN]`, the hash code is computed by the following equation.

$$h(\omega) = \sum_{i=0}^{N-1} X[i]p^i$$

For example, using $p = 7$ for the string $\omega =$ "aaei," the computation of the polynomial hash code is as follows:

1. From the string, an array of integers is computed for $\omega =$ "aaei." The array is X = [0, 0, 1, 2].
2. Next, the polynomial is computed:

$$h(\omega) = 0 \cdot 7^0 + 0 \cdot 7^1 + 1 \cdot 7^2 + 2 \cdot 7^3 = 735$$

Hashing Composite Keys

When using a key that has several fields, the first step would be to compute a hash code for each field that consists of an integer value. A common strategy to create a hash code for the integer fields is called a folding method. **Folding method** refers to a way to combine all different keys though an arithmetic operation and then reduce it using modulo m, where m is a parameter based on the length of the data array.

For example, suppose that a key value is composed of a name, surname, and country code. The first step to compute a hash code using the folding method would be to hash each field into a numeric value. Consider a record of a person named Melinda, surname Pack, and country code 612. Suppose it is converted using a polynomial hash function for the string fields and nothing for the numeric field into (19291, 2921, 612). Using a parameter $m = 111$, the resulting hash code is:

$$h(x) = (19291 + 2921 + 612) \bmod 111 = 69$$

Another option is using a variation of polynomial hashing. Once the composite key value is transformed into an array of integers using other hash functions, the procedure is the same as for the integer array generated in the polynomial hashing for strings.

Note	You should be careful when using hash functions because there is more than one kind. The functions discussed in this chapter are designed to be used with hash tables or indices. But other types of hash functions have different purposes.
	Another type of hash function is a cryptographically secure hash function. A **cryptographically secure hash function** always generates a fixed-length hash code from arbitrary data. The key point for a cryptographically secure hash function is that the probability of artificially creating a collision is very low.
	Cryptographically secure hash functions can be used to sign a document, preventing a third party from altering its content. This is done by computing a cryptographically secure hash code for the complete message and storing it to validate the document's authenticity. If someone alters the content of the message, the resulting function won't be the same. Another application is when storing a password in a database, it is common to store the hash code instead of the plaintext password. In such cases, only the hash code is visible even if someone gains access to the file with the passwords. By design, it is very hard to find a text whose hash code is the same as the one stored.

7.4 Compressing Hash Codes

The previous section described some techniques for computing integer hash codes. A key characteristic for keeping a fast searching, insertion, and deletion is that the hash code should point directly to the position in the data array associated with the key value.

The functions described in the previous section generate an integer hash code, but a hash code might need to be in the adequate range to be used directly into the data array of the hash table. One way to solve this is to use a modulo operator directly, in the same manner as it was done in Table 7-2. Unfortunately, this simple method usually produces a high number of collisions.

Hence, it is necessary to apply some procedure to reduce the hash code into a range of values adequate for the hash table at hand. **Compressing hash codes** refers to reducing an integer hash code or key into a given range, reducing the number of possible collisions.

Residue or Division Method

The simplest way to reduce a hash code is using modulo division with m, where m is the array's size. To reduce the potential of collision, it is possible to use a random parameter k and compute the compressed hash code as follows:

$$h(x) = k \pmod{m}$$

When you do not have much information on the keys, the best bet is to randomly choose k as one of the values from 1 to m-1.

Multiplication Method

Before describing the method, it is necessary to introduce the floor and fractional part functions. The **floor function** denoted by $\lfloor x \rfloor$ is the integer k such that $k \leq x < k + 1$. Below are some examples of the floor function applied to several numbers.

$$\lfloor 1.212 \rfloor = 1 \quad \lfloor 3.712 \rfloor = 3 \quad \lfloor 9.9991 \rfloor = 9 \quad \lfloor 0.212 \rfloor = 0$$

The **fractional part function** denoted by $\{x\}$ is defined as $\{x\} = x - \lfloor x \rfloor$; that is, the part left after the floor is removed. As its name indicates, you can think of it as leaving only the digits after the decimal point. You can see some examples below. They are the same numbers used in the example for the floor function so that you can relate the two functions.

$$\{1.212\} = 0.212 \quad \{3.712\} = 0.712 \quad \{9.9991\} = 0.9991 \quad \{0.212\} = 0.212$$

The multiplication method uses a real number $0 < A < 1$ as a parameter and the size of the target array m. The computation is as follows:

$$h(x) = \lfloor m\{Ax\} \rfloor$$

So first, the integer key x is multiplied by A, then its fractional part is extracted. At last, the value is multiplied by m, and the floor function is applied. One great advantage of this method is that it seems to produce good results independently of the choice of m as long as m is a relatively large number.

For the value of A, a common value is:

$$A = \frac{\sqrt{5} - 1}{2} \approx 0.6180339887$$

Table 7-6 shows the result for $m = 31$ and several key values.

Table 7-6   The hash code for several different integer values using the multiplication method

x	10	11	21	71	102	9381	817161
Ax	6.18033989	6.79837388	12.9787138	43.8804132	63.0394668	5797.77685	505033.272
{Ax}	0.18033989	0.79837388	0.97871376	0.8804132	0.03946685	0.77684799	0.27224008
$\lfloor m\{Ax\} \rfloor$	5	24	30	27	1	24	8

Quick Check 7-4

What is the value of the multiplication compression for $x = 87$? Use a parameter of $m = 37$ and $A = 0.6180339887$.

Answer: 28

The answer follows these computations:

$$Ax = 53.7689570169$$
$$\{Ax\} = 0.7689570169$$
$$m\{Ax\} = 28.4514096253$$
$$[m\{Ax\}] = 28$$

Note	The value

$$A = \frac{\sqrt{5} - 1}{2} \approx 0.6180339887$$

is the inverse of $\phi = \frac{\sqrt{5} + 1}{2}$, known as the golden ratio. The golden ratio is related to the Fibonacci sequence, and the proportion between two consecutive Fibonacci numbers approaches the golden ratio as the numbers become larger. The golden ratio is also important in art where it seems that making some proportions close to the golden ratio makes them more appealing. In mathematics it is a common proportion used in search processes. It is possible to split a sorted sequence in a golden ratio proportion instead of two, as in binary search, and get better results in the searching algorithm.

7.5 Handling Hash Collisions

A collision occurs when two different key values have the same hash code or the same index associated with the data array of a hash table. Even with a good hash function where you do not know exactly all the keys to be stored, the possibility of a collision still exists.

To handle a collision, there are two types of approaches:

- **Chaining** is a technique where collisions are handled using a pointer from the array to a separate data structure. You can see a depiction of chaining in **Figure 7-12**.

- **Open addressing** is a technique where a collision is handled by assigning a different array position to the colliding key value. Of course, there is a determined procedure that allows you to search for every key value, even if a collision exists. This is done by creating a sequence of values for each hash code. The sequence is called a probe, usually denoted by $h_0, h_1, \ldots$.

When searching for a specific key value, if the space associated with h_0 is filled with a different key value, then the space h_1 is tested. In case the space associated with h_1 is not the required key value, then the space h_2 is tested. This process is repeated until the desired value is found or there are no more elements in the probing sequence to be tested.

Figure 7-12   A hash table where collisions are resolved using chaining. In this case, the external data structure used to solve the collision is a linked list

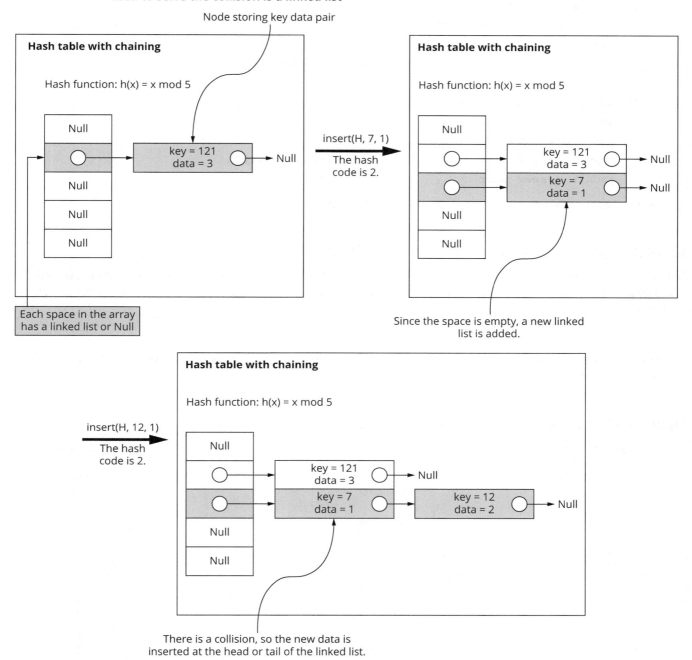

Solving Collisions with Chaining

Chaining is a technique for resolving collisions where all colliding elements are stored in a single linked list. When using this technique to solve collision, each place in the data array stores the head of a linked list. Each time a new element is inserted into the hash table, it is inserted into the linked list corresponding to the index associated with the hash code of its key.

The following code shows an implementation of a hash table that handles collisions by chaining.

```
chained_hash_insert(H, key, data)
    hash_code = H.hash_function(key)
    idx = hash_code mod H.m
    insert_llist(H.data_array[idx], new pair(key,data))


chained_hash_search(H, key)
    hash_code = H.hash_function(key)
    idx = hash_code mod H.m
    answer_pair = llist_search(H.data_array[idx], key)
    return answer_pair
```

Notice that the operations are based on a linked list's search and insert operations.

Open Addressing Using Linear Probing

When using **linear probing**, an additional parameter k is used. Now the computation of the corresponding position is made with a hash function $h(x)$, called an **auxiliary hash function**, and m the length of the data array of the hash table as follows:

$$h(x,n) = (h(x) + kn) \bmod m$$

The auxiliary hash functions can be given by any type of hash function. You can see an example of how linear probing works in **Figure 7-13**.

Figure 7-13 The process of insertion in case of collision when using linear probing

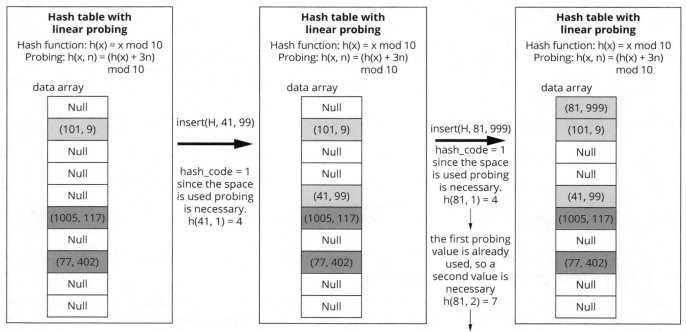

Notice how the probing sequence takes all index values. For example, when $m = 10$ and $k = 3$, you can see the sequence of probing values for each value of x from 0 to 9 in **Table 7-7**.

Table 7-7 Each column of the table shows the probing sequence for a different value of x

x/n	0	1	2	3	4	5	6	7	8	9
0	0	1	2	3	4	5	6	7	8	9
1	3	4	5	6	7	8	9	0	1	2
2	6	7	8	9	0	1	2	3	4	5
3	9	0	1	2	3	4	5	6	7	8
4	2	3	4	5	6	7	8	9	0	1
5	5	6	7	8	9	0	1	2	3	4
6	8	9	0	1	2	3	4	5	6	7
7	1	2	3	4	5	6	7	8	9	0
8	4	5	6	7	8	9	0	1	2	3
9	7	8	9	0	1	2	3	4	5	6

Quick Check 7-5

For $x = 7$, $k = 11$, and $m = 20$, what are the first four terms of the probing sequence using linear probing?

Answer: 7, 18, 9, 0

$$h(7,0) = (7 + 11 \cdot 0) \bmod 20 = 7$$
$$h(7,1) = (7 + 11 \cdot 1) \bmod 20 = 18$$
$$h(7,2) = (7 + 11 \cdot 2) \bmod 20 = 29 \bmod 20 = 9$$
$$h(7,0) = (7 + 11 \cdot 3) \bmod 20 = 40 \bmod 20 = 0$$

Note | Implementing delete when using open addressing is more complicated than for the perfect hashing case. When using probing, it is necessary to mark a place as used before. Otherwise, the searching would stop at that position; however, there might be more used positions of the probing sequence.

Open Addressing Using Double Hashing

As its name indicates, **double hashing** uses two auxiliary hash functions $h_1(x)$ and $h_2(x)$. To compute the probing sequence of hash codes, the following equation is used:

$$h(x, n) = [h_1(x) + nh_2(x)] \bmod m$$

Double hashing has almost the same characteristics as a random function. In **Figure 7-14**, you can see the probing sequences for a set of keys that collide.

Figure 7-14 Some values for the probing sequence in a double hashing scheme using modular hashing functions as a base

$h_1(x) = 3x \mod 20$ $h_2(x) = 7x \mod 20$

$h(x, n) = (h_1(x) + nh_2(x)) \mod 20$

	n = 0	n = 1	n = 2	n = 3
x = 11	13	10	7	4
x = 21	3	10	17	4
x = 72	16	0	4	8

7.6 Hash Efficiency

One of the key points in using a hash table is that insertion and searching under ideal conditions can achieve constant time complexity $O(1)$.

The previous sections show that collisions might interfere with the ideal. Hash tables are extremely efficient, given that the conditions discussed in the previous section are met. When a collision occurs, additional steps other than access to the array are necessary. Fortunately, a good hash function that produces the indices on the array with almost the same probability for all indices allows for a very efficient data structure.

Static Hashing

When the complete set of keys is small and known beforehand, the programmer can write a simple hash function that assigns every possible key to a single index. In such cases, the hash key is static and the hashing is perfect. When hashing is perfect, the searching and insertion time are $O(1)$.

In a previous section, it was mentioned that algorithms exist that receive a set of keys as input and then provide a set of parameters for modular hash functions that produce perfect hashing as output. In such cases, the cost of writing the hash function is absorbed by the computer, but it is still necessary to know the complete set of keys to be used and to invest the resources necessary to build the perfect hashing function.

Collisions and Efficiency in Chaining

Notice that in the worst case, the searching operation takes $O(\alpha_k)$, where α_k is the length of the linked list stored at the position k on the array. Supposing that $N > m$ keys are stored in the hash table, then $\alpha_k \approx \alpha = N / m > 1$. This parameter α is called the **loading factor** of the hash table.

So, for example, if you expect to have 128 different key values using chaining and use a data array of 32, then the loading factor $\alpha = 128/32 = 4$. That means that on average you might expect that when inserting 128 values into the table, each position holds a linked list with approximately four elements each.

The performance of the hash table will depend on how well distributed the hash codes are. If, due to a bad design or luck, all key values have the same hash code, then instead of working with a hash table, the result will be the same as using a linked list.

Collisions and Efficiency in Open Addressing

To use open addressing, the number of available places in the array m must be larger than or equal to the number of keys N. In such cases, the load factor $\alpha = N / m \leq 1$.

To avoid the possibility that the hash table is full, it is convenient to have an $\alpha < 1$.

Assuming the hash function uniformly distributes the hash values, each key will have approximately the same number of collisions. It is possible to prove that under such circumstances, the number of probes required is approximately $1/(1-\alpha)$. Hence, the time complexity of searching and inserting will be, on average, $O(1+1/(1-\alpha))$.

Best Practices

In practice it is considered ideal to use a loading factor of less than one; that is, to have more spaces in the data array than keys present in the hash table. The idea is to reduce the probability of collision as much as possible. In most cases a good value for the loading factor is 0.75. That means that the data array should be only up to 75% full.

When the number of keys in the hash table grows larger than the desired loading factor, a strategy commonly used is to construct a new hash table with a larger size for the data array. This keeps the searching process efficient because it reduces the probability of using chaining or probing; although this approach should be weighted based on the conditions of the problem at hand. It might be that the hash table won't grow any larger, in such a case it might not be worth it to go through the process of creating a new hash table and copying all data.

Note   Notice that the complexity of the open addressing is based on the fact that the probability of getting an index is evenly distributed. A phenomenon occurring when the distribution of the index values is not evenly distributed is that after the first collision occurs more key values collide with values used in the probing sequence. These values colliding and requiring probing of more positions are called a cluster. The formation of clusters in hash tables is a complicated problem to solve, but it could be prevented with a hash function that behaves almost randomly or with hash codes distributed evenly.

Summary

- Arrays are fast, stable structures. It is only possible to access them through the position index of the desired data.

- An associative array is an ADT that extends the benefits of an array by allowing it to access data from a key value. This way, it is possible to organize information like a phone book, where you get the number and related data from a name.

- One way to implement an associative array is using a normal array and creating a function that associates an index to each possible key value where the data associated with a key value might be found.

- Such functions that transform key values (that might be of any user-defined or built-in data type) into an integer are called hash functions. These hash functions are combined with a data array to build an associative array called a hash table.

- Hash tables are ideal when the number of keys used is small compared to the set of all possible keys and want almost equal random access to the data.

- Hash tables implemented using arrays can provide equal random time access, provided there is a good-enough hash function. A good hash function avoids collisions. A collision is when two different key values are associated with the same hash code.

- It is possible to have a perfect hashing function, which means there are never collisions. These are, however, usually built from a perfectly known set of key values.

- An associative array and hence a hash table have the basic insertion, deletion, and search operations.

- Hash functions for any user-defined data type can be built from other hash functions defined for basic data types. The main data types used in keys are strings and integers. For integers, the simplest and very effective hash function is modular hashing, defined by:

$$h(x) = (k\ x) \bmod m$$

- To add more randomness, there is also the mid-square method. The mid-square method can be applied several times. Each time it is combined in some way it seems to produce more random patterns. You can see this being effectively applied when using double hashing.

- For string values, a common strategy is to use a mapping from the set of possible characters to a set of integers. In other words, each character in the string is assigned a numeric value. Then a polynomial-like function is applied. The method is known as polynomial hash coding.

- Having a way to transform all integer and string fields into a hash code, it is possible to create a hash function for the whole key. One method to do that is folding, which consists of combining the hash code of the fields into a single number through an arithmetic operation such as adding, multiplying, or modular arithmetic.

- Strategies such as mid-square and polynomial hash produce integers that might be too large for the associated data array of a hash table. To make use of the hash code as an index in the array, an extra compression step is necessary. Two very effective strategies for compressing the hash code are the residue (also called division) method and the multiplication method.

- There are two general strategies to use when facing a collision: chaining and open addressing.

- In chaining, an auxiliary data structure stores all the key-data pairs that have the same code. Usually, a linked list is used, but more sophisticated data structures could also be used.

- In open addressing, when a collision occurs, a new index is chosen from a sequence called a probing sequence. In this way, no auxiliary data structure is used but only the data array associated with the hash table. Two ways to produce the probing sequence are by using linear probing or double hashing.

- Hash tables are very efficient in searching and inserting, even when collisions occur. When using a handwritten or static hash function, perfect hashing is ensured and a constant running time is always guaranteed.

- In the cases of chaining, it might be necessary to traverse an additional data structure but smaller than the complete table. The quotient between the number of keys to store and the size of the data array is called the loading factor of the hash table. When the loading factor is larger, the number of collisions increases.

- When using open addressing, the complexity is also related to the loading factor. In this case, the estimation of the running time is more complex but it relates to $O(1 + 1/(1 - \alpha))$, where α is the loading factor.

Key Terms

associative array	floor function	linear probing
auxiliary hash function	folding method	loading factor
chaining	fractional part function	mid-square method
collision	frequency histogram	modular hashing
compressing hash codes	hash code	open addressing
cryptographically secure hash function	hash function	perfect hash function
double hashing	hash table	polynomial hash codes
	index	

Review Questions

1. In which of the following structures can you use string values as keys to access associated data?

   a. Linked list

   b. Array

   c. Associative array

   d. Hash table

2. Suppose that `h(x) = len(x)` is a hash function used to create hash codes for the key values `"val"`, `"vector"`, `"comm"`, `"cat"`, `"commt"`. How many collisions occur?

   a. 0

   b. 1

   c. 2

   d. 3

3. Which of the following is the main reason for not using hash functions with floating point numbers?

   a. They are too big to use hash functions.

   b. Nobody will make a search based on a decimal value.

   c. The rounding error might lead to inconsistencies in hashing.

   d. Hash functions only work with integer keys.

4. Which of the following is the recommended option for the parameter k in modular hashing?

   a. Zero

   b. The size of the data array

   c. Power of 2

   d. A random integer

5. Which of the following best describes the purpose of compressing hash codes?

   a. Save storage space

   b. Create an index appropriate for the data array

   c. Reduce the number of possible collisions

   d. Increase the randomness of the hash code

6. When using open addressing, which of the following must be a characteristic of the load factor α?

   a. It must be exactly 1.

   b. It must be a lot larger than 1.

   c. It must be smaller than 1.

   d. Open addressing doesn't have a loading factor.

7. Why is polynomial hashing using a parameter $p = 0$ not ideal?

8. Using mid-square hashing for $x = 81$ and the middle two digits, what is the hash code for x?

9. Using the multiplication method for hash compression, what is the index associated with $x = 282$ using $A = 0.61803$ and $m = 64$?

10. Suppose that you use linear probing:

$$h(x)_n = (h(x) + n) \bmod m$$

   with $m = 5$ and $x = 12$ with hash code 4. What is the probing sequence generated by the key x?

Programming Problems

1. Implement the search function for a hash table that uses chaining with a linked list. **(LO 7.1, 7.2, 7.3, 7.5)**

2. Create a user-defined data type to identify college courses as keys in a hash table. The courses have a department code given as a string in uppercase letters such as "MATH," "CHEM," "PHY," "MD." The courses also have a code number like 101, 203, and 302 and a field that specifies whether the course is an honors course. Combine the `poly_hash(txt)`, `hash0(txt)`, and an integer value to produce a hash value for the data type defined using folding and an array size of 2048. **(LO 7.1, 7.3, 7.5)**

3. In the **Ch7_votes.csv** data file is a list of votes in an assembly to elect first, second, and third place for a prize. There are 10 candidates. Use a hash table to compute how many votes each candidate receives. **(LO 7.1, 7.2, 7.3)**

    To access data files, sign up or sign in at http://www.cengage.com/ and search for the Additional Student Resources folder of the Instructor Center, or contact your instructor.

4. Suppose the user-defined data type product contains the fields department, inventory, and state. All products are stored in a hash table with a key value and an integer product code. Suppose that the array `state_list` provides all the possible values for the state field. Create an index for the hash table based on the state using another hash table; that is, an associative array that points from each state to a list of pointers of all products in a given state. **(LO 7.1, 7.2, 7.5)**

Projects

Project 7-1: Extended Hash Table Operations

(LO 7.1, 7.2, 7.5) A hash table is very efficient for basic operations, but there are some other useful operations that are desirable for it. Given a hash table that solves collisions using chaining, write a function that returns all the key values present in the hash table.

Project 7-2: Hash with Linear Probing

(LO 7.5) Create an implementation of a hash table that uses linear probing to handle collisions. Implement the insert and search operations on it. Recall sending an error code when the hash table is full.

Project 7-3: Studying Collisions

(LO 7.3, 7.4) In the **Ch7_names.csv** data file is a list of names. Implement a hash function that combines polynomial hashing and mid-square hashing. As mentioned in the chapter, the mid-square can be applied several times. Apply the mid-square after the polynomial hashing zero, one, two, and three times. Compress the hash code to an array of 128. Count the number of collisions in each case.

To access data files, sign up or sign in at http://www.cengage.com/ and search for the Additional Student Resources folder of the Instructor Center, or contact your instructor.

Project 7-4: Creating Perfect Hashing

(LO 7.1, 7.3, 7.4) Suppose that an array with all the possible key values is given. For simplicity, suppose that the values are all different integers. Write a program that computes up to 31 different values for the parameter *m* and chooses the number with the least number of collisions, assuming that the value of the parameter *m* is approximately two times the size of the key array. To compute the compression, use the multiplication method for a data array of the same size as the key array.

Chapter 8

Trees

Learning Objectives

Upon completion of this chapter, you will be able to:

8.1   Discuss different types of tree data structures.

8.2   Identify in-order, pre-order, and post-order traversal tree processes.

8.3   Design and implement a binary search tree.

8.4   Design and implement an AVL tree.

8.5   Construct an algorithm for adding, removing, and retrieving an element using a heap data structure.

8.6   Integrate the trie data structure for string data storage.

8.1 Introduction to Trees

When working with data, sometimes you need more complex relationships than linear data structures such as lists, queues, or stacks. One such instance is when the information has a hierarchical structure. For example, an organizational chart in a company is usually represented not simply by listing all positions but by listing the position and whom the person in that position should report to. You can see an example of such representation in **Figure 8-1**.

Another example of hierarchical data organization is how files and folders are presented in an operating system. In **Figure 8-2**, you can see a file system representation of the folders and files stored in a computer.

In these cases, the non-linear tree ADT is ideal for organizing the data and keeping the relevant relationships. Trees are a special type of graph, and they share some common terminology. Moreover, some techniques and algorithms applicable to graphs can be used for trees. The next sections present some of the characteristics unique to trees and their applications. In a future chapter, you can find a more in-depth discussion on graphs.

Figure 8-1 An organizational tree representing which employees are under the supervision of whom, or equivalently, to whom each employee should report directly

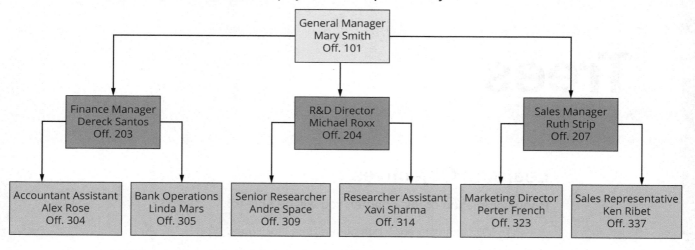

Figure 8-2 A file system organization depicted as a tree in the way it is commonly found in a modern OS

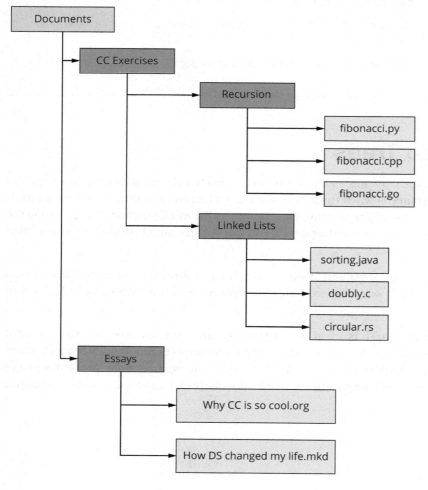

A tree like the ones presented in the previous examples is also a graph, since it is composed of vertices joined by edges. So, you can consider a tree a special type of graph. What characterizes a tree is that any two vertices are joined by exactly one edge. From a theoretical point of view, you can also think of a singly linked list as a tree and a graph. The implementation of linked lists, trees, and graphs significantly differs from the practical perspective.

Main Characteristics of Trees

As noted, a tree is a set of vertices and edges. The **vertices**, also called nodes, hold the data that is stored in the tree, The vertices are joined by edges to other vertices to provide the tree with the hierarchical structure. Hence, an **edge** is characterized by a pair of vertices, the pair that it joins. Each vertex has a set of vertices connected to it called its children. Following a pragmatic convention, `children(v)` is used to refer to the data structure where the children of vertex v are stored. In a tree, there is one vertex that is not a child of any other vertex in the tree. This vertex is called the **root** of the tree. Every other vertex is a child of one other vertex. In such cases, it is said that it is the parent of the vertex, denoted by `p = parent` or `p = parent(v)`. When a vertex has no children, it is called a **leaf**. You can see a depiction of a tree compared with a real tree in **Figure 8-3**.

Figure 8-3   A tree ADT is similar in form to a physical tree, though an ADT tree is usually depicted with the root at the top

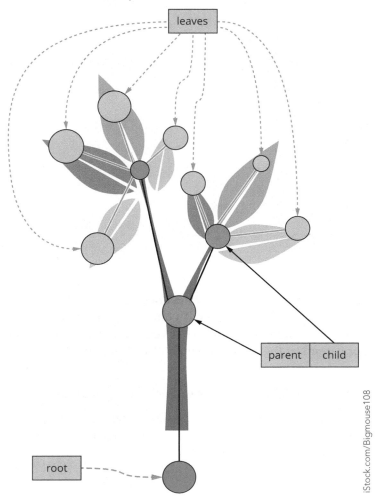

iStock.com/Bigmouse108

Despite the relation of the terminology with parts of a physical tree, it is not common to see a tree depicted as in Figure 8-3. Notice that the properties described in the previous paragraph are abstract and unrelated to how you draw or represent the set of vertices and edges. **Figure 8-4** shows three ways that one tree could be portrayed.

Figure 8-4   Three ways of portraying the same tree. Notice that one of them is not represented in a way easy to recognize as a tree

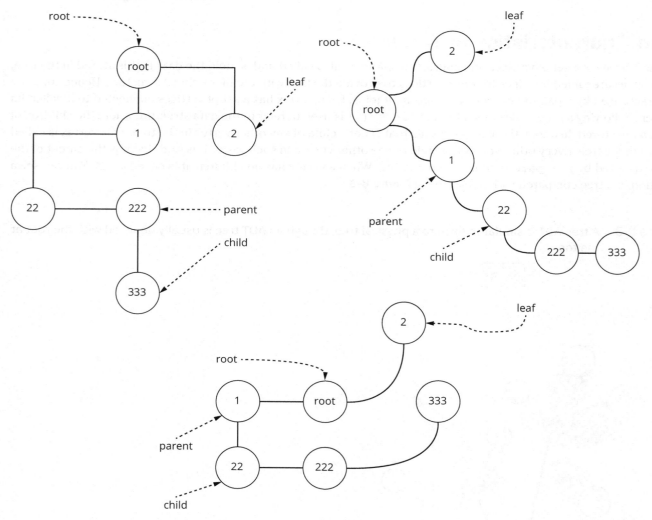

As you can see, drawing the set of vertices and edges in a random place in a plane does not convey the natural organization of trees, such as the ones presented at the beginning of the chapter. A common convention to make such representations easier to read is to represent parents followed by their children in one direction. For example, displaying children below parents from top to bottom, or parents at the right of their children from right to left. You can see such an example in **Figure 8-5**.

In what follows the convention is to draw the root at the top of the tree and draw parents above children.

A point to notice here is that when working with data structures, vertices are not only points but nodes. That means they usually contain user-defined data types useful for a particular application. For instance, in the file system example, each vertex has a name, a type, and a physical location in a hard drive for files.

Figure 8-5   The same tree depicted in different ways. The top two do not follow any convention and the bottom two use the convention of direction from parent to children, but in different orientations

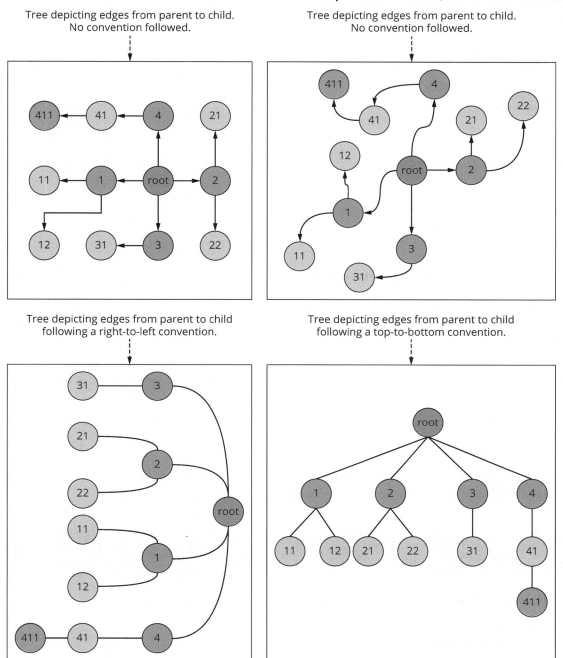

Tree depicting edges from parent to child.
No convention followed.

Tree depicting edges from parent to child.
No convention followed.

Tree depicting edges from parent to child
following a right-to-left convention.

Tree depicting edges from parent to child
following a top-to-bottom convention.

Also, notice that the edges are considered bidirectional, which means they link a parent with its children and a child with its parent. But for some applications, you might have to consider that the link can only connect a parent to their child. For example, when you give a new user permission to modify the files in a folder, you do not want the user to have permission to modify the parent folder. In such cases, it is better to store the information of such permissions with links that work only from parent to child.

A **path** in a tree is a sequence of edges $(v_0, v_1), (v_1, v_2) \dots, (v_{n-1}, v_n)$ where each vertex v_i is parent to the next one v_{i+1}. The **length of a path** is the number of edges, not vertices used. Thus, the length of the path is n. It is also possible to describe paths from children to parents, as it might be convenient sometimes. Notice that it is not always possible to build a path joining any two vertices of a tree. You can see such a situation illustrated in **Figure 8-6**.

Figure 8-6   It is impossible to create a path to join two vertices if they are at the same level, according to the definition of a path for a tree

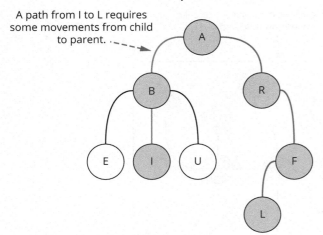

A path from I to L requires some movements from child to parent.

In order to describe some algorithms with trees, it is necessary to introduce some terminology. Given a tree T:

- The **descendants** of a vertex v are those vertices u such that there is a path from v to u. The set of descendants of v is referred to as `descendants(v)`.

- The **ancestors** of v are those vertices p such that there is a path from p to v. The set of ancestors of v is referred to as `ancestors(v)`.

- The **siblings** of a vertex v are those that have the same parent. The set of siblings of v are referred to as `siblings(v)`.

- A **subtree** of tree T is a tree composed of a vertex v of T, its descendants, and all the edges relating them.

Figure 8-7 illustrates these definitions.

All the previous definitions give rise to relationships between the vertices. For example, in Figure 8-7, 8 and 12 are siblings. These siblings 8 and 12 have a common ancestor, and so on.

Quick Check 8-1

Consider the tree depicted in **Figure 8-8**. Which of the following is accurate about the tree?

> **1.** Vertex X has 3 descendants and 2 ancestors.
> **2.** Vertex X has 2 descendants and 2 ancestors.
> **3.** Vertex X has 3 descendants and 5 ancestors.
> **4.** Vertex X has 4 descendants and 2 ancestors.

Answer: 4

Notice that from the root to the vertex X there are only two nodes, 2 and 1. Those are its ancestors. From X there are paths to 7, 8, 9, and 10. Those are its descendants.

Figure 8-7   Using the top-to-bottom convention to follow the edges from parent to child makes it easier to recognize ancestors and descendants, since the ancestors are at a higher level and the descendants are at a lower level

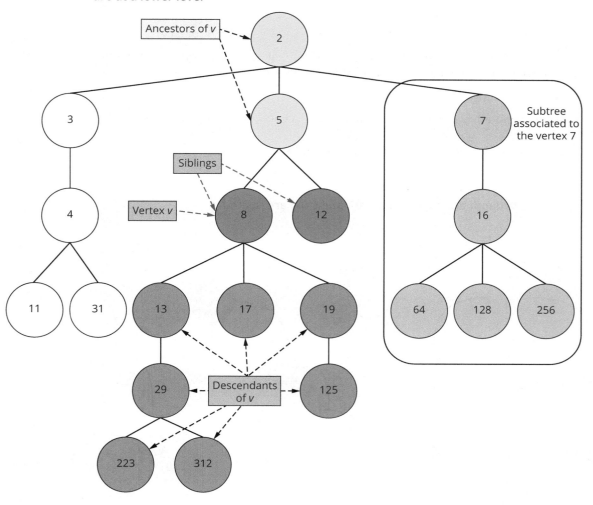

Figure 8-8   Tree used in Quick Check 8-1

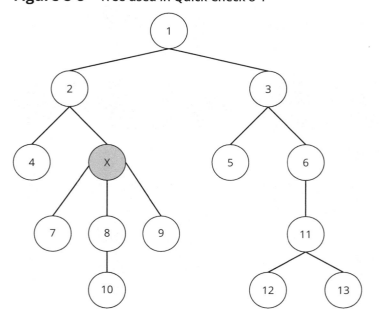

Types of Trees

To classify trees for purposes of studying algorithms, it is convenient to define some quantitative measures. Suppose T is a tree with vertices $\{v_1, v_2, \ldots, v_m\}$ and root r.

- The **depth of a vertex v** is the length of the path from r to v. It is denoted by `depth(v)`.

- The **height of a vertex v**, denoted `height(v)`, is the largest among the lengths of the paths from v to all reachable leaves. For the Null value, its height is considered –1.

- `height(r)` is called the **height of the tree**.

- The **size of a vertex v**, denoted `size(v)`, is the number of descendants of v including itself.

In **Figure 8-9**, you can see these definitions illustrated in two graphs.

Figure 8-9   Notice that the depth and height of parent and child are related

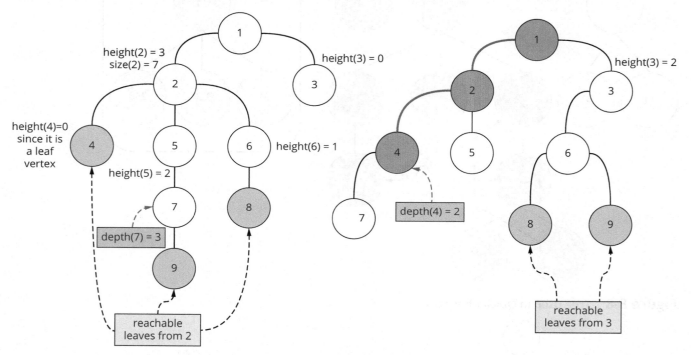

Quick Check 8-2

Consider the graph depicted in **Figure 8-10**. Compute `height(6)`, `size(6)`, and `children(6)`.

Answer: 3, 6, {9}

Notice that the leaf farthest away from the vertex 6 is 16, and the path joining them is 6, 9, 13, 16. The number of edges used is 3. Thus, the length of the path is 3, and hence the height of the vertex 6 is 3. The size of the vertex is the set of all descendants, including the vertex itself, thus 6. Although vertex 6 has more descendants, it is only directly connected to its parent, and vertex 9, thus 9, is its only child.

Figure 8-10   Tree used in Quick Check 8-2

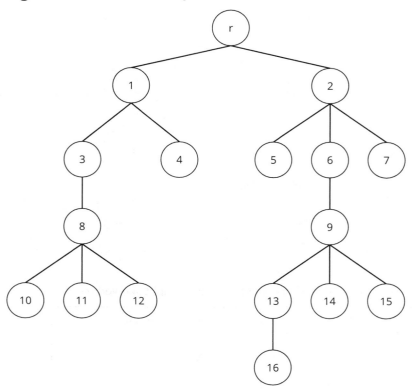

Another concept useful to describe the properties of trees is level. It is said that all vertices with depth k are at level k. For example, in Figure 8-10 you have:

- Vertices at level 1: {1, 2}
- Vertices at level 2: {3, 4, 5, 6, 7}
- Vertices at level 3: {8, 9}
- Vertices at level 4: {10, 11, 12, 13, 14, 15}
- Vertices at level 5: {16}

A tree with the property that each vertex has at most N children is called an **N-ary tree**. A special case is a 2-ary tree called a **binary tree**. In a binary tree, each vertex has at most two children. In such a case, it is common to refer to the children of a vertex as left and right. When depicting a binary tree, the left child is at the left, and the right is at the right. Unlike the binary case for other values of N in an N-ary tree, there is no convention on presenting the children of a vertex. You can see an N-ary tree with $N = 4$ and a binary tree illustrated in **Figure 8-11**.

When every vertex in a tree has at most one child, the tree is called a **skewed tree**. In the case of skewed binary trees, if every vertex with a child has only the left child, then it is called a **left skewed tree**. Similarly, the tree is called a **right skewed tree** if every non-leaf vertex has only its right child. You can see those cases illustrated in **Figure 8-12**.

Note | Notice that a skewed tree can be seen essentially as a singly linked list. If the data is related so that the tree results skew, a linked list might be a better tool than a tree. Implementing a tree requires more technical details than a linked list and uses more memory. Moreover, some care must be taken when considering the data arranged in a tree when using the structure.

Figure 8-11 A N-ary tree with $N = 4$ and a binary tree

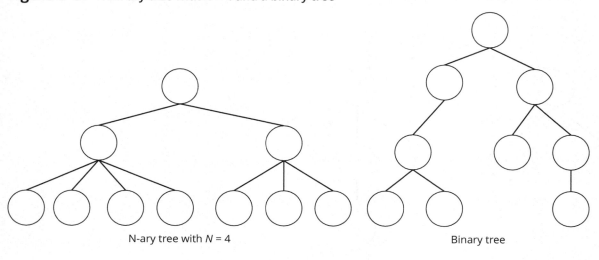

N-ary tree with $N = 4$ Binary tree

Figure 8-12 A skewed tree that is not left or right skewed, a left skewed tree, and a right skewed tree

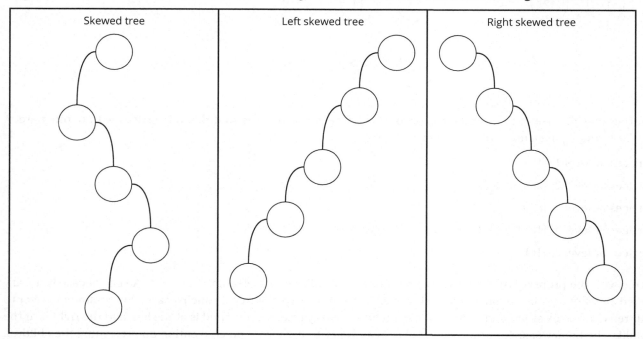

Among the binary trees, some classifications are based on how many children each vertex has. The first is the **full binary tree**. A full binary tree is one with all leaves at the same level, and every non-leaf vertex has exactly two children. The definition implies that if the trees have h levels, then all vertices at the level h are leaves and, at the level $h - 1$, every vertex has exactly two children. Thus, a full binary tree has exactly $2^h - 1$ vertices. You can see the possible full binary trees for several values of h in **Figure 8-13**.

A less restrictive classification is the strict binary tree. A binary tree is a **strict binary tree** if each vertex has exactly two or zero children. Notice that a full binary tree is a strict binary tree. You can see some illustrations of strict and nonstrict binary trees in **Figure 8-14**.

When drawing a binary tree, it is possible to list the vertices at level m from left to right so that you can speak of the position k at level m. You can see this terminology illustrated in **Figure 8-15**.

Figure 8-13   Full binary trees for *h* = 2, 3, and 4

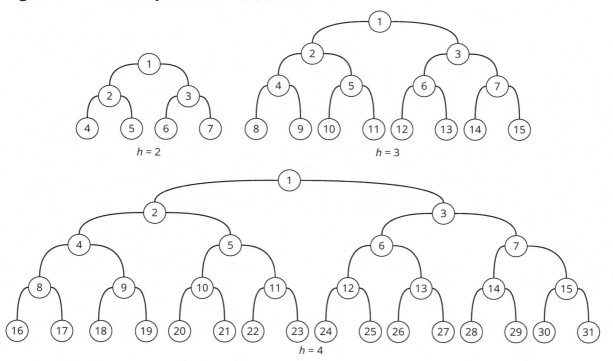

Figure 8-14   Several possible strict binary trees that are not full binary trees, and some nonstrict binary trees

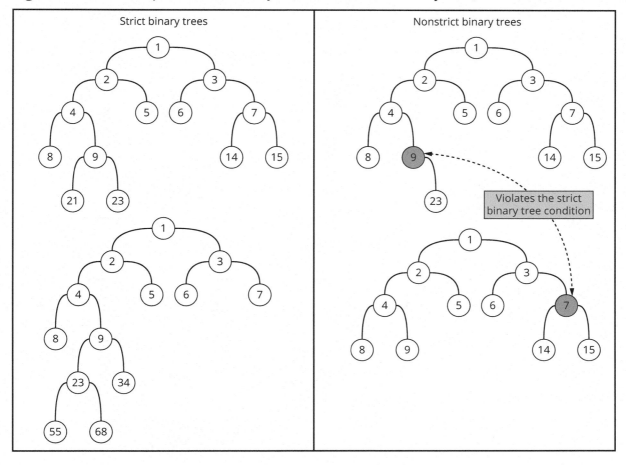

Figure 8-15   The vertices at positions 1 and 2 of level 2, position 4 of level 3, and position 11 of level 4 colored in a binary tree

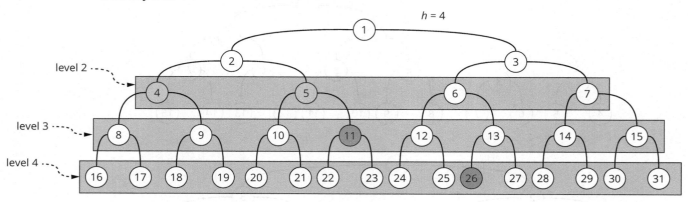

A **complete binary tree** is a tree of height h such that every leaf is at the level $h-1$ or h and that at level h all positions from 1 to k are filled from left to right, while positions $k+1$ to the end are empty. **Figure 8-16** shows three complete binary trees and one incomplete binary tree.

Figure 8-16   To check if a binary tree is complete, it is necessary but not sufficient to check that every vertex that has a right child has a left child

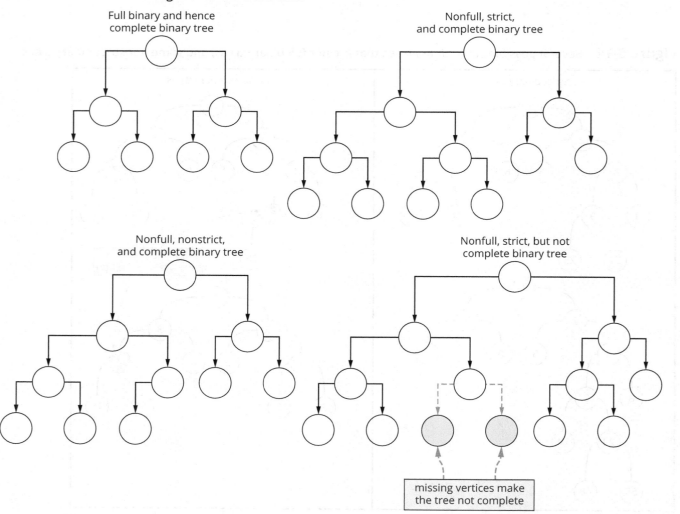

Tree ADT and Implementation

As an ADT, a tree T usually has a set of operations that act on the tree as a whole, but there are also operations that act on each of the vertices individually. The essential operations of an ADT tree are:

- `root(T)` that returns the root of the tree.
- `size(T)` that returns the total number of vertices in the tree.
- `parent(v)` that returns the parent vertex of v.
- `children(v)` that returns a linear data structure, such as an array or list, containing the children of v.
- `is_leaf(v)` that returns True if the vertex v is a leaf and False if not.
- `is_root(v)` that returns True if v is the root vertex and False in other cases.
- `empty(T)` that returns True if the tree T is empty.

It is common to require that a tree ADT has the operations `vertices(T)` that returns a linear data structure with all the vertices of the tree, `depth(v)` that returns the depth of a vertex, and `height(v)`. Although it happens commonly with complex ADTs such as a tree, you can write some operations using others, so authors tend to require the ones that are more convenient for a given set of applications. For example, suppose that you want to represent a file system storage as a tree. In such a system, a non-leaf node represents a folder and a leaf node represents a file. A common operation will be to display all the files and folders in the system. For that propose it is more efficient to use a linear data structure that points to the vertices and helps in the display process. If traversal or verification of certain properties over all vertices is common, it might be convenient to include the `vertices(T)` operation in the implementation of the tree data structure, rather than have it as an implemented function as shown here.

```
list_vertices(v, current_list)
    for x in children(v)
        add(current_list,x)
        list_vertices(x, current_list)


vertices(T)
    r = root(T)
    vertices_llist = new LinkedList()
    addv(vertices_llist, r)
    list_vertices(r, vertices_llist)
    return vertices_llist
```

In a similar way, it is possible to implement `height(v)` as follows:

```
height(v)
    if v = Null
        return -1
    if is_leaf(v)
        return 0
    else
        max_height = 0
        for x in children(v)
            cur_height = height(v)
            if cur_height > max_height
                max_height = cur_height
        return max_height + 1
```

You can see the work of the `height(v)` algorithms illustrated in **Figure 8-17**.

Figure 8-17 Vertices and height can be computed using other operations and recursion

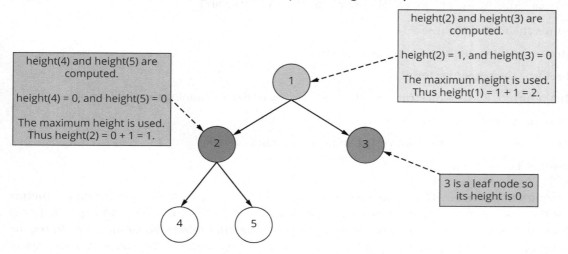

When implementing a tree for a specific application, more information than just the vertex or the edge is often necessary. In such cases, a graph is called a labeled graph when additional information is added to each vertex. In practice, this is achieved by using a node in each vertex. Several key values that might be used for purposes other than identifying a vertex can be stored in the node. For example, in the organizational diagram presented at the beginning of the chapter, each node has much more information, such as the name of the employee in the given position, the office number, and the official title.

Thus, to describe the implementation of a tree, it is better to suppose that each vertex or node will only include a key value or data and information about the links. More fields can be added to the node if necessary for a particular application.

The two implementations discussed here are based on how the node will handle the link information. The first approach is called an **array of pointers implementation**. The array of pointers implementation of a tree uses an array of pointers to store the link to each child of a node. This means that there is a fixed size for the array of children. The size of the array B is called the **branching factor** of the tree, so with a branching factor of B, it is only possible to represent B-ary trees. A declaration for a node in an array of pointers implementation and a tree is as follows.

```
type node
    fields
        data ;; the user defined data type to store the data
        children = new array[B] ;; A fixed size array for each child
        parent = Null ;; pointer to the parent node


type tree
    fields:
        root = Null, B
```

To insert new nodes into a tree, it will be necessary, at least at this stage, to specify to which node the new node is going to be attached and at which position of the array. A procedure to insert a new node could be implemented as follows:

```
insert(parent, new_node, child_num)
    if child_num >= parent.B
        return -1
    parent.children[child_num] = new_node
```

On the other hand, when deleting a node, you need to decide how to proceed with all the node descendants being deleted. The complete subtree associated gets removed. But in some applications the information in the subtree is still necessary, so further modifications to the tree are necessary.

Figure 8-18 shows how a tree can be constructed using the insert procedure for a branching factor of 2.

Figure 8-18   Binary tree constructed using the insert procedure

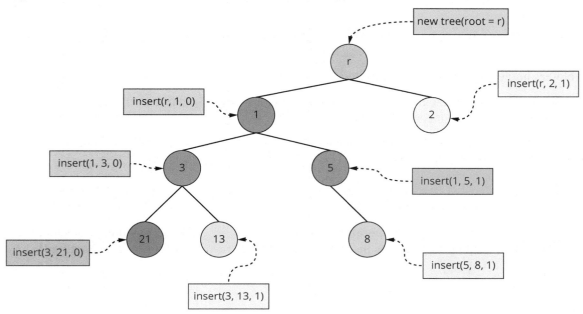

Notice that there is not a single order for using the insertion operations to create a tree.

Quick Check 8-3

Consider the tree depicted in **Figure 8-19**. What does foo(9) return for the following function?

```
foo(v)
    if is_root(v)
        return 1
    return 2*foo(v.parent) + 1
```

Figure 8-19   Binary tree for Quick Check 8-3

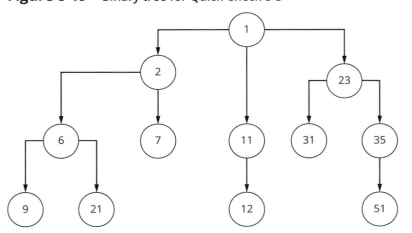

(continues)

The array of pointers implementation has two problems.

- If the branching factor B is large, but if many nodes have fewer children than B, a large portion of the space reserved for the pointers is wasted since all are Null.

- The branching factor is fixed. Thus, if you choose a small B and the needs of your application change, you might face problems since it is impossible to change it.

Another way to implement an N-ary tree is called **leftmost right sibling**. In this approach each node stores two pointers, one to its leftmost child and one to its right sibling. You can see such an implementation in **Figure 8-20**.

The following code implements an insertion operation in a tree using a leftmost right sibling implementation. Notice that the insertion is done sequentially, always inserting a new child to the right of the last one inserted.

```
type node_lmrs
    fields
        data
        left_most = Null
        right_sibling = Null
        parent = Null


insert(parent, new_node)
    curr = parent.left_most
    if curr = Null
        ;; when there are no children new_node
        ;; will be the left most child
        parent.left_most = new_node

    while not curr.right_sibling = Null
        ;; move curr until reach the last child
        ;; that is the one with no right sibling
        curr = curr.right_sibling

    curr.right_sibling = new_node

    new_node.parent = parent
```

The leftmost right sibling approach gives a solution to the problem of deciding the branching factor in advance since it uses a dynamic approach to the number of children a node can have. It also saves memory space since more memory space is added only if necessary.

Figure 8-20   How to implement two trees using the leftmost right sibling approach

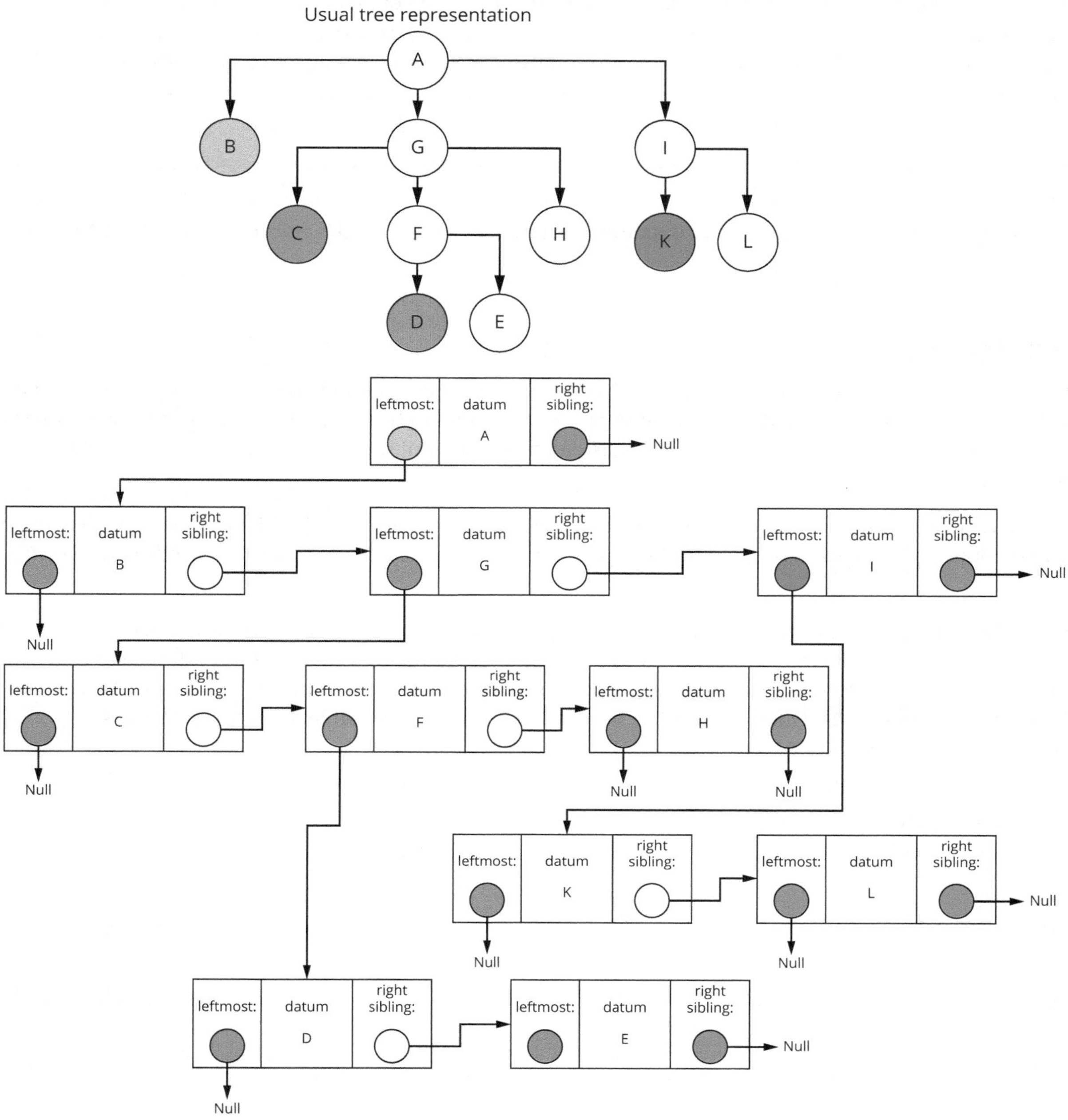

Usual tree representation

![Best Practice banner]

Best Practice

When using a tree to solve a problem, it is worth taking some time to choose the best implementation for the tree. Some aspects to consider are the following.

- Can you use a constant branching factor?
- Do most of the nodes, except leaves, have a number of children close to the branching factor?

(continues)

When the answer to the previous questions is positive, then using an array of pointers for the children is possible and, in most cases, it will be very efficient in terms of memory use and speed because arrays have constant random access time. When using the leftmost right sibling implementation, you gain a dynamic branching factor but searching requires a linear search in the children since they are stored in a linked-list-like structure.

In the case of binary trees, it is customary to simply declare the left and right children as fields of the node data type.

Recursion in Trees

As you might have noticed, operations on trees work well with recursion. For example, to compute the depth of a vertex, it is possible to compute it using the depth of its parent. And to compute the height of a vertex, it is necessary to have the height of its children. In each case, recursive calls can be made until the function reaches a leaf or the root, depending on the problem.

There are two possibilities for using recursion when working with trees: one is to build a tree from the leaves to the root and the second is to build from the root to the leaves in a recursive manner. For simplicity, let's consider only binary trees.

Given an arithmetical expression such as $3^*5 + 7^* (9 - 4)$, it is possible to represent it as an expression tree. An **expression tree** is a tree in which every non-leaf node represents an operation between its two children, and each leaf node represents a value or variable to be operated on. Such constructions are made from leaves to roots. You can see the process illustrated in **Figure 8-21**. Once the tree has been constructed, it is possible to evaluate it recursively from the root to the leaves, as shown in the figure.

Figure 8-21   The expression tree for $3^*5 + 7^* (9 - 4)$

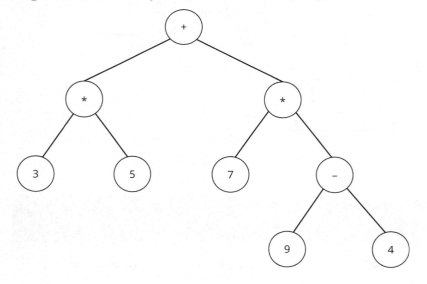

Another example of the recursive nature of building trees is the one used in backtracking or when enumerating a set of possibilities. For example, when analyzing the N-sum problem, a tree structure appears naturally. The N-sum problem is the problem of finding a subset of a set of positive numbers that sum to N. A solution using backtracking requires that you choose some numbers from a given set in such a way that the sum of the elements is N. The backtracking strategy keeps trying possibilities as long as the sum doesn't equal N (this is called a bounding condition). For each stage of testing, two options were used, including the number $X[k]$ or not in the subset. Hence, each new child represents a new subset built from its parent. The left one for the new set includes a number and the right one for a set that doesn't include the number. You can see such a construction illustrated in **Figure 8-22**.

Figure 8-22   A tree that enumerates all subsets of a set of positive integers. Only the colored nodes satisfy the bounding condition for the problem, so they represent the feasible solutions

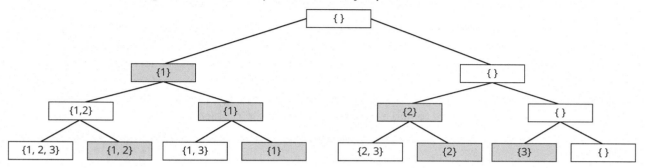

It is possible to think of each child as a subtree when building a tree from the leaves to the root. Thus, it is possible to define functions over a complete tree by recursively defining them over each subtree. The following is an example of how to apply the `invert()` operation over a tree.

```
invert(v)
    tmp = v.left
    v.left = v.right
    v.right = tmp.left
    invert(v.right)
    invert(v.left)
```

The invert operation reflects a tree, changing the order of every child. You can see the result of the invert operation illustrated in **Figure 8-23**.

Figure 8-23   A tree and its inversion

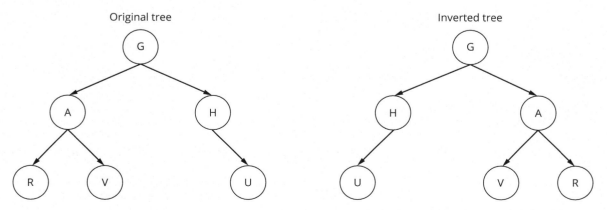

> ## Technical Interview

In order to use the algorithmic tools and data structures at your disposal when solving a programming problem, two powerful strategies are:

- Create a user-defined data type to store the characteristics of the data related to the problem. By doing this you can think of the objects and data related to the problem as nodes in a data structure.

- Focus on the arithmetic properties of the data, such as the size and any sorting function that might be in use, to relate the data to a data structure or algorithm that might help you solve the problem.

For example, suppose that you have contiguous spaces of size 1024, followed by a reserved memory space and then the rest of the memory stack. You are given a set of arrays of size $l_1, l_2, .., l_m$. Your task is to write a program to use the whole contiguous space to store some of the arrays. By abstracting the problem and forgetting that you are working with arrays of data in a computer, you might find that the problem can be reduced to finding numbers that added give 1024. That is precisely the N-sum problem. Thus, you can use backtracking and a binary tree structure to find a possible solution to the problem.

8.2 Tree Operations and the Traversal Process

In a tree, unlike an array or list, there is no standard method to enumerate all elements stored in the data structure. Moreover, even if all the data stored in the tree is enumerated, how do you do it in a way that reflects the relationships described by the links in the tree?

There is no universal way to traverse the tree. It depends on the applications at hand. For example, in **Figure 8-24**, a tree is used to store several three-digit numbers, with each digit at a different level.

Figure 8-24 Several three-digit numbers stored in a tree. Each digit is stored in a different level. Each leaf represents a two- or three-digit number

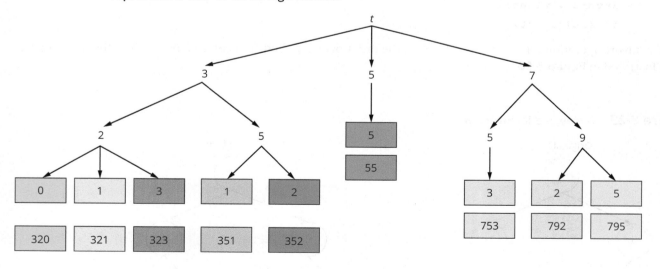

A way to present the numbers stored in the tree in Figure 8-24 is to traverse the tree from the root to each leaf one at a time.

A particular way to traverse might be useful for an algorithm, but some ways are commonly used. These ways of traversal are discussed in the following sections. When traversing a tree, at each step the traversal procedure gets a pointer to a node, and in the following descriptions such a node is usually referred to as the current node.

Depth-First and Breadth-First Traversal

Depth-first traversal starts at a parent node and explores each child before moving to the next sibling. Depth-first traversal allows for variations depending on whether the parent node is presented before or after exploring all children and the order in which children are explored. **Figure 8-25** illustrates some variants of this process.

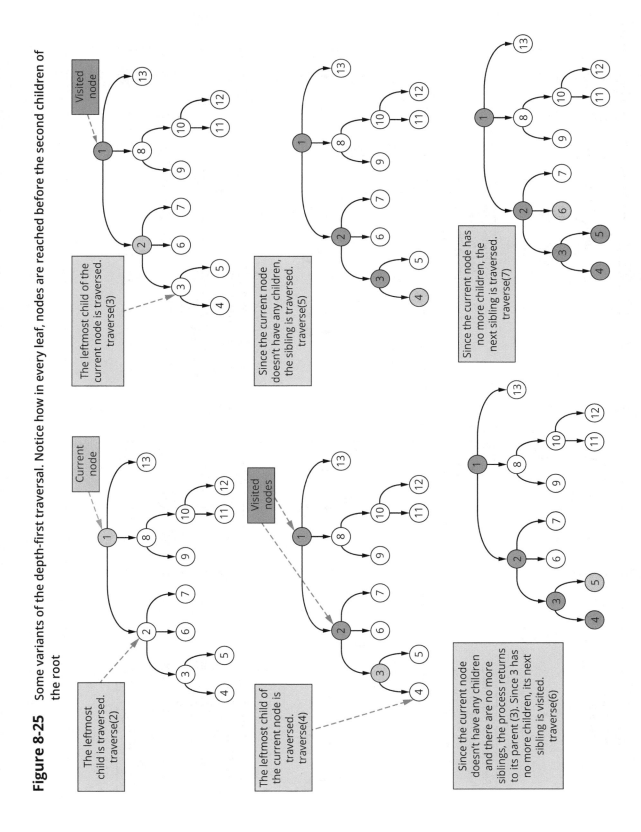

Figure 8-25   Some variants of the depth-first traversal. Notice how in every leaf, nodes are reached before the second children of the root

Figure 8-25 Some variants of the depth-first traversal. Notice how in every leaf, nodes are reached before the second children of the root—Continued

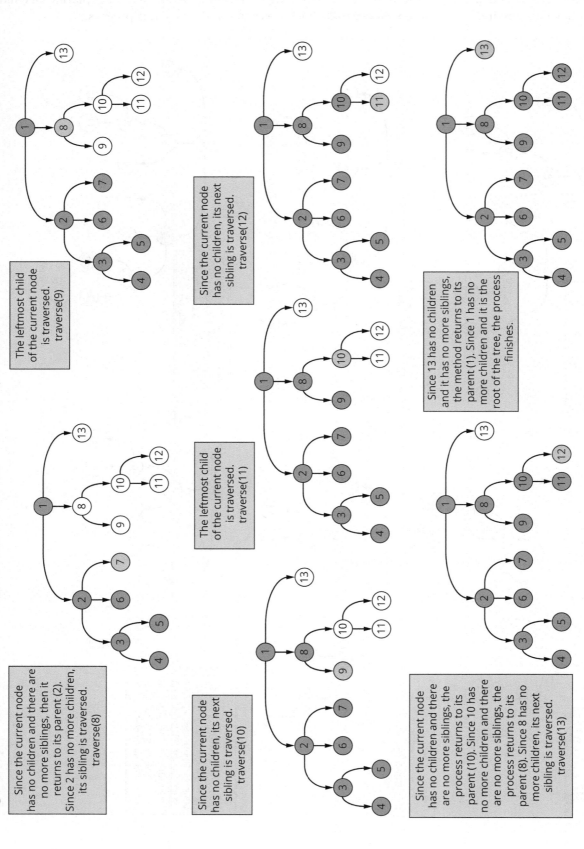

Since the current node has no children and there are no more siblings, then it returns to its parent (2). Since 2 has no more children, its sibling is traversed. traverse(8)

The leftmost child of the current node is traversed. traverse(9)

Since the current node has no children, its next sibling is traversed. traverse(10)

Since the current node has no children, its next sibling is traversed. traverse(11)

Since the current node has no children, its next sibling is traversed. traverse(12)

The leftmost child of the current node is traversed. traverse(11)

Since the current node has no children and there are no more siblings, the process returns to its parent (10). Since 10 has no more children and there are no more siblings, the process returns to its parent (8). Since 8 has no more children, its next sibling is traversed. traverse(13)

Since 13 has no children and it has no more siblings, the method returns to its parent (1). Since 1 has no more children and it is the root of the tree, the process finishes.

It is straightforward to implement depth-first traversal recursively, as shown in the code snippet below.

```
depth_first(v)
    display(v.data)
    for c in children(v)
        depth_first(c)
```

To implement it without recursion, it is necessary to use an auxiliary data structure to store the nodes that are children to a traversed node but are waiting to be traversed. Since the siblings of a node are traversed only after the children have been traversed, the first to be discovered are the last to be traversed. Hence, a LIFO structure is more appropriate. Here is an iterative implementation of the depth-first traversal:

```
depth_first(v)
    aux_stack = new stack()
    push(aux_stack, v)
    while not empty(aux_stack)
        curr = pop(aux_stack)
        for c in children(curr)
            push(aux_stack, c)
        display(curr.data)
```

The depth-first traversal can be used to enumerate the elements stored in the tree shown in Figure 8-24. During the traversal algorithm, a string of digits can be stored and, when the algorithm reaches a leaf node, the complete string can be displayed. You can see an implementation in the following code snippet.

```
display_element(v, str)
    if is_leaf(v)
        display(str + v.data)
    else
        for c in children(v)
            display_element(c, str + v.data)
```

Breadth-first traversal consists of visiting each child of a parent node before visiting the rest of the descendants. Hence, a parent node p gets all its children v traversed, then each element in children (v) gets traversed. You can see the breadth-first traversal process illustrated in **Figure 8-26**.

An arbitrary tree used to store keys and search for them works essentially as a linked list for that aspect. Since no additional restriction on the way the keys are stored is imposed, to search it is necessary to start traversing the structure until a match is reached or the structure has been completely traversed. Thus, the two general approaches to search are depth-first search and breadth-first search.

In-Order Traversal

In a binary tree it is common to impose additional conditions on the keys, for example, to require that `node.left.key < node.right.key`. In such a case, it is meaningful to say that the nodes are going to be traversed in order. **In-order traversal** in a binary tree is to traverse the left node, visit the parent, and then visit the right node. You can see the process illustrated in **Figure 8-27**.

Other Traversals in Binary Trees

In a binary tree, it is possible to be more specific about how each element is displayed or traversed during the traversal process. The two general types of traversal are depth-first traversal and breadth-first traversal. In addition, for each case for a binary tree, it is possible to describe in which order the elements are displayed or traversed by the three possible nodes: the parent, the left child, and the right child.

Figure 8-26   Breadth-first traversal of a tree. Notice how each child of the root is visited before any leaf is visited

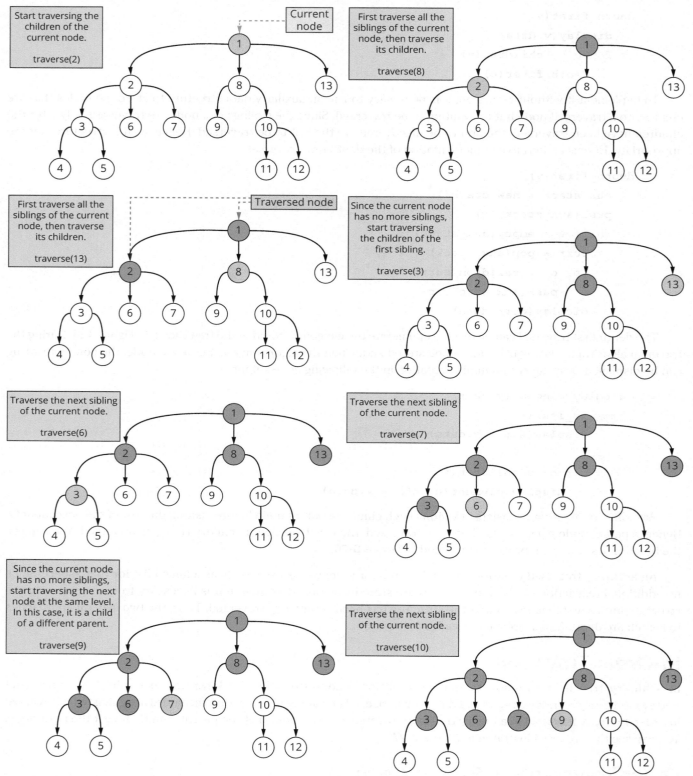

Figure 8-26 Breadth-first traversal of a tree. Notice how each child of the root is visited before any leaf is visited—Continued

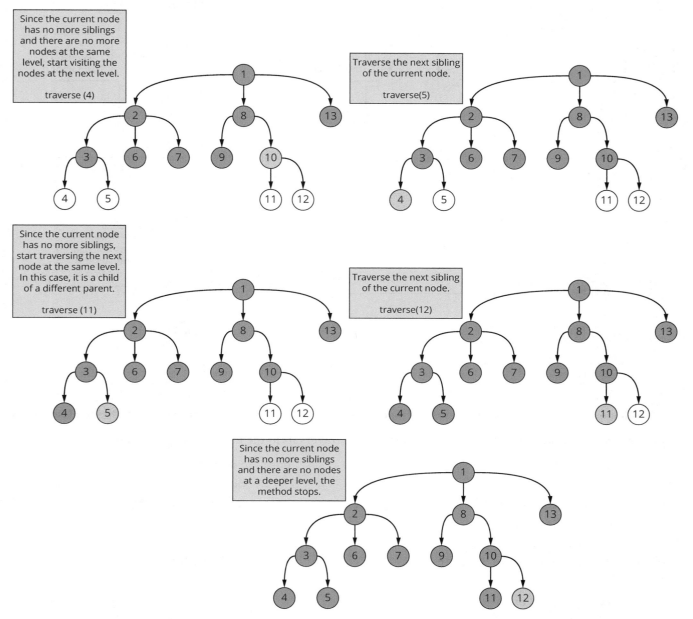

When using depth-first traversal, one child is traversed before its sibling is displayed. The order in which this operation can be executed is:

- Traverse left child, display current node, traverse right child. This is called **in-order traversal**, **in-fix traversal**, or **symmetrical traversal**.

- Traverse right child, display parent, traverse left child.

- Display the current node, traverse the left child, traverse the right child. This is known as **pre-order traversal** or **prefix traversal**.

- Traverse the left child, traverse the right child, display current node. This is known as **post-order traversal** or **post-fix traversal**.

Figure 8-27 Notice that the tree has some conditions imposed in the way the keys were inserted in the tree

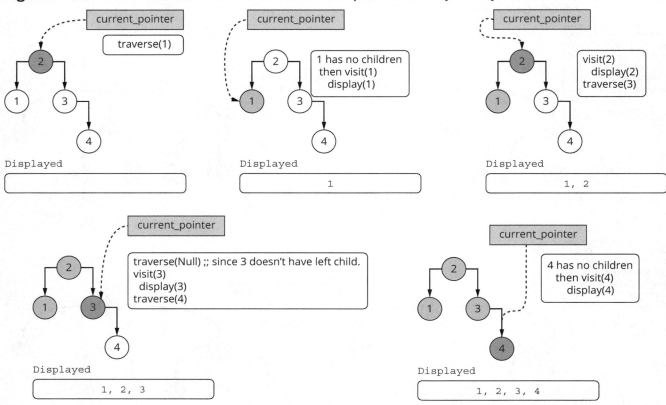

The elements of a tree displayed when traversed in-order, pre-order, and post-order are illustrated in **Figure 8-28**.

You can see recursive implementations of the different traversals in the following code snippet.

```
in_order(v)
    if not v.left = Null
        in_order(v.left)
    display(v.data)
    if not v.right = Null
        in_order(v.right)


reverse_order(v)
    if not v.right = Null
        in_order(v.right)
    display(v.data)
    if not v.left = Null
        in_order(v.left)


pre_order(v)
    display(v.data)
    if not v.left = Null
        in_order(v.left)
    if not v.right = Null
        in_order(v.right)
```

```
post_order(v)
    if not v.left = Null
        in_order(v.left)
    if not v.right = Null
        in_order(v.right)
    display(v.data)
```

Figure 8-28   The same tree traversed in-order, pre-order, and post-order

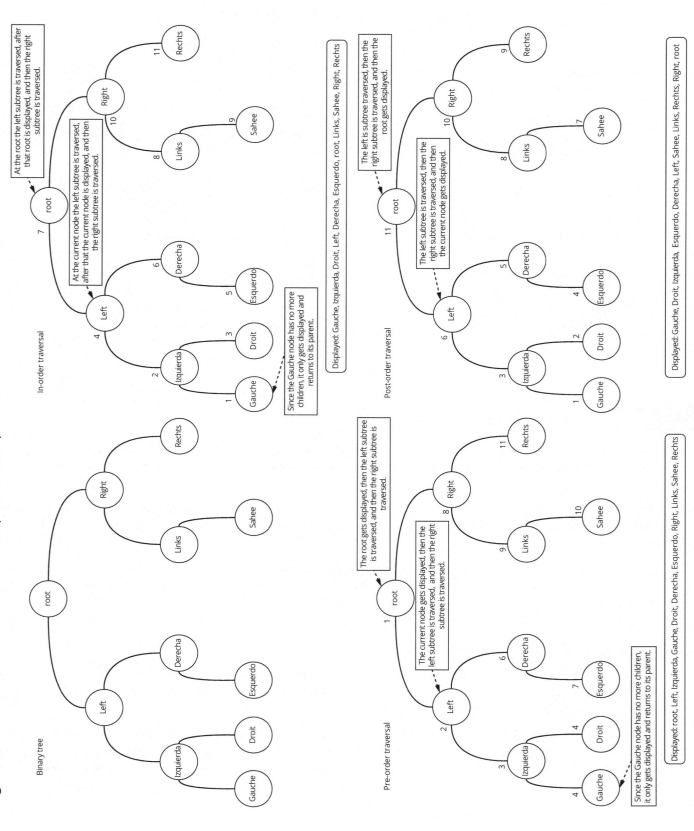

Note

Given an expression tree, traversing the tree in an in-fix, pre-fix, or post-fix way gives the operations in the in-fix, pre-fix, or post-fix operations. The reconstruction produced during the traversal is always the same, except possibly for the place of the parentheses and other aggrupation signs. You can see an expression tree for the expressions written in the three ways in **Figure 8-29**.

- in-fix notation: $5 + 7 * 3$
- pre-fix notation: $+(5, *(7, 3))$
- post-fix notation: $(5, (7, 3) *) +$

Figure 8-29 An expression tree traversed in in-fix, pre-fix, and post-fix order. The output provides an arithmetic expression in in-fix, pre-fix, and post-fix notation

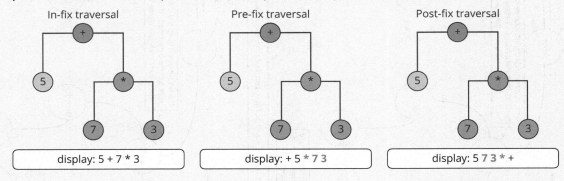

8.3 Binary Search Trees

Binary trees are especially useful to improve the performance of searching, and hence for building associative arrays. This is because you can organize the keys in a binary tree in such a way that the binary search algorithm is easier to implement.

In what follows it is assumed that the key values used in the binary trees are positive integers, but the ideas can be extended to other data types using a comparison function as was done in earlier chapters for searching and sorting algorithms with arrays.

Also, for simplicity, and as long as no confusion might be created, the key value of a node will be referred to simply by the same letter or name as the node. For example, the node x with key value 3 would be referred to simply as $x = 3$.

What Is a Binary Search Tree?

A **binary search tree (BST)** is a binary tree such that for each node p, if node q is in the left subtree `q.key < p.key` and if q is in the right subtree `p.key < q.key` when the children are not `Null`. You can see some examples of binary search and non-binary search trees in **Figure 8-30**.

Suppose that the set of key values of a BST is given $k_1 < k_2 < \ldots < k_N$. The **in-order successor** of a node x, with key value k_j, is the node y with key value k_{j+1}, or Null if the key value of the node x is the largest. In a similar way, the **in-order predecessor** of a node x, with key value k_j, is the node y with key value k_{j-1}, or Null if the key value of the node x is the smallest.

Figure 8-30   Notice how an in-order traversal of a binary search tree gives all the keys in order

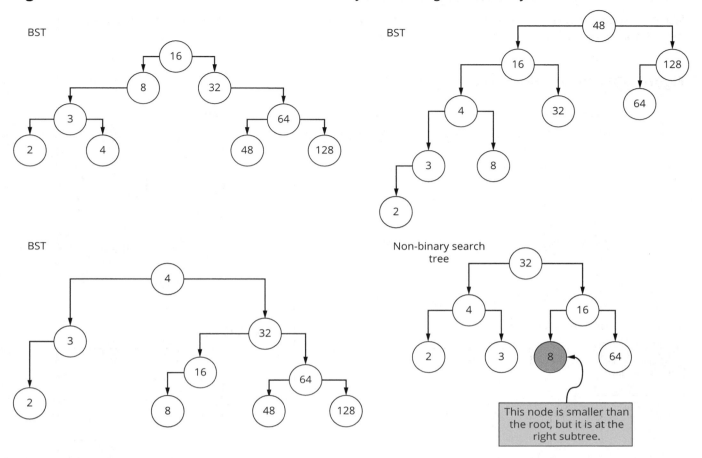

Searching in a BST

A key observation for BST is that if `y.key` > `x.key`, then there can't be a node with key value `y.key` in the left sub-tree of *x*. If there exists a node with key value `y.key`, it must be in the right subtree of *x*. Therefore, when searching for a key value in a BST, it is not necessary to make a complete traversal. It is only necessary to check for the subtrees where it is still possible to find the target key.

You can see an implementation of the searching operation in a BST using the previous observations:

```
search(r, target)
    if r = Null
        return Null
    if r.key = target
        return r
    if r.key > target
        return search(r.left, target)
    else
        return search(r.right, target)
```

Complexity of Searching in BSTs

When searching in BSTs, the worst case is when the key value is not found and the algorithm reaches the maximum height. You can see such cases illustrated in **Figure 8-31**.

Figure 8-31 Worst case for searching in BSTs

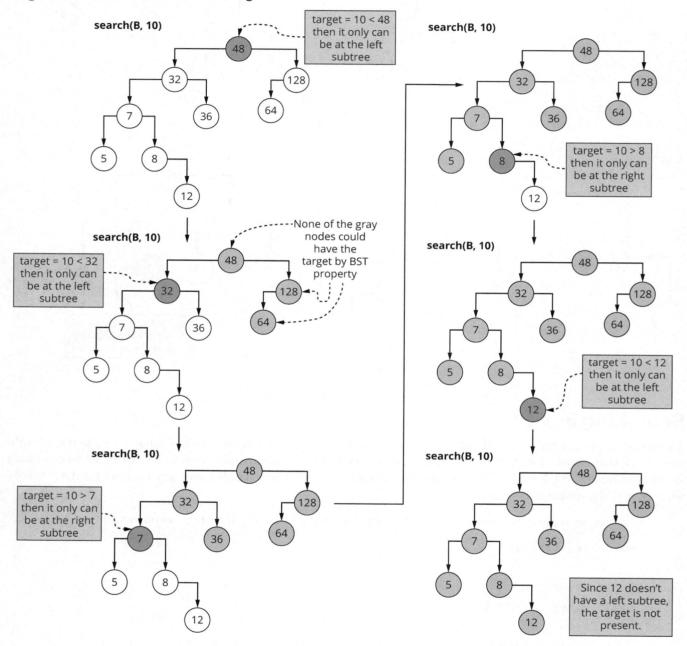

A search in BST might take as much as h comparisons where h is the height of the tree. As mentioned before, when the tree is skewed it is not possible to take advantage of the additional structure of a tree, hence skew trees are not desirable because in such cases the complexity of searching becomes $O(n)$.

If you keep a BST with the least possible height that is approximately $logn$, then the search will have complexity $\Theta(logn)$.

Insertion and Deletion in BSTs

To insert a new element in a BST, it is necessary to ensure that the resulting tree keeps the BST property. That gives you only one possible option to insert a new node without changing the relationships between the previous nodes.

The first step will be to determine if the new node must be inserted into the left or right subtree by comparing the new key value with one of the current nodes. When an empty subtree is reached, the new node can be inserted.

You can see the procedure illustrated in **Figure 8-32**.

Figure 8-32   The process of finding the place to insert a new node is similar to the process of searching for a target value

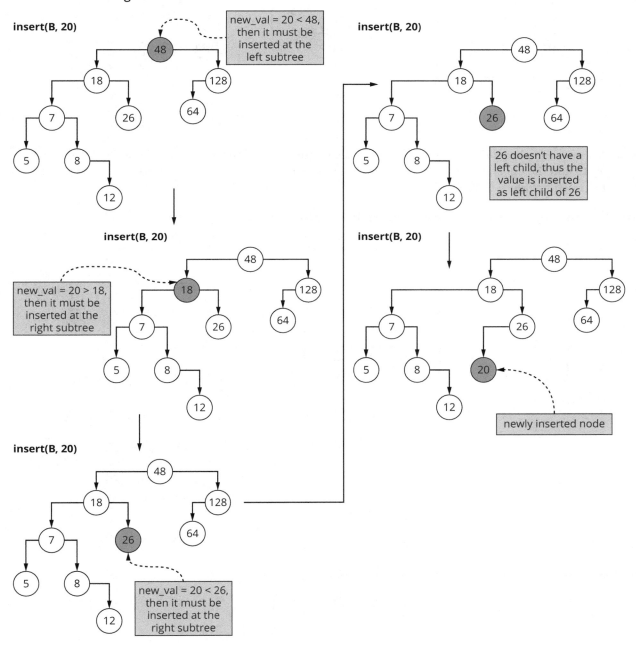

When making a deletion, it is possible that the user provides only the target value. In such cases, it is necessary to search the BST for a reference to the node to delete. Once the reference is made, some rearrangements might be necessary to preserve the BST property and all the rest of the values stored in the tree.

To understand how to keep the BST property when deleting a node, let's split the analysis into the following cases:

- *The node is a leaf node.* In such a case, deleting the node won't affect the BST property. **Figure 8-33a**.

Figure 8-33a   Keeping BST when deleting a leaf node

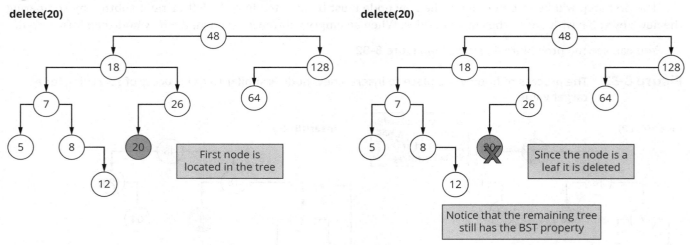

- *The node has only one child either left or right.* In such a case, depending on where the node to be deleted is, it is necessary to add the child as the left or right child to the parent of the node to be deleted. You can see the process illustrated in **Figure 8-33b.**

Figure 8-33b   Keeping BST when deleting a node with only one child

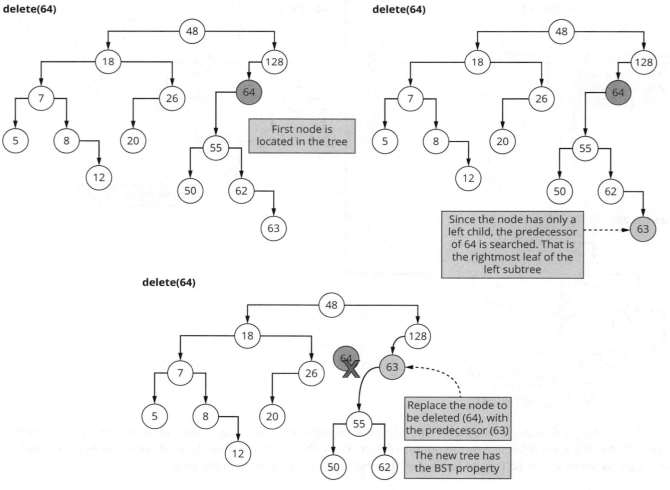

- *The node has two children.* In this case, one possible strategy is as follows. First find the in-order successor of the node to be deleted; let's call it node x. The node x is necessarily in the right subtree of the node to be deleted, since its key value must be larger than the key to be deleted. Moreover, the node x can't have a left child. If it has a left child, then the key value of its left child would be greater than the value to be deleted and smaller than the key value of x; hence, x couldn't be the successor of the node to be deleted. The node x can be deleted from the tree using the previous case, then replace the node to be deleted with the node x. You could use a similar strategy using the in-order predecessor instead of the successor. You can see the process illustrated in **Figure 8-33c**.

Figure 8-33c Keeping BST when deleting a node with two children

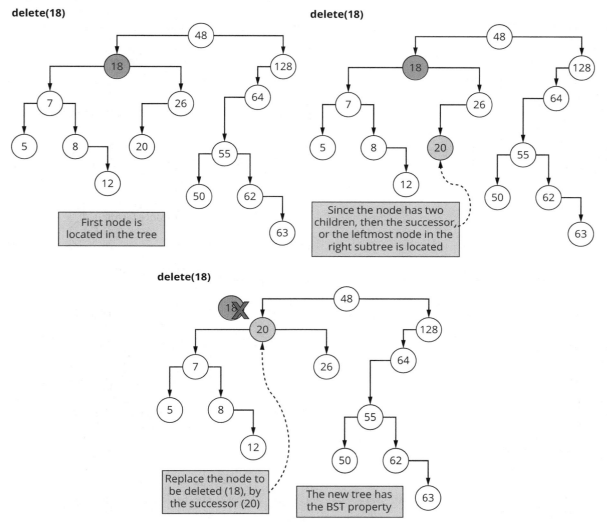

Note When working with BSTs and key values, it is assumed that there are no repeated keys. If it were necessary to deal with repeated keys, one strategy might be to use a linked list to store the different data associated to a key value.

8.4 Adelson-Velsky-Landis (AVL) Trees

In the previous section, the analysis showed that the complexity of the main operations of searching, inserting, and deletion are affected by the height of the tree. In ideal conditions, the tree should be full. In that way, the tree will have the minimum possible height. But that is not possible in all cases.

If a tree is not full, it is possible to measure how far from being full the tree is. This measure is called the balance factor. The **balance factor** of a node is the difference in the height of the left and right subtrees of the node. When a tree has a balance factor of the root of 0 it is said that it is perfectly balanced. In **Figure 8-34**, you can see some trees and the balance factors of each node.

Figure 8-34 Trees with different balance factors. Notice that the balance factor is higher for skewed subtrees

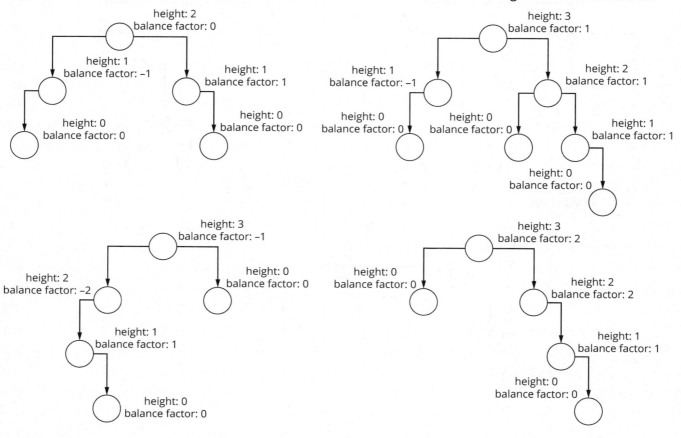

Note | AVL trees are named after Georgy Adelson-Velsky and Evgenii Landis, who first proposed the algorithm in a 1962 paper. AVL trees were the first self-balanced trees to be proposed.

Properties of AVL Trees

A tree is said to be an **AVL tree** when each node has a balance factor of –1, 0, or 1. What that means for each node is that it either has two subtrees of the same height or it only has one child (left or right) and the child is a leaf node.

In **Figure 8-35**, you can see AVL trees with balance factors of −1, 0, and 1.

Figure 8-35   AVL trees have differences of height only at the last level of the tree

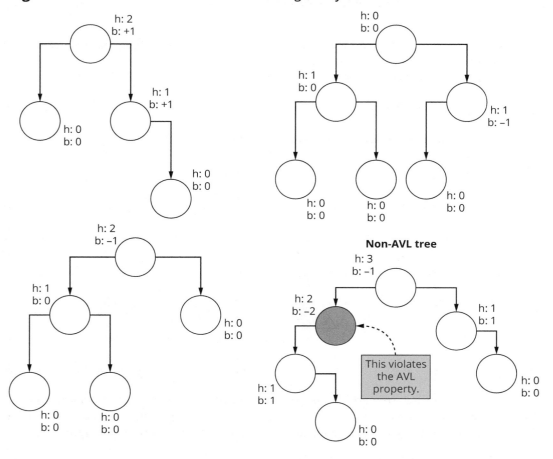

Quick Check 8-4

Suppose that you execute the following insertions in a BST *T*:

```
insert(T, 12)
insert(T, 15)
insert(T, 5)
insert(T, 3)
insert(T, 17)
insert(T, 2)
```

What is the balance factor of the nodes 12, 15, and 5 at the end of the insertions?

Answer: −1, 1, −2.

Notice that before inserting node 2 the tree is an AVL tree. After the insertion of node 2, node 12 has a balance factor of −1. But node 5 now has a balance factor of −2. The root node 12 has a balance factor of −1 since the height of the left subtree is 3 and the height of the right subtree is 2, but the tree is no longer AVL since node 5 has a balance factor of −2.

Balancing a Tree by Left and Right Rotation

When an operation such as insertion or deletion is made on an AVL tree, the balance factor of the children's nodes is not affected. But the balance factor of any of the nodes in the path from the root to the affected node might be –2 or 2.

To reduce the balance factor on the nodes affected by an insertion it will be necessary to move some nodes to reduce the balance factor of predecessor nodes. One key observation is that when moving child nodes, including their associated subtrees, their balance factors won't be affected.

The basic cases are illustrated in **Figure 8-36**.

Figure 8-36   In each case, moving at most two nodes results in an AVL tree

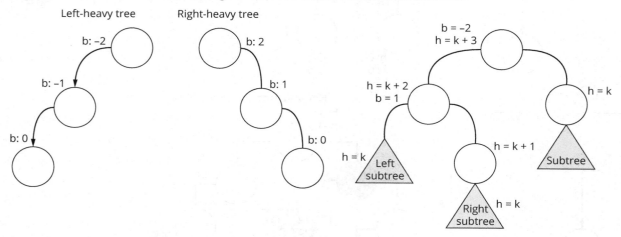

The two basic operations to balance an AVL tree are the left and right rotation. In a **left rotation**, a node with a balance factor of 2 is moved into the left child of its right child. In a **right rotation**, a node with a balance factor of –2 is moved into the right child of its left child. You can see a schematic of the left and right rotations in **Figure 8-37**.

An implementation of the right rotation can be seen in the following:

```
right_rotation(v)
    ;; The left child of v will replace the place of v in the tree
    parent = v.parent
    new_root = v.left
    if parent.key < new_root.left
        parent.right = new_root
        new_root.parent = parent
    else
        parent.left = new_root

    ;; v will become the right child of new_root
    temp = new_root.right
    new_root.right = v
    v.parent = new_root

    ;; the previous right subtree of v will be the left subtree of v
    v.left = temp
    temp.parent = v
```

Figure 8-37   Notice that the new balance factors make the tree AVL, and that the balance factors in all subtrees are not affected

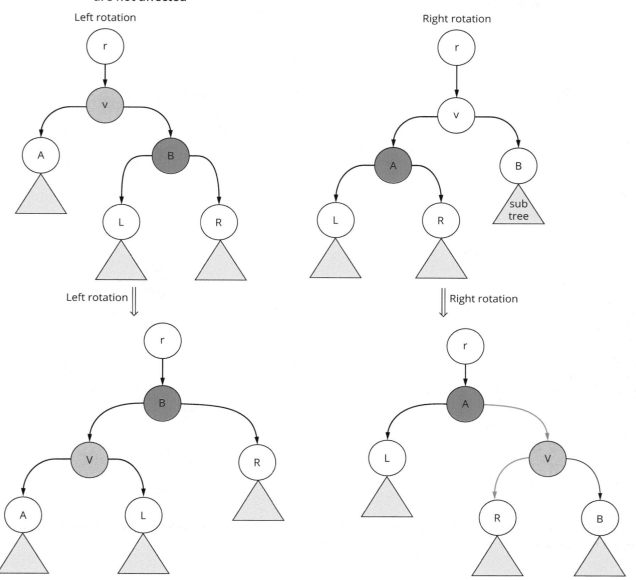

The case where a right rotation fixes an unbalanced node in a tree is shown in **Figure 8-38** with the result of the right rotation, and the case where a left rotation fixes an unbalanced node.

Figure 8-38   **Under the specific configurations shown, a single rotation fixes the unbalance**

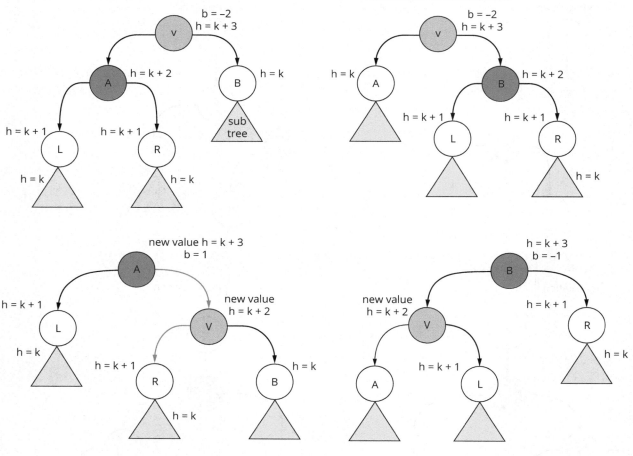

A < V, R < V, and V < B, so the BST property still holds.

Notice that a key feature is that the height at the node where the rotation was performed is reduced. Other cases require two rotations, such as the ones shown in **Figure 8-39**.

Figure 8-39   **The trees are balanced by performing a left rotation followed by a right rotation**

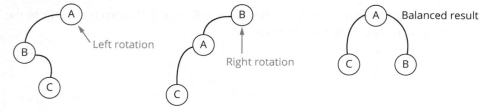

Insertion in AVL Trees

An insertion in AVL trees starts in the same way as in any BST. When inserting a new leaf into a BST, it is possible to increase the height of a subtree. That is what causes the imbalance. So, one of the following cases might occur.

1. A node is inserted and increases the height of the right subtree of a node v that has a balance factor 1.
2. A node is inserted and increases the height of the left subtree of a node v that has a balance factor −1.

Case (1) has two possible subcases:

a. The new node x is inserted at the right subtree of v.right. In this case, a single left rotation of v fixes the tree. This is illustrated schematically in **Figure 8-40**.

b. The new node x is inserted at the left subtree of v.right. In this case, a double rotation at v fixes the unbalance. You can see the procedure illustrated schematically right-left in **Figure 8-41**.

Case (2) also has two subcases that are symmetrical to those for case (1).

For implementation purposes, you can see that knowing the height of a node is important. So, it is common to use a height field in the nodes of the AVL tree.

Figure 8-40   A single rotation reduces the balance factor

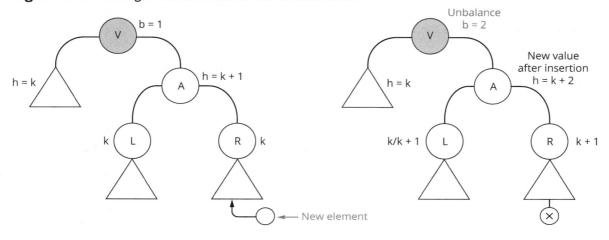

Figure 8-41   A double rotation is required to reduce the balance factor

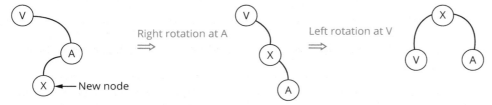

Deletion in AVL Trees

Deletion in AVL trees is performed in the same way as in BSTs. The deletion process implies that a leaf node, the in-order successor of the deleted node, is moved to the place of the deleted node if the deleted node is not a leaf. Such deletion can only affect the balance factor of some nodes if the parent node of the in-order successor is the only child of its parent.

There are two cases where the imbalance occurs:

1. The deletion reduces the height of the right subtree of a node with a balance factor of −1.
2. The deletion reduces the height of the left subtree of a node with balance factor 1.

These two are symmetrical to each other and have similarities to the insertion cases. Let's analyze case (1).

Suppose that the node where the imbalance occurs is V. For an imbalance to occur, the height of the right subtree $B = V$.right is k, while the height of the left subtree $A = V$.left is $k + 2$. This can happen in one of the following cases:

a. The left subtree $L = A$.left has height $k + 1$ and the right subtree $R = A$.right has height k. In this case, a single right rotation resolves the imbalance. You can see this illustrated in **Figure 8-42**.

Figure 8-42 The single rotation solves the unbalance at the node V

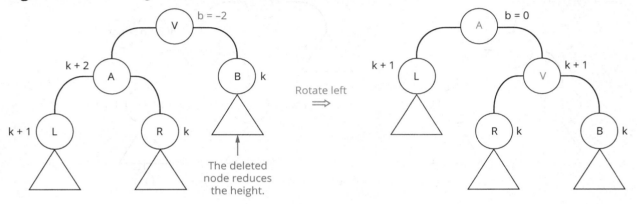

b. The right subtree $R = A$.right has height $k + 1$ and the left subtree L = A.left has height k. Then a double right rotation resolves the imbalance. You can see this illustrated in **Figure 8-43**.
c. The last case is when both $R = A$.right and $L = A$.left have height $k + 1$. In this case, a single right rotation solves the unbalance.

You can see this illustrated in **Figure 8-44**.

The possible subcases for case (2) are symmetrical and are solved using single left rotations or double left–right rotations.

8.5 Heaps and Treaps

One structure that is useful in developing simulations and other algorithms is a priority queue. A **priority queue** is an ADT where each element is sorted not just by the time of arrival but also by a priority value. The highest-priority elements leave the queue first.

An example of priority queue usage is for a shared resource. Suppose that in an office everybody shares a printer. To have the largest number of clients satisfied it might be a good idea to give small documents a higher priority, so a brief letter would be printed before a long report.

A priority queue has the `insert` operation, where an element is inserted into the queue with an associated priority. The `delete_max` operation is where the element with the highest priority is returned and deleted from the queue. The `empty` operation returns True if the queue is empty. It is common to include a `get_max` operation to get the next element to be deleted from the queue without removing it from the queue.

Using a priority queue, it is possible to sort the elements of an array in the following way.

Figure 8-43 The double right rotation solves the unbalance

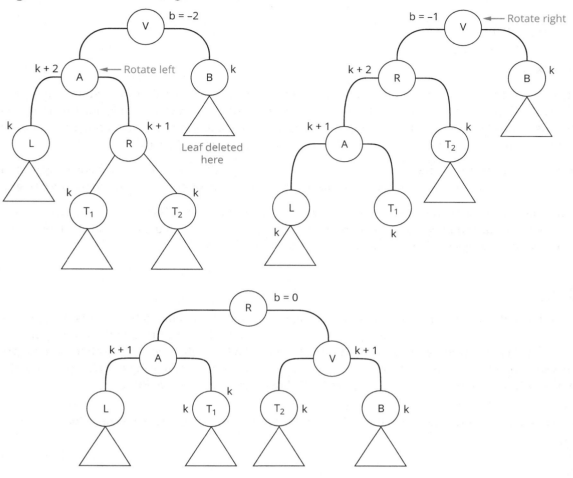

Figure 8-44 The single right rotation solves the unbalance

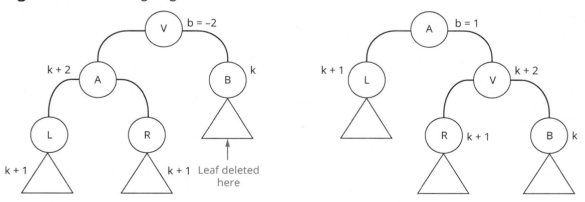

Suppose you have an array X of size N. Traverse the array and insert each element into a priority queue Q with a priority equal to the value of the element. When all the elements of the queue are returned, they are in descending order. You can see an implementation of such a procedure in the following code.

```
Q = new priority_queue()


for i = 0 to N step 1
    ;; The element X[i] is inserted with priority X[i]
```

```
        insert(Q, X[i], X[i])
    idx = 0
    while not empty(Q)
        X[idx] = delete_max(Q)
        idx = idx + 1
```

If you implement a priority queue using an unsorted array, each `delete_max` operation will require finding the maximum in the array. That operation has complexity $O(n)$. If a dynamic structure such as a linked list is used, it is possible to make the insertions in a way that the list stays sorted and the maximum is at the tail of the list, hence the `delete_max` operation will have $O(1)$ complexity but the insertion will have complexity $O(n)$.

By using a BST, it is possible to reduce the `insert` and `delete_max` complexities to $O(logn)$ on average. By using a balanced version of the BST, such as an AVL tree, both insertion and deletion are guaranteed to have complexity $O(logn)$.

One thing to notice about the implementation of a priority queue using a balanced BST is that the strict order is not necessary. It is only necessary to have fast access to the largest element in the queue, not to keep all elements sorted at all times. A creative strategy to achieve that is described in this section.

What Is a Heap?

An auxiliary structure for understanding priority queues and one very efficient implementation of it is the partially ordered tree. A **partially ordered tree (POT)** is a binary tree where each node has a priority, and the priority of each node is larger than or equal to every descendant. Notice that the nodes of a POT might hold data other than the priority. One key observation on POTs is that the root is always the max element. So, when using a POT, retrieval of the element with maximum priority can be done in $O(1)$. **Figure 8-45** shows some examples of POTs.

Figure 8-45   Notice that a POT might not have the BST, so in some sense it is a more relaxed condition

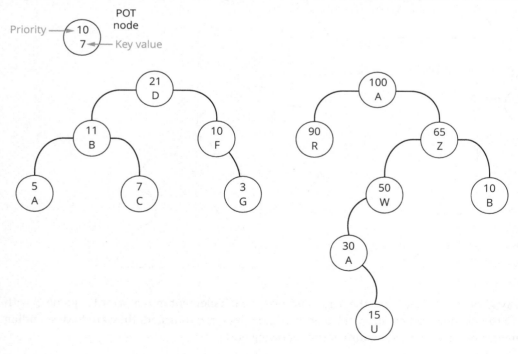

To get the most benefits from a POT it is desirable to have the least number of levels or minimum height possible, as was pointed out with the AVL trees. A **heap** is a tree with the POT property that is complete. Recall that a complete binary tree is a binary tree where each leaf is at the height of the tree h or at $h-1$. In **Figure 8-46**, you can see some illustrations of heap trees.

Figure 8-46 Heap and non-heap trees

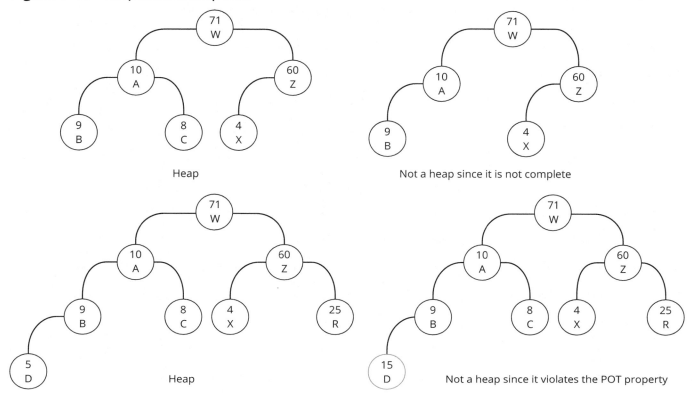

As in the case of sorting problems, it is possible to transform a heap or a POT to have the minimum at the root by changing the definition of the properties. Since the minimum and maximum could be of particular interest in different applications, it is common to refer to each case separately.

- A **min heap** is a complete binary tree where each node has a priority smaller than or equal to all its descendants.

- A **max heap** is a complete binary tree where each node has a priority higher than or equal to all its descendants.

Heaps are usually represented as arrays where the elements are presented following a breadth-first traversal. So, the elements are presented in an array from left to right one level of the tree at a time. In **Figure 8-47**, you can see an illustration of heaps and their array representation.

It is common to allow access to the elements of a heap through an index (the index that the element has in the array representation). In Figure 8-44, the root is at position 1. Heaps usually start at index 1 to make implementations about parents easier, the elements at level 1 are from 1 to 2, the elements at level 2 from 3 to 7, and the elements at level 3 from 8 to 15.

The Heapify Operation

When inserting or deleting an element from a heap, the POT property might not be fulfilled. To restore the property once a node that violates the POT property has been found, it is possible to exchange the nodes to recover the heap property. The process of creating a heap from a BST is called the **heapify operation**.

There are two methods used in the heapify operation:

- **Bubble down** or **percolate down** is swapping a node with its largest children until the heap property is fulfilled.

- **Bubble up** is swapping a node with its smallest children until the heap property is fulfilled.

Figure 8-47   Heaps and their array representation. Notice that the links drawn in the array representation are not usually shown; they are in the figure to highlight the tree structure

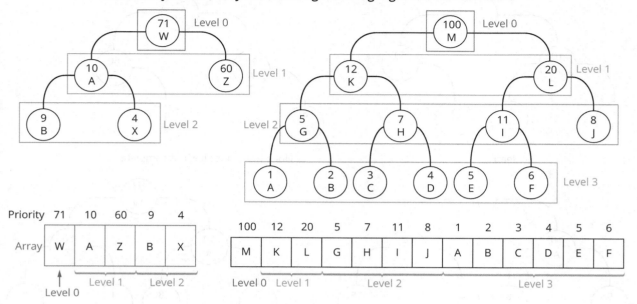

The following code shows an implementation of bubble down for a heap.

```
heapify(v)
    ;; heapify by bubble down
    ;; Check if the heap property is violated  if leaf(v)
        ;; If it has no children then it can't violate the heap property
        return

    ;; Choose the child with largest priority
    max_children = Null
    if not v.right = Null
        max_children = v.right
    if not v.left = Null
        if not max_children = Null
            if max_children.priority < v.left.priority
                max_children = v.left
        else
            max_children = v.left

    ;; If v.priority is greater or equal than max_children the
    ;; heap property holds

    if v.priority >= max_children.priority
        return
    ;; If the heap property doesn't hold swap the nodes
    swap(v, max_children)
    heapify(v)
```

In **Figure 8-48**, you can see the previous implementation illustrated in a tree where the heap property doesn't hold.

Figure 8-48   The heapify operation is applied recursively until *v* becomes a leaf

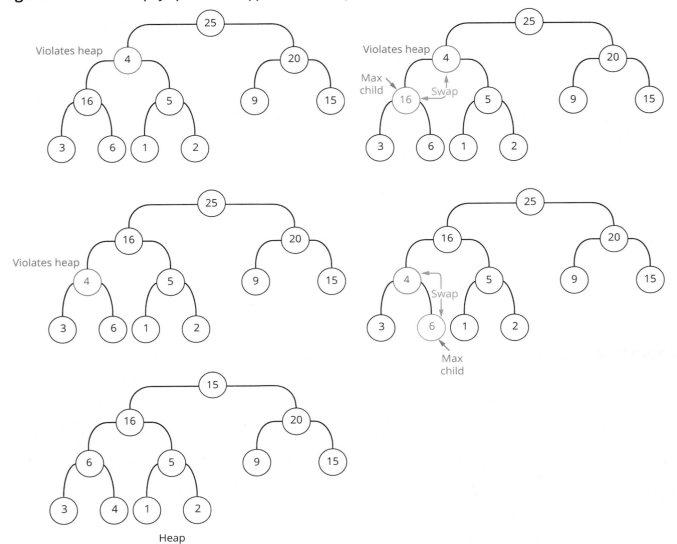

Heap

Insertion and Deletion in a Heap

To insert an element into a heap, the new element is inserted at the end of the heap, which means the last free position at the highest level. After that, the new element is bubbled up until the heap property is restored. You can see an example of the procedure in **Figure 8-49**.

For the heap, the only relevant deletion is deleting the max or removing the root. To keep the tree complete, the last element in the heap, which is the rightmost element in the last level, replaces the root. Then the root is bubbled down until the heap property is restored. You can see the procedure illustrated in **Figure 8-50**.

What Is a Treap?

A **treap** combines the properties of a BST with those of a heap. A treap is a BST where each node has a priority, and the heap property is enforced on the priorities.

Since the data stored in a treap doesn't have a natural or expected priority, the main strategy is using a random choice priority. That means using a sequence of random values as priorities. The main advantage of using a random priority is that the heap property forces the BST to have lower balance factors, like the AVL trees. In **Figure 8-51** you can see some examples of treaps.

Figure 8-49   The new element is bubbled up until the new element heap property is fulfilled

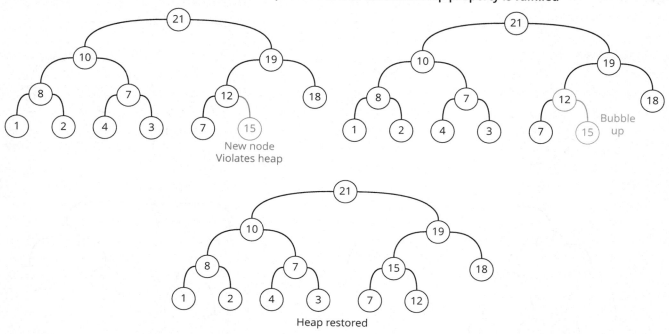

Figure 8-50   A bubble-down process after a deletion to restore the heap property

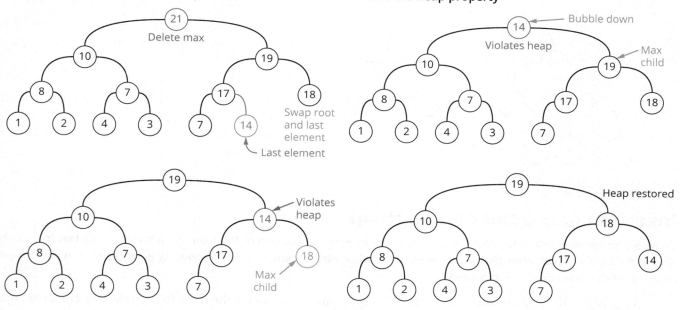

Note that you can always build a treap given a set of key priorities. The procedure is to insert each node in a BST in decreasing order of priority. The result shows that the lower priorities are in lower levels of the BST. You can see the procedure illustrated in **Figure 8-52**.

Insertion and Deletion in a Treap

When a new node is inserted in a treap, the heap property might be violated. In a heap, the operations of bubble up and bubble down were used. However, the bubble up and bubble down operations violate the BST property. Equivalent operations are the right and left rotation used in AVL trees. These AVL rotations always preserve the BST property, but the height of the nodes involves changes, hence the heap property might be restored.

Figure 8-51   Examples of treaps with the same key values but different priorities

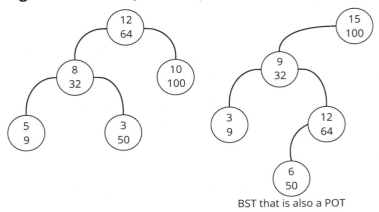

BST that is also a POT

Figure 8-52   How a treap can be constructed by inserting the nodes in decreasing order of priority

key–priority pairs (5, 27), (14, 11), (3, 8), (17, 5), (7, 3)

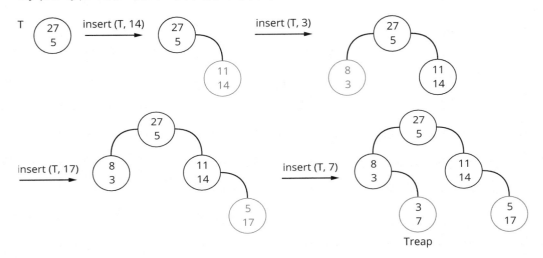

As an example, consider the treap shown in **Figure 8-53** where a new node is inserted.

Figure 8-53   The new node inserted in the treap following the BST procedure violates the heap property

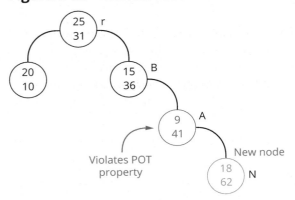

The heap property is violated by the nodes A and N. Thus, a right rotation will exchange the level of the nodes A and N. Now nodes B and N violate the heap property, and one more right rotation restores the heap property. You can see these operations illustrated in **Figure 8-54**.

Figure 8-54 The two rotations restore the heap property

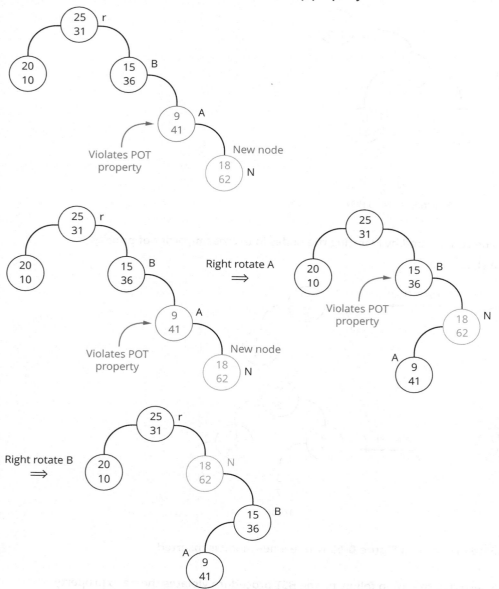

When deleting a node in a treap, the simplest case is when the node is a leaf. In such cases, the deletion won't affect the heap property or the BST property. If the node to be deleted is not a leaf, a series of rotations can move the node to a leaf position. To choose which rotation (left or right) should be done, you must consider the priority of the children. If the left child has the highest priority, rotate to the left, and if the right has the highest priority, rotate to the right. In this way, the heap property is kept for the rest of the nodes. You can see the procedure illustrated in **Figure 8-55**.

8.6 Tries

A tree can store a sequence of values in each path from the root to the leaves. For example, in **Figure 8-56**, each path from the root to a leaf spells a word.

Notice that it is easy to determine that the word *space* is not in the tree since, after the second letter, it is not possible to find a match in any of the nodes. An improvement in the previous descriptions is described in the following sections. This structure allows you to do faster searches over strings.

Figure 8-55   The series of rotations put the node to be deleted in a leaf position and keeps the heap property

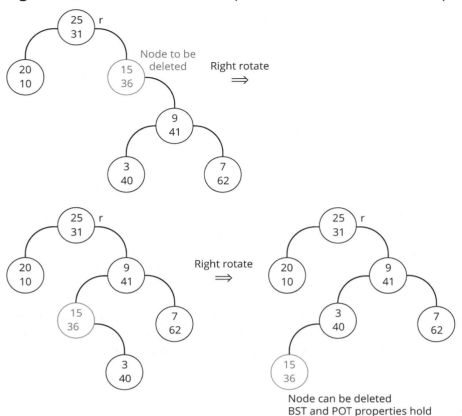

Figure 8-56   A tree with characters at each node where each path from root codifies a word

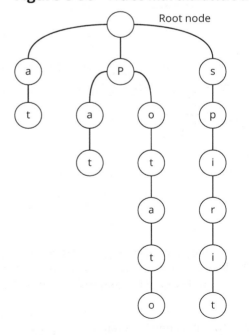

What Is a Trie?

A **trie** is a data N-ary tree that stores characters as keys at each node and an additional binary flag to indicate if the node is the last character of a word. Tries are designed to store strings and make searching for strings more efficient than by direct comparison or by sorting through lexicographical order. In **Figure 8-57**, you can see how a set of words is stored in a trie.

Figure 8-57 Each word in the trie finalizes at a node with the word flag at 1

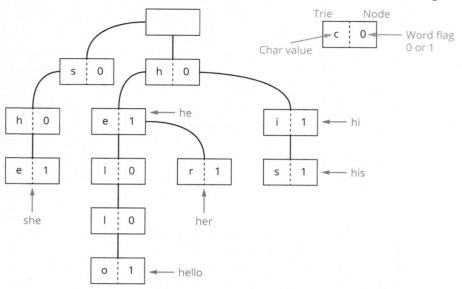

To search for a string in a trie starting from the root, each character is searched in the list of children until a character is not found. When the target string is over and there is a match in the last character, the word flag must be checked to see if the word is actually stored in the trie. The procedure is illustrated in **Figure 8-58**.

Figure 8-58 A search process in a trie

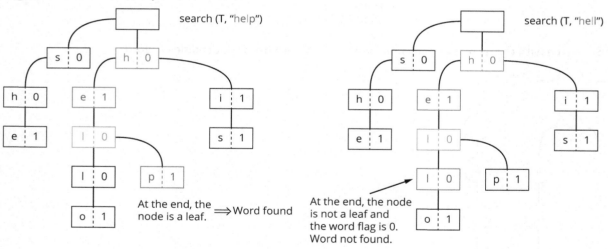

Time Complexity of Search in a Trie

Notice that when comparing two strings it is necessary to make a character-by-character comparison. Thus, in its simplest form, the equality of two strings has complexity in the worst case the length of the strings being compared. But in a list of k strings, the comparison will require k comparison, each with the complexity of the length of the target string. Hence, the complexity would be $O(kn)$.

In the case of using an array of pointers to implement the trie, it is possible to determine if a character is present as a child of a node in constant time. This can be achieved, for example, by using a function like the $ord(char)$ function that transforms characters into integers. The previous observation results that the worst case in searching will require comparing all the characters of the target string; therefore, the complexity is $O(k)$.

Fortunately, you can likely determine that a string is not present in the trie before reaching the end of the target string.

Insertion and Deletion in a Trie

When inserting a string x into a trie, each character is inserted as a node if it is not already present. When inserting a new string into a trie, there are two possibilities. The first one is that the string is a substring of an already inserted string. In such a case, every character of the string x is already in the trie, so when the end of the string x is reached, it is only necessary to set the word flag of the node to one. The second case is when the string x is not a substring of an already inserted string. Then it will be necessary to insert at least one new character to the trie, and the node with the last character inserted gets its word flag set to one. You can see the process illustrated in **Figure 8-59**.

Figure 8-59   Inserting a new string in a trie. Notice that to insert a new string it is only necessary to traverse the string along with the trie

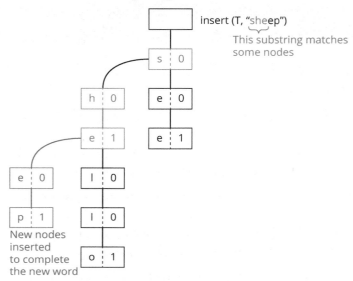

To delete a string from a tree, the path from the root to the last character of the string must be found in the tree. If the node is not a leaf node, then only the word flag is changed. If the node is a leaf, it is deleted from the tree, and then all nodes in the path that don't have children or a word flag are deleted. The process is illustrated in **Figure 8-60**.

Figure 8-60   Delete process of a string in a trie

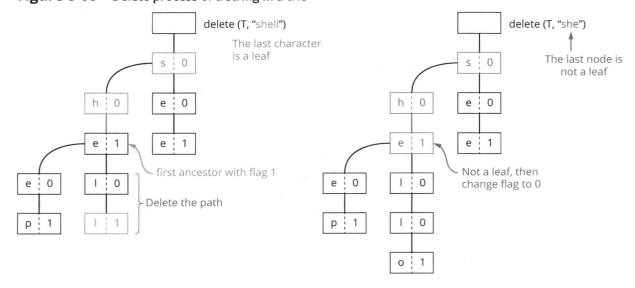

Best Practice

When implementing a trie, a single node will not usually have all letters following it, thus using an array of pointers will result in having a large number of null pointers. To avoid this, the simplest approach is to use a leftmost-right sibling approach, although there are other approaches such as a ternary trie.

Summary

- A tree is a data structure that can represent hierarchical information. Trees are not linear; thus, they are better suited to express more complex relationships between stored elements.

- A tree is mainly composed of a root and nodes. Each node has a set, possibly empty, of children. A node without children is called a leaf node.

- A special convention when drawing trees is used. In this convention, the root is at one extreme and the leaves at the other. This way, it is possible to recognize which nodes are children and parents.

- Among the useful classifications of trees are the N-ary and binary trees. These differ by the maximum number of children each node can have.

- A binary tree is called skewed when each node has zero or one child. One characteristic of a skewed binary tree is that the tree's height is larger than that of a non-skewed tree with the same number of elements.

- N-ary trees can be implemented using pointers to represent edges and user-defined data types of modeling the vertices. Two ways to do it are through an array of pointers where the size of the array used to store the children is called the branching factor.

- Another tree implementation is the leftmost-right sibling implementation, where in a node only a pointer to the left-most children and a pointer to its right sibling is stored. So, to traverse the set of children of a node, you follow the leftmost pointer and, from this node, you use the right sibling pointer to move to the next children.

- Trees are closely related to recursion in two ways. Recursion facilitates the application of functions to all the tree elements. Also, the relation between a tree and a subtree is recursive, since each subtree is itself a tree.

- Since a tree does not have an expected way to traverse the tree, there are various ways of traversing it. The two general ways that are most popular are depth-first and breadth-first.

- In depth-first traversal, the children of a node are traversed before the node's siblings. In breadth-first, all the siblings of a node are traversed before any of the children are traversed.

- In the case of a binary tree, it is possible to distinguish other ways to traverse the tree. When traversing the tree in a depth-first way in a binary tree, it is possible to follow an in-order, post-order, or pre-order way.

- A binary search tree (BST) is a special kind of tree. A BST is characterized by the binary search property. That requires that each node x be larger than its left child and smaller than its right child.

- The structure of a BST allows to eliminate the possibility that a target value is in the right or left subtree of a node. The searching process in a BST has a complexity of $O(h)$, where h is the tree's height.

- The observations about the complexity of the search, insertion, and deletion of nodes in a BST point out that having skewed subtrees is undesirable, and the ideal is to have full binary trees.

- To guarantee that the BST is as close to a full binary tree, AVL trees enforce the condition that every node has a balance factor of –1, 0, or 1. Under such conditions, it is ensured that the tree is very close to a full binary tree.

- To restore the AVL property in a tree after an insertion or deletion, two types of operations are used: a single left rotation or a single right rotation. The combinations of the left and right rotations can be used to restore the balance in a tree after insertion or deletion.

- A priority queue is where each element has a datum and a priority. In a priority queue, the first element to get out of the queue is the one with the highest priority.

- An efficient way to implement priority queues without using the full properties of a BST is the use of a partially ordered tree (POT). The property of a POT is that every node has a higher priority than all its descendants.

- A heap combines the POT and the advantages of a complete binary tree. When inserting or deleting a node in a heap, the POT property is restored by using a heapify operation. Heapify is done through the bubble up or down operations, where each node is swapped until the property is restored.

- A treap is a data structure that combines the properties of a BST and a heap. When inserting or deleting the heap property might get violated, and to restore it instead of bubble up or down, rotations are used.

- A trie is a data structure that stores strings so that each path from the root to a node with a word flag set to True represents a string in the data structure.

Key Terms

ancestor	heap	path
array of pointers implementation	heapify operation	post-fix traversal
AVL tree	height of a vertex v	post-order traversal
balance factor	height of the tree	pre-fix traversal
binary search tree (BST)	in-fix traversal	pre-order traversal
binary tree	in-order predecessor	priority queue
branching factor	in-order successor	right rotation
breadth-first traversal	in-order traversal	right skewed tree
bubble down or percolate down	leaf	root
bubble up	left rotation	sibling
complete binary tree	left skewed tree	size of a vertex
depth of a vertex v	leftmost right sibling	skewed tree
depth-first traversal	length of a path	strict binary tree
descendant	max heap	subtree
edge	min heap	symmetrical traversal
expression tree	N-ary tree	treap
full binary tree	partially ordered tree (POT)	vertices

Review Questions

1. Which of the following are characteristics of a tree?

   a. Every node has at least one child.

   b. Every node except the root has a parent.

   c. Every non-leaf node has at least one child.

   d. Every root has at least one parent.

2. Which of the following correctly defines the height of a tree T with root r?

   a. The maximum height of the height of all the children of the root r plus one.

   b. The maximum height of all the children of the root r plus one.

   c. The largest set of connected vertices from the root to a leaf.

   d. The maximum depth of all leaves.

3. Suppose that x is an ancestor of y and y is an ancestor of z. Which of the following conclusions is correct?

   a. x is an ancestor of z.

   b. z is an ancestor of y.

   c. z is a descendant of x.

   d. x is a descendant of z.

4. How many pointers are used in a tree implemented using array pointers if it has five nodes and a branching factor of 3? Consider only the parent-to-child pointers. Disregard the child-to-parent pointers.

   a. 3

   b. 5

   c. 8

   d. 15

5. If a leftmost child-right sibling implementation is used, how many pointers are used for a tree with 10 nodes, excluding the child-to-parent pointers?

   a. It is only possible to calculate by knowing the number of levels.

   b. 100

   c. 20

   d. 10

6. What is the minimum height possible to store 29 elements in a binary tree?

   a. 15

   b. 8

   c. 4

   d. 3

7. Let T be an empty tree BST. Draw the resulting tree after inserting nodes with key values 12, 15, 16, 11, 4, and 12.

8. Consider the tree shown in **Figure 8-61** and compute each node's height and balance factor.

Figure 8-61   Binary tree for Review Question 8

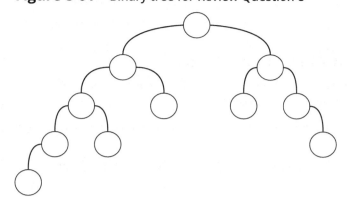

9. Consider the following set of key priority pairs. Draw a treap that stores all values.

    (10, 9), (21, 11), (31, 7), (35, 12), (33, 5)

10. Consider the AVL tree shown in **Figure 8-62**. After inserting a new node with key value 10, describe the rotations necessary to restore the AVL property.

Figure 8-62   AVL balancing in Review Question 10

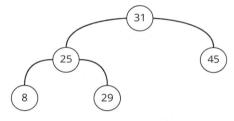

Programming Problems

1. Given a BST and a target value of x that is in the tree, write a program that finds the least node v such that $x < v$ or Null if x is larger than any value in the tree. **(LO 8.1, 8.2, 8.3)**

2. Given an N-ary tree, write a program that traverses the tree in a breadth-first tree in an iterative way. **(LO 8.1, 8.2)**

3. Given a tree, T, write a program that prints the keys of the tree in reverse level order. That means printing the leaves first, then the next level, until the root is reached. **(LO 8.1, 8.2)**

4. Given two BSTs A and B, write a program to determine if the two trees have the same elements. Make sure that your implementation has complexity $O(n + m)$, where m, and n are the number of vertices of the BSTs. **(LO 8.1, 8.2, 8.3)**

5. Given a BST, write a program that computes the balance factor of each node. **(LO 8.2, 8.4)**

6. Suppose that tree T contains the organizational structure of a project, where each node represents a member of the developing team. You need to write a program that generates a list of permissions for a file. A new user-defined data type `file_object` has two lists: `file_object.writers` that records who has the authorization to write the content of the file and `file_object.readers` that records who has authorization to only read the content. When a new `file_object` is created by a team member with `create(new_file, node)`, only the creator (node) and its parent should have write permission and all persons to whom the creator responds must have permission to read the file. Write a routine to set the permissions correctly. Suppose the new file is simply created by using `create_new_file(new_file)`. **(LO 8.1, 8.2, 8.4)**

Projects

Project 8-1: Largest Smaller Key and Smaller Largest Key

(LO 8.2, 8.3) Consider a BST and a target value of x. The largest value smaller than x in the tree is the node v such that v is less than or equal to x, but such that if w is less than x, then w is less than v.

Similarly, the smaller value larger than x in the tree is the node v such that v is larger than x, but such that if w is larger than x, then v is smaller than w.

For example, in a tree with the values 8, 12, 20, 25, and 32, the largest value smaller than 15 is 12 and the smaller value larger than 15 is 20.

Write a program to compute the lvs (largest values smaller than x) and the svl (smaller value larger than x).

Project 8-2: AVL Implementations

(LO 8.3, 8.4) Write a complete implementation of the AVL trees, including the insert and delete operations. For this implementation, also write the rotation operations necessary to balance the tree.

Project 8-3: Expression Trees

(LO 8.1, 8.2) An arithmetic expression like $3 + 2 * 9$ is said to be in in-fix notation. In in-fix notation means that the operator $*, +, -, \div$ is between the two operands.

1. If a character is a number, for simplicity, you can assume that only single digits are used. Then, push any to the operand stack number.

2. If a character is an operand, then (a) If the operator stack is empty or the top is an operator with less precedence, then push the character to the operator stack. (b) If the operator stack top has more or equal precedence than the character, then pop from the operands and operate and calculate the result accordingly to the operator at the top. Push the result to the operand stack. And repeat until the top of the operator stack has less precedence or is empty.

3. If a character is a parenthesis, then (a) If it is (, push it to the operator stack. (b) If it is), pop the operators and two operands. Compute the result of the operation over the operands and push it to the operands stack. Repeat until a (is found and pop it.

You can see the procedure illustrated in **Table 8-1** for the expression $3^*((3+1)*5+7)-11$.

Write a program that receives a string `exprs` with an arithmetic expression and using the previous procedure builds an expression tree and then uses the tree to compute the result.

Project 8-4: Associative Arrays with Tries

(LO 8.6) In an associative array, each key value—in this case, a string—is associated with a pointer storing the data. Implement an associative array using a trie to store the key values and, instead of a word, flag the index in an array to access the associated data to the key. Recall implementing the insert and delete operations and creating a mechanism to assign an associate index to each new string key inserted.

Table 8-1   Procedure for Project 8-3

Index	Character	Execute	S1(operand)	S2(operator)
0	3	push(3) to S1	3	
1	*	push(*) to S2	3	*
2	(	push("(") to S2	3	*(
3	(	push("(") to S2	3	*((
4	3	push(3) to S1	3 3	*((
5	+	push(+) to S2	3 3	*((+
6	1	push(1) to S1	3 3 1	*((+
7	)	pop 3,1 from S2 and + from S1	3	*((
7	)	compute 3 + 1 pop "(" from S2	3	*(
7	)	push(4) to S1	3 4	*(
8	*	push(*) to S2	3 4	*(*
9	5	push(5) to S1	3 4 5	*(*
10	+	+ has less precedence than *	3 4 5	*(*
10	+	pop * from S2 and 4,5 from S1	3	*(
10	+	compute 4*5 and push to S1 push(+) to S2.	3 20	*(+
11	7	push(7) to S1	3 20 7	*(+
12	)	pop until a) is found	3 20 7	*(+
12	)	pop 7, 20, and +	3	*(
12	)	compute and push 7 + 20	3 27	*(
12	)	pop (from S2	3 27	*
13	–	– has less precedence than *	3 27	*
13	–	pop 27, 3, and * stack empty		
13	–	compute 27*3 and push	81	–
14	11	push(11)	81 11	–
14	END	pop 11, 81, and – operate	70	

Chapter 9

Graphs

Learning Objectives

Upon completion of this chapter, you will be able to:

9.1   Discuss the importance of graphs as data structures for connected items.

9.2   Describe graph terminologies such as vertices, edges, adjacency matrix, and adjacency lists.

9.3   Design and implement depth-first traversal for graphs.

9.4   Design and implement breadth-first traversal for graphs.

9.5   Illustrate the differences between directed and undirected graphs.

9.6   Illustrate the differences between weighted and unweighted graphs.

9.1 Introduction to Graphs

Graphs are non-linear data structures that can represent complex relations between data that lists or trees can't capture. A graph is composed of a set of vertices and edges. Each edge joins two vertices. There is no restriction on what vertices are joined by an edge. The lack of restrictions on organizing the connections allows graphs to represent complex structures.

Network Connections

A **network** is a set of interconnected people or things. This broad definition allows for representing many kinds of relationships, from computer networks to social networks.

The first part of a network is the people or things that can be modeled as simple elements of a set or, if necessary, using a more complex user-defined data type. The second part is the connection, which the edges can model.

In **Figure 9-1**, you can see a network of roads connecting some cities and an abstract representation of this network as a graph of vertices and edges.

Figure 9-1   Depiction of a network of cities and its graph representation

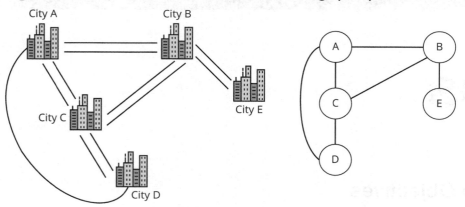

| **Note** | The theory of graphs can be traced back to mathematician Leonhard Euler, who created an abstract description of the bridges of the German city of Königsberg (now a part of Russia). You can see a depiction of the Königsberg bridges in **Figure 9-2**. |

Figure 9-2   Depiction of the Königsberg bridge problem and a graph representation of the problem

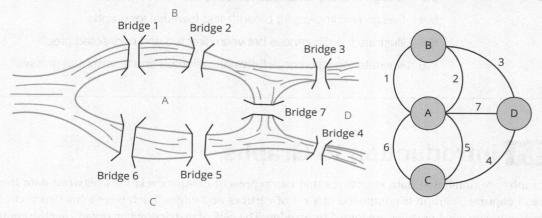

The problem posed to Euler by the people of Königsberg: Find a route in the city that crosses each of the seven bridges exactly once.

The representation of such networks as graphs is useful for creating a computer model of the network. Nevertheless, a variety of graphical representations is common. In **Figure 9-3**, you can see three different representations of the same graph.

Figure 9-3   The same graph relationships can be drawn in different ways

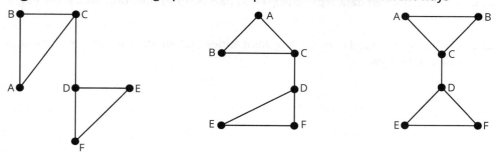

The connections between the vertices are what characterize a graph.

Additional Examples

To illustrate the concepts behind graphs, let's consider a couple more practical examples: a park with a network of paths and a social network.

Consider a natural park with several attractions joined by paths. A map of attractions and the paths can be seen in **Figure 9-4**.

Figure 9-4   Illustration of a park and different attractions connected by paths

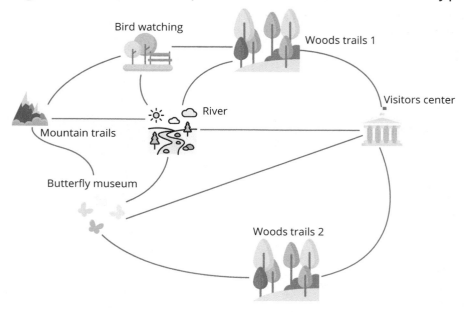

To conceptualize the map's information in a graph data structure, you can think of it in terms of the two parts of a graph:

- Each attraction will be a user-defined data type. These user-defined data types will be the vertices of the graph.
- Each trail will be an edge joining two vertices.

A simple representation of this model is shown in **Figure 9-5**.

Figure 9-5   An abstract graph representation of the park depicted in Figure 9-4

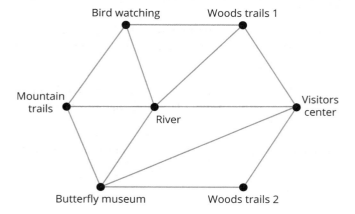

However, this model lacks important information, such as the distance between each attraction. This information can be attached to each edge joining two attractions, which leads to a graph that is not characterized completely by the connection between its vertices but also by the number associated with each edge.

In a more abstract situation, graphs are a great tool to represent the data stored about the relationship between different people in a social network. One way to relate a social network to a graph is by associating each user with a vertex. Then an edge between two vertices is added if the two corresponding users are friends in the social network. **Figure 9-6** illustrates these relationships.

Figure 9-6   A graph representing persons as vertices and edges as the connection of two persons as friends

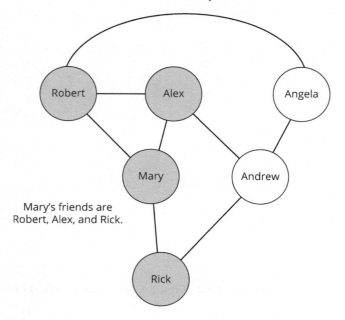

Mary's friends are Robert, Alex, and Rick.

9.2 Graph Terminologies

As an abstract data type (ADT), a graph represents vertices and their connections. Recall that the vertices might be any data type. That means they may be simple references to a set's abstract points or arbitrary elements. Or they could be user-defined data types that, at the same time, are part of another data structure. For example, you could think of all the vertices of a graph as part of a set, the set of all vertices.

The main type of graph used in programming is a directed graph in discrete mathematics. A **directed graph** is a graph where each edge is completely characterized as an ordered pair of vertices. That means the edge joining a and b differs from the edge joining b and a. However, only one edge can join a and b.

Depending on the application, there may be an associated edge value or weight. The **weight of an edge** is a real number assigned to the edge. This weight might represent the distance between two places on roads or the time it takes to send data through a link in a computer network.

In **Figure 9-7**, you can see a directed graph. Notice how an arrow indicates the order of the pair that represents each edge.

Figure 9-7 The set of ordered pairs that compose the edges of a graph and its graphical representation

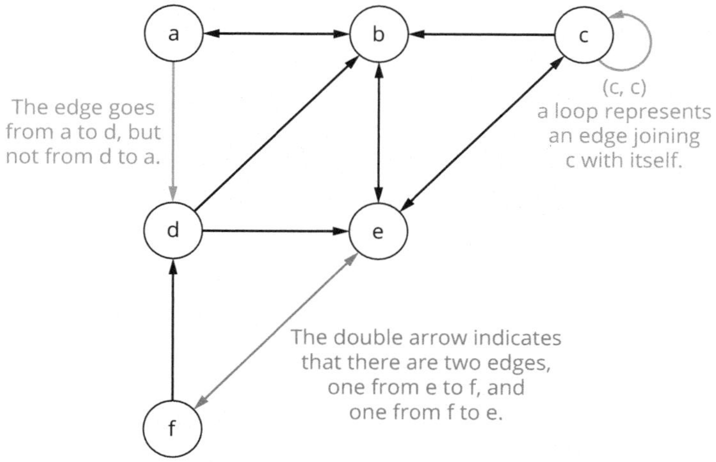

The edge goes from a to d, but not from d to a.

(c, c) a loop represents an edge joining c with itself.

The double arrow indicates that there are two edges, one from e to f, and one from f to e.

The set of edges is represented by {(a, d), (a, b), (a, d), (b, a), (b, e), (c, b), (c, c), (c, e), (d, b), (d, e), (e, b), (e, c), (e, f), (f, d), (f, e)}

A Graph as an Abstract Data Structure

A graph G, as an ADT, consists of a set of vertices V and a set of pairs E, representing all edges. Additionally, it might have an additional function that assigns a weight or value to each edge.

The operations commonly required for a graph ADT are:

- `vertices(G)` return a linear data structure containing all the graph's vertices
- `edges(G)` return a linear data structure containing all the graph's edges
- `add_vertex(G, u)` adds the vertex u to the set of vertices of G
- `adjacent(G, u, v)` returns True if the pair (u,v) is an edge in G and False in another case. If the pair (u,v) is an edge of a directed graph, it is said that u is **adjacent** to v or that v is a **neighbor** of u
- `add_edge(G, u, v)` adds the pair (u,v) to the set of edges
- `remove_edge(G, u, v)` removes the pair (u,v) from the set of edges
- `remove_vertex(G, u)` removes the vertex u from the set of vertices and all the edges related to u
- `neighbors(G, u)` return a linear data structure of all the vertices v such that (u,v) is an edge of G, which means all other vertices with an edge from u

Depending on how the graph is implemented, it might be necessary to have an explicit function to set the values of the weight of an edge (u,v). If the edge is implemented as a user-defined data type with other fields, then the weight can be set by `e.weight = val`.

In **Figure 9-8**, you can see an illustration of a graph and all the previous operations.

Figure 9-8   Operations to add and remove edges and vertices and specify neighbors are illustrated for a graph

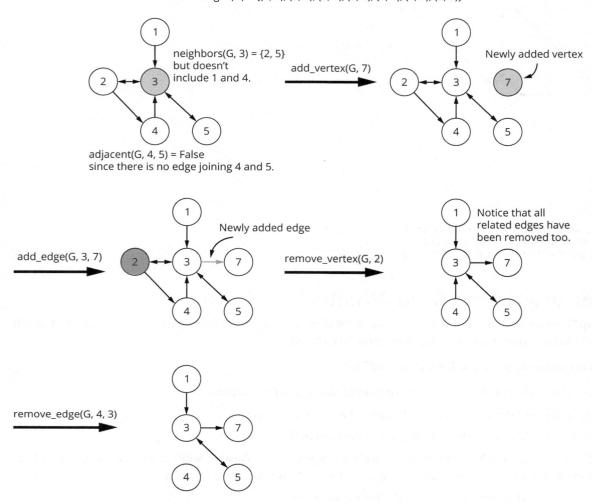

vertices(G) = {1, 2, 3, 4, 5}
edges(G) = {(1, 3), (2, 3), (2, 4), (3, 2), (3, 5), (4, 3), (5, 3)}

neighbors(G, 3) = {2, 5} but doesn't include 1 and 4.

add_vertex(G, 7)

Newly added vertex

adjacent(G, 4, 5) = False since there is no edge joining 4 and 5.

add_edge(G, 3, 7)

Newly added edge

remove_vertex(G, 2)

Notice that all related edges have been removed too.

remove_edge(G, 4, 3)

The Adjacency Matrix

One way to implement the graph ADT is by using a two-dimensional data structure known as a matrix. A **matrix** is a data structure composed of rows and columns that associates data with each row and column.

Commonly a matrix is represented as a rectangular array or table. Matrices have several implementations, but the simplest way to implement them is through a two-dimensional array. That array has as elements arrays of a given size. It is common to associate the entry $M[i, j] = M[i][j]$ with the jth element of the ith array. Although this is a common way to implement matrices, it is not the only one. The ideas of associative arrays and other specialized structures might be used. You can see a matrix represented as an array of arrays in **Figure 9-9**.

Figure 9-9   A matrix represented as an array of arrays

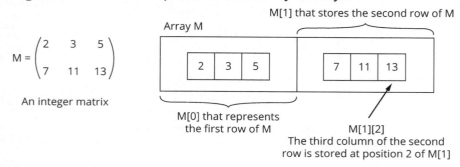

$$M = \begin{pmatrix} 2 & 3 & 5 \\ 7 & 11 & 13 \end{pmatrix}$$

An integer matrix

Array M

M[1] that stores the second row of M

M[0] that represents the first row of M

M[1][2]
The third column of the second row is stored at position 2 of M[1]

Matrices can be used to implement graphs through the adjacency matrix. The **adjacency matrix** of a graph is a matrix where the rows and columns are a list of the graph's vertices, and the data associated is 1 if an edge joins the row vertex with the column vertex and 0 in another case. **Figure 9-10** shows a graph and its adjacency matrix.

Figure 9-10   Two graphs and their adjacency matrices

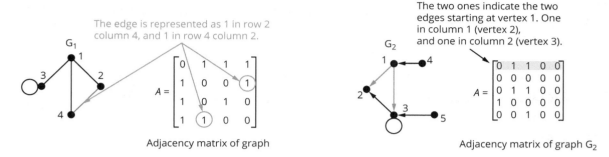

Adjacency matrix of graph   Adjacency matrix of graph G₂

To have a dynamic graph using an adjacency matrix, it is necessary to have a dynamic matrix implementation. That means implementing a matrix where a new row and column can be added or removed.

Supposing that the set of vertices V is given, an implementation of graph G might follow the code described in this snippet.

```
type graph
    fields
        N ;; The number of vertices
        ;; The list of vertices starts as an array of Null values
        ;; or an associative array of Null values
        vertex_array = new array[N]
        ;; The adjacency matrix starts as a new array of zeros
        adjacency_matrix = integer array[N][N]
```

With the previous implementation, to access a vertex it is necessary to identify it with an integer value. A way to avoid that is to use a hash function that transforms the key values into indices for the adjacency matrix. In the following pseudocode you can see the add_vertex, add_edge, adjacent, and neighbors operations.

```
add_vertex(G, v, node)
    ;; the node is added to the vertex list.
    ;; There is no need to modify
    ;; the adjacency matrix
    vertex_array[v] = node ;; add the node into the list of vertices

add_edge(G, u, v)
    ;; the creation of the node is reflected in the adjacency matrix
    A = G.adjacency_matrix
    A[u][v] = 1

adjacent(G, u, v)
    if A[u][v] = 1
        return True
    else
        return False
```

```
neighbors(G, v)
    N = G.N
    A = G.adjacency_matrix
    answ = new list()
    total = 0
    for u = 0 to N-1 step 1
        if A[v][u] = 1
            ;; if a 1 entry is found in the adjacency matrix
            ;; an integer identifying the vertex is inserted
            add(answ, total, u)
            total = total + 1
    return answ
```

Quick Check 9-1

Consider the graph depicted in **Figure 9-11**.

Figure 9-11 **Graph associated with Quick Check 9-1**

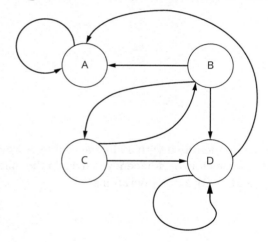

Provide its adjacency matrix.

Answer:

	A	B	C	D
A	1	0	0	0
B	1	0	1	1
C	0	1	0	1
D	1	0	0	1

Notice that the loop that starts and ends at vertex D is represented in the adjacency matrix as a one in the fourth row and fourth column.

Notice that the adjacency matrix implementation of a graph makes the search for neighbors and insertion relatively simple. One drawback of this implementation is that to delete a vertex, it is necessary to modify all the entries in the adjacency matrix related to the deleted vertex. You can see an implementation of `remove_vertex` here.

```
remove_vertex(G, v)
    G.vertex[v] = Null
    N = G.N
    A = G.adjacency_matrix
    for j = 0 to N - 1 step 1
        ;; set all entries at row v to zero
        A[v][j] = 0
        ;; set all entries in column v to zero
        A[j][v] = 0
```

Notice that the index i of the `vertex_array` is now free to be filled with a new vertex.

The adjacency matrix representation can be made very efficient since each entry doesn't need to be an integer but only a Boolean value, True or False. But if the number of edges is much smaller than the number of vertices squared, there will be a large number of zero entries in the matrix. A matrix where most entries are zero is called a **sparse matrix**.

Best Practice

There is a complete family of algorithms dedicated to efficiently working with sparse matrices. But if the number of edges is closer to n than to n^2, then it is usually better to use the adjacency list implementation. The other factor to consider is if the set of vertices changes dynamically. When changes in the set of vertices are small or nonexistent, and the number of edges is larger than n, then using an adjacency matrix is more convenient. But if the set of vertices changes frequently, the adjacency list implementation is preferred.

The Adjacency List

Another implementation for a graph is the **adjacency list**. In the adjacency list implementation, the graph has a linear structure storing all the vertices and associated to each vertex v is a linked list of all the vertices u such that the edge (v,u) is part of the graph (in other words, a list of adjacent nodes). **Figure 9-12** shows a graph and its adjacency list.

Figure 9-12   A graph and a depiction of its adjacency list implementation

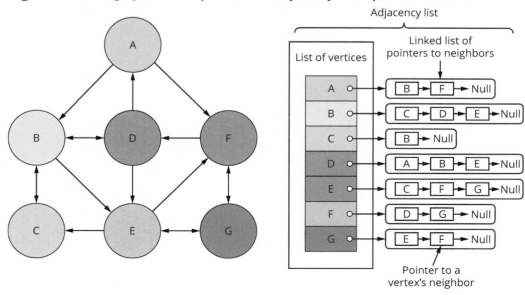

Implementing a graph using adjacency lists saves space since it is only necessary to store pointers to the neighbor vertices. Inserting a new edge (u,v) requires adding a new node to the adjacent vertices of u. But to remove a vertex v, it is necessary to search for v in the adjacency list of each vertex u. You can see an implementation of a graph using adjacency lists here.

```
type graph_node
    fields
        ;; each field has a key
        key
        ;; and a list of adjacent nodes
        pointer_list = new list()


type graph
    fields
        ;; An empty list of vertices is used
        V = new list()
```

Using the operations over a list, which could be implemented using a singly linked list, a doubly linked list, or a binary tree, it is possible to describe the main operations of a graph ADT. The following is an implementation for the add_edge and remove_vertex operations.

```
add_edge(G, key1, key2)
    u = search(G.V, key1)
    v = search(G.V, key2)

    add(u.pointer_list, v)

remove_vertex(G, key1)
    remove(G.V, key1)
    for v in G.V
        remove(v.pointer_list, key1)
```

Notice that the complexity of the operations depends on the structures used to implement the set of vertices and the list of adjacencies. For example, if a linked list is used, the search and remove operations have $O(n)$ complexity, where n is the number of neighbors a vertex has. But if a balanced binary tree is used, the search operation has $O(\log n)$ complexity. Recall that that comes with the overhead that the insertion will also have a $O(\log n)$ complexity.

Quick Check 9-2

Given the following adjacency matrix:

	A	B	C	D
A	1	0	0	1
B	1	0	1	0
C	0	1	0	1
D	1	0	1	1

What are the elements of the `pointer_list` of vertex D? What are the elements of the `pointer_list` of A?

Answer:

```
D.pointer_list = [ A, C, D ]
A.pointer_list = [ A, D ]
```

Notice that the pointer list for each vertex is a simplified representation of the corresponding row of the adjacency matrix.

9.3 Depth-First Traversal

Since a graph might have complex connections between its nodes, there is no expected way to traverse such nodes. Like other non-linear data structures, the data can be traversed in arbitrary order. Nevertheless, some ways have been proven useful in some applications.

Depth-first graph traversal refers to a way of traversing graph nodes where, starting at node u, all nonvisited adjacent nodes v are traversed in a depth-first way.

Notice that the definition of depth-first has a recursive nature. Keeping track of all visited nodes is necessary to avoid entering an infinite loop. In **Figure 9-13**, you can see how the depth-first traversal is executed over a graph.

Figure 9-13   Depth-first traversal of a graph

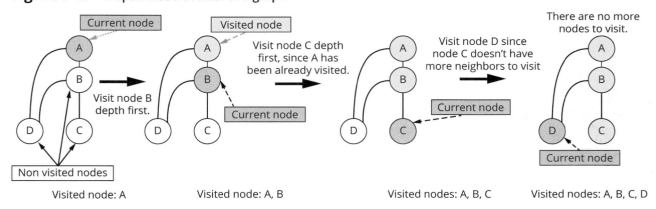

Notice that how the adjacent nodes are listed is relevant to the result. You can see two different results of the depth-first traversal for the same graph in **Figure 9-14**.

Figure 9-14 Depth-first traversal for the same graph using a different order for the neighbors

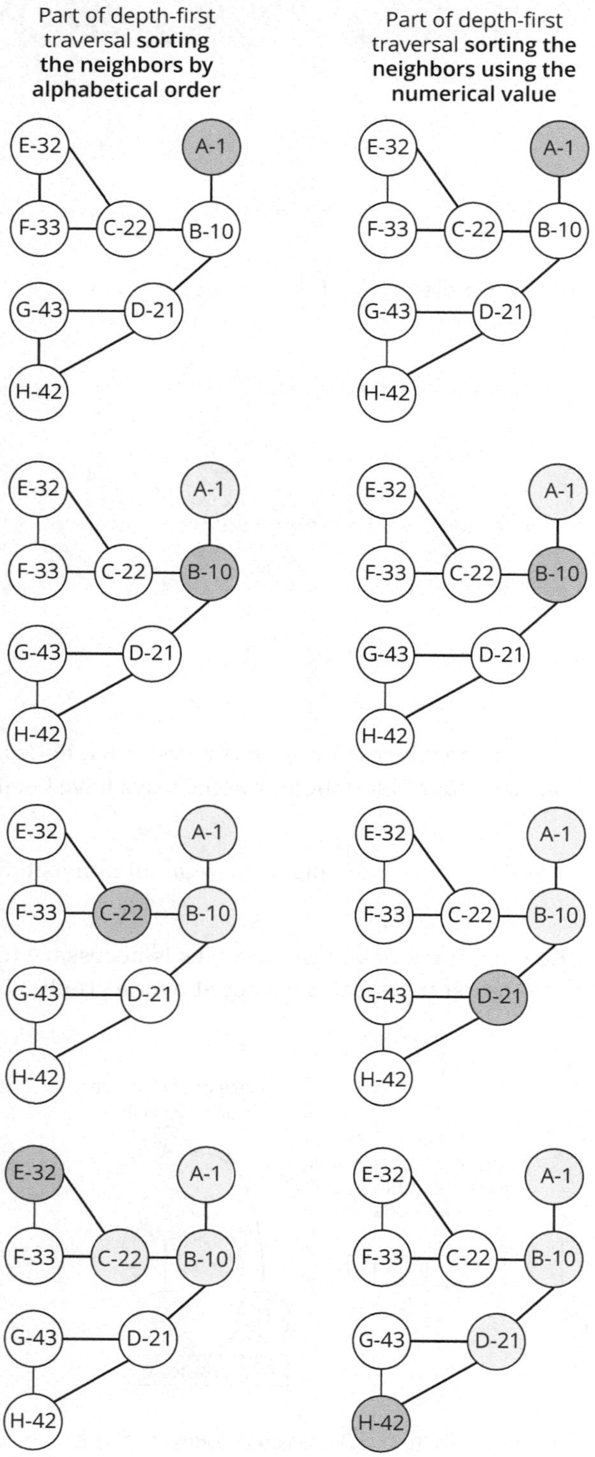

Choosing a way to sort the nodes is relevant to the traversal result. That means that how the adjacent nodes are presented or sorted might significantly affect the result of an algorithm.

| Note | The term *depth-first* is used also in the context of trees. The common terminology is due in part to the fact that a tree can also be considered a graph. Since a tree is composed of vertices and edges joining parents to children, it can be considered a graph. On the other hand, not every graph can be considered a tree. The key observation is that in a tree two siblings can't be connected by an edge. A consequence of the previous restriction in trees is that it is not possible to have a set of vertices $v_1, v_2, \ldots, v_N = v_1$ all distinct, such that $(v_1, v_2), (v_2, v_3), \ldots, (v_N, v_1)$ form a path starting and ending at v_1. |

Best Practice

When solving a problem that involves the use of nodes and connections between them, the more general data type to model the data is a graph. Nevertheless, a careful analysis should be made to determine if a linked list or a tree data type would be more appropriate, since trees and linked lists have more specialized methods. In large-scale problems (such as in databases) and in applications where performance is crucial (such as with embedded devices and medical hardware), using a more specialized data structure such as a tree instead of a graph can have a great impact. For example, although linked lists, trees, and graphs all have traversal procedures, the graph traversal is more complex and requires more resources (storing the visited nodes and checking the list). The extra complexity might affect performance in critical tasks, making another data structure a better choice for some situations. However, you should not shy away from the use of graphs where the scale is smaller and/or performance is not as critical.

Implementing Depth-First Traversal

The following code shows an implementation of the depth-first traversal for a graph that uses an associative array `visited` to keep track of the visited nodes. During the first call to `depth_first_recursive(G, v, visited)`, the `visited` array has all the vertices associated with False values since no vertex has been visited.

```
;; start with a call with v the starting node
;; and visited a linear data structure with all initialized to False
depth_first_recursive(G, v, visited)
    visited[v] = True
    display(v.data)
    for u in neighbors(G, v)
        if visited[u] = False
            depth_first_recursive(G, u, visited)
```

You can see an example of how the procedure works in **Figure 9-15**.

Figure 9-15   Recursive calls made during a depth-first traversal

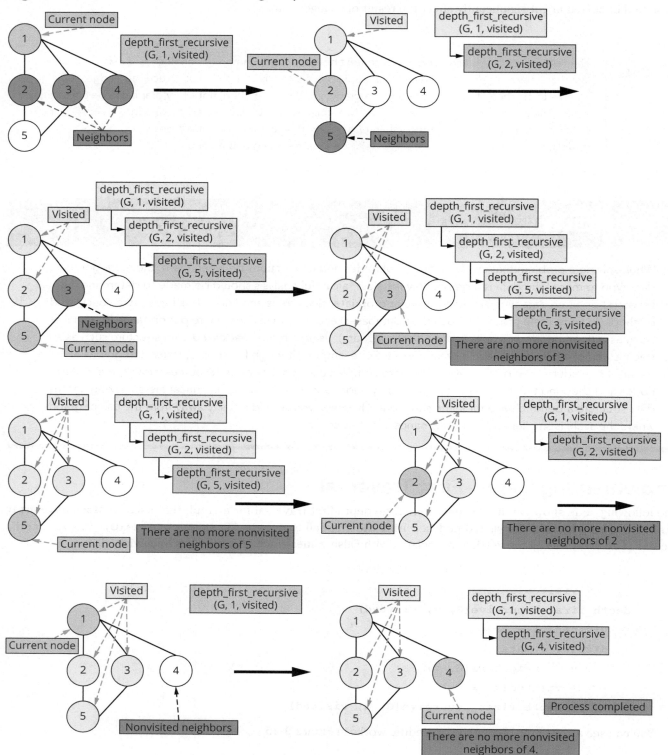

To implement a nonrecursive version of the depth-first traversal, an auxiliary data structure must store the nodes that haven't been visited. In **Figure 9-16**, you can see an illustration of the idea. The auxiliary data structure stores the nodes adjacent to a visited node but is pending to be traversed.

Figure 9-16   Depth-first traversal of a graph and the stack used to make the procedure iterative

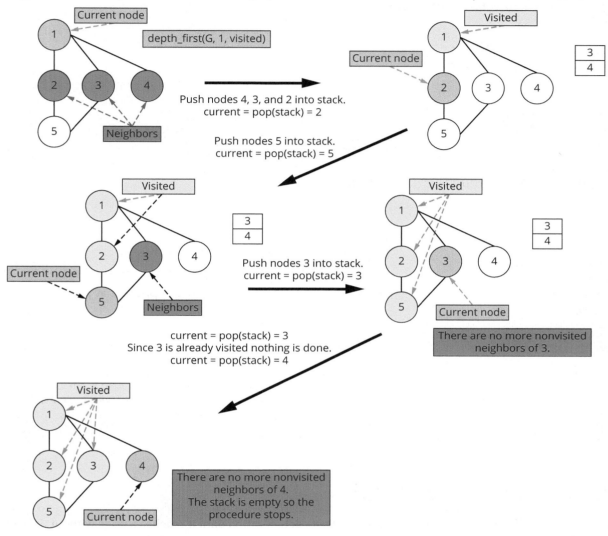

Here is an iterative implementation of the depth-first traversal:

```
depth_first_traverse(G, u)
    ;; the visited structure is set to all False
    visited = new Array[G.N]
    curr = u
    ;; the pending stack will hold the nodes
    ;; that have not been visited
    pending = new stack()
    push(pending, curr)
    while not empty(pending)
```

```
;; while there are still nodes pending to visit
curr = pop(pending)
display(curr.data)
visited[curr] = True
for v in neighbors(G, curr)
    ;; add only the neighbors that have not been visited
    if visited[v] = False
        push(pending, v)
```

Quick Check 9-3

Consider a graph with the following adjacency matrix:

$$
\begin{array}{c c c c c}
 & A & B & C & D \\
A & 1 & 0 & 1 & 1 \\
B & 1 & 0 & 1 & 0 \\
C & 0 & 0 & 0 & 1 \\
D & 1 & 0 & 1 & 0 \\
\end{array}
$$

In which order are displayed the nodes if the graph is traversed in a depth-first order, suppose that you start with the node A?

Answer: A, C, D, B

Since the nodes are visited in a depth-first order after the node A is visited, the node C and all its neighbors are visited. Since the node C has D as a neighbor, this node is visited. At this point, there are no more neighbors to visit for C. Hence, the node D should be visited, but it was already visited. Thus, its neighbors are visited, which means that B is visited. Since B has no neighbors that haven't been visited, the procedure is complete.

9.4 Breadth-First Traversal

Depth-first traversal moves further away from the initial node at each iteration until it reaches a node without links or connected to an already visited node. Another approach to traversing a graph might be visiting all adjacent nodes to a given node first and then moving to the children. **Breadth-first graph traversal** is a way of traversing a graph where all adjacent nodes are visited and then all the nodes adjacent to a neighbor are traversed. You can see an illustration of a breadth-first traversal in **Figure 9-17**.

When traversing the graph using a breadth-first approach, notice that the nodes that are closer to the starting node are the ones that are visited first. You can see the breadth-first traversal compared to the depth-first in **Figure 9-18**.

The fact that the nodes closer to the starting one are visited first makes the breadth-first traversal ideal for discovering the shortest paths. That means finding a sequence of edges that joins the starting vertex u with another vertex v.

Figure 9-17   Breadth-first traversal of a graph

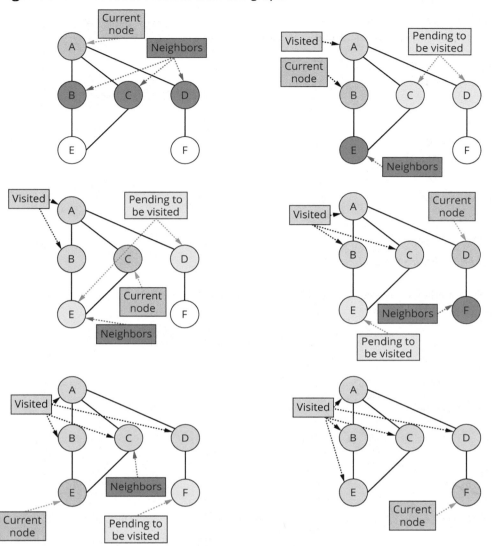

Figure 9-18   Depth-first traversal and breadth-first traversal for the same graph

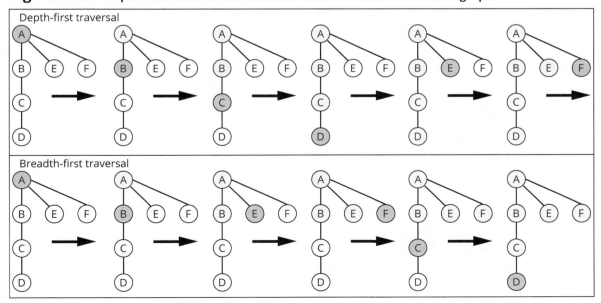

Implementing Breadth-First Traversal

To implement a breadth-first traversal, two additional data structures are used, one to record which nodes have been visited and one to store the nodes adjacent to the ones already visited.

```
breadth_first_traversal(G, u)
    visited = new array[G.N]
    pending = new queue()
    enqueue(pending, u)
    while not empty(pending)
        curr = dequeue(pending)
        visited[curr] = True
        for v in neighbors(G, curr)
            if visited[v] = False
                enqueue(pending, v)
```

You can see this code illustrated in **Figure 9-19**.

Figure 9-19   Breadth-first traversal and the queue used to make the procedure iterative

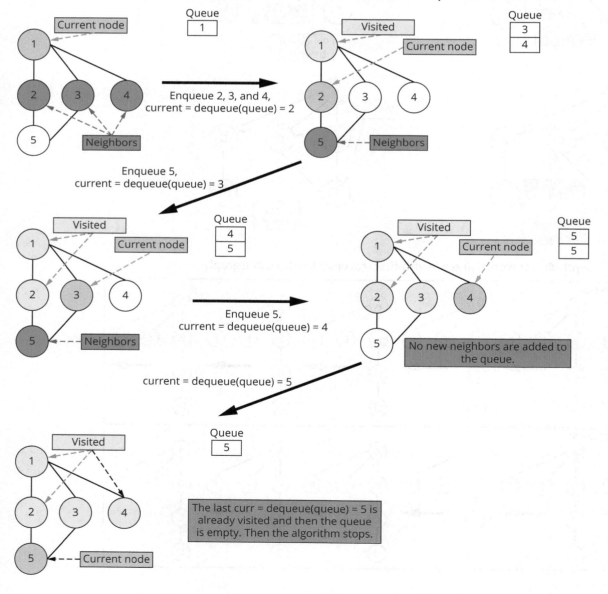

Notice that the traversal might be affected by the order in which the neighbor vertices of a given vertex v are listed during the innermost loop in the previous implementation.

9.5 Directed and Undirected Graphs

In a network of connections, it is common to have an edge joining a with b but no edge joining b with a. When the order of the vertices that form an edge is relevant, it is said that the associated graph is directed.

When the edges of a graph are represented through ordered pairs, then:

$$(a,b) \neq (b,a)$$

unless $a = b$. The set of ordered pairs in such cases represents the directed graph.

Generally, a set of ordered pairs is called a **binary relation**. In the case of a graph, the binary relation is over the set of vertices.

As the name suggests, binary relations help describe relations between elements of a set. For example, given the set $X = [4, 3, 12, 20, 24, 36]$, it is possible to define a relation by saying that a is related to b if a is a proper divisor of b. In **Figure 9-20**, all pairs or elements compose the relation.

Figure 9-20   Set of pairs of the relation: "a is a proper divisor of b"

(3, 12)   (3, 24)   (3, 36)

(4, 12)   (4, 20)   (4, 24)   (4, 36)

(12, 24)   (12, 36)

A slightly easier-to-read representation is the graph representation of the relation. You can see this in **Figure 9-21**.

Figure 9-21   Graph representation of the relation "a is a proper divisor of b"

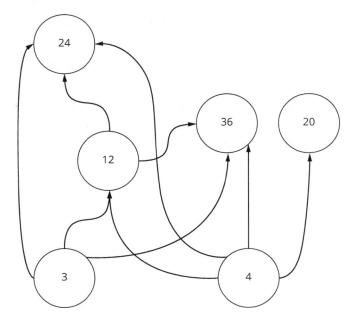

Notice that the order of the elements is relevant since 4 divides 12, but 12 does not divide 4. The graph has arrows pointing from one vertex to the adjacent one. When applying a traversal starting at a node—for example, 3—not all the graph nodes are visited. This is because the edges are followed in the direction represented by the arrows. It is only sometimes possible to reach all the nodes of the graph. In **Figure 9-22**, you can see the breadth-first traversal of the graph starting at node 3.

Figure 9-22   A breadth-first traversal of the graph representing the divisibility relation

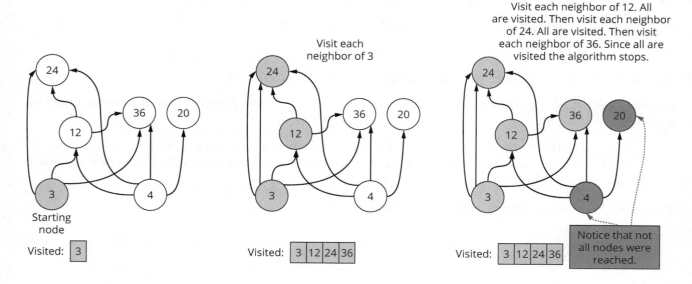

When the order of the vertices that compose an edge is not relevant, it is said that the graph is an **undirected graph**. Another way of making a graph undirected is to ensure that each time an edge from a to b is inserted, the corresponding edge from b to a is also inserted.

In terms of the relations that a graph represents, every undirected graph represents a relation with the **symmetric property**. A relation is said to be symmetric if the ordered pair (a,b) is part of the relation, then the pair (b,a) is also part of the relation.

The main difference between directed and undirected graphs is that all edges can be traveled in two directions in an undirected graph.

In a directed graph, if (a,b) is an edge, it follows that (b,a) is also an edge. The adjacency matrix must be symmetric, which means that if you switch rows and columns, the matrix results in the same. You can see an illustration of a directed and undirected graph with the corresponding adjacency matrices in **Figure 9-23**.

Figure 9-23   Directed and undirected graphs, with their respective adjacency matrices. Notice that the directed matrix is not symmetrical

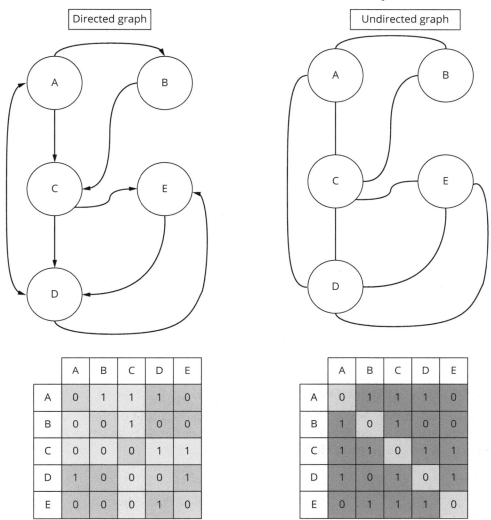

	A	B	C	D	E
A	0	1	1	1	0
B	0	0	1	0	0
C	0	0	0	1	1
D	1	0	0	0	1
E	0	0	0	1	0

	A	B	C	D	E
A	0	1	1	1	0
B	1	0	1	0	0
C	1	1	0	1	1
D	1	0	1	0	1
E	0	1	1	1	0

9.6 Weighted Graphs

When representing a network such as a network of roads, it is sometimes necessary to have additional information about the edges. For example, it might be necessary to have the distance that a road, represented by an edge, extends or the gasoline cost of traveling on such a road. When such information is necessary, it is said that a graph is weighted.

A **weighted graph** comprises the set of vertices V, the set of edges represented by pairs of vertices, and a weight function or association that assigns a weight or cost to each edge in the graph. The cost or weight of an edge is usually denoted by $d(a,b)$ or $w(e_i)$.

Figure 9-24 shows a graph where the weight of each edge represents the distance that separates different attractions in a park.

Figure 9-24 A graph representing attractions in a park. The weight of the edges represents the distance between the attractions

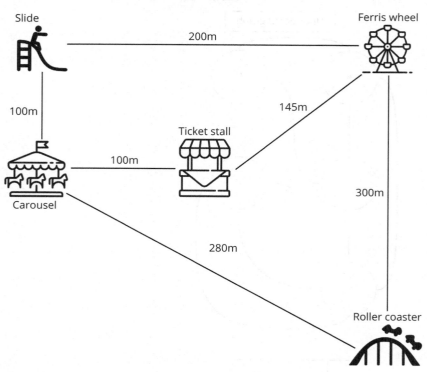

Describing the Cost of Travels in a Network

Recall that a path in a graph is a sequence of edges $e_1, e_2, \ldots, e_N$ where each edge e_i joins u, v and e_{i+1} joins v, w. In other words, the path describes a sequence of edges that can be traversed, moving from one node to an adjacent one. You can see an illustration of some paths in a weighted graph in **Figure 9-25**.

Figure 9-25 Two paths in weighted graphs

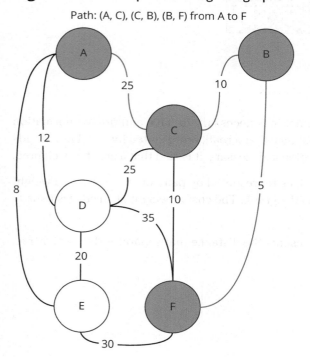

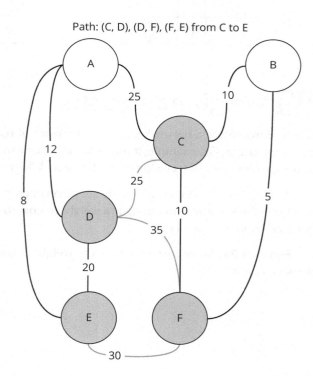

Notice that even if two paths have the same starting and final vertices, they differ from an application point of view. For example, they differ when the weight represents the distance necessary to move from one vertex to an adjacent one. **Figure 9-26** shows two paths joining vertices A and B, but g_1 is shorter than g_2.

Figure 9-26   Two paths joining the vertices A and B

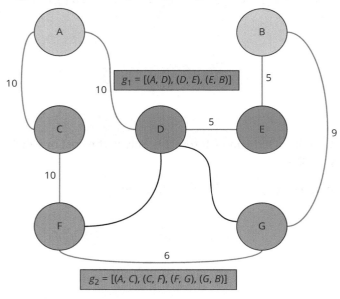

In general, given a path $g : e_1, e_2, \ldots, e_n$, the cost of the path, or the cost of traveling such path, is:

$$w(g) = w(e_1) + w(e_2) + \cdots + w(e_n)$$

For example, in Figure 9-26, the cost of g_1 is 20, while the cost of g_2 is 35. The word *cost* should not make you believe that the objective is always to have a lower cost. The objective will depend on the application. For example, if the cost of each edge represents the total payment received after traveling an edge, you would want to maximize the path's cost.

The adjacency matrix is a way to implement and represent a weighted graph. Instead of storing binary values for whether an edge joins two vertices, its weight is stored in the matrix. You can see a weighted graph and its adjacency matrix used to store the weights in **Figure 9-27**.

Figure 9-27   A weighted graph and its adjacency matrix. The infinity weight is used in the places where there is no edge joining two vertices

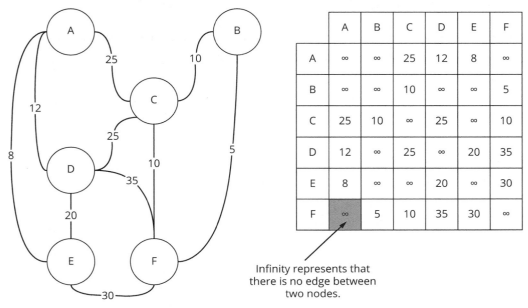

	A	B	C	D	E	F
A	∞	∞	25	12	8	∞
B	∞	∞	10	∞	∞	5
C	25	10	∞	25	∞	10
D	12	∞	25	∞	20	35
E	8	∞	∞	20	∞	30
F	∞	5	10	35	30	∞

Infinity represents that there is no edge between two nodes.

Multigraphs

When describing connections between places, like the case of a road network, there is likely to be more than one road from one city to an adjacent one. In such cases, the description of an edge as an ordered pair needs to be revised.

A **multigraph** is a structure composed of a set of vertices V and a set of edges E, where each edge e has the following properties:

- source(e) the starting vertex
- target(e) the target vertex
- weight(e) the weight of the vertex
- key(e) a unique key identifier or label

The key value is only useful to refer to a specific edge. It is omitted if the main interest is only in the cost or weight of the edge. You can see an illustration of a multigraph in **Figure 9-28**.

Figure 9-28   A multigraph. Notice that there is more than one edge joining the vertices 3 and 5

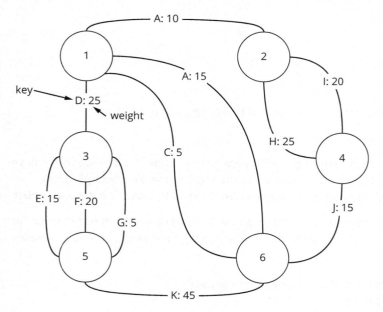

A possible implementation of a multigraph that uses a user-defined data type for the edges and an adjacency list is shown here:

```
;; user defined data type
;; edge with all the properties associated with it
type edge
    fields
        s ;; pointer to source edge
        t ;; pointer to target edge
        w ;; weight
        k ;; label or key
```

```
type vertex
   fields
       key   ;; unique identifier
       data ;; data stored in vertex
       neighbors = new list()

type multigraph
   fields
       V = array vertices[]
       E = array edges[]

add_vertex(G, u)
   add(G.V, u)

adjacent(G, u, v)
   for x in u.neighbors
      if x.t.key = v.key
         return True
   return False

add_edge(G, source, target, weight, key)
   new_edge = new edge(source, target, weight, key)
   add(source.neighbors, new_edge)
   add(G.E, new_edge)

remove_edge(G, key)
   e = get(G.E, key)
   s = e.s
   delete(s.neighbors, key)
   delete(G.E, key)
```

Technical Interview

When using recursion to solve a problem that uses a graph, keep in mind that a data structure keeping record of the visited nodes is necessary. Failing to keep track of the visited or processed nodes might lead to infinite loops, which are not usually present in a tree.

Summary

- A graph is a non-linear data structure representing node relations using edges. A graph is a more general structure than a tree.

- Graphs can be used to represent networks of computers, roads, and even social network connections.

- The two main classifications of graphs are directed and undirected and, within these, weighted and unweighted.

- In a directed graph, each edge has an orientation. Thus, an edge from a to b is different from an edge from b to a.

- In a weighted graph, each edge has an associated number called a weight. The weight is useful to represent additional data, such as distance or cost.

- The graph ADT has some common operations such as `edges(G)` that returns the set of all edges, `adjacent(G, u, v)` that returns True if the two vertices u and v are adjacent, and `neighbor (G, u)` that returns a data structure with all adjacent vertices to u.

- There are two main structures used to represent a graph. The adjacency matrix is a matrix with 1 at the row u and column v if there is an edge joining u with v. An adjacency list uses a list associated with each node to store all neighbors of a node.

- A graph can be traversed in a depth-first way where each adjacent node to a node u is traversed in a depth-first way. You can think of depth-first traversal as getting away from the initial node before exploring all other possibilities.

- The breadth-first graph traversal visits the set of all siblings of a node before visiting the neighbors of each one.

- When more information than just the nodes it connects is necessary for an edge, it might be associated with a label, a weight, and even additional data. In such instances, more than a single edge can join two vertices. Such a structure is known as a multigraph.

Key Terms

adjacency list	directed graph	symmetric property
adjacency matrix	matrix	undirected graph
adjacent	multigraph	weight of an edge
binary relation	neighbors	weighted graph
breadth-first graph traversal	network	
depth-first graph traversal	sparse matrix	

Review Questions

1. The graph in **Figure 9-29** depicts friends in a social network.

Figure 9-29   Graph depicting a social network for Review Question 1

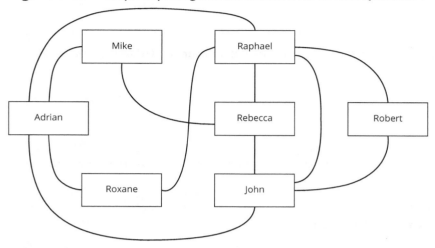

Who are Raphael's friends?

    a. Roxane, Rebecca, Adrian, Robert

    b. Roxane, Rebecca, Mike, Robert

    c. Roxane, Rebecca, Adrian, Robert, John

    d. Rebecca, Mike, John

2. Consider the graph depicted in **Figure 9-30**. Which of the following is correct?

Figure 9-30   Graph for Review Questions 2–4

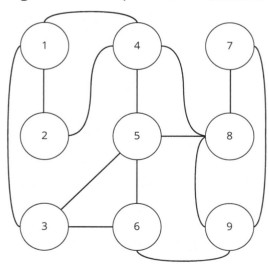

    a. $neighbors(G,8) = \{4,5,7,9\}$

    b. $neighbors(G,5) = \{3,4,8,\ 9\}$

    c. $neighbors(G,8) = \{4,5,6,7,9\}$

    d. $neighbors(G,6) = \{3,5,8\}$

3. Create an adjacency matrix for the graph depicted in Figure 9-30.

4. Suppose an alphabetical order to list the nodes during depth-first traversal is used. What is the order in which the graph nodes in Figure 9-30 are visited starting at *A*? Assume depth-first traversal is used.

    a. A, B, C, D, E, F, G, H, I
    b. A, B, D, E, C, F, I, H, G
    c. A, B, D, E, F, I, G, H, C
    d. A, B, C, D, E, F, H, I, G

5. In the breadth-first traversal of a graph, the neighbors of each visited node are added to what data structure?

    a. queue
    b. associative array
    c. stack
    d. adjacency matrix

6. Suppose an nondirected graph is represented using its adjacency matrix. Which of the following must always be true?

    a. Every node *a* is adjacent to itself.
    b. Every node is adjacent to at least one other node.
    c. If *a* is adjacent to *b*, then *b* is adjacent to *a*.
    d. If *a* is adjacent to *b*, then *b* might not be adjacent to *a*.

7. Consider the graph depicted in **Figure 9-31**. Write the paths joining nodes *A* and *B* without repeated edges.

8. Suppose the implementation used in the text for a multigraph is used. Draw the graph resulting after the following code.

Figure 9-31   Graph for Review Question 7

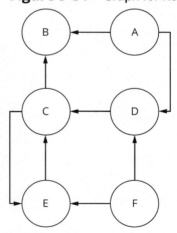

```
M = multigraph()
for i = 0 to 3 step 1
    u = new vertex(i, i)
    add_vertex(M, u)
```

```
for j = 0 to 10 step 1
    idx0 = j mod 4
    s = M.V[idx0]
    idx1 = (j*2) mod 4
    t = M.V[idx1]
    add_edge(M, s, t, 2*j, j)
```

9. Consider the graph shown in **Figure 9-32**. What is the cost of the path [(1, 6), (6, 5), (5, 4), (4, 2)]?

Figure 9-32   Graph for Review Question 9

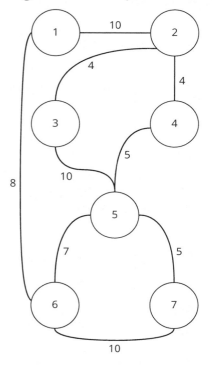

10. Suppose a graph has many vertices but fewer edges. What specialized data structure is the most efficient for storing the graph's adjacency matrix?

Programming Problems

1. Suppose graph G describes a set of roads connecting different buildings. Write a program that uses depth-first traversal to find a path from two given buildings, A and B. **(LO 9.1, 9.2, 9.3)**

2. Given a directed graph G, write a program that reverses the graph. Construct a graph G' with the same set of vertices; for each edge (u,v) in G, there is an edge (v,u) in G'. **(LO 9.1, 9.2)**

3. Write a program that determines if, in a given graph G, there is a path that starts at a node and ends at the same node. **(LO 9.2, 9.4, 9.5)**

4. In a weighted graph G, its vertices represent cities in a state. The edges represent roads connecting two cities directly. The weight of an edge is the time it takes to travel the road. Write a program that receives an origin city and displays all cities that can be visited during the same day (that can be visited in less than 24 hours). Assume that the weights are given in hours. **(LO 9.1, 9.5, 9.6)**

5. To implement a graph with a dynamic set of vertices and an adjacency matrix, it is necessary to implement a dynamic matrix. Recall that a matrix can be implemented as an array $M[\,]$ where each entry $M[i]$ is an array. Hence, a dynamic matrix can be implemented using a dynamic array instead of a static array. Write an implementation for a dynamical matrix using a linked list instead of an array that stores integer values using integer keys for its indices. Assume default values of 0 when they are not specified. Include operations to add a new row and a new column and to get a specific entry on the matrix.

Projects

Project 9-1: Squaring a Graph

(LO 9.1, 9.2, 9.4) The square of graph G is a new graph S with the same set of vertices such that the edges of S are all (a, c) such that for some vertex b, (a, b) and (b, c) are edges of G. Write a program that constructs the square of a graph G.

Project 9-2: Maze to Graph

(LO 9.1, 9.2, 9.3) Consider a matrix A of zeros and ones that describes a maze. A player can only move from a position with a 1 to another position above, below, to the right, or to the left if there is a 1 in that position. Write a program that converts the maze matrix into a graph representing the original matrix, as shown in **Figure 9-33**.

Figure 9-33 A matrix representing a maze and its graph representation

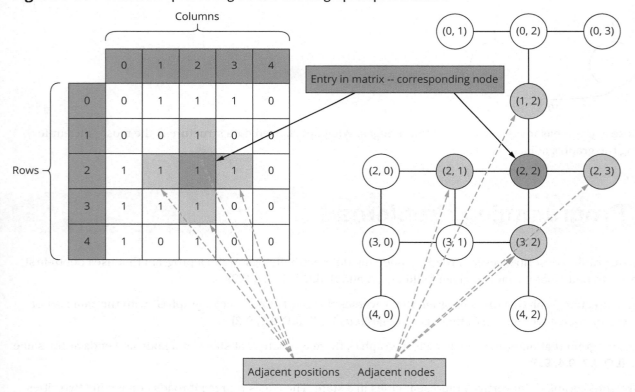

Project 9-3: Coloring Graphs

(LO 9.1, 9.2, 9.4) A common problem is assigning colors to the vertices of a graph in such a way that two adjacent vertices have different colors. A special type of graph called bi-partite can be colored with only two colors. Write a program determining if graph G can be colored with only two colors.

Project 9-4: Finding All Paths

(LO 9.2, 9.4) Write a program that enumerates all paths from a given node A to any other node in graph G that uses exactly m steps. Don't count paths that pass through the same edge more than once.

Chapter 10

Advanced Algorithms

Learning Objectives

Upon completion of this chapter, you will be able to:

10.1   Describe the design and implementation of greedy algorithms.

10.2   Construct a solution using dynamic programming.

10.3   Design and implement a graph's shortest path using Dijkstra's algorithm.

10.4   Design and implement the KMP algorithm to identify a string pattern.

10.5   Implement algorithms to compute the minimum spanning tree of a graph.

10.6   Implement algorithms to label regions and find contours in binary images.

10.1 Greedy Algorithms

Optimization is one of the most difficult problems in computer science. An **optimization problem** maximizes or minimizes a quantity, subject to certain conditions.

Suppose you have 100-, 50-, and 10-dollar denomination bills. Your task is to choose five bills of one denomination, eight of a second denomination, and 10 of the third denomination. The selection of denominations should be such that the total gathered with the 23 bills is the maximum amount of money possible.

In an optimization problem, the **objective function** is the quantity to maximize or minimize. The objective function of the problem described in the previous paragraph would be the total sum of the 23 bills.

One attempt to solve the problem might be to take five 100-dollar bills, eight 50-dollar bills, and five 10-dollar bills. That gives a total of 950 dollars. This solution doesn't provide the maximum amount possible or even use all the available bills, but it satisfies the constraint of the maximum number of possible bills to pick. A set of values that satisfies the given set of constraints of an optimization problem is called a **feasible solution**. The solution to an optimization problem only comes from the set of feasible solutions.

A **greedy algorithm** divides a problem into subproblems and builds a feasible solution for each subproblem that maximizes or minimizes the objective function.

To illustrate why a greedy algorithm works, consider the problem of the bills previously described. The problem can be divided into subproblems of choosing the denomination of the 10 bills, then the denomination of the eight bills, and finally, the denomination of the five bills. When choosing the denomination of the 10 bills, the choice is made so the total is maximized. This means the 100-dollar denomination is chosen for the first 10 bills. The next choice made is the denomination for the eight bills. The choice that maximizes the total is to use the 50-dollar denomination. That leaves only the possibility of choosing the 10-dollar denomination for the remaining five bills.

At each step, the previously taken steps, or how the current decision might affect the following steps, are not considered. Only maximizing the objective function under the current constraints is considered. This strategy is called the local best choice.

Parts of a Greedy Algorithm

Not all problems can be solved using the local best choice strategy. One such case is the traveling salesperson problem. Suppose you are given a list of cities and the distances between them, as described in the graphs in **Figure 10-1**. The problem consists of finding a route that starts at A and ends at A, visiting every city once, in such a way that the cost is minimized. In this problem, the best local choice lets you visit another city traveling the least distance. But the best choice of locals might put you in a position where in order to reach the next city the distance would increase much more than what you saved using the local best choice.

Figure 10-1 When searching a path that traverses all vertices of a graph with minimum cost, using a greedy choice can result in a nonoptimal solution

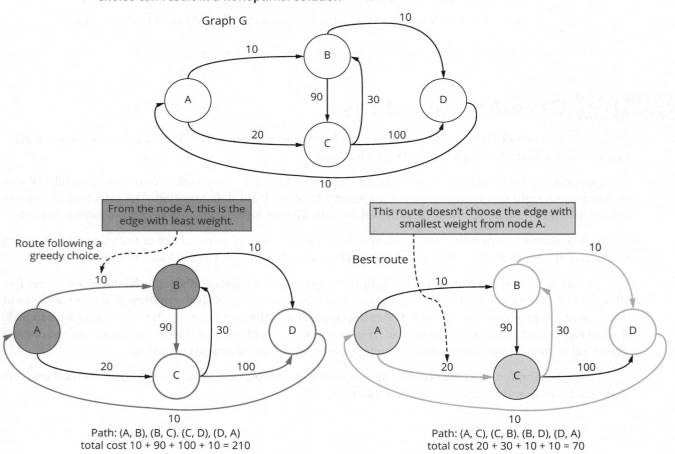

Path: (A, B), (B, C). (C, D), (D, A)
total cost 10 + 90 + 100 + 10 = 210

Path: (A, C), (C, B). (B, D), (D, A)
total cost 20 + 30 + 10 + 10 = 70

Following the local best choice might not lead to an optimal solution in this example. To have a globally optimal solution using a greedy strategy, the problem must have two properties: the greedy choice property and the optimal sub-structure property.

The **greedy choice property** means that taking the locally optimal solution at each step of the problem, that is, taking the local best choice, would lead to a globally optimal solution. Since the local best choice must be part of the set of feasible solutions, it might depend on previously taken steps, but it can't depend on future choices.

For example, in the bill choice problem, once the local best choice of using ten 100-dollar bills is taken, the choice in the second step is restricted to bills of 50- or 10-dollar denominations. So once the best local choice is taken, the set of feasible solutions is affected, hence the best local choice.

A problem possesses **optimal sub-structure** when an optimal solution is composed of optimal solutions to its subproblems. To illustrate this, consider the problem of choosing the denominations of bills again. The global problem of choosing all the denominations is composed of several subproblems. One of them is to choose two of the denominations. Once the choice of one of the bills is made, an optimal solution for choosing the two remaining denominations is necessary to build an optimal solution. So, the problem possesses an optimal sub-structure.

Here's another problem that illustrates the parts of a greedy algorithm. You have a conference hall that can be used for only one conference at a time. You are tasked with assigning the largest number of possible activities to the hall from a list. Each activity has a starting time (`start_time`) and a finish time (`finish_time`). You can schedule two activities if the finishing time of the first is less than or equal to the starting time of the second. An example of a possible list of activities is given in **Table 10-1**.

Table 10-1   A list of possible activities, each with its starting time and its end time

Name	Start Time	Finish Time
AB	6	8
AC	7	9
AE	6	7
CE	8	10
DF	9	10
RE	10	11
TA	11	12

Notice that once a choice has been made for the time interval from 6 to 9—for example, scheduling activities AB and AC—then the subproblem of the assignment left is only for the interval from 9 to 12. If the assignment made from 6 to 9 is optimal, to have an optimal solution, the assignment from 9 to 12 must be optimal also. Hence, the problem has an optimal sub-structure.

A greedy choice for this problem must maximize the number of possible activities to assign. One way of making such a choice is to use the least amount of resources possible, assigning the activity with minimum finish time. That guarantees that the maximum number of assignments is possible in the remaining time slots.

For the given table you can see the greedy algorithm choices made in **Figure 10-2**.

An implementation of the algorithm can be made using a minimum priority queue. The minimum priority queue has the `delete_minimum()` method that returns and deletes the element in the queue with minimum priority, as shown in the following code.

```
type activity
    fields
        start_time
        finish_time
    ;; Make sure that start_time < finish_time


activity_queue = new minimum_priority_queue()
```

```
for activity in activity_list
    add(activity_queue, activity, activity.start_time)

start_time = 6 ;; start_time will mark the least
                ;; possible time to start a new activity

keep_searching = True
solution = new List()

while keep_searching
    greedy_activity = delete_minimum(activity_queue)
    if start_time >= greedy_activity.finish_time
        keep_searching = False
    else
        add(solution, greedy_activity)
        start_time = greedy_activity.finish_time
```

Figure 10-2   Creating a schedule following a greedy strategy

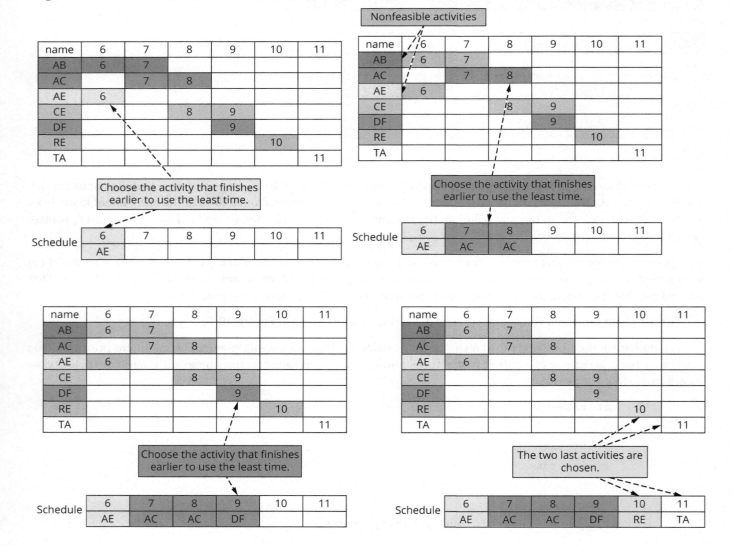

> ## Technical Interview

When faced with a complex optimization problem, a good starting point might be to create a feasible non-optimal solution. By studying why the feasible solution is not optimal, it is possible to gain insight into how to create the optimal solution.

Although not all optimization problems can be solved by a greedy strategy, a greedy strategy can help you produce a feasible solution. Hence, designing a solution that uses a greedy strategy to produce a feasible solution can be a good starting point. Also, in practice, a feasible non-optimal solution is better than no solution.

In the context of a technical interview, writing code or describing the process of searching for a solution indicates your skills in solving problems. Solving problems is one of the most important skills for any programmer, developer, or software engineer, and one of the main reasons to learn algorithms and data structures.

Huffman Coding Algorithm

A common problem when working with data is that of compression. **Data compression** refers to building a new representation of the information that requires less space but conveys the same information. For example, when working with strings and characters in a computer, each character is stored as a number. Usually, all characters use an 8-bit representation; thus, the string "Hello" uses five characters and 40 bits of space.

One way to compress information is to use **variable-length codification** or variable-length code. Variable-length codification uses a representation of characters from 6 to 9, which is optimal. To have an optimal solution, the assignment from 9 to 12 must also be optimal. In both cases, a "1" separates two different symbols, but the order in which each symbol is assigned is random. **Table 10-2** shows two ways of coding the characters in "Hello".

Table 10-2   Two possible codifications for the characters in "Hello"

Character	Code 1	Code 2
H	01	01
E	001	001
L	1	0001
O	0001	1

When a chain of digits like "100110001" is received, it is necessary to know what code was used to reconstruct the represented text. If Code 1 was used, then $1 = L, 001 = E, 1 = L$, and $0001 = O$, so the original text was LELO. But if Code 2 was used, then $1 = O, 001 = E, 1 = O$, and $0001 = L$, so the original text was OEOL.

Notice that the representation using the first code for "Hello" is "01001110001" of length 11. Furthermore, the representation for "Hello" using the second code is "01001000100011" of length 14. The difference in the lengths of representations is due to the representation used for the letters L and O. Because the letter L repeats, a greedy strategy to reduce the length of the final representation is to use the smaller possible representation for it.

Huffman coding uses a greedy strategy to build a codification for the characters of a file in such a way that characters with a higher frequency use the smallest possible code. With Huffman coding, building a frequency histogram for each character in the text is necessary.

A frequency histogram for a text is built simply by counting how many times a character is repeated in a text. For example, in the sentence "I love my mom," the characters present are e, I, o, m, y, l, v and white space. I, e, v, and y have a frequency of 1 since they appear only once in the text. The white space and the m character have frequencies of 3.

You can see a frequency histogram for a larger text in **Table 10-3**.

Table 10-3 A sample frequency histogram for a long text.

Character	Frequency
a	7
e	11
i	19
o	13
u	5
m	23
space	31
Total	109

The first step is to sort the characters in increasing order of frequency, as shown in **Figure 10-3**.

Figure 10-3 Sample frequency table used to exemplify the Huffman coding construction

char	frequency
u	5
a	7
e	11
o	13
i	19
m	23
space	31

You start by building a binary tree where the root is a node associated with the Null value and a value equal to the sum of the frequencies of the two first characters. The children of this new node are the two first characters. You can see the construction in **Figure 10-4**.

Figure 10-4 Initial step to construct the Huffman code, starting with the two characters with least frequency

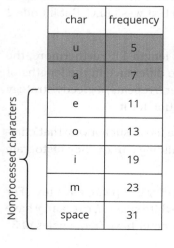
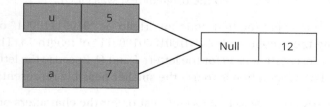

The next steps are to create a new node with the Null value and a frequency equal to the sum of the previously created node plus the frequency of the following nonprocessed character. This process is repeated until the root has a frequency equal to the total, 109, in this case. You can see the procedure illustrated in **Figure 10-5**.

Figure 10-5 Construction of the tree representing the Huffman code

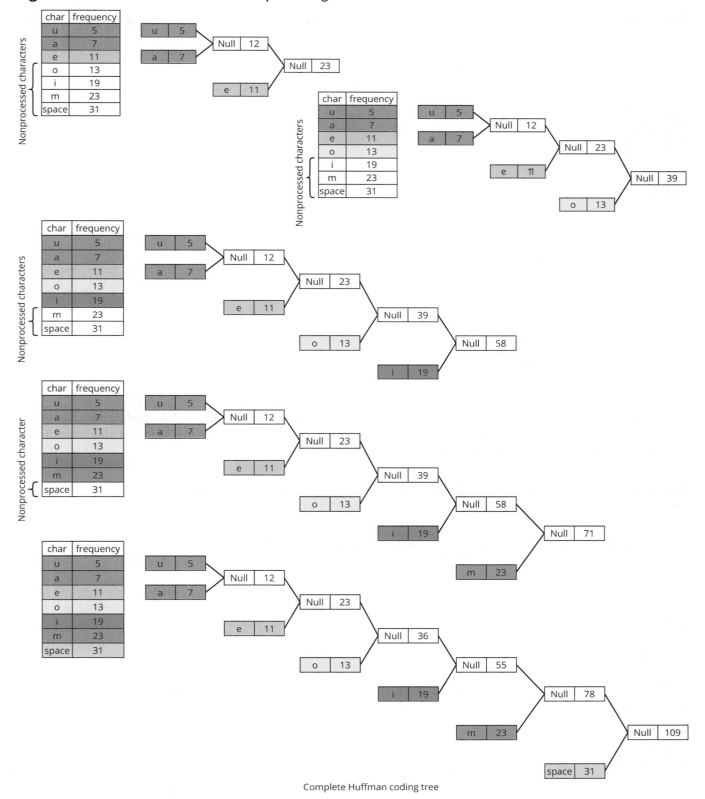

Complete Huffman coding tree

Once the binary tree is built, the code associated to each character is computed by traversing the tree in a breadth-first way. Each time the left child is traversed, a 0 is concatenated to the representation and, when the right is traversed, a 1 is concatenated to the representation. When a leaf is reached the representation is completed. You can see an illustration of the procedure in **Figure 10-6**.

Figure 10-6   Huffman code represented in a tree. Each character and its coding are presented in a leaf node of the tree

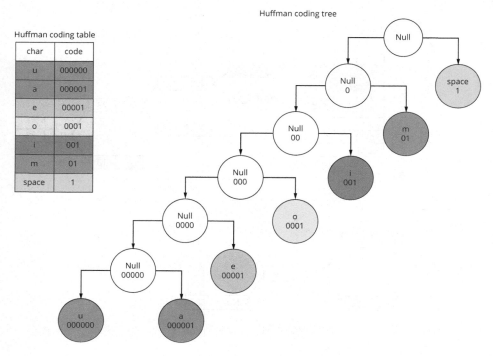

To get the original text back, the tree built before is used. For each 0 you move to the left child, and for each 1 you move to the right child. Once a leaf is reached, that character is part of the original message and you return to the root. You can see the procedure illustrated in **Figure 10-7**.

Figure 10-7   Part of decodification after a message has been transformed using a Huffman code

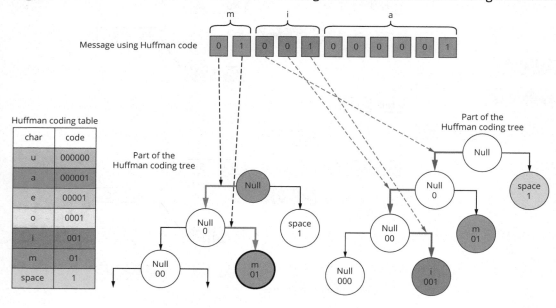

> ## Quick Check 10-1

Given the Huffman coding described in the previous example, what is the original text associated to "0000000001000001"?

Answer: "uoa"

Notice that 000000 corresponds to the leaf associated to u, 0001 to the leaf associated with o, and 000001 to a. Hence, the original text was "uoa".

| Note | The application of the greedy principle has been a key element in the development in the field of artificial intelligence, specifically in the use of artificial neural networks. The principle is applied in a slightly different way there. It usually consists of creating an objective function that measures the error in the desired neural network results, usually called the cost. The behavior of an artificial neural network is based on the choice of a family of numbers called its weights or parameters. The process of adjusting weights is usually called training. So, at each training step, the parameters are modified so that the cost is reduced. To know how to modify the weights to reduce the cost, a mathematical object called the gradient of the cost is used. The gradient has the property that its negative value indicates a direction in which the value of the cost will decrease faster. |

10.2 Dynamic Programming

Dynamic programming is a technique to solve problems that breaks a larger problem into subproblems in a recursive manner and simultaneously avoids recalculating previously solved subproblems.

Dynamic programming uses a convention of recursion and memorization to solve a problem. To see how the dynamic strategy could be used, consider the **0-1 knapsack problem**. (The knapsack problem was introduced in an earlier chapter on designing efficient algorithms.) The 0-1 knapsack problem consists of selecting from a set of n elements, with a given profit and weight, the elements that fit in a bag with a maximum capacity of W and that maximize the total profit.

Consider a knapsack problem for $n = 3$ and $W = 5$. Weights and profits are given in **Table 10-4**.

Table 10-4   The weights and profits of a set of objects for the 0-1 knapsack problem

Element	Weight	Profit	Available
A	1	3	1
B	2	2	1
C	4	1	1

You can see a tree that enumerates all feasible solutions with their profit values in **Figure 10-8**.

Figure 10-8 Enumeration tree showing all possible combinations in a knapsack problem

As you can observe in the previous table, some subproblems are repeated in the tree analysis. Hence, storing or memorizing the result of such problems can help reduce the number of cases necessary when searching for the optimal solution.

Note | One thing that makes computers and computer algorithms so powerful is that the problems they solve are abstract. The abstract part of the algorithms allows you to use them in a large set of actions and objects.

The knapsack problem is one such example problem stated in abstract terms but is almost universally applicable. You have a limited capacity to carry out some tasks, take actions, or use resources, and a list of options for the tasks, actions, or use of the resources, and you want to maximize the benefit you get. One application is to fill out a list of investments. Each possible investment has a cost and a reward or return on the investment. Since the funds to invest are usually limited, you have a maximum to invest. You are choosing the investments that will provide the largest reward. This problem is a knapsack problem where you have a list of investments with a maximum budget instead of a bag with a maximum capacity.

This application can get more sophisticated. For example, if instead of a safe return, you have only an estimate; if you invest in a company, you only have the promise of profit, which is nonexistent at the moment of investment.

Parts of Dynamic Programming

Dynamic programming is a powerful solution strategy that can only sometimes be applied. Two conditions are necessary to apply dynamic programming. The problem must have an optimal sub-structure and there must be **overlapping subproblems**.

The optimal sub-structure of a problem was discussed in the previous section. The overlapping subproblems refer to the fact that other smaller cases appear in more than one subproblem when solving some subproblems. This property makes memorization a way to reduce the complexity of the solution-searching process.

To exemplify the dynamic programming technique, it's better to start with a simpler example. Suppose that three dice with eight faces are numbered from one to eight. The problem consists of finding all the possible ways in which the sum of the three eight-sided dice sums a given number. For simplicity, consider the desired number as 15. The naive approach would be to list all possible result combinations for a roll of the three dice and check them for the desired result. You can see part of a tree enumerating the possibilities in **Figure 10-9**.

Notice that the number of cases for this problem is $8 * 8 * 8 = 512$ to check. Thus, such an algorithm would generally have complexity $O(f^n)$, where f is the number of faces and n is the number of dice. Hence, it has exponential complexity.

To write a recursive solution to the problem, suppose that `S(n, f, t)` denotes the number of ways n dice with f faces sum t. Notice that to get 15, if the first die is set to a value—for example, 3—then it is only necessary to find how many ways two dice can sum to 12, that is, `S(2, 8, 15-3)`. Hence, when taking different values for the first die, you can compute the total number of ways the three dice can sum to 15, as shown in **Figure 10-10**.

A recursive implementation is shown here.

```
S(n, f, t)
  if n = 1
    if t > 0 and t <= f
      return 1
    return 0
  total = 0
  for k = 1 to f step 1
    if t - k > 0
      total = total + S(n-1, f, t-k)
  return total
```

Figure 10-9   Part of the enumeration tree of possibilities for the dice sum problem

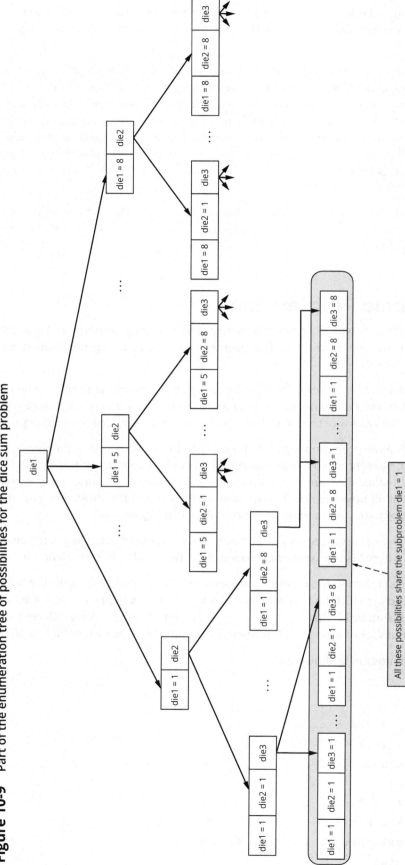

Figure 10-10   Possible cases for the dice sum problem solution

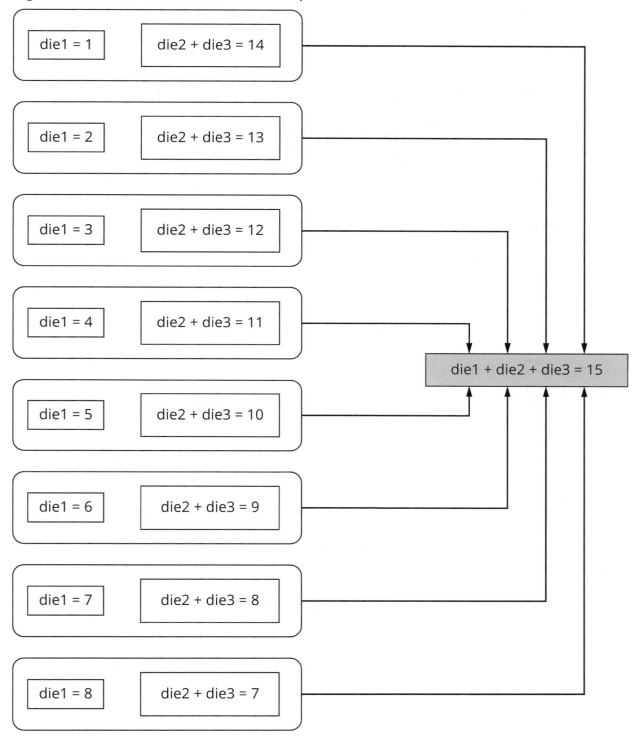

An enumeration tree showing the recursive calls necessary to solve the dice problem for S(3, 4, 5) is shown in **Figure 10-11**.

Figure 10-11   Recursive calls made to compute S(3, 4, 5). Notice that there are repeated computations in the recursive procedure

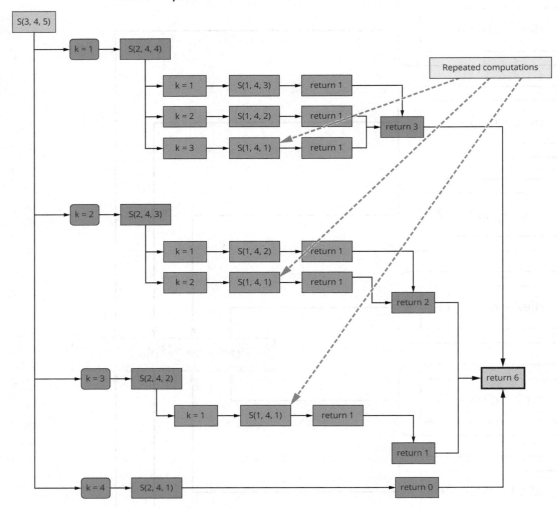

Notice that in this recursive depiction, there are repeated calls to S(1, 4, 1), and this is not the only one. That means the problem shows the overlapping property necessary to use the dynamic programming approach successfully.

To solve the problem for S(3, 8, 15), the first step would be solving problem S(1, 8, r) for *r* from 1 to 15. A table like the one shown in **Figure 10-12** shows the results of this step.

Figure 10-12   First row of the dice sum problem solution using a dynamic programming solution

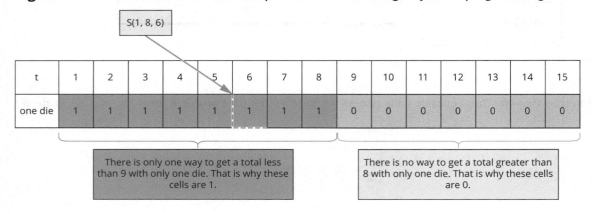

t	1	2	3	4	5	6	7	8	9	10	11	12	13	14	15
one die	1	1	1	1	1	1	1	1	0	0	0	0	0	0	0

There is only one way to get a total less than 9 with only one die. That is why these cells are 1.

There is no way to get a total greater than 8 with only one die. That is why these cells are 0.

The next step would be solving problem S(2, 8, r) for *r* from 1 to 15. To compute those values, it would be necessary to use the values of S(1, 8, r). You can see the updated table in **Figure 10-13**.

Figure 10-13   Second row of the dice sum problem solution when using a dynamic programming solution

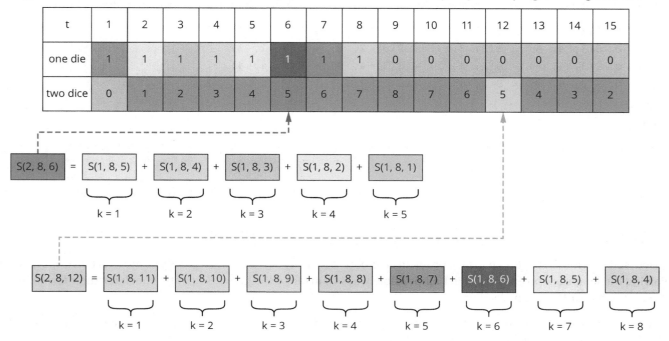

t	1	2	3	4	5	6	7	8	9	10	11	12	13	14	15
one die	1	1	1	1	1	1	1	1	0	0	0	0	0	0	0
two dice	0	1	2	3	4	5	6	7	8	7	6	5	4	3	2

S(2, 8, 6) = S(1, 8, 5) + S(1, 8, 4) + S(1, 8, 3) + S(1, 8, 2) + S(1, 8, 1)
   k = 1   k = 2   k = 3   k = 4   k = 5

S(2, 8, 12) = S(1, 8, 11) + S(1, 8, 10) + S(1, 8, 9) + S(1, 8, 8) + S(1, 8, 7) + S(1, 8, 6) + S(1, 8, 5) + S(1, 8, 4)
   k = 1   k = 2   k = 3   k = 4   k = 5   k = 6   k = 7   k = 8

The last step is to compute the values of S(3, 8, r) for *r* from 1 to 15. And as in the previous iteration, this would require using the values of S(1, 8, r). The final table is shown in **Figure 10-14**.

Figure 10-14   Third and last row of the dice sum problem solution when using a dynamic programming solution

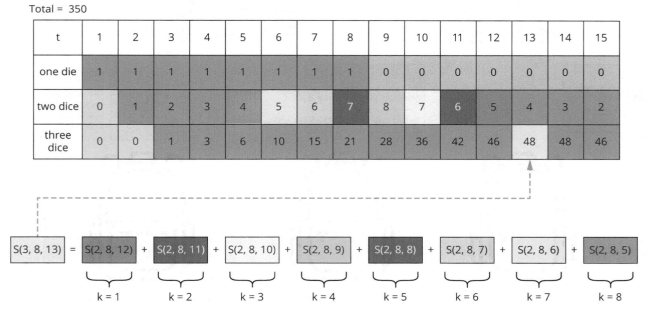

Total = 350

t	1	2	3	4	5	6	7	8	9	10	11	12	13	14	15
one die	1	1	1	1	1	1	1	1	0	0	0	0	0	0	0
two dice	0	1	2	3	4	5	6	7	8	7	6	5	4	3	2
three dice	0	0	1	3	6	10	15	21	28	36	42	46	48	48	46

S(3, 8, 13) = S(2, 8, 12) + S(2, 8, 11) + S(2, 8, 10) + S(2, 8, 9) + S(2, 8, 8) + S(2, 8, 7) + S(2, 8, 6) + S(2, 8, 5)
   k = 1   k = 2   k = 3   k = 4   k = 5   k = 6   k = 7   k = 8

Notice that the complexity of a solution constructed using the table described before is $O(f * n * t)$, a polynomial complexity.

The previous solution uses a table to store the values for some subproblems. This transforms the original recursive procedure into an iterative method using the subproblems table. That is the key to dynamic programming.

Quick Check 10-2

Using the notation in this section about the function `S(n, d, r)`, which of the following identities is true?

    a. `S(3, 4, 4) = S(2, 4, 3) + S(2, 4, 2) + S(2, 4, 1)`
    b. `S(3, 4, 4) = S(3, 3, 3) + S(3, 2, 2) + S(3, 1, 1)`
    c. `S(3, 4, 4) = S(3, 4, 1) + S(3, 4, 2) + S(3, 4, 4)`
    d. `S(3, 4, 4) = S(2, 4, 2) + S(1, 4, 2)`

Answer: a

Since `S(3, 4, 4)` is the number of ways three four-face dice can sum 4, once the value of one die is fixed to k, then to get a result of 4, the remaining two dice have to add $4 - k$. Hence, `S(3, 4, 4) = S(2, 4, 3) + S(2, 4, 2) + S(2, 4, 1)`.

0-1 Knapsack Dynamic Programming Solution

As discussed previously, the 0-1 knapsack problem cannot be optimally solved using a greedy strategy. A naive approach to solving the knapsack problem is to list all possible ways to arrange the given elements, check for their feasibility, and search later for the optimal solution.

You can see a list of possible combinations in **Figure 10-15** for a 0-1 knapsack problem with a maximum weight of 6; objects of weight 2, 3, and 4; and profits 4, 3, and 8.

Figure 10-15   Some possible solutions for the 0-1 knapsack problem

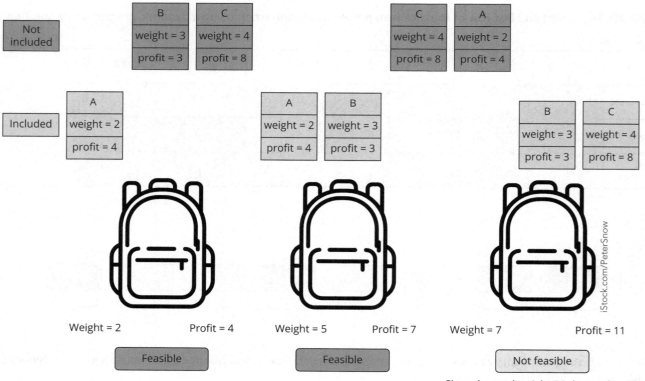

Since the total weight 7 is larger than the maximum weight 6, the solution is not feasible.

iStock.com/PeterSnow

Notice that the total number of options to analyze for a 0-1 knapsack problem with n objects is 2^n. Hence, a naive solution to the 0-1 knapsack problem would be exponential.

To apply dynamic programming to solve the 0-1 knapsack problem, let's start with a recursive approach. Suppose that K(W, [w1, w2, …, wn], [p1, p2, …, pn]) is the maximum value solution to the 0-1 knapsack problem for a maximum weight W, weights w1, …, wn, and profits p1, …, pn. Unlike in the greedy approach, all possibilities must be analyzed when deciding whether an object is included. You can see an enumeration tree for the possible combinations in **Figure 10-16** for the specific example described in previous paragraphs.

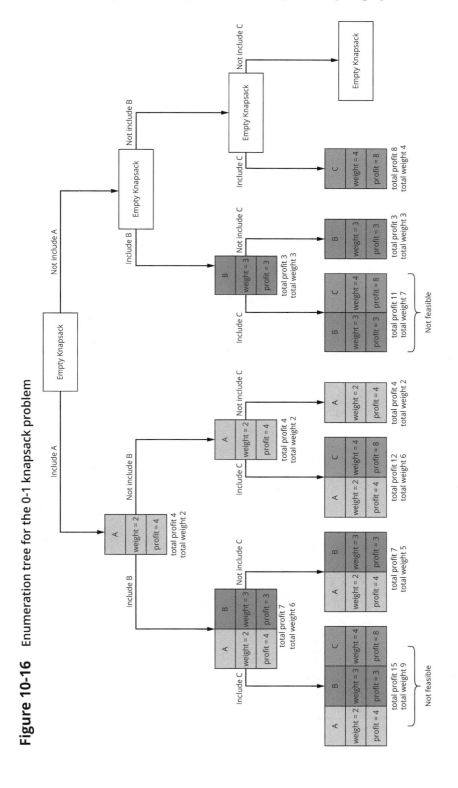

Figure 10-16   Enumeration tree for the 0-1 knapsack problem

From the tree you can see that the problem can be solved recursively. When deciding whether to include an object or not, it is analyzed at each level of the tree in Figure 10-16. The two options are studied and, if both are feasible, the one with the maximum total profit is chosen. For example, for the previous example, to decide if the third object should be used or not, the two magnitudes $K(6, [2, 3], [4, 3])$ and $8 + K(6 - 4, [2, 3], [4, 3])$ are evaluated. The first one uses a weight of 6 since no weight is used if the third object is not included. The second expression uses a maximum weight of $6 - 4$ since the third object has a weight of 4, and the profit of the third object is added. A tree depicting the recursive calls necessary to solve the 0-1 knapsack problem is shown in **Figure 10-17**.

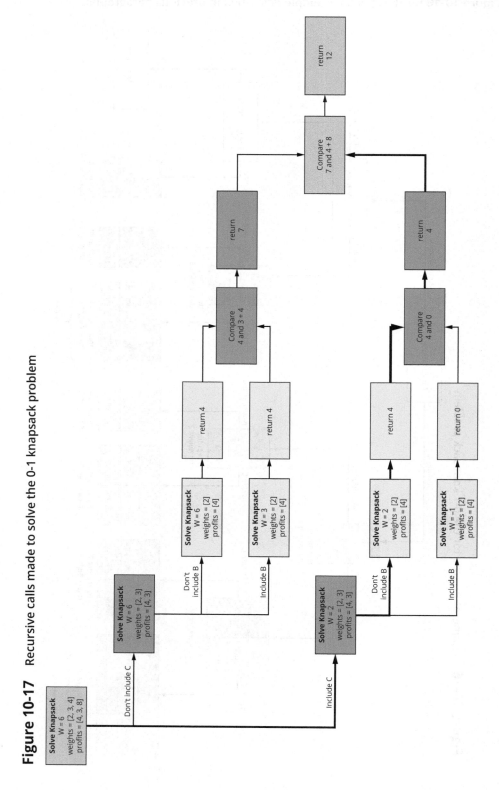

Figure 10-17 Recursive calls made to solve the 0-1 knapsack problem

Notice that this problem also shows the overlapping subproblem property since some calculations are repeated. The recursion also makes evident the optimal sub-structure property of the problem. Therefore, it makes sense to use a data structure to store the solution to the subproblems. To simplify the algorithm, it is convenient to sort the objects in an increasing weight value. Hence, starting with the object of weight 2, the table starts computing `K(r, [2], [4])` for r from 0 to W. You can see the computations in **Figure 10-18**.

Figure 10-18 First row of the 0-1 knapsack problem solution when using dynamic programming to solve it

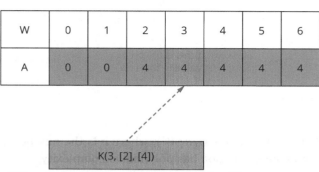

W	0	1	2	3	4	5	6
A	0	0	4	4	4	4	4

	A	B	C
	weight = 2	weight = 3	weight = 4
	profit = 4	profit = 3	profit = 8

Maximum weight = 6

K(3, [2], [4])

With only object A and a maximum weight of 3,
the maximum possible profit is 4.

Once the first row of the table is filled, the values of `K(r, [2, 3], [4, 3])` are computed for r from 0 to W. You can see the results of the computations in **Figure 10-19**.

Figure 10-19 Second row of the table used to solve the 0-1 knapsack problem when using dynamic programming to solve it

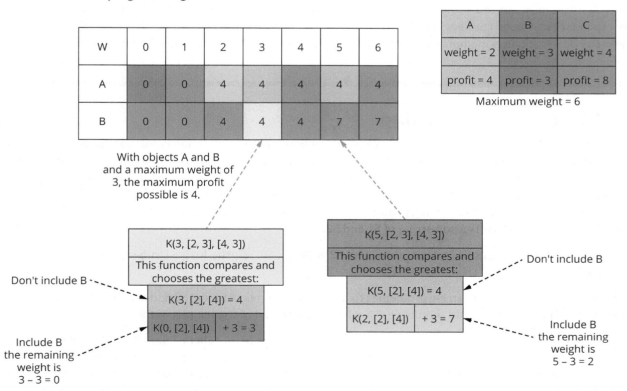

The last step provides the values of `K(r, [2, 3, 4], [4, 3, 8])` for r from 0 to 6. You can see the table completed in **Figure 10-20**.

Figure 10-20   Third row of the 0-1 knapsack problem solution when using dynamic programming to solve it

W	0	1	2	3	4	5	6
A	0	0	4	4	4	4	4
B	0	0	4	4	4	7	7
C	0	0	4	4	8	8	12

A	B	C
weight = 2	weight = 3	weight = 4
profit = 4	profit = 3	profit = 8

Maximum weight = 6

Notice that this is the only interesting value in this row.

K(6, [2, 3, 4], [4, 3, 8])

Notice that the complexity of the solution using dynamic programming is $O(n * W)$, where n is the number of objects and W is the maximum weight. Hence, the dynamic programming solution has polynomial complexity.

Best Practices

Dynamic programming is a powerful technique to solve problems that require enumerating many options. When facing a problem with many cases to analyze, even if it might be computationally expensive, designing a solution that enumerates each possibility and evaluates it is a good starting point.

As you might have noticed in the previous examples, a recursive procedure was designed once the enumeration task had been studied. Then the overlapping property of the problem becomes clearer. With the previous observations, a memorization application can be designed to produce a solution using dynamic programming.

Longest Common Sub-String

When you have a long list of text—for example, descriptions of books or courses—one common task is to search for specific content. It is not always the case that you can write the precise text that you are looking for; you may just have a set of words or a sentence. By searching such strings that match as much as possible, the search results can be more useful than searches on only 100% exact matches. This gives rise to the problem of finding the longest match possible, also known as the longest sub-string problem. Given two strings, S1 and S2, the **longest sub-string problem** is finding the longest string S that is a sub-string of S1 and S2.

For example, given the strings S1 = "acdaabca" and S2 = "cacdaabac", the longest sub-string between both of them is "acdaab".

One way to solve the longest sub-string problem is to find all sub-strings of S1 and S2 and search in the intersection for the longest one. This process would require $O(2^r)$, where r is the sum of the lengths of the strings.

To understand how the procedure works, consider the two strings S1 = "abcde" and S2 = "babcda". You can analyze if a sub-string of S1 is a sub-string of S2 by comparing the characters S1[j] with each of the characters S2[i]. If there is a match, then they have a sub-string of length 1 in common. For example, S1[0] matches S2[1] and S2[5]. Since this is the first character of S1, it is impossible to be part of a larger sub-string. When comparing S1 with S2, there are matches for S2[0], and S2[2]. Now it is possible to deduce that the match at S2[2] is part of a longer sub-string since S2[1] was also a match. However, S2[0] couldn't be part of a longer sub-string.

All the previous comparisons could be summarized in a table like the one shown in **Table 10-5**.

Table 10-5   Summary of single-character matches between S1 and S2

	b	a	b	c	d	a
a	0	1	0	0	0	1
b	1	0	1	0	0	0
c	0	0	0	1	0	0
d	0	0	0	0	1	0
e	0	0	0	0	0	0

Table 10-5 shows that the diagonal from row a and column a to row d and column d describe the longest sub-string. A way to keep track of the length of the sub-string is by adding the number of previous matches to each match. This could be done by adding to the entry (i, j) on the table the value of the entry $(i-1, j-1)$ if the characters match in other cases. You can see a table filled that way in **Table 10-6**.

Table 10-6   Result of the table used to find the longest common sub-string

	b	a	b	c	d	a
a	0	1	0	0	0	1
b	1	0	2	0	0	0
c	0	0	0	3	0	0
d	0	0	0	0	4	0
e	0	0	0	0	0	0

This procedure has complexity $O(n * m)$, where n and m are the lengths of the compared strings.

Quick Check 10-3

Can a greedy algorithm be considered a way of dynamic programming? Why or why not?

Answer: Yes

Recall that a greedy algorithm has the optimal sub-structure property. The overlapping subproblem property is only partially evident in a greedy algorithm since there is only one subproblem for each step. And the given subproblem is solved by using the local best choice. The local best choice ensures you don't need to memorize the solutions to subproblems using a table.

Note | American mathematician Richard E. Bellman first studied and developed dynamic programming theory. In his book *Dynamic Programming*, Bellman presented the basis of the dynamic programming technique and a series of applications ranging from scheduling to mathematical economics.

Best Practices

The complete table of cases was built in the examples discussed in this section, which means that a bottom-up approach, also called a tabulation method, was used. You start to solve a problem by computing the solution for the smaller cases and incrementally reach the final state. This is common in optimization problems, where analyzing almost all feasible solutions is necessary. But there are other options for starting from the larger case into smaller cases, similar to a simple recursion. But a caching or memorization process is used in building the smaller solutions, so all the computations necessary for the intermediate steps are computed only once and reused, if necessary. The latter approach is sometimes called a top-down approach, and the method of saving the intermediate results is called memorization.

When choosing the approach to implement a solution, you must remember that the top-down approach still requires recursion, so the memory overhead of the recursive calls might affect the performance. But as you saw in the previous examples, a bottom-up approach requires more memory, and the computations transition from one row of a table to the next one, which might result in less readable code than using recursive calls.

Hence, you should think about which aspects between code readability, memory usage, and time complexity have a higher priority to pick the best route to implement a solution.

10.3 Dijkstra's Algorithm for the Shortest Path

A weighted graph can be used to represent a network composed of cities and roads, where each city represents a vertex and each road represents an edge. The weight of each edge represents the distance or cost of using that given road. You can see an example of such a graph in **Figure 10-21**.

Figure 10-21   Graph representing cities and distances between them

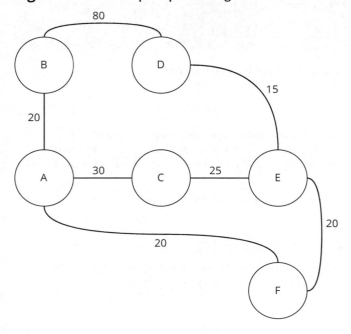

A natural question for somebody traveling from city A to city D would be: What is the shortest or the least expensive path to reach city D? Dijkstra's algorithm is precisely designed to answer that question. Moreover, the algorithm also computes the shortest path to every other vertex in a given graph.

> **Note** | Dijkstra's algorithm was invented by computer scientist Edsger Wybe Dijkstra. Dijkstra received the 1972 Turing Award, an award considered to be like the Nobel prize for computer science. He was an influential figure in the development of structured programming languages.

Technical Interview

A key to using computers to solve problems is to create adequate representations. That means choosing the correct data structure to represent the parts of the problem. A graph will likely be a useful data structure when facing a problem that directly speaks of any form of network, social networks, relations (binary relations), and roads. And in that context, a good question is, "How can the shortest path be interpreted?"

Dijkstra's Algorithm Examples

Dijkstra's algorithm is a combination of breadth-first search and the use of a priority queue. To better understand this algorithm, start with a table, or associative array, to store the minimum distance between a source vertex A and any other vertex v. Let's refer to the table as the distance table. A field `visited` that indicates if a given vertex has been visited will be stored in the distance table to make the procedure easier. Let's start by setting all distances in the search table to ∞ (infinity) to indicate no way to reach a given vertex. **Table 10-7** describes the distance table for a graph with four vertices.

Table 10-7   The distance table at the beginning of Dijkstra's algorithm

Vertex	Distance	visited
A	0	False
B	∞	False
C	∞	False
D	∞	False

Dijkstra's algorithm analyzes the vertex v with the minimum distance that has not been visited. For a neighbor vertex u of v, a potentially new path to u follows the already described path from A to v and then uses (u, v). The length or cost of the previously described path is `distance = distance_table[v].distance + w(G, v, u)`, where `w(G, v, u)` is the weight of the edge (v, u). If `distance < distance_table[u]`, a shorter path to u has been found and the table is updated. Dijkstra's algorithm repeats this step until there are no non-visited vertices. An illustration of this algorithm is shown in **Figure 10-22**.

Figure 10-22 A graph where a greedy choice doesn't lead to an optimal solution

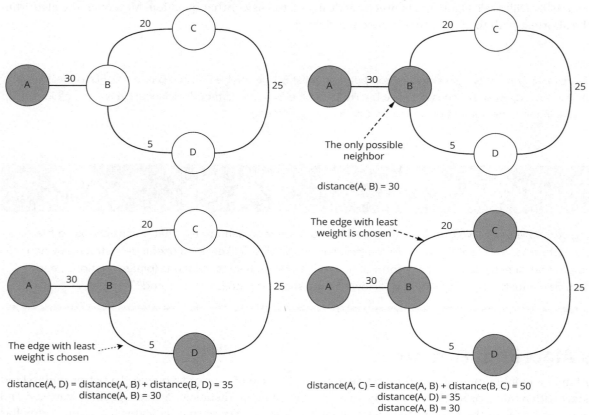

distance(A, B) = 30

distance(A, D) = distance(A, B) + distance(B, D) = 35
distance(A, B) = 30

distance(A, C) = distance(A, B) + distance(B, C) = 50
distance(A, D) = 35
distance(A, B) = 30

Dijkstra's Algorithm Details

Suppose that G is a weighted graph with adjacency matrix $G.M$. For simplicity, let's assume that the vertices are represented by integer values from 0 to N and that the source vertex is $A = 0$. The first part of Dijkstra's algorithm is to initialize all the data used in the algorithm. Here is an implementation of the initial step.

```
;; Use a list of non-visited vertices
not_visited = new Set()

;; Create an array of the previous vertices in
;; the shortest path
prev_vertex = new array[size(G)]
;; Create an array to store the minimum distances
distance = new array[size(G)]

;; Set the distances

for i = 0 to size(G)-1 step 1
    ;; Set the value of the distance to infinite
    distance[i] = infinite
    ;; Set the previous vertex to -1 to indicate that
    ;; that it has not been found
    prev_vertex[i] = -1
    ;; Add all vertices to the non-visited list
    add(not_visited,i)

distance[0] = 0
prev_vertex[0] = 0
```

You can see an illustration of how the data structures are initialized for a weighted graph in **Figure 10-23**.

Figure 10-23   A graph and its initial data structures to apply Dijkstra's algorithm

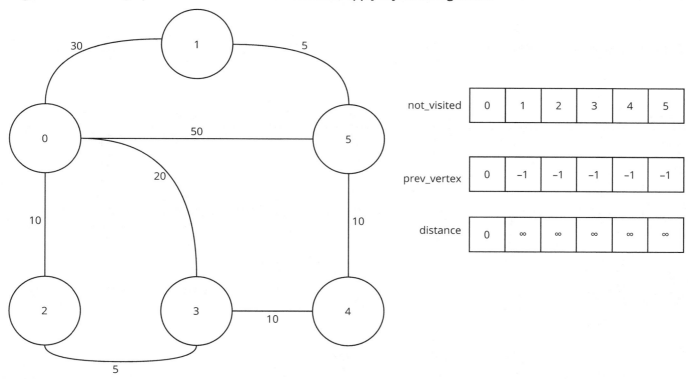

Once the data is initialized, each vertex's minimum distance is computed until there are no more non-visited vertices. This step is implemented as follows.

```
dijkstra(G, not_visited)
   while len(not_visited) > 0
      ;; Search for the vertex with minimum distance
      min_dist = infinite
      min_idx = 0
      for i in not_visited
         if distance[i] < min_dist
            min_idx = i
            min_dist = distance[i]
      ;; Remove the vertex with minimum distance
      delete(not_visited, min_idx)

      for j = 0 to size(G)-1 step 1
         ;; Check all neighbors of the min_idx vertex
         if G.M[min_idx][j] < infinite
            new_dist = G.M[min_idx][j] + min_dist
            ;; Update the distance and previous vertex
            ;; if a new minimum is found
            if new_dist < distance[j]
               distance[j] = new_dist
               prev_vertex[j] = i
   return
```

You can see an illustration of the previous implementation in **Figure 10-24**.

Figure 10-24 Illustration of how Dijkstra's algorithm works

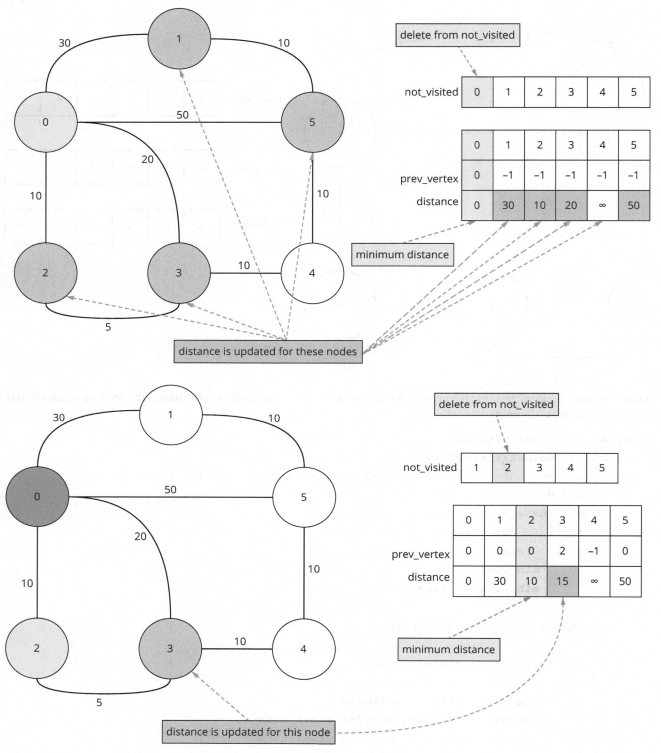

Figure 10-24   Illustration of how Dijkstra's algorithm works—continued

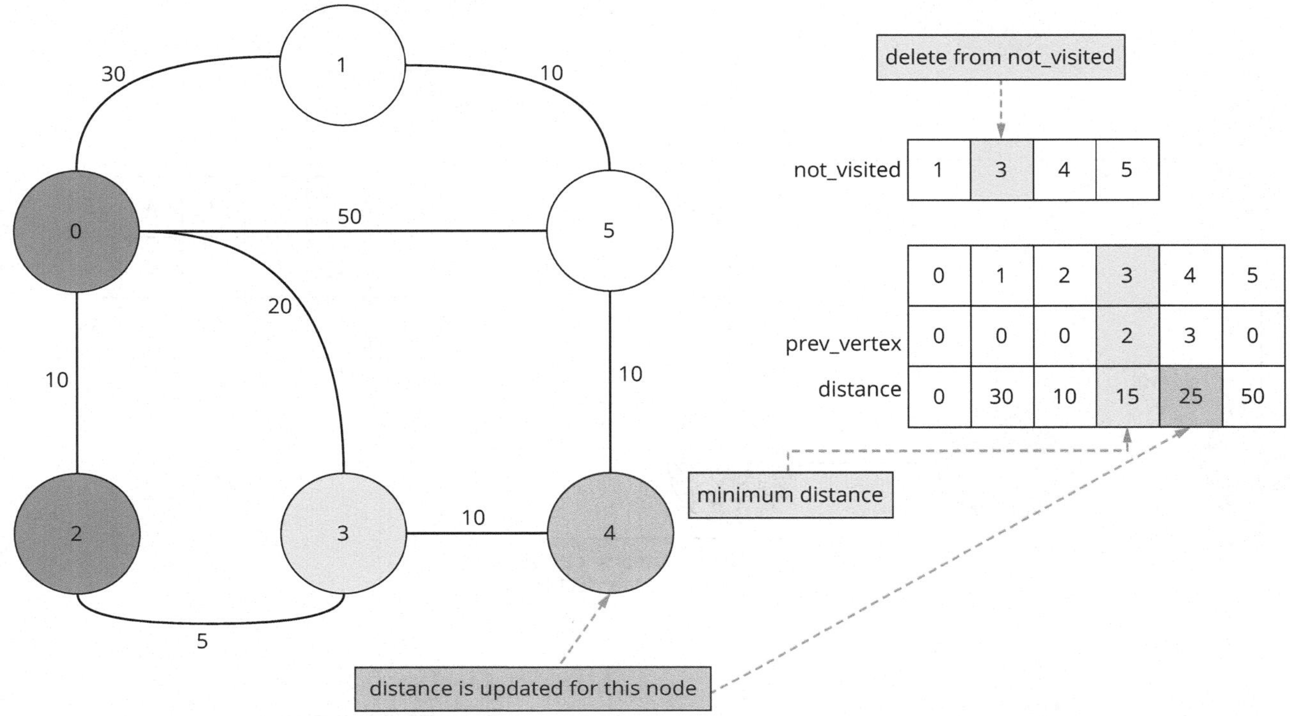

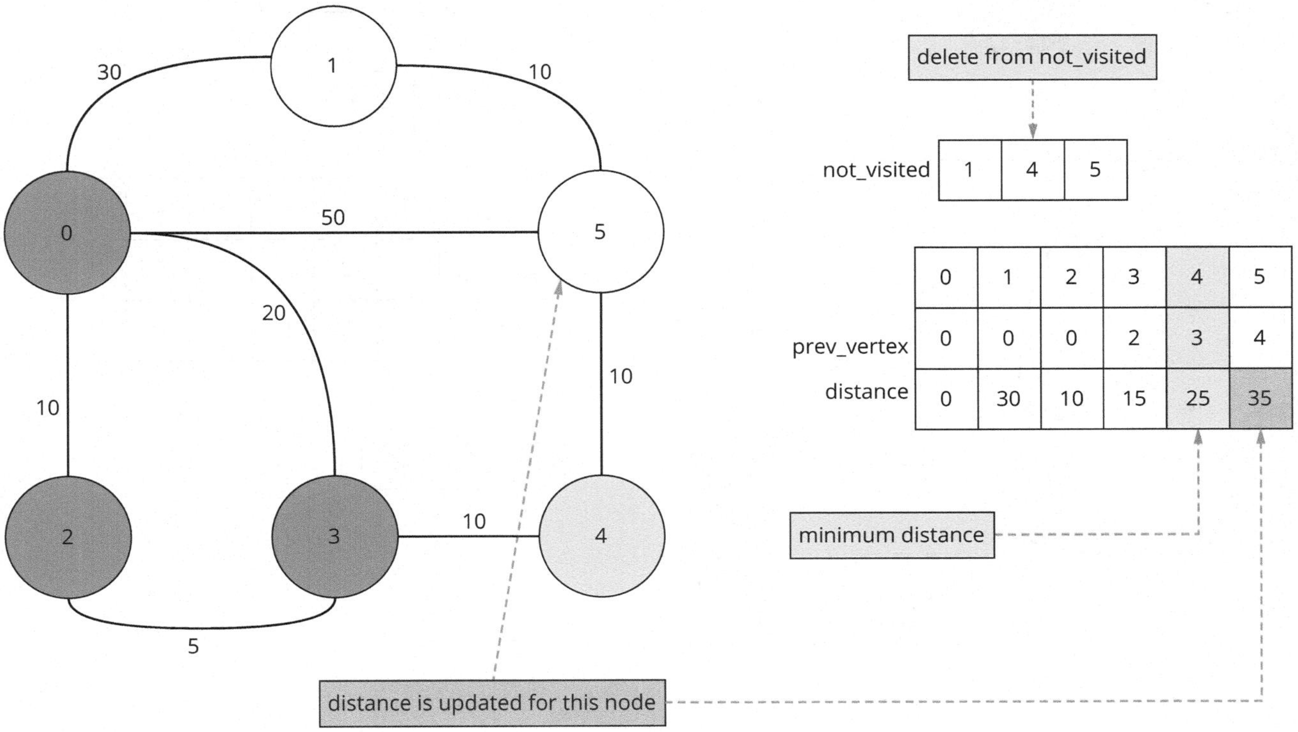

(continues)

Figure 10-24 Illustration of how Dijkstra's algorithm works—continued

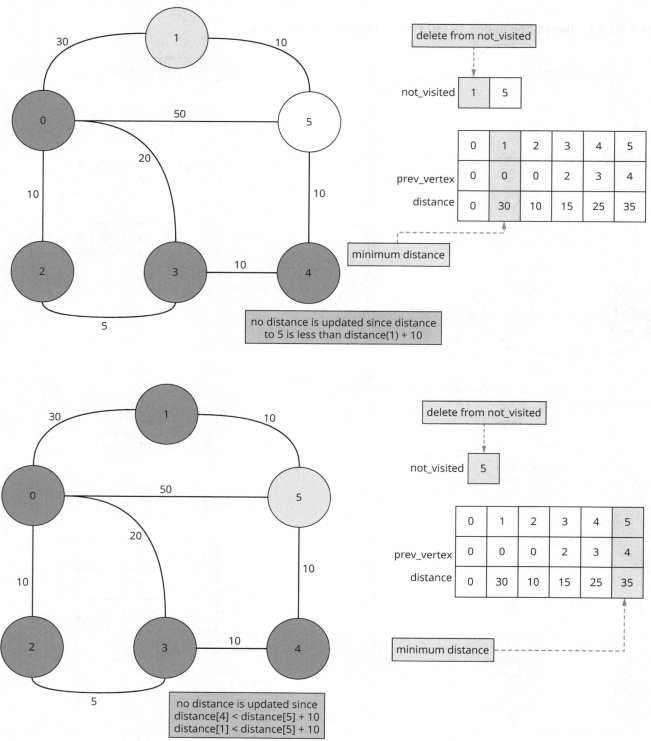

The previous implementation has a loop that iterates `size(G)` times as it empties the `not_visited` list. Inside the loop are two loops, one that iterates over the `not_visited` set and one with `size(G)` iterations. Then the algorithm has complexity $O(N * N) = O(N^2)$, where N is the size of the graph or the total number of vertices.

> **Note** | An implementation where the graph uses an adjacency list does not require a loop with size(G) iteration. Instead, it is possible to iterate only through the list of neighbors. Moreover, the search for the minimum can be made using a priority queue (probably implemented through a heap) where each updated distance is added to the queue, even if a vertex with a different distance is already inserted. Since a priority queue has operations with complexity $O(n)$, then an implementation of Dijkstra's algorithm using a priority queue will have complexity $O(N + M \log(N))$, where M is the number of edges and N is the number of vertices.

10.4 Knuth–Morris–Pratt (KMP) Algorithm

String algorithms are a family of algorithms specialized in operating over strings. When you start typing a URL in the search bar of your web browser, a string algorithm presents you with suggestions of previously visited sites.

When using string algorithms in applications, speed is an important factor since suggestions on completing the string should appear almost immediately. Hence, the use of good algorithms is extremely important when working with strings.

Pattern Searching

When you have a long string, such as an essay or paper, in a word processor, it is common to use a search tool to locate specific text. The target text or word you search on the document is called a **pattern**. Finding a pattern in a string is called **pattern matching**.

One aspect that makes pattern matching difficult is that checking if two strings are equal is a character-by-character comparison. So, for example, to compare if two strings, s1 and s2, are equal, the more elementary way is by comparing each character of s1 and s2 for equality, like this:

```
equal_strings(s1, s2)
    N = len(s1)
    if not len(s2) = N
        return False
    for i = 0 to N-1 step 1
        if not s1[i] = s2[i]
            return False
    return True
```

Another aspect of pattern matching that creates difficulties is that the length of the text where the pattern is being searched might be large, such as looking for a specific word in an essay with thousands of words.

Naive Pattern Searching

The following code snippet describes a naive approach to pattern matching for a pattern *p* of length *n* and a text *txt* of length *m*.

```
naive_search(p, txt)
    n = len(p)
    m = len(txt)
    if n > m
        ;; There cannot be a match if
        ;; the length of p is larger than
        ;; the length of m
        return -1
```

```
i = 0
found = False
while i < m - n and not found
    found = True
    for j = 0 to n-1 step 1
       if not p[j] = txt[i+j]
           ;; If there is a mismatch between
           ;; the pattern and the substring
           ;; stop the search and move to the next position
           found = False
           break
       ;; If the for loop is completed without a mismatch
       ;; then a match is found beginning at j
    if found
        return i
    else
        return -1
```

You can see this algorithm illustrated in **Figure 10-25**.

Figure 10-25 Naive comparison method illustrated for txt = aaeeaaeaa and *p* = aaea

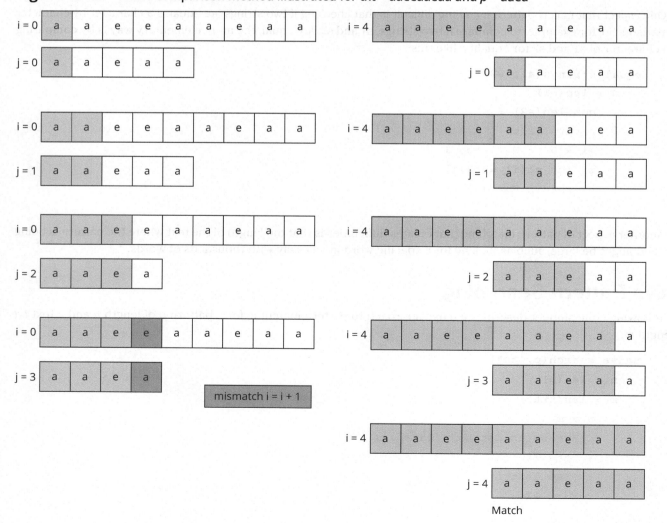

Figure 10-25   Naive comparison method illustrated for txt = aaeeaaeaa and *p* = aaea—continued

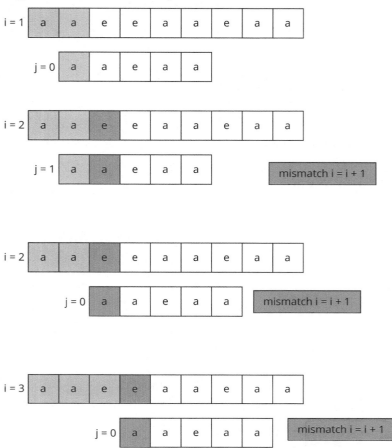

The worst case for the previous algorithm is when there is no match. In such a case, the outer `while` loop will be executed $m - n$ times, while the inner loop might be executed up to n times. Hence, the complexity of the algorithm is $O((m-n)*n) = O(m*n - n^2) = O(m*n)$.

Rabin–Karp String Matching Algorithm

One of the main drawbacks of the naive approach is that for each position j, it is necessary to make a comparison with complexity $O(n)$. The Rabin–Karp algorithm uses a polynomial hash code to work around the $O(n)$ comparison.

For simplicity, suppose that the only available characters are *a, e, i, o, u,* and *m*. To each character, assign a number between 0 and 5. A possible assignment of values is shown in **Table 10-8**.

Table 10-8   The values of the `ord` function for the characters in the alphabet *a, e, i, o, u,* and *m*

char	a	e	i	o	u	m
ord(char)	0	1	2	3	4	5

For the pattern *mia*, the polynomial code would be:

$$ord(m)\,6^2 + ord(i)\,6^1 + ord(a)\,6^0 = 192$$

Since the polynomial hash code is collision-free, comparing two codes is equivalent to comparing two strings. Here is a modification of the naive approach that uses the polynomial hash code instead of a character-by-character comparison.

```
poly_hash(s, N, start, end)
    ;; Computes the polynomial hash code
    ;; for the string s from position start to position end
    if start = end
        return ord(s)
    return N*poly_hash(s, N, start, end-1) + ord(s[end])


naive_hash_match(p, txt)
    ;; Let N be the number of characters available
    n = len(p)
    ;; Compute the polynomial hash code for p
    x = poly_hash(p, N, 0, n-1)
    found = False
    while i < m - n and not found
        y = poly_hash(txt, N, i, i+n)
        if x = y
            return i
    return -1
```

You can see an illustration of the procedure in **Figure 10-26**.

Figure 10-26 Comparisons made using a hash code

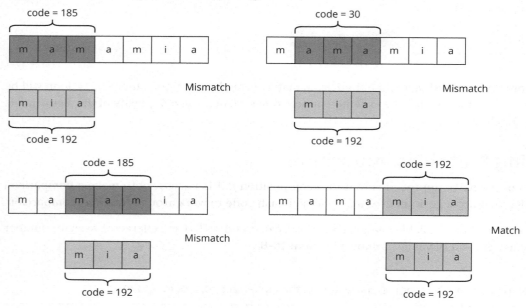

Notice that computing the polynomial hash code of a string of length k has complexity $O(k)$. Hence, comparing the hash codes is less efficient than a character-by-character comparison. However, from the illustration, notice that the computation of poly_hash (txt, N, i, i+n) and poly_hash (txt, N, i+1, i+n+1) have some parts in common, as shown in **Figure 10-27**.

Figure 10-27 Notice how the two substrings share similar terms when computing the hash code

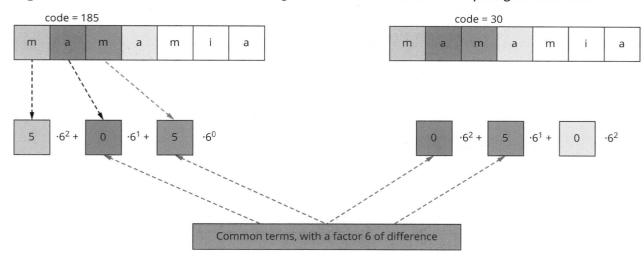

The previous observation can be used to compute `poly_hash(txt, N, i+1, i+n+1)` from `poly_hash(txt, N, i, i+n)`. The relation is expressed in the following code snippet.

```
y = poly_hash(txt, N, i, i + n)
    ;; z will hold poly_hash(txt, N, i+1, i+n+1)
z = N*y - ord(txt[i])*N^(n-1) + ord(txt[i+n+1])
```

Therefore, the computation of `poly_hash (txt, 0, 0, n-1)` is done at the beginning of the procedure, and every new iteration can be done using the previous relationship with complexity $O(1)$.

The Rabin–Karp algorithm uses the polynomial hash code for comparison and the previous relation to compute the hash codes efficiently. Hence, the Rabin–Karp algorithm has a complexity of $O(m + n)$ since the operations require the computation of the two hash codes once.

One problem with the previously shown version of the Rabin–Karp algorithm is that if the size of the set of characters used as the alphabet is large, then the hash function values are large. In a computer, an integer number is usually stored in a register of 32 or 64 bits. That means the largest possible value for an integer is $2^{64} \approx 1.8 \times 10^{19}$. If the pattern is a string of length 100 and the set of used characters has size $256 = 2^8$, then the polynomial hash code might reach

$$255 * 256^{99} + 255 * 256^{98} + \ldots + 255 \approx 6.66 \times 10^{240}$$

That is much larger than what can be stored in an integer. One approach to work around this problem is to use hash compression. For example, the polynomial hash code can be reduced modulo r, where r is an integer. The use of compression causes collisions. Hence, when a match between the codes is obtained, you can only partially confirm that there is a match between the strings. In that case, it is necessary to make a character-by-character comparison to ensure a match.

Overview of the KMP Algorithm

The Knuth–Morris–Pratt algorithm is independent of the alphabet used and reduces the number of comparisons made when searching. To better understand how the KMP algorithm works, consider the naive approach to `p = "aaia"` and `txt = "aaaaia"`. You can see the comparisons illustrated in **Figure 10-28**.

Figure 10-28 When doing naive pattern matching, notice how some sub-strings are already matched, and it is not necessary to restart from position 0

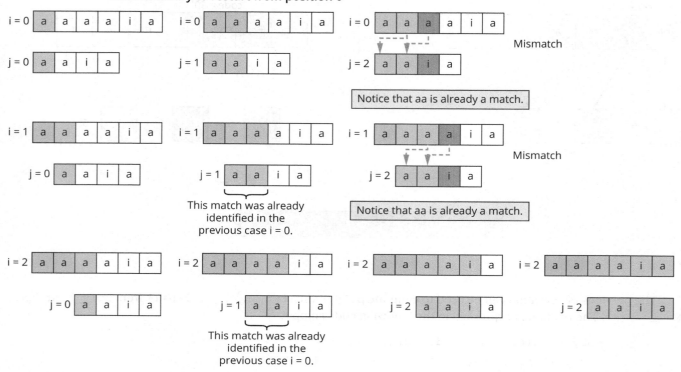

Notice that some comparisons can be avoided if it is recognized that after a mismatch, some characters might be part of a match. Hence the KMP algorithm first creates an auxiliary data structure to know how many characters can still be considered a match when a mismatch character is found. The structure is called a **prefix table**. The prefix table stores information on how many positions of a part of the pattern are a prefix of itself. A **prefix** of a string p is a sub-string of p that starts at position 0. **Figure 10-29** shows a list of prefixes of $p =$ "miamama".

Figure 10-29 A string and a list of all its prefixes

m	i	a	m	a	m	a

Prefixes

m

m	i

m	i	a

m	i	a	m

m	i	a	m	a

m	i	a	m	a	m	a

The prefix table stores information on how prefixes of *p* can be found in *p* in positions that do not start at position 0. You can see the previous concept illustrated for *p* = "mmiammiamo" in **Figure 10-30**.

Figure 10-30   Notice how using a register of an already matched prefix is not necessary to start the comparisons

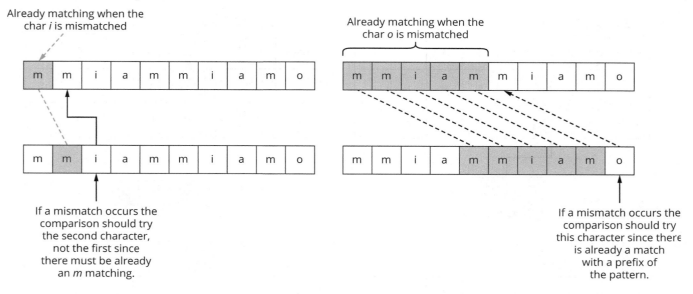

The pointers shown in Figure 10-30 can be computed using the algorithm shown in the following code snippet. The result is the prefix table of a string *p*.

```
prefix_table(p)
    n = len(p)
    table = new array[n]
    j = 0
    i = 1
    while i < n
        if p[i] = p[j]
            table[i] = j + 1
            j = j + 1
            i = i + 1
        else if j > 0
            j = table[j-1]
        else
            table[i] = 0
            i = i + 1
    return table
```

You can see how the `prefix_table(p)` functions work in **Figure 10-31** for *p* = "aaiaaiu".

Figure 10-31   How to fill the prefix table

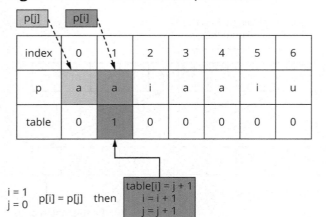

p[j]   p[i]

index	0	1	2	3	4	5	6
p	a	a	i	a	a	i	u
table	0	1	0	0	0	0	0

i = 1
j = 0   p[i] = p[j]   then   table[i] = j + 1
i = i + 1
j = j + 1

p[j]   p[i]

index	0	1	2	3	4	5	6
p	a	a	i	a	a	i	u
table	0	1	0	0	0	0	0

i = 2
j = 1   p[i] ≠ p[j]   then   j = table[j-1] = 0

p[j]   p[i]

index	0	1	2	3	4	5	6
p	a	a	i	a	a	i	u
table	0	1	0	0	0	0	0

i = 2
j = 0   p[i] = p[j]   then   table[i] = 0
i = i + 1

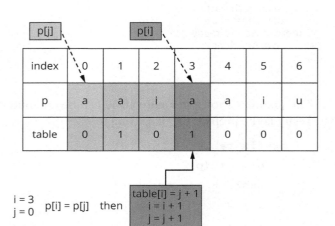

p[j]   p[i]

index	0	1	2	3	4	5	6
p	a	a	i	a	a	i	u
table	0	1	0	1	0	0	0

i = 3
j = 0   p[i] = p[j]   then   table[i] = j + 1
i = i + 1
j = j + 1

p[j]   p[i]

index	0	1	2	3	4	5	6
p	a	a	i	a	a	i	u
table	0	1	0	1	2	0	0

i = 4
j = 1   p[i] = p[j]   then   table[i] = j + 1
i = i + 1
j = j + 1

p[j]   p[i]

index	0	1	2	3	4	5	6
p	a	a	i	a	a	i	u
table	0	1	0	1	2	3	0

i = 5
j = 2   p[i] = p[j]   then   table[i] = j + 1
i = i + 1
j = j + 1

Quick Check 10-4

Build the prefix table for the pattern p = "aeuaaeui".

Answer: See **Figure 10-32**.

Figure 10-32   Prefix table for p = "aeuaaeui"

index	0	1	2	3	4	5	6	7
p	a	e	u	a	a	e	u	i
table	0	0	0	1	1	2	3	0

Implementing the KMP Algorithm

Once the prefix table has been computed for the pattern p, the KMP algorithm traverses the characters' prefix table to know from which position the character-by-character comparison should proceed. In the following code snippet, you can see an implementation of the second part of the KMP algorithm that uses the already-built prefix table.

```
KMP(p, txt)
    table = prefix_table(p)
    i = 0
    j = 0
    n = len(p)
    m = len(txt)
    while i < m
        if p[j] = txt[i]
            ;; there is a matching character
            if j = n-1
                ;; if p[j] is the last character of the pattern
                ;; then a match has been found
                return i-j
            else
                ;; there is no match yet
                i = i + 1
                j = j + 1
        else if j > 0
            ;; If there is mismatch between the characters
            ;; the prefix table is used to know from which character
            ;; restart the comparisons
            j = table[i-1]
        else
            ;; If there is no prefix match, then just move one position
```

```
                    ;; the comparison of txt
                i = i + 1
            return -1
```

You can see the process illustrated in **Figure 10-33**.

Figure 10-33   Illustration of the KMP algorithm

index	0	1	2	3	4
p	a	i	a	i	e
table	0	0	1	2	0

j = 0

index	0	1	2	3	4	5	6	7	8	9	10	11	12
txt	a	i	a	i	o	a	i	a	i	a	i	e	e

i = 0

index	0	1	2	3	4
p	a	i	a	i	e
table	0	0	1	2	0

j = 1

index	0	1	2	3	4	5	6	7	8	9	10	11	12
txt	a	i	a	i	o	a	i	a	i	a	i	e	e

i = 1

index	0	1	2	3	4
p	a	i	a	i	e
table	0	0	1	2	0

j = 2

index	0	1	2	3	4	5	6	7	8	9	10	11	12
txt	a	i	a	i	o	a	i	a	i	a	i	e	e

i = 2

index	0	1	2	3	4
p	a	i	a	i	e
table	0	0	1	2	0

j = 3

index	0	1	2	3	4	5	6	7	8	9	10	11	12
txt	a	i	a	i	o	a	i	a	i	a	i	e	e

i = 3

Figure 10-33   Illustration of the KMP algorithm—continued

index	0	1	2	3	4
p	a	i	a	i	e
table	0	0	1	2	0

j = 4

index	0	1	2	3	4	5	6	7	8	9	10	11	12
txt	a	i	a	i	o	a	i	a	i	a	i	e	e

i = 4

The mismatch considers the prefix table to avoid returning to i = 0.

index	0	1	2	3	4
p	a	i	a	i	e
table	0	0	1	2	0

j = 2

index	0	1	2	3	4	5	6	7	8	9	10	11	12
txt	a	i	a	i	o	a	i	a	i	a	i	e	e

i = 4

j = 0 indicates that there are no possible prefix matches

index	0	1	2	3	4
p	a	i	a	i	e
table	0	0	1	2	0

j = 0

index	0	1	2	3	4	5	6	7	8	9	10	11	12
txt	a	i	a	i	o	a	i	a	i	a	i	e	e

i = 5

index	0	1	2	3	4
p	a	i	a	i	e
table	0	0	1	2	0

j = 1

index	0	1	2	3	4	5	6	7	8	9	10	11	12
txt	a	i	a	i	o	a	i	a	i	a	i	e	e

i = 6

(continues)

Figure 10-33 Illustration of the KMP algorithm—continued

index	0	1	2	3	4
p	a	i	a	i	e
table	0	0	1	2	0

j = 2

index	0	1	2	3	4	5	6	7	8	9	10	11	12
txt	a	i	a	i	o	a	i	a	i	a	i	e	e

i = 7

index	0	1	2	3	4
p	a	i	a	i	e
table	0	0	1	2	0

j = 3

index	0	1	2	3	4	5	6	7	8	9	10	11	12
txt	a	i	a	i	o	a	i	a	i	a	i	e	e

i = 8

index	0	1	2	3	4
p	a	i	a	i	e
table	0	0	1	2	0

j = 4

index	0	1	2	3	4	5	6	7	8	9	10	11	12
txt	a	i	a	i	o	a	i	a	i	a	i	e	e

i = 9

The prefix table indicates where the comparison should continue

index	0	1	2	3	4
p	a	i	a	i	e
table	0	0	1	2	0

j = 2

Notice that the prefix is not checked again.

index	0	1	2	3	4	5	6	7	8	9	10	11	12
txt	a	i	a	i	o	a	i	a	i	a	i	e	e

i = 9

Figure 10-33   Illustration of the KMP algorithm—continued

index	0	1	2	3	4
p	a	i	a	i	e
table	0	0	1	2	0

j = 3

index	0	1	2	3	4	5	6	7	8	9	10	11	12
txt	a	i	a	i	o	a	i	a	i	a	i	e	e

i = 10

index	0	1	2	3	4
p	a	i	a	i	e
table	0	0	1	2	0

j = 4

index	0	1	2	3	4	5	6	7	8	9	10	11	12
txt	a	i	a	i	o	a	i	a	i	a	i	e	e

i = 11

Complete match

The KMP algorithm needs to construct the prefix table, and the procedure has complexity $O(n)$. The KMP function described in the previous code snippet makes, at most, $m + n$ iterations. Thus, the complexity of the KMP algorithm is $O(m + n)$, but it is not affected by the number of characters used as the alphabet.

Note | The KMP algorithm was proposed by James Morris and Donald Knuth independently. In 1977, Knuth, Morris, and Vaughan Pratt published the algorithm in the paper "Fast Pattern Matching in Strings" in the *Journal on Computing of the Society for Industrial and Applied Mathematics*. The KMP algorithm was the first pattern-matching algorithm with linear time complexity.

10.5 Spanning Trees

Every tree is a graph since it is composed of vertices and edges. But not every graph is a tree since the main characteristic of a tree is that every vertex has only one parent, and there is only one node with no parent.

A way to characterize a tree is by saying it has no closed path composed of different edges. A closed path is a path that starts and ends at the same vertex. Given a tree, creating a path that starts and ends in the same vertex is impossible without passing through the same edge twice.

A graph is called a **connected graph** if a path joins every pair of vertices. You can see an example of connected and unconnected graphs in **Figure 10-34**.

Figure 10-34 Examples of connected and unconnected graphs

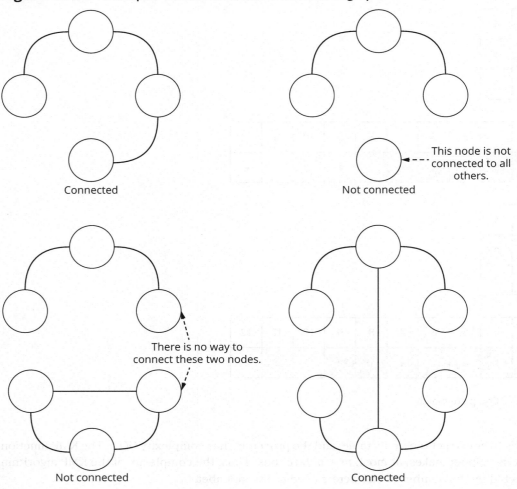

Given a connected graph G, the common problem is constructing a tree T that uses all the vertices of G and some edges of G. Such a tree is called a **spanning tree**. You can see some examples of spanning trees in **Figure 10-35**.

Figure 10-35 A graph, a spanning tree, and an additional representation of a spanning tree

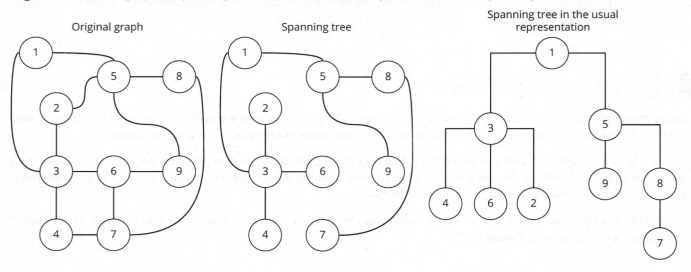

A key feature of a spanning tree is that it has the minimum set of edges necessary to connect every pair of vertices.

Minimum Spanning Trees

Additionally, it is relevant to compute a spanning tree with a minimum cost to find a spanning tree when graph G is a weighted graph. A **minimum spanning tree** is a spanning tree T such that the sum of the weights of its edges is minimum. **Figure 10-36** shows a graph G, a minimum spanning tree for G, and a nonminimum spanning tree for G.

Figure 10-36   A graph and two spanning trees. One is not minimum

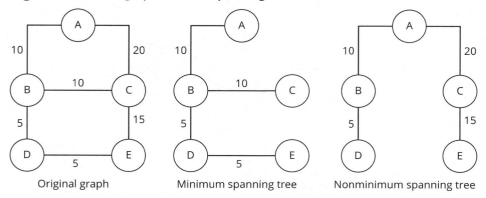

A minimum spanning tree also provides the minimal set of edges necessary to connect all edges of G, but at the least possible cost. Although the minimum spanning tree and the shortest path problem are related, a minimum spanning tree might not provide the shortest path between the root and any other edge. You can see that illustrated in **Figure 10-37**.

Figure 10-37   A graph illustrating how a minimum spanning tree might not generate the shortest path possible between two nodes

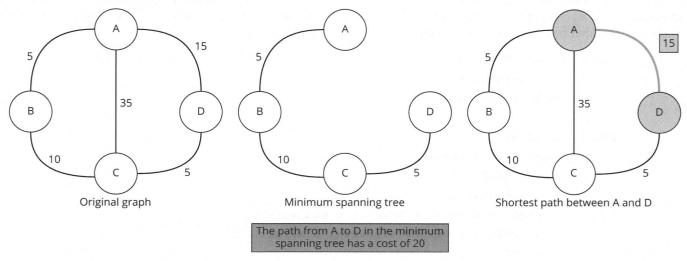

Minimum spanning trees are helpful when building physical networks. Suppose that a new telecommunications service is necessary for several places in a house. The service is provided through a wire, and this wire is going to be installed through pipes that are already in the walls of the house. You can see an example of some rooms in a house and a graph representing the places in the house and the pipes that join them in **Figure 10-38**.

To use the least amount of wire, and since the service has a single point of origin, a minimum spanning tree should be computed to connect all rooms to the service.

Figure 10-38 A depiction of a house with cable pipes and its abstract representation using a graph

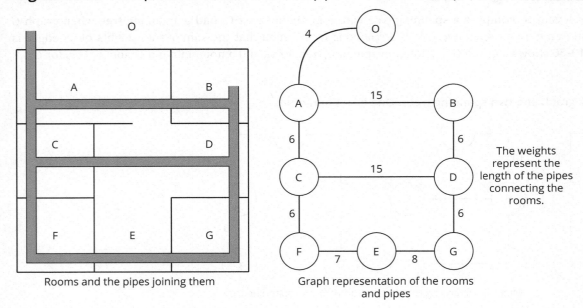

Rooms and the pipes joining them

Graph representation of the rooms and pipes

The weights represent the length of the pipes connecting the rooms.

Prim's Algorithm

Prim's algorithm uses a greedy strategy to build a minimum spanning tree. The algorithm uses a list of non-visited nodes. The algorithm starts with the edge with the smallest weight. After that, new edges are added until there are no non-visited nodes. At each step, the edge added is one such that the cost of the algorithm is minimized.

You can see how Prim's algorithm works in **Figure 10-39**.

Prim's algorithm can use a minimum priority queue for the possible edges to add at each step. Since a priority queue has $O(\log n)$ complexity for its operations, it is much faster than doing a sequential search for a minimum edge. In the code snippet below, you can see an implementation of this algorithm.

```
add_neighbors(G, u, Q)
    for v in neighbors(G, u)
        add(Q, weight(u,v), (u, v) )


get_min_edge(G)
    min_weight = infinite
    min_edge = Null
    for e in G.edges()
        if weight(e.source, e.target) < min_weight
            min_weight = weight(e.source, e.target)
            min_edge = e
    return min_edge


init_visited(G)
    visited = new associative_array[size(G)]
    for v in vertex(G)
        visited[v.key] = False
    return visited
```

Code continues on p. 330

Figure 10-39 How Prim's algorithm works

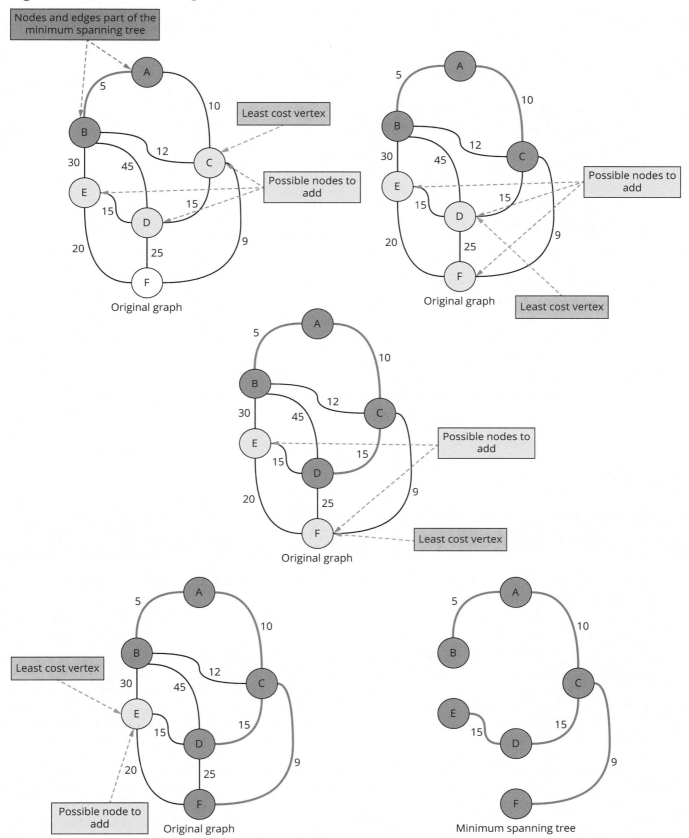

```
prim_min(G)
    T = new Graph() ;; A graph to store the spanning tree
    e = get_min_edge(G) ;; Start with the minimum weight edge

    ;; Add the neighbors of the starting vertices
    Q = new min_priority_queue()
    add_neighbors(G, e.source, Q)
    add_neighbors(G, e.target, Q)

    ;; Add the starting vertices and edge
    visited = init_visited(G)
    visited[e.source.key] = True
    visited[e.target.key] = True

    add_vertex(T, e.source)
    add_vertex(T, e.target)
    add_edge(T, e.source, e.target, weight(e))
    while size(T) < size(G)
        x = delete(Q)
        if not visited[x.target.key]
            add_vertex(T, x.target)
            add_edge(T, x.source, x.target, weight(x, x.target))
            add_neighbors(G, x, Q)

    return T
```

Figure 10-40 shows an implementation of Prim's algorithm.

Quick Check 10-5

Suppose that a weighted graph has all its weights equal. Then any spanning tree is a minimum spanning tree for this graph. True or False?

Answer: True

If all weights in the graph are equal, then the sum of a tree's weights will equal the number of edges it has times the weight of an edge. Since any spanning tree must have $N - 1$ edges, where N is the number of vertices in the graph, then the cost of every spanning tree is $(N - 1)* w$, where w is the weight of an edge. Hence, every spanning tree for this graph will be a minimum spanning tree.

Note | When a graph is not connected, there can't be a single spanning tree. When a graph is not connected, it can be divided into several subgraphs, each one connected. In such a case, a family of spanning trees might be constructed—one tree for each connected subgraph. Prim's algorithm can't work on a non-connected graph to produce several trees. But other algorithms, such as Kruskal's algorithm, can be used to find more than one spanning tree. Kruskal's algorithm uses a greedy strategy by choosing the minimum-weight edge.

Figure 10-40   Prim's algorithm and the auxiliary data structures used

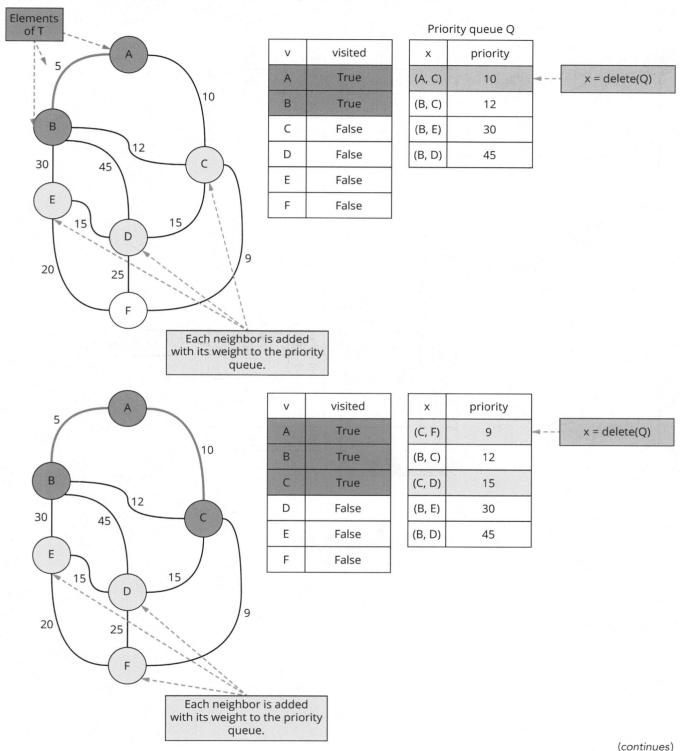

Figure 10-40   Prim's algorithm and the auxiliary data structures used—continued

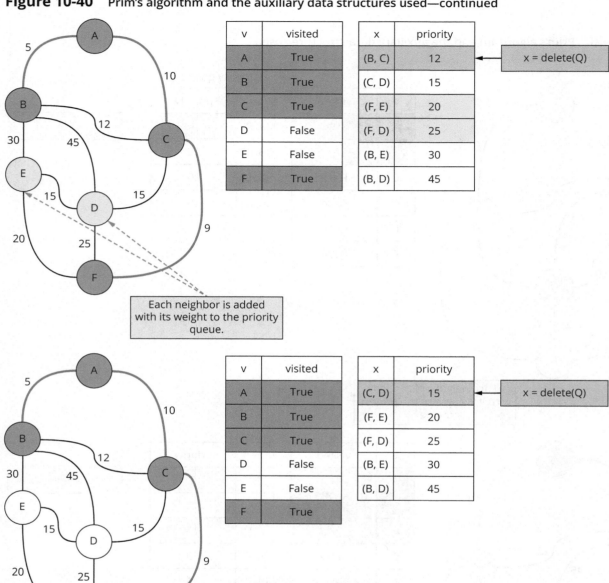

v	visited
A	True
B	True
C	True
D	False
E	False
F	True

x	priority
(B, C)	12
(C, D)	15
(F, E)	20
(F, D)	25
(B, E)	30
(B, D)	45

x = delete(Q)

Each neighbor is added with its weight to the priority queue.

v	visited
A	True
B	True
C	True
D	False
E	False
F	True

x	priority
(C, D)	15
(F, E)	20
(F, D)	25
(B, E)	30
(B, D)	45

x = delete(Q)

C was already visited so a new node is searched.

Figure 10-40   Prim's algorithm and the auxiliary data structures used—continued

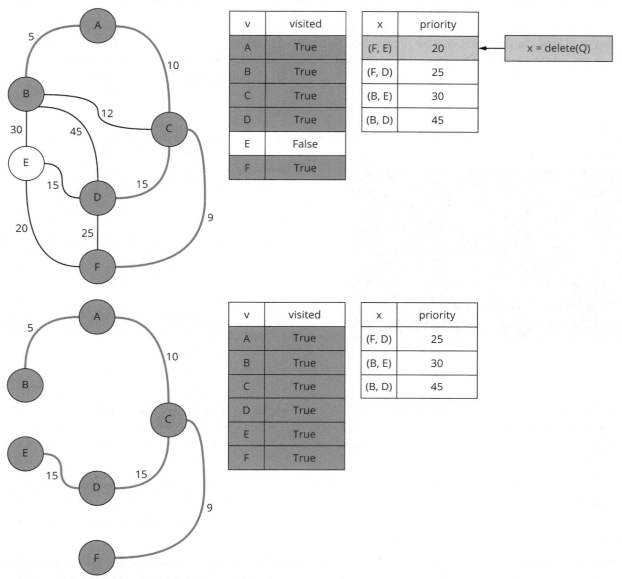

There are no more vertices to add. The result is a minimum spanning tree.

10.6 Contours and Regions in Binary Images

A binary image is a digital image, usually a bidimensional array $I[y][x]$, that takes only values of 0 or 1. The pixels (x, y) such that $I[y][x]$ is 1 are called positive pixels. Binary images are useful for separating different objects in an image. You can see an illustration of how a binary image is used to separate objects of interest from the background in **Figure 10-41**.

Figure 10-41 A binary image used to delimit the space where a pen and some coins are present in the image on the right

Binary Image to detect coins and pen

Original image

Renata Photography/Shutterstock.com

Some techniques, such as searching for a particular color or texture, derive a binary image from a picture. The idea is to create a binary region to represent an object. A binary region is a set of positive pixels such that each pair of pixels can be joined by a line of positive pixels. You might say that a binary region is a set of positive pixels that are next to each other.

Unfortunately, the result of creating binary images to separate objects in an image is not always perfect. Hence, more than one region is created in the binary image. Moreover, in some problems, knowledge of the shape of an object, its orientation, or properties such as its area is required. In such cases, the simple structure of a binary image is not sufficient, and some auxiliary constructions are necessary.

One problem that commonly arises when using binary regions is region labeling. Region labeling refers to creating a data structure that associates each pixel in an image with a specific object, represented by a binary region. You can see an illustration of a binary image with all its regions labeled in **Figure 10-42**.

Figure 10-42 Labels, represented by numbers and colors, associated with several regions in an image

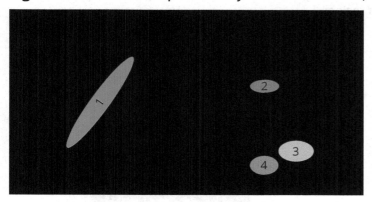

Another problem is finding the contour of a region. Unfortunately, the problem of what makes up the contour of a region might be complicated in the case of digital images. You can see a binary image and the contour pixels for different regions illustrated in **Figure 10-43**.

Figure 10-43 Example of binary regions and their contours

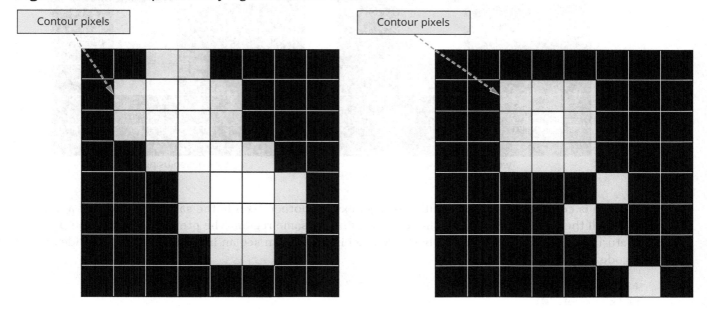

Flood Filling

Given a binary image, the definition of a region depends on when two pixels are considered to be next to each other. The precise definition of when two pixels are considered adjacent is given regarding a neighborhood. In **Figure 10-44**, you can see an illustration of the pixels in the neighborhood of a given pixel and how it affects what is considered a region.

Figure 10-44   Illustration of the N4 and N8 definitions of neighbors. Notice how using different neighbors may lead to having a different number of regions

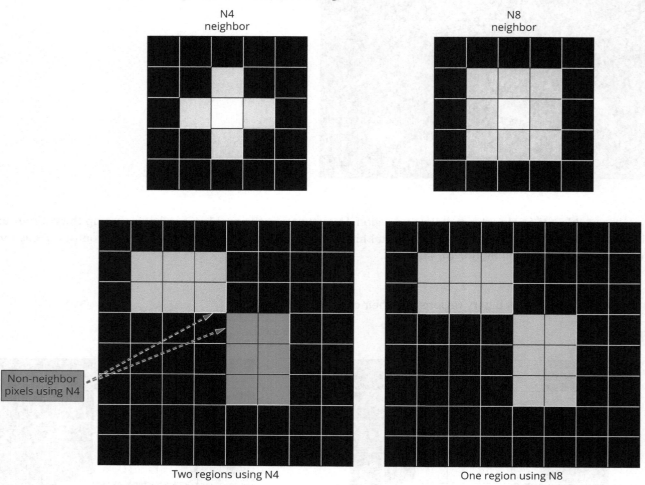

So, a region is considered a set of positive pixels next to another pixel in the same set. Hence, if a pixel (x, y) is positive, all the pixels in its neighborhood are part of the same region. The previous observation provides a way to return all the pixels in a region given any pixel in it. You can see an implementation of the idea in the following code.

```
;; n4 returns a list with the neighbor's pixels
n4(x, y, H, W)
    ;; x, y are the column and row of the pixel
    ;; H, W is the number of rows and columns of the image
    nl = new list()
    if y  < H-1
        add(nl, tuple(x, y+1))
    if y > 0
        add(nl, tuple(x, y-1))
    if x  < W-1
        add(nl, tuple(x+1, y))
    if x > 0
        add(nl, tuple(x-1, y))
    return nl
```

```
flood_fill(I, S, x, y, H, W)
    ;; x, y are the column and row of the pixel
    ;; I is the binary image. It will be altered to
    ;; mark a pixel as processed
    ;; S is a set of pixels that compose the region
    ;; H, W are the number of rows and columns of the image
    if I[y, x] = 1
        add(S, tuple(x, y))
        I[y, x] = 0 ;; the pixel is marked as processed
        for p in n4(x, y, H, W)
            if not p in S and I[p.y, p.x] = 1
                flood_fill(I, S, p.x, p.y, H, W)
    return S
```

The algorithm implemented in the previous code snippet is called **recursive flood filling**. The previous algorithm is based on the graph representation of the binary region. The flood filling is just a traversal of the graph representation. **Figure 10-45** shows a graph associated with a binary image.

Figure 10-45   A binary region and its graph representation

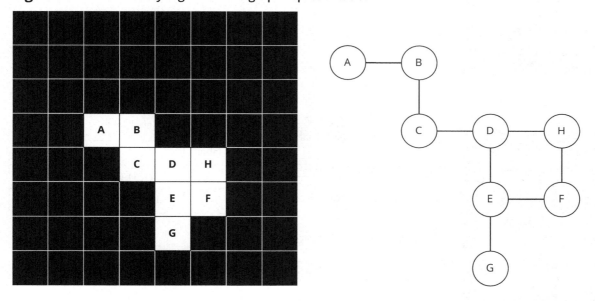

To label each region in a binary image, it is necessary to use a copy of the image to mark the pixels that have already been added as part of a region. To save and associate a label to each pixel in the region, it is possible to use a hash table to keep track of the pixels associated with each region. Another approach is to use an image with the same shape as the original where each value is an integer associated with each region. The following is an implementation of a region labeling procedure for image *I*.

```
region_labeling(I, H, W)
    ;; I is a binary image with the region to label
    ;; H, W are the number of rows and columns of I
    J = copy of I
    label_table = new hash_table()
    curr_label = 2 ;; start from 2 since 1 is positive
    ;; and 0 is a background
    for i = 0 to H-1 step 1
        for j = 0 to W-1 step 1
            if J[i, j] = 1
```

```
        S = new set()
        flood_fill(J, S, j, i, H, W)
        add(label_tabel, curr_label, S)
        curr_label = curr_label + 1
    return label_table
```

You can see an illustration of the previous function in **Figure 10-46**.

Figure 10-46   How region labeling works on a binary image

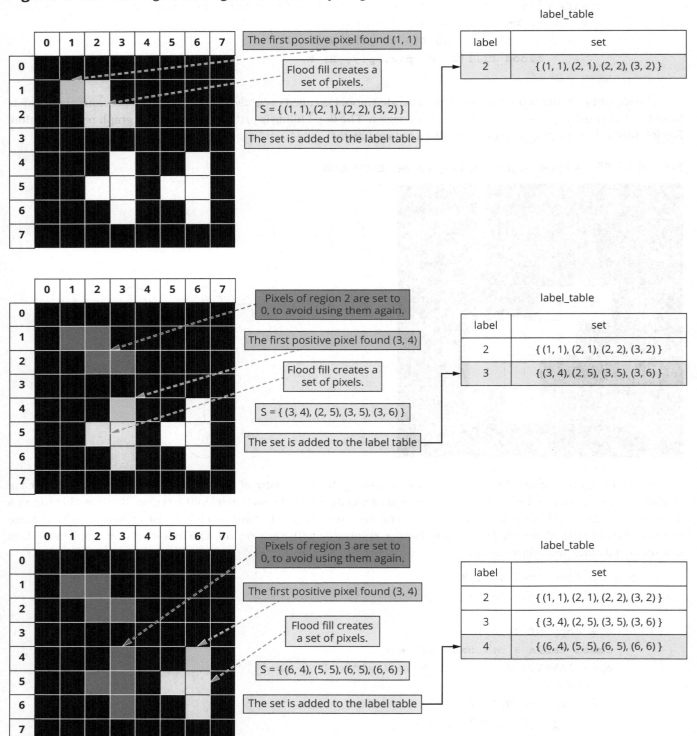

Notice that it is possible to use a different approach where each pixel is altered by the `flood_filling` procedure instead of using a set structure.

Contour Finding

If you are given a single region in a binary image, finding its contour is easily described, but its implementation has several difficulties. The first one is how to start the contour description. Finding a contour requires starting with a pixel belonging to the region. But only some pixels might be useful. If the pixel is not part of the contour, it can't be used immediately to describe the contour. On the other hand, if the pixel is part of the contour, then a description of the contour can be given by simply following the contour.

Another aspect to remember is the possibility that a region might have more than one curve describing its contour. This situation occurs when the region is not simply connected. A **simply connected region** has no holes. You can see the difference between a simply connected region and one that is not simply connected in **Figure 10-47**.

Figure 10-47   A simply connected region and a multiply connected region

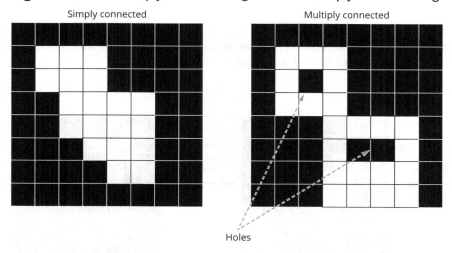

A non–simply connected region is called a **multiply connected region**. Multiply connected regions have two contours: one external contour and possibly multiple internal contours. The algorithms that follow ignore the holes in multiply connected regions, thus requiring an additional hole-searching process to produce the internal contours.

A precise definition of the contour is necessary to avoid errors in reasoning. A **contour pixel** is a pixel in a region where at least one neighbor pixel is not part of the same region. You can see some illustrations of the contour pixel definition and how it depends on the definition of neighbors in **Figure 10-48**.

Figure 10-48   Contour pixels in binary images. Notice how the classification of a pixel as contour pixel or not depends on the neighbor definition

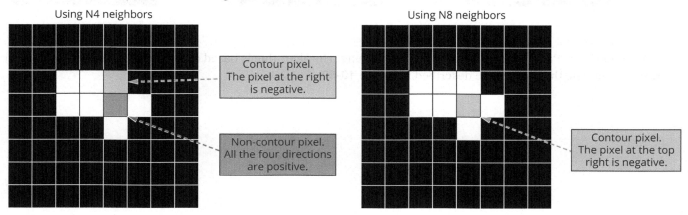

To find an initial pixel, it is possible to use the pixel (x, y) in the region such that y is the minimum possible and x is the minimum possible for the given y. Here is a procedure to find such pixels.

```
init_pixel(I, H, W)
    ;; I is a binary image containing only one region
    ;; H, W are the number of rows and columns of I
    for j = 0 to H-1 step 1
        for i = 0 to W-1 step 1
            if H[j, i] = 1
                return tuple(i, j)
```

Once the initial pixel has been found, the following algorithm describes the contour from the point of view of someone traveling the contour. To better understand the algorithm, consider how the contour of a region is described in terms of instructions to move in different directions. **Figure 10-49** illustrates how to describe such contours.

Figure 10-49 How the contour can be described using directions relative to the current pixel. The directions depend on the position and orientation of the current pixel

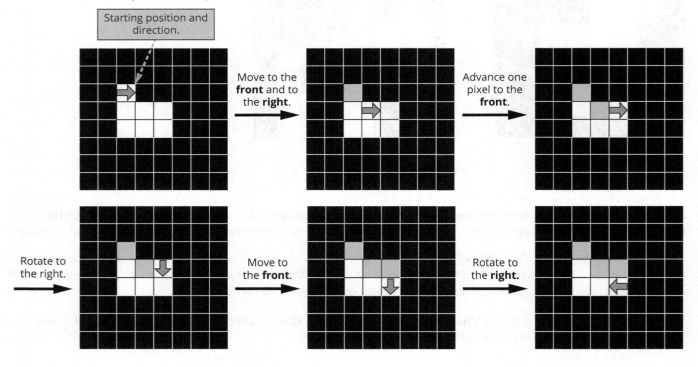

The following is Pavlidis' algorithm for contour tracing. The algorithm is based on moving the current pixel based on three cases. The three cases are described in **Figure 10-50**.

Figure 10-50   The base cases used to trace the contour of a binary region

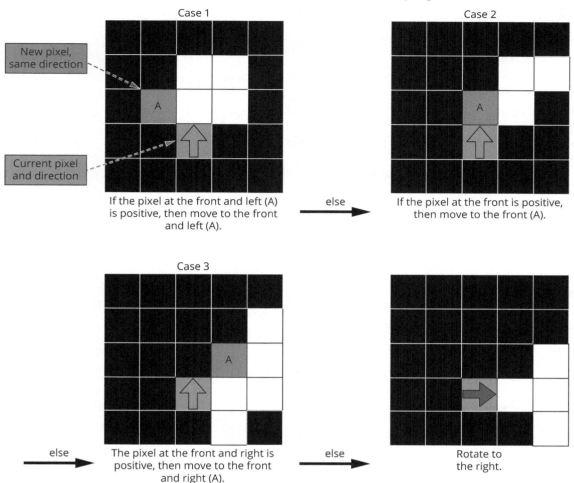

Case 1

New pixel, same direction

Current pixel and direction

If the pixel at the front and left (A) is positive, then move to the front and left (A).

else →

Case 2

If the pixel at the front is positive, then move to the front (A).

Case 3

else →

The pixel at the front and right is positive, then move to the front and right (A).

else →

Rotate to the right.

Notice that if none of the three cases occurs, you can turn 90 degrees to the right and start again. In order to simplify the implementation, a code for the eight possible directions is used. The code is shown in **Figure 10-51**.

Figure 10-51   The eight directions in which a pixel might move

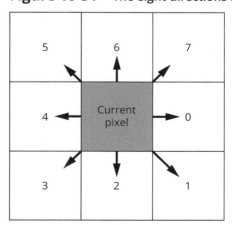

After turning 90 degrees three times, all possible directions must have been covered. So, if no new pixel is found after three turns, the current pixel must be isolated. The procedure find_next(p, d, I, H, W) implements these ideas.

```
turn_90(d)
    ;; H, W are the number of rows and columns of I
    ;; d is an integer describing the direction
    ;; d ranges from 0 to 7
    return (d + 2) mod 8

pixel_at_dir(p, d, H, W)
    x = p.x
    y = p.y
    if d = 0 or d = 7 or d = 1
        new_x = x + 1
    else if d = 3 or d = 4 or d = 5
        new_x = x - 1
    else
        new_x = x
    if d = 5 or d = 6 or d = 7
        new_y = y - 1
    else if d = 1 or d = 2 or d = 3
        new_y = y + 1
    else
        new_y = y
    if x < 0 or x > W-1
        return Null
    if y < 0 or y > W-1
        return Null
    return tuple(x,y)

find_next(p, d, I, H, W)
    ;; d is returned by reference
    ;; In that way, the value of d holds the new direction
    turns = 0
    while turns < 3
        ;; Check the pixel at the front left position
        n = pixel_at_dir(p, (d - 1) mod 8, H, W)
        if not n = Null and I[n.y, n.x] = 1
            return p
        ;; Check the pixel at the front position
        n = pixel_at_dir(p, d, H, W)
        if not n = Null and I[n.y, n.x] = 1
            return p
        ;; Check the pixel at the front right position
        if not n = Null and I[n.y, n.x] = 1
            return p
        turns = turns + 1
        d = (d + 2) mod 8
    ;; If all directions were checked, then there are
    ;; no more points
    return p
```

When creating the contour, Pavlidis' algorithm uses the starting pixel with direction $d = 0$. That choice ensures that no pixel will be ignored. Each new pixel you get from the find_next function is added to a list describing the contour. The algorithm finishes when the find_next function gives the starting pixel with direction $d = 0$. Another way to stop the algorithm is to use the starting pixel s and the result of first = find_next (s, 0, I, H, W) as the first pixel on the contour. The algorithm stops when the pixel *s* is visited with the next pixel first. The following is a complete implementation.

```
pavlidis_contour(s, I, H, W)
   ;; s is the starting position
   ;; I the binary image with only one region
   curr_d = 0
   f = find_next(p, d, I, H, W)
   c = new list() ;; the contour
   add(c, f)
   if curr_d = f
      return c
   curr_pix = f
   back = False
   while not back
      nex_pix = find_next(curr_pix, curr_d, I, H, W)
      if nex_pix = f and curr_pix = s
         back = True
      curr_pix = next_pix
      add(c, curr_pix)
```

The Pavlidis algorithm is illustrated in **Figure 10-52**.

Figure 10-52   How the Pavlidis algorithm works

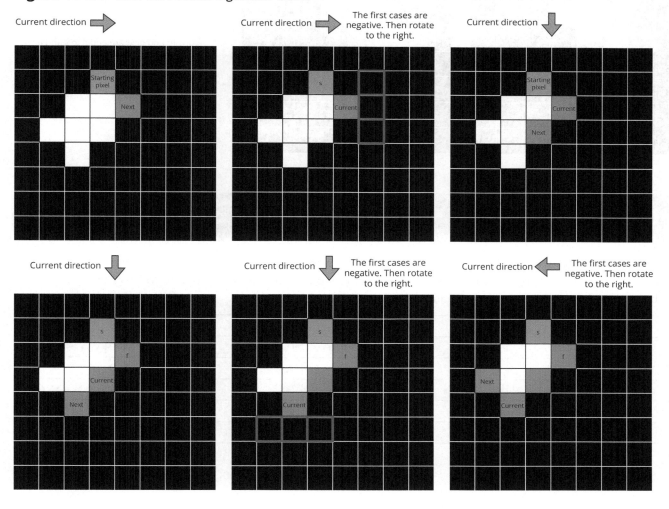

Figure 10-52 How Pavlidi's algorithm works—continued

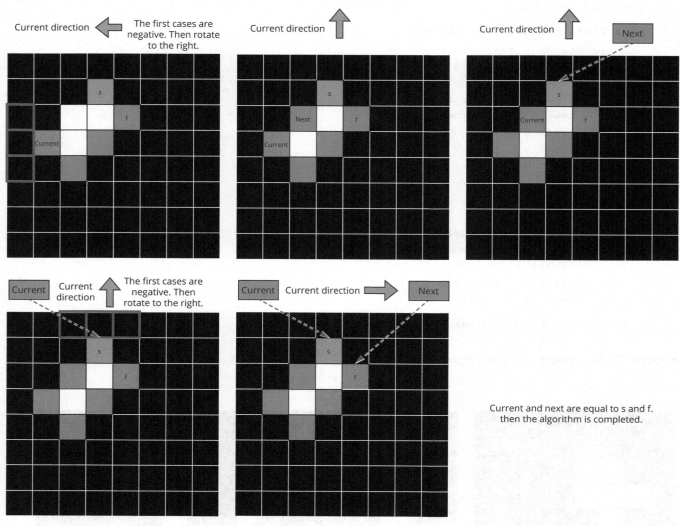

Current and next are equal to s and f.
then the algorithm is completed.

Quick Check 10-6

Consider the Pavlidis algorithm where the current pixel is marked with X in the table below. If the current direction is to the left, which is the next pixel to be added to the contour of the region? Which of the three basic cases is this? Consider that all named pixels are positive.

	0	1	2	3	4	5
0	0	0	0	0	0	0
1	0	0	0	A	1	0
2	0	0	<- X	B	1	1
3	1	D	0	C	1	0
4	1	1	0	0	0	0
5	0	0	0	0	0	0

(continues)

Answer: D. This is Case 1.

Based on the current direction, the pixel at the front left direction is positive, thus that becomes the next pixel in the contour. The first case of the basic cases to determinate the next pixel is when the pixel at the front left corner is positive. This pixel is determined based on the current direction of the trace; hence, it becomes the pixel at the bottom left direction of X.

Summary

- Optimization problems are problems where a magnitude, called the objective function, is maximized or minimized given a set of restrictions.

- An algorithm that solves a problem that takes at each step the local best choice and produces a globally optimal solution is called a greedy algorithm.

- For the greedy strategy to be applied, the problem must have two characteristics, the greedy choice property and the optimal sub-structure property. The greedy choice property ensures that the local best choice exists when solving each step of the problem. And the optimal sub-structure property guarantees that a globally optimal solution is made from optimal subproblems.

- Greedy algorithms are helpful when solving assignment problems such as scheduling activities for a single common resource.

- Huffman coding uses a greedy strategy and a frequency histogram to compress text data. Huffman coding assigns to the character with the highest frequency the smallest possible coding. The result is code that reduces the size of a message.

- Dynamic programming is a problem-solving strategy that uses memorization to reduce the complexity of a recursive procedure. To apply dynamic programming, a problem must be divided into similar subproblems. Given the recursive nature of the divide-and-conquer approach, studying all possible options leads to a solution with exponential complexity. If the computation of optimal solutions to different cases shares some subproblems, then memorization can be used to avoid having to compute each subproblem several times. This property is called overlapping subproblems. When the optimal sub-structure property is also present, it is possible to use memorization and recursion to construct an optimal solution with polynomial time.

- String algorithms are present in daily tasks, such as when a word is searched in a document. That means that the performance of such a search is a priority.

- Pattern matching is the problem of searching a string p, called a pattern, in a larger text. Two effective pattern-matching algorithms are the Rabin–Karp and Knuth–Morris–Pratt (KMP) algorithms.

- The Rabin–Karp algorithm uses a polynomial hashing function to reduce the complexity of comparing two strings. To compute the hash function for several sub-strings of a text, it uses a property of polynomials that makes the computation of new hash values have constant time complexity.

- The KMP algorithm uses a prefix table to avoid having to completely restart a search each time a mismatch between the characters of the pattern and of the text happens.

- Dijkstra's algorithm is used to find the shortest path joining a source node A with any other node in graph G.

- Dijkstra's algorithm applies to any network problem using a weighted graph. For example, it applies to roads and cities. It is also used in computer networks and route planning for robot movement.

- Dijkstra's algorithm uses a greedy approach and breadth-first traversal. At each step of the algorithm, the distance to each node is updated based on the newly analyzed node.

- Given a connected graph G, a spanning tree is a tree that contains all vertices of the original graph and is composed of some edges of G. When graph G is a weighted graph, a minimum spanning tree is a spanning tree where the sum of the weight of the edges is minimum.

- Prim's algorithm finds a minimum spanning tree from a graph. The algorithm uses a greedy strategy to add an edge that joins a new vertex at each step. That means that the edge with minimum weight is added at each step.

- Using a binary or bilevel image when working with a digital image or even game development is common; that is, a digital image where each pixel has a value of 0 or 1. Given a binary image, two important problems are finding connected sets of pixels called regions and finding the border or contour of each region.

- An effective way to construct the sets that compose different regions is to use the graph representation of a binary image. With the graph representation, it is possible to use any way of traversal. In particular, when recursive traversal is used, the algorithm is called recursive flood filling.

- Pavlidis' algorithm uses the idea of finding the next pixel in a contour depending on the direction in which the search is going. The pixels are analyzed from left to right at each step relative to the current search direction. Once the algorithm returns to the starting position and indicates the initial search direction again, the algorithm stops.

Key Terms

0-1 knapsack problem	local best choice	positive pixel
binary image	longest sub-string problem	prefix
binary region	minimum spanning tree	prefix table
connected graph	multiply connected region	recursive flood filling
contour pixel	objective function	region
data compression	optimal sub-structure	region labeling
dynamic programming	optimization problem	simply connected region
feasible solution	overlapping	spanning tree
greedy algorithm	subproblems	string algorithms
greedy choice property	pattern	variable-length
Huffman coding	pattern matching	codification

Review Questions

1. In any optimization problem, which of the following are characteristics of a solution to the problem?

    a. It must be unique.

    b. It must be real.

    c. It must be feasible.

    d. It must be bounded.

2. Which of the following are necessary to apply a greedy algorithm to an optimization problem?

    a. A set of feasible solutions

    b. Optimal sub-structure

    c. Overlapping subproblems

    d. The greedy choice property

3. Which of the following are necessary to apply dynamic programming to a problem?

    a. A set of feasible solutions

    b. Optimal sub-structure

    c. Overlapping subproblems

    d. The greedy choice property

4. In the 0-1 knapsack problem, a greedy choice always leads to an optimal solution.

    a. True

    b. False

5. How many prefixes can the string p = "abacdabc" have?

    a. 0   **b.** 3   **c.** 4   **d.** 8

6. Which of the following is true for any weighted graph G where all weights are 1?

    a. It has only one minimum spanning tree.

    b. The Prim's algorithm doesn't work on it.

    c. G doesn't have a spanning tree.

    d. Any spanning tree is a minimum spanning tree.

7. For the graph shown in **Figure 10-53**, use Prim's algorithm to compute its minimum spanning tree.

Figure 10-53   Graph for Review Question 7

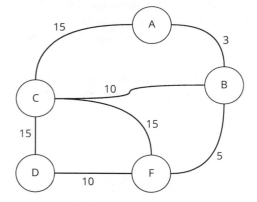

8. Suppose that the pixels marked as A, B, C, and D in **Figure 10-54** are positive in a binary image. If the current pixel in Pavlidis' algorithm is D and the current direction is 7, which is the next pixel on the contour?

Figure 10-54   Binary region and named pixels for Review Question 8

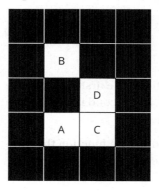

9. For the pattern $p =$ "mamaemamamia", compute the prefix table used in the KMP algorithm.

10. Given a maximum weight of 10 and objects with weights 8, 5, 2, 4, and 6 with profits 5, 3, 1, 4, and 6, solve the 0-1 knapsack problem using the dynamic programming solution discussed in the text.

Programming Problems

1. Suppose a programmer wants to invest computation time from one of its servers while idle. The programmer has *N* hours to invest. The programmer decides to use the computation time to mine some crypto coins. There is a list of computational tasks and a payment for each one of them given in an array of tuples `arr = [(max_time1, payment1), (max_time2, payment2), …, (max_timem, paymentm)]`. There is the option to get paid for partially completed jobs, not only completed jobs. For example, if the programmer uses the server to compute a task with a max_time of 3 hours and payment of $60 but only does it for 1 hour, payment is $20. Use a greedy algorithm to compute what jobs the programmer should take and for how much time to maximize payment. **(LO 10.1, 10.2)**

2. Suppose that an array *X* of length *N* is given. Let's call a good subsequence to a set of indices `i1, i2, i3, …`, such that `i1 < i2 < i3 < … im` in such a way that `X[i1] < X[i2] < X[i3] < … X[im]`. Write a program that finds the length of the longest possible good subsequence of an array *X*. **(LO 10.2)**

3. A natural park has a list of attractions *A*, such as ponds and gardens. Each attraction is joined by one or several other attractions through trails prone to accidents. The park administration has decided to build roads over the existing trails so visitors can use the roads to reach any attraction in the park. The set of attractions and the cost of building the roads over the nature trails is given as a weighted graph *G*. Write a program that computes what roads should be built so every attraction can be reached and the cost is minimum. **(LO 10.5)**

4. A binary region marks an island on a map, the island is connected, and no other region exists in image *X*. It is known that each pixel in the image is equivalent to $20m \times 20m$. Write a program approximating the length of the island's coastline and land area. **(LO 10.6)**

Projects

Project 10-1: Huffman Coding and Decoding

(LO 10.1) Suppose that you are given a text *txt*. Write functions to compute the Huffman coding associated with the text, a function to translate text to a representation using Huffman coding, and a function to translate the Huffman coding representation back to the original text.

Project 10-2: Dijkstra's Complete Path Algorithm

(LO 10.1, LO 10.3) Two features mentioned in the text make Dijkstra's algorithm more practical. The first one is to use a priority queue or heap to keep track of the distances to get the minimum distance faster. The second is to compute the sequence of edges necessary to provide the path from source node *A* to any other node.

Modify Dijkstra's algorithm implementation given in the text to use a priority queue and write a function that provides the sequence of edges that makes the shortest path between the source and any other node.

Project 10-3: Knapsack Problem

(LO 10.2) Suppose you have a knapsack with maximum capacity W. There is also a set of objects with a given weight, a profit, and a maximum number of objects of the given type. Hence, you might have a knapsack with a maximum capacity of 100. And you are given three types of objects with weights 1, 2, and 3; profits of 10, 40, and 5; and 10, 20, and 25 objects of each type.

Write a program that finds a combination of objects such that the profit is maximum. Suppose that the array wt gives the weight of each object, the array pr the profit of each object, the array sup the number of available objects of each type, W the maximum capacity, and N the number of objects.

Project 10-4: Robot Trajectory Planning

(LO 10.3, LO 10.6) Write a program that creates the inner contour of a region. The inner contour is the contour of the hole in a non–simply connected region. Assume that the binary image I has only one region.

A robot has a designated area where it can move in a room. The areas allowed for the robot to move are given in a matrix $R[][]$ where 1 means that it can move in that pixel and 0 that it can't. The robot uses less than half an energy unit moving north or south in one position. It uses one energy unit moving left and right, and it uses two energy units when moving in a diagonal direction. Given a map R of the region allowed for the robot to move, write a program that computes the minimum units of energy necessary for the robot to reach from position $R[i][j]$ position $R[k][l]$.

Glossary

A

0-1 knapsack problem A problem that consists of selecting from a set of n elements, with a given profit and weight, the elements that fit in a bag with a maximum capacity of W and that maximize the total profit.

abstract data type (ADT) Logical description of how data is stored and the operations you can perform with it.

adaptive sorting algorithm A sorting algorithm whose complexity changes based on whether the array is presorted.

adjacency list A graph implementation where the vertices are stored in a linear data structure and associated with each vertex v is a linked list of all the vertices u such that the edge (v, u) is a part of the graph.

adjacency matrix A matrix where the rows and columns are a list of a graph's vertices, and the data associated is 1 if an edge joins the row vertex with the column vertex and 0 in another case.

adjacent When two vertices are joined by an edge.

algorithm A set of instructions that uses a set of input values to produce a result. The result produced by an algorithm is called the output. The set of output values satisfies a given constraint, making them a solution to a given problem.

analysis of algorithms The process of finding the more efficient algorithm, usually measuring how long it will take to produce a solution.

ancestor In a tree structure, an ancestor of a vertex v is a vertex p such that there is a path from p to v.

array A fixed-size data structure that stores elements of a fixed type.

array of pointers implementation An implementation of a tree that uses an array of pointers to store the link to each child of a node.

associative array An abstract data structure that stores pairs of key and data values so that each key appears at most once in the abstract data type.

asymptotic analysis A set of techniques to describe the limit behavior of a function.

auxiliary hash function A hash function used when computing a linear or double-hashing probing sequence.

average-case running time The average of the complexity of all possible cases for an algorithm.

AVL tree A tree where each node has a balance factor of -1, 0, or 1.

B

backtracking A strategy to find solutions to problems that incrementally build solutions. The search for a solution can be recursive or not.

balance factor The difference in the height of the left and right subtree of the node.

base case In a recursive function, the case in which the function will no longer call itself (recurse). It is expected that a recursive function reaches a base case.

best-case running time When an algorithm executes the least number of instructions.

best-case scenario or **best case** The input configuration for which the running time is the best.

Big O notation Gives an asymptotic upper bound for a function. The upper bound for a function $f(n)$ is usually represented by $f(n) = O(g(n))$.

binary image A digital image, usually a bidimensional array $I[y][x]$, that takes only values of 0 or 1.

binary region   A set of positive pixels such that each pair of pixels can be joined by a line of positive pixels.

binary relation   A set of ordered pairs.

binary search   A search algorithm for sorted arrays that finds the target value by splitting the array in two at each iteration.

binary search tree (BST)   A binary tree such that for each node p, if q is in the left subtree $q < p$ and if q is in the right subtree $p > q$.

binary tree   A 2-ary tree, which means that each vertex has at most two children.

bounding function or condition   A function or condition that is used during backtracking to determine if the search must continue or not.

branching factor   In the array of pointers implementation, the maximum number of children a node has.

breadth-first graph traversal   A way of traversing a graph where all sibling nodes are visited and then all the nodes adjacent to each sibling are traversed.

breadth-first traversal   Traversing a tree where each child of a parent node is traversed before visiting the rest of the descendants.

bubble down or **percolate down**   Swapping a node with its largest children until the heap property is fulfilled.

bubble sort   A simple sorting algorithm that traverses parts of the input array, swapping elements to put the largest of the current sub-array at the last position.

bubble up   Operation of swapping a node with its smallest children until the heap property is fulfilled.

built-in type   A data type that is supported by the language without the use of additional libraries.

by reference   Term used to describe when a reference or pointer to a parameter is passed to a function. In this case, any change made to the parameter in the function's code affects the parameter's value outside of the function.

by value   Term used to describe when a new copy of a parameter is passed to a function. Hence, every change made to the copy inside the function won't affect the copy outside the code.

C

chaining   A technique where collisions are handled by using a pointer from the array to a separate data structure.

circular linked list   Linked list where the next pointer of the tail points to the head and the previous pointer of the head points to the tail.

collision   The case when two different key values have the same hash code.

comparison function   A function used to sort a certain type of object that follows a set of rules to ensure coherent results.

complete binary tree   A tree of height h such that every leaf is at the level $h-1$ or h and that at level h has all positions from 1 to m filled. However, all positions from m to the last position at level h are empty.

complexity of an algorithm   A function that measures the number of resources needed by an algorithm as a function of the input size.

compressing hash codes   The procedure of reducing an integer hash code or key into a given range by trying to reduce the number of possible collisions.

computational process   A set of instructions that uses input values to produce output values, but it is not designed to halt or stop after a finite number of steps.

connected graph   A graph in which a path joins every pair of vertices.

container   A data structure that holds objects of the same type.

contour pixel   A pixel in a region where at least one neighbor pixel is not part of the same region.

cryptographically secure hash function   A function that generates a fixed-length hash code from arbitrary data with very little probability of a collision.

D

data compression   The procedure of building a new representation of the information that requires less space but conveys the same information.

data structure   A particular implementation for storing and managing data.

data type   A particular set of values and operations allowed on those values that programming languages specify.

depth of a vertex v   The length of the path from the root vertex r to v.

depth-first graph traversal   A way of traversing the nodes of a graph where, starting at node u, all nonvisited adjacent nodes v are traversed in a depth-first way.

depth-first traversal   A way of traversing a tree where the traversal starts at a parent node and explores each child before moving to the next sibling.

descendant   In a tree, the descendants of a vertex v are the vertices u such that there is a path from v to u.

direct recursion   When a function calls itself directly.

directed graph   A graph where each edge is completely characterized by the ordered pair of vertices that it joins.

double hashing   A technique to compute a probing sequence of hash codes, defined by the equation $h(x,n) = [h_1(x) + nh_2(x)] \bmod m$, where $h_1(x)$ and $h_2(x)$ are auxiliary hash functions.

doubly linked list   Linked list where each node has an additional previous pointer.

dynamic data structure   A data structure with a nonfixed size.

dynamic programming   A technique to solve problems that breaks a larger problem into subproblems in a recursive manner while simultaneously avoiding recalculating previously solved subproblems.

dynamic set   An abstract data type where data can be added, retrieved, and removed from the set.

E

edge   A link between two nodes in a tree or graph.

equal-time random access   Refers to the time complexity of retrieving an element independent of the place where the element is positioned in the data structure.

expression tree   A tree in which every nonleaf node represents an operation between its children and each leaf node represents a value or variable to be operated.

external sorting algorithm   A sorting algorithm that uses external memory, such as hard drives or cloud storage.

F

feasible solution   A set of values that satisfies the constraints of an optimization problem.

FIFO   Stands for first in, first out; meaning that the first element inserted is the first one deleted or retrieved from a data structure.

floor function   A mathematical function denoted by $\lfloor x \rfloor$ and defined as the integer k such that $k \le x < k+1$.

folding method   A method to combine several different fields that compose keys through an arithmetic operation and then reduce them module m.

fractional part function   A mathematical function denoted by $\{x\}$ is defined as $x - \lfloor x \rfloor$.

frequency histogram   A function or table that counts how many times certain values repeat in an object.

full binary tree   A binary tree with all leaves at the same level and every nonleaf vertex has exactly two children.

G

garbage collector   Subroutine in charge of analyzing which parts of reserved memory are no longer being used and freeing them.

graph   An abstract data type is described by a set of vertices V and a set of edges E that connect two vertices.

greedy algorithm   A strategy to solve a problem through dividing a problem into subproblems and for each subproblem building a feasible solution that maximizes or minimizes the objective function.

greedy choice property   When choosing the locally optimal solution at each step of a problem, that is, taking the local best choice, leads to a globally optimal solution.

greedy heuristic   Observes that choosing the locally optimal solution might lead to a globally optimal one.

growth rate   The grow rate of a function $f(n)$ is the type or order of the highest-order term.

H

hash code   The value returned by a hash function for a specific key value.

hash function   A function from a set of keys K to a set of integers $V = \{0, 1, \ldots, N-1\}$.

hash table An implementation for an associative array that uses a hash function to create an integer key value to store the data associated with a key value.

head pointer Pointer or reference to the first element in a linked list.

heap A tree with the POT property complete.

heapify operation A sequence of exchanges or swaps between nodes designed to restore the POT property in a heap.

height of a vertex v The largest among the lengths of the paths from v to all reachable leaves. For the Null value, its height is considered –1.

height of the tree The height of the tree's root node.

heuristic A strategy or pattern that has proven effective when solving one problem.

Huffman coding Coding built for the characters of a file using a greedy strategy. The code is built so that characters with a higher frequency use the smallest possible code.

I

index A data structure that associates to values of a field with the set of key data pairs where the value is present.

indirect recursion When a function calls to itself but in an indirect manner.

in-fix traversal A traversal exclusively defined for binary trees where the left node is traversed, visits the parent, and then traverses the right node.

in-order predecessor For node x of a binary search tree, the element with the largest key smaller than the key of x.

in-order successor For node x of a binary search tree, its in-order successor is the element with the smallest key greater than the key of x.

in-order traversal A traversal exclusively defined for binary trees where the left node is traversed, visits the parent, and then traverses the right node.

in-place sorting algorithm An algorithm that has space complexity $O(l)$ or $O(logn)$, which means that most of the operations are done without using additional memory space.

insertion sort A sorting algorithm that creates a sorted array by sequentially inserting each new element in the appropriate position in the previously sorted sub-array.

inverse comparison The inverse of comparison function `comp(x,y)` is one that returns `'lesser'` when `comp(x,y)` is `'greater'`, and `'greater'` when `comp(x,y)` is `'lesser'`.

inversion A change in the order of elements of the sequence where the kth element is put in the jth position and the jth element in the kth position. Also known as *swap*.

K

key A field from a data type that is used to retrieve an element from a data structure; in order to have consistency the key value should be unique to each element; also, a set of fields used to compare two objects to search and sort algorithms.

knapsack problem Finding a combination of elements that doesn't exceed the given weight and provide the most profit.

L

leaf A vertex that has no children.

left rotation Movement in a tree where a node with a balance factor of 2 is moved into the left child of its right child.

left skewed tree A binary tree where every vertex with a child has only the left child.

leftmost right sibling An implementation of a tree where each node stores two pointers, one to its leftmost child and one to its right sibling.

length of a path The number of edges, not vertices, that compose a path.

LIFO Stands for last in, first out; meaning that the last element inserted is the first to be removed.

linear data structure A data collection where the elements are stored sequentially.

linear probing A technique to construct a probing sequence using $h(x,n) = (h(x) + kn) \bmod m$, where $h(x)$ is called an auxiliary hash function and m is the length of the data array.

linked list A non-fixed-size structure that stores elements sequentially in nodes where each node points to the next one.

list An abstract data type formed by a sequence of elements (this includes the empty list) $a_0, a_1, a_2, \ldots, a_N, a_0, a_1, a_2, \ldots, a_n$ where more elements can be added.

loading factor The ratio of keys to be stored and the size of the data array of a hash table $\alpha = N / m$.

local best choice   Maximizing the objective function under the current constraints without considering future or previous steps.

longest sub-string problem   The problem of finding the longest string S that is a sub-string of S1 and S2.

M

matrix   A data structure composed of rows and columns that associate data with each row and column.

max heap   A complete binary tree where each node has a priority higher than or equal to all its descendants.

memory fragmentation   When holes of free memory exist between reserved spaces in memory.

memory leakage   Problem that happens when your program keeps memory reserved even when it is no longer using it and can no longer access the stored content.

merge sort   A not in-place sorting algorithm that splits an array recursively into smaller parts; each part is sorted and then joins the parts to produce the desired sorted array.

mid-square method   Algorithm to produce a hash code by squaring the key value and using the middle digits as hash code.

min heap   A complete binary tree where each node has a priority smaller than or equal to all its descendants.

minimum spanning tree   A spanning tree that has minimum cost or sum of the weights of the edges that compose it.

modular hashing   A hashing technique that uses the residue of a key modulus m. To reduce the possibility of collisions, a parameter k is used as $h(x) = (kx) \bmod m$, where x is the key value.

multigraph   A structure composed of a set of vertices V and a set of edges E, where each edge e has the following properties: `source(e)`, `target(e)`, `weight(e)`, and `key(e)`.

multiply connected region   A non–simply connected region.

N

N-ary tree   A tree in which each vertex has at most N children.

neighbors   The set of vertices that are adjacent to a given vertex u.

network   A set of interconnected people or things.

node   A term used to refer to the data of a user-defined data type inside a larger data structure such as a linked list, an array, or a queue; also called a *record*. Also, an element used to store data in a linked list that usually contains links or pointers to other nodes as part of the linked list.

non-linear data structure   A data structure where the data is not structured in sequential order.

Null   Term used to denote a reference to an invalid or nonexistent object.

O

objective function   In an optimization problem, the magnitude that is to be maximized or minimized.

Omega notation   Gives an asymptotic lower bound for a function; it is usually represented by $f(n) = \Omega(g(n))$.

online sorting algorithm   A sorting algorithm that executes with partial knowledge of the data it needs to sort.

open addressing   A technique where a collision is handled by using a different position in the array.

optimal sub-structure   The property of an optimization problem that guarantees that an optimal solution is composed of optimal solutions to its subproblems.

optimization problem   A problem that searches to maximize or minimize a quantity subject to certain conditions.

overflow   When you try to insert a new element to a data structure with a size limit after it has reached its maximum capacity.

overlapping subproblems   A property of a problem where a given subproblem appears in many feasible solutions.

P

parallel algorithm   Runs several pieces of code simultaneously.

partially ordered tree (POT)   A binary tree where each node has a priority datum and the priority of each node is larger than or equal to every descendant.

path   In a tree, a sequence of edges $(v_0, v_1), (v_1, v_2), \ldots, (v_{n-1}, v_n)$ where each vertex v_k is parent to the next one v_{k+1}.

pattern   In a string algorithm, the target text or word searched on.

pattern matching   Finding a pattern in a string.

perfect hash function   A hash function $h(x)$ over a set of key values S such that there are no collisions.

pivot value   An element of an array (it could be a multidimensional array like a matrix) selected as reference to perform certain operations.

polynomial hash codes   Algorithm to compute hash codes for strings that convert each character into a numerical value and then computes a polynomial function using the numerical value of each character as the coefficients.

`pop()` **operation**   Operation that removes an element from a stack.

positive pixel   A pixel (x, y) such that $I[y][x]$ is 1.

post-fix traversal   A traversal where the left child is traversed, the right child is traversed, and then the parent is traversed.

post-order traversal   A traversal where the left child is traversed, the right child is traversed, and the parent is traversed.

prefix   A prefix of a string p is a sub-string of p that starts at position 0.

prefix table   An auxiliary data structure with information on how many characters can still be considered a match after a mismatch character is found.

pre-fix traversal   A traversal where the parent is traversed, the left child is traversed, and then the right child is traversed. Also known as *pre-order traversal*.

pre-order traversal   A traversal where the parent is traversed, the left child is traversed, and then the right child is traversed. Also known as *pre-fix traversal*.

previous pointer   Pointer in the nodes of a doubly linked list that points to the previous element in the list.

primitive data type   A data type or range of values defined by the programming language or compiler. Most programming languages provide primitive data types that allow you to store only one number or character.

priority queue   An abstract data type where each element is sorted not just by the time of arrival but also by a priority value.

profiling   A type of analysis in software engineering where speed of execution, memory usage, and other factors are measured.

`push()` **operation**   Operation that adds a new element to a stack.

Q

queue   A data structure that can be fixed or nonfixed in size, where the elements are stored and retrieved following a first in, first out order.

quicksort   A sorting algorithm that divides an array in two parts then applies the same strategy to each part to sort the whole array, which means that it uses the strategy of divide and conquer.

R

random access policy   Policy where no specific order exists to insert or retrieve an element.

record   A term used to refer to the data of user-defined data type used inside a larger data structure such as a linked list, an array, or a queue; also called a *node*.

recursion   A technique to solve problems where the case at hand is divided into smaller subtasks similar to the original one.

recursive flood filling   An algorithm that uses the graph representation of a region in a binary image to label each pixel in the region.

recursive function   A function that calls itself and ultimately reaches a base case.

region   In a binary image, a set of positive pixel neighbors to another pixel in the same set.

region labeling   Creating a data structure that associates each pixel in an image to a specific object or region.

right rotation   Movement in a tree where a node with balance factor −2 is moved into the right child of its left child.

right skewed tree   A binary tree where every vertex with a child has only the right child.

root   The single vertex of a tree with no parent.

S

schedule policy   Rule that dictates in which order the elements in a data structure are retrieved.

search algorithm   An algorithm designed to provide a way to access a particular record or node in a data structure.

search process   The operation of retrieving a specific element from a data structure.

selection sort   A sorting algorithm that iteratively searches for the smallest element and swaps it into the appropriate place.

sequential search   A search algorithm implemented for a linear data structure where the data structure is traversed until the record with the matching key is found.

sibling   In a tree, two vertices are siblings if they have the same parent.

simply connected region   A region that has no holes.

size of a vertex   The size of a vertex v is the number of descendants of v including itself.

skewed tree   A tree where each vertex has at most one child.

sorting algorithm   An algorithm that solves the sorting problem.

sorting problem   The problem of producing from an array of elements a new array with the elements in a predetermined order.

space complexity   A function that relates the amount of memory an algorithm uses as a function of the input size.

spanning tree   Given a connected graph G, a spanning tree is a tree T that uses all the vertices of G and some edges of G.

sparse matrix   A matrix where most entries are zero.

stable sorting algorithm   An algorithm that keeps the relative order of the input values in the output sequence for elements with the same key value.

stack   An abstract data type where elements of the same type can be stored and retrieved following last in, first out order.

stack overflow   An error that occurs when the special space of memory in a computer called a stack lacks space to store necessary data.

state of infinite recursion   The state of a program or procedure where it keeps making recursive calls forever.

static data structure   A data structure with a fixed size.

strictly binary tree   A tree where each vertex has exactly two or zero children.

string algorithms   The family of algorithms specialized in operating over strings.

string-matching algorithm   An algorithm that finds if a given string is part of a larger text.

subtree   For a tree T, a tree composed of a vertex v of T, its descendants, and all the edges relating them.

swap   A change in the order of elements of the sequence where the kth element is put in the jth position and the jth element in the kth position; also known as *inversion*.

symmetric property   The property of a relationship where if the ordered pair (a, b) is part of the relationship, then the pair (b, a) is also part of the relation.

symmetrical traversal   A traversal exclusively defined for binary trees where the left node is traversed, visits the parent, and then traverses the right node.

T

tail pointer   Pointer or reference to the last element of a list.

tail recursion   When a function finishes with the recursive call.

target value   The key of interest in the search algorithm.

Theta notation   Gives an asymptotic equivalence, $f(n) = \Theta(g(n))$, when $f(n) = O(g(n))$ and $f(n) = \Omega(g(n))$.

time complexity   Measures the computational time needed by the algorithm.

traversing a data structure   The term used for the operation of enumerating or iterating over all the elements of the data structure.

treap   A binary search tree that enforces the POT and heap property.

tree   A data structure where data is organized hierarchically through links. In a tree, the data is encapsulated in nodes composed of the datum and the links to other nodes.

trie   A data N-ary tree that stores characters as keys at each node and an additional binary flag to indicate if the node is the last character of a word.

U

underflow   When you try to retrieve an element from an empty data structure.

undirected graph   A graph where the order of the vertices that compose an edge is not relevant.

user-defined data type   A structure that uses primitive or other user-defined data types to represent more complex data.

V

variable-length codification   A codification that represents characters with variable lengths.

vertices   In a tree, nodes that hold the data that is stored in the tree.

W

weight of an edge   A real number assigned to the edge in a graph.

weighted graph   Comprises a set of vertices V, a set of edges represented by pairs of vertices, and a weight function or association that assigns a weight or cost to each edge in the graph.

well-defined recursion   A term used to describe a recursive algorithm that reaches an end state in a finite time and that every time it is used returns the same value.

worst-case running time   When an algorithm executes the greatest number of instructions.

worst-case scenario or **worst case**   The input configuration for which the running time is the worst.

Index